THE STUDENTS MANUAL OF ANCIENT HISTORY

D1882530

Owing to the antiquity and rarity of this book, certain pages are regrettably absent, and readability is compromised due to the blurring of the original text. If you possess any insights regarding the availability of these missing sections, kindly inform us. Your assistance is crucial in ensuring the completion of this significant work for the benefit of future generations.

THE STUDENTS MANUAL OF ANCIENT HISTORY

W. COOKE TAYLOR

GYAN

Published by

GYAN

Gyan Publishing House
5, Ansari Road
Daryaganj, New Delhi-110002
Phone: 011-47034999, 9811692060
E-mail: books@gyanbooks.com

Distribution Network
gyanbooks.com
India, USA, Canada, UK, Australia

© Publisher

All rights reserved. No part of this work may be reproduced, stored, adapted, or transmitted in any form or by any means, electronic, mechanical, photocopying, micro-filming, recording or otherwise, or translated in any language, without the prior written permission of the copyright owner and the publisher.

ISBN: 978-93-7447-019-0 (PB)

First Published, 1877

2nd Impression 2026

Printed at: Gyan Press, Delhi.

The book is sold subject to the condition that it shall not, by way of trade or otherwise, be lent, resold, hired out, or otherwise circulated without the prior publisher's written consent.

THE STUDENTS MANUAL OF ANCIENT HISTORY
Author: W. COOKE TAYLOR

THE

STUDENT'S MANUAL

OF

ANCIENT HISTORY:

CONTAINING THE

POLITICAL HISTORY, GEOGRAPHICAL POSITION, AND SOCIAL STATE OF THE PRINCIPAL NATIONS OF ANTIQUITY, DIGESTED FROM THE ANCIENT WRITERS, AND ILLUSTRATED BY THE DISCOVERIES OF MODERN SCHOLARS AND TRAVELLERS.

BY

W. COOKE TAYLOR, LL.D.

NEW EDITION.

LONDON:
LONGMANS, GREEN, AND CO.
1877.

TO

THE RIGHT HONOURABLE

THE MARQUIS OF LANSDOWNE, K.G.

THIS WORK

IS RESPECTFULLY DEDICATED

BY HIS OBLIGED AND GRATEFUL SERVANT,

THE AUTHOR.

PREFACE.

The plan of the following work is briefly explained in the Introductory Chapter, and may easily be understood by a glance at the Table of Contents. The author's design was to present students with a survey of ancient history, containing not merely a simple record of facts, but some notice of the natural and moral causes that produced the chief revolutions of antiquity. For this purpose he has described the geographical position, the social state, the commercial condition, and the progress in civilisation of the leading empires and republics. In this he has only followed the example of Heeren, whose *Manual*, an invaluable treasure to historical lecturers, is unsuited to the use of students, requiring a stock of information not to be expected in youth, and referring to a great number of volumes that could not be comprised in ordinary libraries. Though restricted to narrow limits, the author trusts that no important omission will be detected; while, at the same time, he trusts that he has opened to youthful students new and valuable stores of information, which were hitherto available only to the learned; among these subjects he may mention, as particularly interesting to British youth, the chapters on the trade of Asia and Africa, and on the colonial policy of the Greeks.

Some important documents are added in the Appendix, especially the first commercial treaty between Rome and Carthage, and Hanno's Periplus, the earliest account of a voyage of discovery that has come down to our times.

It will be observed, that in the chapters on Asiatic history, the author has consulted the oriental writers, as well as the western historians. From the importance that attaches to the age of Cyrus, on account of his connexion with sacred history, a brief dissertation respecting the various narratives given of his career has been inserted; and the author trusts it will be found to corroborate, in no slight degree, the historical verity of the Old Testament.

It would be a mere parade of learning to enumerate the works used in the preparation of this Manual; but respect to the memory of a dear friend justifies the mention of the late Professor Shea's excellent translation of *Mirkhond;* and very extensive obligations demand the special mention of the three great German historians, Heeren, Niebuhr, and Washsmuth. The author is himself responsible for the theory, that there was some connexion in origin between the dominant races of Persia and India; but it was suggested by a dissertation of Schlegel's in the Reports of the Royal Society of Literature, and seems to be hinted at in Burnouf's Dissertations on the Zend language.

In conclusion, the author begs leave to express a hope, that while this will be found to contain sufficient information respecting the ancient world for the use of ordinary students, it may serve as a guide and stimulus to those who have taste and leisure for more extensive investigations.

From the great number of names and dates in these pages, it is probable that some typographical errors may have escaped detection; but it is hoped that none will be found of sufficient magnitude to produce inconvenience.

London, August 1836.

TABLE OF CONTENTS.

Chapter V.—*Palestine.*

Chapter VI.—*The Empire of the Medes and Persians.*

Chapter VII.—*Phœnician Colonies in Northern Africa.*

Chapter VIII.—*The Foundation of the Grecian States.*

Chapter IX.—*History of the Grecian States and Colonies before the Persian War.*

CHAPTER XV.—*History of the Roman Republic.*

CHAPTER XVI.—*Geographical and Political Condition of the Roman Empire.*

CHAPTER XVII.—*History of the Roman Empire.*

APPENDIX.

INTRODUCTION.

A complete Universal History, a record of all the events that have passed in all nations, would be a work impossible to execute, and unprofitable if it were possible to be accomplished. The use of history is not to load the memory with facts, but to store the mind with principles,—to collect from the experience of past ages rules for our conduct as individuals and as members of society. Every historical work, therefore, professes to give only a selection of events; and the writer's choice is determined by the nature of his history: the general historian directs attention to the occurrences that have changed the general aspect of society, the revolutions of states and empires, the causes that led to them, and the consequences by which they were followed. The special historian confines his attention to one class of facts, specified in the title of his work: thus the ecclesiastical historian writes only of the affairs of the church; the military historian confines his narrative to wars and battles; and the commercial historian devotes his attention exclusively to trade.

But even general histories may, in some degree, be regarded as special; their object may be called "political," that is, they profess to describe the destinies of nations, both in their external relations with foreign states, and in their internal affairs. Under the first head are comprised wars, treaties of peace or alliance, and commercial intercourse; under the second, governments, institutions, and manners. Such a history must, to a certain extent, be a history of civilisation; for it will describe the progress of social improvement, and the progress of the human mind. These essential parts of civilisation must not be confounded; for we shall have more than once occasion to remark, that the social system, or, in other words, the relations between the different parts of society, may display great wisdom and justice, while men, in their individual capacity, continue the slaves of ignorance and superstition.

A distinction is usually made between the narrative and the philosophy of history: in the former are included the actions of kings and rulers, the accounts of wars and treaties, the rise and fall of empires; in the latter are comprehended descriptions of the political and religious institutions, the organisation of society, the amount of knowledge, the state of industry and the arts, the morals, the habits, and the prevailing prejudices in any age or nation; and the facts, thus ascertained by philosophy, are shewn to be the causes of the events detailed in the narrative. It is possible to go back a step farther, and to trace the origin of these institutions and manners in the succession of opinions and gradual development of the human intellect. But unassisted reason can go no farther; the law fixed by Providence for the succession of opinions, and development of mind, can only be known to its omniscient Author; but that such a law exists is proved to us by the fulfilment of prophecy, by the frequent instances of unconscious agents working out the great designs of God.

It is proposed in the following pages to unite the philosophy with the narrative of history, to combine events with their causes, and direct occasionally the attention of the student to the progress of civilisation, both in its effects on society and on individuals. Sacred history, the account of the direct operations of the Divine agency on his chosen servants and chosen people, is necessarily excluded from a political history; but the general course of Providence displayed in the moral government of his creatures is an essential element of our plan; it is, in fact, the principle of unity that binds together its several parts.

The necessary companions of history are chronology and geography; they determine the time when, and the place where, each event occurred. The difficulties of chronology arise both from the imperfection of records, and from varieties in the mode of computation: the former cannot be remedied;

but, to prevent the mistakes which may arise from this cause, uncertain dates have been marked with an asterisk: the second source of confusion is removed by using throughout solar years for a measure of time, and the birth of Christ as an era from which to reckon.

Instead of constructing a general system of ancient geography, it has seemed better to prefix a geographical outline to the history of each separate country, and to combine with it some account of the nature of the soil, and its most remarkable animal and vegetable productions. There is no doubt that the position, climate, and fertility of a country have a powerful influence over the character, condition, and destiny of its inhabitants, and ought not to be omitted in the consideration of their history.

The arrangement of this work is both chronological and geographical; the history of each country is given separately, but the states are arranged in the order of their attaining a commanding influence in the world. To this there are two exceptions — Egypt, which is placed first, on account of its being the earliest organised government of which we have any authentic record; and India, which is placed last, because it exercised no marked influence over the most remarkable nations of ancient times.

The history of Greece in this volume has a less orderly appearance than in most similar works, because it contains not merely the histories of Athens and Sparta, to which most writers confine their attention, but also those of the minor states, the islands, and the colonies. A chapter has been added on the colonial policy of the Greeks; a subject of great importance in itself, and peculiarly interesting to a commercial country.

To the Roman history there is prefixed a brief account of the ancient inhabitants of Italy before the era usually assigned for the foundation of Rome. In the earlier period of the republic notice is taken of the reasonable doubts that have been raised respecting the authenticity of the common narrative; but care has been taken to avoid an excess of scepticism, which is at least as bad as an excess of credulity.

In the chapter on India attention has been directed to the ancient routes of trade between that country and eastern Europe; many of these subsist to the present day; projects have been formed for re-opening others; some account of them consequently appears necessary for illustrating both ancient commerce and modern policy.

In a general summary, restricted within narrow limits, it is scarcely possible to avoid dryness of details; notes have therefore been added, consisting for the most part of illustrations and anecdotes, that may serve both to relieve the mind, and to place important traits of character, national and individual, in a clearer light.

An appendix of tables has been added, in which the student will find much chronological and genealogical information condensed into forms convenient for reference.

It has been deemed advisable to take some notice of the mythology, as well as the real history, of nations; for though mythic traditions may in many or in most instances have had no foundation, yet they should not be wholly neglected by the historian, for they had a share in forming, and they help to illustrate, the character of the nation by which they were once believed. At the same time, care has been taken to separate these traditions from the authenticated narrative, and to discriminate between those that have and those that have not some probable foundation in fact.

Political reflections and moral inferences from the narrative have, in general, been avoided: the instructive lessons of history are, for the most part, found on the surface, and may best be collected by the students themselves. It is not quite fair to prejudge questions for the mind; the chief business of those who write for the young should be to make them think, not to think for them.

The author has to acknowledge his great obligations to the works of Professor Heeren, whose volumes on the "Politics, Intercourse, and Trade of Ancient Nations," should form part of every historical library: he has also borrowed very copiously from the valuable essays that have appeared in the "Memoirs of the French Academy of Inscriptions;" his particular obligations in the several chapters need not be specified, most of them being mentioned in the notes.

The design of this Introduction is merely to explain the plan of the work; some few suggestions, however, may be added on the mode of using it. Students should compare the geographical chapters with maps, and fix in their minds the most characteristic natural features of the country whose history they are about to commence. One division should be thoroughly mastered before another is begun; and when the whole is gone through, it will be found a most useful exercise to synchronise the events in the history of one country with the events in the history of another. For instance, to trace the condition of the Roman republic at the time of the battle of Arbela.

Should the work be found as useful as it is expected to be, care will be taken in each successive edition to introduce such corrections as may be derived from the additions made to our stores of knowledge by the discoveries of travellers, and the researches of antiquaries.

The design of the work having been now explained, the author has only to hope that its execution may be found to correspond with his intentions, and that it may afford pleasure and profit to his readers.

CHAPTER I.

EGYPT.

Section I. — *Geographical Outline.*

Egypt is the country in which we first find a government and political institutions established, though we cannot affirm with certainty that they did not earlier exist in India. The probable cause of this early advancement in civilisation may be found in the nature of the country: civilisation every where seems to have commenced in the formation of agricultural associations on the banks of rivers; and the Nile, the great river of Egypt, invites men to tillage more forcibly than any other. This river is not only the most important feature in the geography and natural history of the country,—Egypt itself having been called from the earliest antiquity "the gift of the Nile,"—but its annual inundations have had a vast influence over the lives and customs, the religion and science, indeed, we may say, the entire social existence of the people. It appears that civilisation advanced northwards along the valley of the river; and we shall therefore commence our examination of the land and river at the southern frontier of Egypt.

The Nile enters Egypt near the city of Syene, below the cataracts, and flows through a narrow valley, about nine miles in breadth, to Chemmis; there the valley begins to widen, and the river continues in an uninterrupted course to Cercasorus, about sixty geographical miles from its mouth. At Cercasorus the stream divides, and encloses in its branches a triangular piece of country, commonly called the Delta, from its resemblance to the Greek letter of that name. The narrow valley from Syene to Chemmis was called Upper Egypt; the wider valley was named Middle Egypt; and the Delta formed Lower Egypt.

Rain seldom falls in Lower Egypt, and is almost unknown in the upper regions; the fertility of the country therefore depends on the annual overflowing of the river, without which the fertile valley would speedily become a barren desert. These inundations are caused by the heavy rains that fall in the districts of Upper Ethiopia during the wet season, from May to September.

The rivers in these southern regions, which have been only partially explored by ancient or modern travellers, pour their floods into the Nile, which begins to rise sensibly about the middle of June: it continues to increase during the month of July; and early in August it overflows its banks, and gives the valley of the Nile the appearance of an inland sea, in which the cities seem like islands. Towards the beginning of October the waters subside, but so gradually do they retire, that the river is not confined to its ancient channel before the end of that month. The fertility of Egypt extends as far as this inundation reaches, or can be continued by artificial means. From the earliest ages canals have been dug to carry the waters to the distant soil, and to retain a supply after the inundation has subsided. So great is the productiveness of the soil thus irrigated, that two crops of pulse or corn have been obtained in the same year.

The eastern side of the valley of the Nile is a mountainous range of country, extending to the Red Sea, and presenting, in different parts, remarkable varieties of geological structure. There are some districts in it suited for pasturage, but it is wholly unfit for agriculture: here, however, are to be found the rich quarries of marble and building-stone that formed the inexhaustible magazines for the architectural wonders of Egypt. In the south-eastern part of these mountains, towards Philæ and the cataracts, the prevailing rock is oriental granite, called Syenite, from the city of Syene. From the granite quarries the ancient Egyptians obtained the enormous masses requisite for their monoliths, or monuments of a single block; and in them, even now, are found the forms whence the obelisks and colossal statues have been hewn out. Extending from Syene, in a northern direction, to Latopolis, is a range of sandstone rocks, varying in colour, but chiefly of a whitish or grayish hue. Of this stone all the temples in Upper Egypt are built; and as it is not very hard, the immense number of sculptures found upon the walls of these temples did not require the labour that must have been bestowed on the granite. The most northern part of these mountains is composed of calcareous rocks, and from these the materials of the pyramids were derived. It is necessary to add, that these mountain ranges are not continuous, but are crossed by valleys running from east to west, and extending to the Red Sea, which opened practicable roads for commercial purposes.

On the western side of the Nile the valley is bounded by a stony ridge, covered with sand, which slopes on its remote side into the Great Desert. But this ridge does not precisely mark the limit between fertility and desolation. For the most part, but particularly in Middle Egypt, where the valley begins to widen, there is a barren sandy strip, from one to three miles in breadth, intervening between the base of the mountain-chain and the land, suited to husbandry. This solitary waste is at once the image and the abode of death, the sandy plain and the hills being filled with countless graves and sepulchres, accumulated during a hundred generations; and this proximity of the living and the dead—this contact of all that is most delightful with all that is most gloomy—has had the most powerful effect in impressing on the Egyptians their very peculiar national character. The western ridge of hills protects the valley of the Nile from the invasion of the sands of the desert, which, without such a barrier, would have desolated the entire country. On some points this protection has proved insufficient, for there are many Egyptian edifices, pyramids, and colossal statues, found buried to the middle in sand; but in general this destructive enemy has been shut out by the mountain-barrier.

The desert beyond the western frontiers of Egypt may be termed a great sandy ocean, in which there are several fruitful spots, or islands of fertility, called oases. Two of these, celebrated for their fruitfulness and abundant springs from remote antiquity, are usually included in Egypt by ancient geographers.

Upper Egypt contains far the most numerous and interesting monuments. Just beyond the first cataract are the islands of Philæ and Elephantine, both of which contain the proudest edifices of antiquity. They stand surrounded by palm-groves, amid the ruins of buildings erected by Greeks, Romans, and Arabs, which have all yielded to the destroying hand of time. Below Syene, the ancient frontier-town of Egypt, are Ombos, Silsilis, and Eliethyia; and further down, the great city of Apollo, containing the most perfect of all the temples, except that of Thebes. Proceeding northwards, we pass the remains of Chnubis, Latopolis, and Hermonthis, before arriving at the metropolis of this region of wonders, "giant Thebes," which has been well called "the mammoth of human works."

Thebes, called also Diospolis, the city of Jupiter or of Ammon, was in the days of Homer regarded as the great wonder of the world, and it continues to be so at the present day. The entire breadth of the valley on both sides of the river, an area of about nine miles, is covered with enormous temples, that seem more like mountains than human edifices, with colossal statues, sphinxes, and obelisks, whose magnitude ensures their duration. Where the habitations of the living end, the dwellings of the dead begin, and extend a considerable distance into the western mountains. The city was built on both sides of the river, which is here about half a mile wide, and its parts were not, as far as we know, connected by a bridge. The western bank, being almost wholly occupied by public monuments, could not have contained many private houses; but on the eastern bank the monuments are all close to the river, and the space between them and the Arabian mountains was open for habitations. On the western side are the palace and temple now called Medínet Abú, the colossus of Memnon,* the palace and tomb of Osymandyas, and the temple of Gurnû. These are all covered with a profusion of sculptures, depicting scenes in Egyptian history. It has been calculated that the largest of the colossal statues, when complete, weighed more than eight hundred tons. On the east side are the stupendous ruins usually called Luxor and Karnac, covered with historical

* This was the celebrated vocal statue supposed to utter a sound at the rising of the sun. Mr. Wilkinson, from whose excellent work on Thebes our description of the city is chiefly taken, ascribes the sound to the contrivance of the priests.

sculptures of great interest and beauty. In the Libyan mountain-chain, on the western bank of the river, are the catacombs,—stupendous caverns excavated in the limestone-rock as sepulchres for the kings, the nobles, and the people, covered with sculptures and paintings that illustrate the public transactions and the domestic habits of the ancient Egyptians.

Below Thebes is Tentyris, the modern Dendera, celebrated for the zodiac sculptured on its mighty temple,—the first specimen of the gigantic and massive architecture peculiar to Egypt, that meets the eye of European visitors.

Middle Egypt is a wider valley than that just described. It contains the lake Mœris, an immense reservoir, partly natural and partly artificial, for retaining the waters of the Nile after the subsiding of the inundation. From the facilities afforded by canals for regulating the irrigation in this part of the valley, it was the most fruitful of the provinces, especially the district called Fayúm, in the neighbourhood of the ancient Arsinoë, called also the city of the crocodiles. The labyrinth, so renowned in antiquity, was near Arsinoë; it is now a shapeless mass of ruins.

Below Arsinoë, on the western bank of the Nile, stood Memphis, the capital of Middle Egypt, and, for a time, the successful rival of Thebes. There are now but slight remains of its temples and palaces; the mountains in its vicinity, however, are filled with catacombs, similar to those of Upper Egypt. But the most remarkable monuments of this district are the pyramids, which extend singly, or in groups, over the rocky Libyan hills between Memphis and the Delta. The area covered by the great pyramid of Cheops was about 570,000 square feet.

Lower Egypt, or the Delta, possesses, from the extension of the river, a greater quantity of fertile land than the other districts. The western chain of mountains turns off here into the Libyan desert, and the eastern ridge terminates near the modern city of Cairo. But the whole space enclosed by the extreme branches of the Nile is not fertile; many barren tracts are found in the Delta and the districts on either side of it: still, this division of Egypt, though civilised at a much later period than the other districts, was covered with flourishing cities, of which it is sufficient to name Sais, Naucratis, and Alexandria. There have been great changes made by the lapse of time, and the neglect of the canals and dams, in this district, more especially along the coast-line: the remains of cities must frequently be sought beneath the waters of the sea that formerly enriched them with commerce. The extreme city on the Syrian side was Rhinocorura, the modern Al Arísh, a good roadstead, though not a safe harbour. On the western side, at the frontier of the desert, is Alexandria, still retaining the name of its great founder, and proving by its extensive trade the wisdom that dictated its position.

Section II.—*Political and Social Condition of the Egyptians.*

From the monumental remains, and from the writings of historians, it appears that the Egyptians were a brown race of people, and that the higher castes of priests and warriors were fairer than the other classes. It seems probable that this difference of colour marked a difference of descent, and that the ruling race descended the Nile from Meroë, bringing with them the peculiar system of religion and government which subsequently prevailed along the course of the river. More than this cannot now be ascertained. It has indeed been conjectured that the Egyptians may have derived their system of civilisation from the Hindús; and there are doubtless many striking analogies between the institutions of both nations; but it is difficult to conceive how any great migration could have taken place from Hindústan, a country that never possessed a navy. There is certainly evidence of some small colonies having come from the mouth of the Indus to the shores of Africa, and penetrated thence to the Nile, south of the Egyptian frontiers; but it is improbable that these few wanderers could have become the founders of ruling tribes and the masters of a nation. There is now no doubt that the Hindús, or at least the higher castes, were a conquering nation that entered India from the north-west; and having penetrated to the Ganges, established on its fertile banks the centre of their religion and their government. It is impossible to discover the parent-country of these victors, or to determine whether they were originally connected with the dominant race in Egypt.

Local circumstances produced marked differences in the habits and manners of the Egyptian people. In the mountainous eastern districts, and in the fens of the Delta, agriculture was impossible, consequently the inhabitants led a pastoral life. Close to the Nile, and along the coast, were tribes of fishermen and mariners. In the rich plains of the valley dwelt the civilised part of the nation, whose great advance in the social arts, and every branch of domestic life, has only been recently discovered.

This difference in manner of life, and perhaps of descent, led to the institution of castes, which this nation had in common with the Hindús. The priests and warriors were the most honourable; next to them ranked the agriculturists, the merchants, the mariners, and the artisans; but their order varied at different times. The lowest caste was that of the shepherds; for "every shepherd was an abomination to the Egyptians."

The migrations of the priestly caste from their native regions in the south were not simultaneous: they formed settlements at different times in the most fertile portions of the valley; the central point of the colony was always a temple, round which, as the inhabitants became accustomed to agriculture, and fixed their dwellings, cities were gradually formed. These settlements, when Egypt became united under one government, led to the division of the country into *nomes*,—most of which, as we have seen, were originally separate states. Even in the latest periods, traces might be discovered of the origin of these divisions. "A nome," says St. Cyril, "is the name given by the Egyptians to a city, its environs, and the villages that own its supremacy."

There was a religious, as well as a political distinction between these nomes; for, though one general form of worship prevailed from Meroë to the Mediterranean, it was modified in each locality by circumstances that cannot now be satisfactorily explained. Every city had its own presiding deity, and the animals regarded as sacred in one nome were not respected in another. The particular history of these petty states is unknown; but they were finally absorbed in the dominion of Thebes and Memphis.

The nations bordering on the Egyptians were for the most part barbarous and wandering tribes, whose avarice was roused by the increasing opulence of the valley of the Nile. Arabia, whose nomad hordes have been herdsmen and robbers from the earliest period of history, and continue to be so in our own day, was the parent of the invaders who most severely harassed the ancient Egyptians. They were called the Hyksos, or shepherd-kings; and, after many desultory incursions, they made themselves masters of Lower and Middle Egypt, and erected a strong fortress, called Avaris, near Pelusium, as a place of retreat, and to secure communication with their countrymen.

Egypt became united under one sovereign after the expulsion of the Hyksos; and it appears that it was at this period that the divisions of the people into castes, and of the country into nomes, were permanently fixed. The priestly caste was subdivided into families, each devoted to a separate temple and a particular god. The priest of Ammon at Thebes could not become the priest of the Sun at Heliopolis, nor could the child of the latter dedicate himself to the same service as the former. This restriction arose naturally from the original nature of the nomes, which had been formed by the colonising priests. The founders of each nome had built a temple, had civilised the neighbouring tribes, had rendered the land productive by teaching the art of agriculture, and consequently supremacy over the nome was the natural inheritance of their descendants. Over each of these sacerdotal subdivisions a high priest presided, whose office was also hereditary; and it will readily be believed that the high priests of the metropolitan temples must have enjoyed authority almost equal to that of kings. And this influence was greatly strengthened by their monopoly of every branch of scientific knowledge. They were not merely priests, but also judges, soothsayers, physicians, architects, and sculptors.

The warrior-caste ranked next to that of the priests: the royal family belonged to it; for, in the early ages, the offices of king and general were inseparable. The warriors were subdivided into two classes, whose relative position cannot now be determined; certain nomes were assigned for their support, most of which were in Lower Egypt,—a circumstance easily explained by the fact, that Egypt was most exposed to attack on its Asiatic frontiers, and also by the first settlements on the Upper Nile having been formed by sacerdotal colonies.

The religion and government of Egypt were intimately blended: there were prescribed forms and ceremonies for every important action, which even kings dared not to neglect. This brought the priests into every department of the state, and gave them paramount control over public affairs and domestic life. To preserve this influence, they encouraged all the popular and local superstitions which prevailed among the lower castes, especially animal worship, which has always been common among the savage tribes of Africa. It seems certain that the religion of the priests was more refined and intellectual than the gross idolatry of the lower orders. Without attempting to explain all the mysteries of their mythology, it may be stated, that one general idea pervades the entire system—the importance of agriculture to a state. Hence arises the great influence of astronomy in the Egyptian theology, on account of its application to determining the times and seasons for agricultural operations: and hence the deification of the productive powers of nature, which can be distinctly traced under the symbolic veil that shrouds without wholly concealing them. Astronomy, in every eastern nation, is connected with astrology; but never was there a people more dependent on its priestly astrologers than the Egyptians. The stars were consulted for every public affair and every private undertaking; the priests alone had a right to consult these celestial monitors, and deliver their oracles. Whether they were always the dupes of their superstition, it is not necessary to investigate, because, whether impostors or not, they were equally checks to the king, and masters to the people. The belief in a future state influenced every portion of Egyptian life; but the nature of the creed is very difficult to be explained. In fact, there were two inconsistent creeds — the transmigration of souls, which was probably imported from India, and confined to the priestly caste; and the belief that the soul will continue as long as the body endures, whence the great care in the preparation of mummies, and the vast expense of hewing sepulchres in the solid rock. The latter was the popular opinion: hence, then, arose the importance of the rites of sepulture, and the dread of the trial after death, when a tribunal, under priestly direction, determined whether the body should be placed in the sacred tomb, or left without burial to the natural process of decay.

The relative position of the lower castes varied at different times; but all trades and professions were hereditary. It was probably supposed that this exclusive dedication of families to separate employments would ensure perfection in the arts; and certainly the progress made by the Egyptians, especially in architecture, surpasses that of any other nation. The edifices of Thebes seem the work of enchanters rather than of ordinary human beings; and modern mechanical knowledge fails to explain how the enormous blocks of which they are composed were raised and fixed in their places. The manufacture of glass was not only known, but also the art of staining and gilding it in imitation of precious stones. Their vases and furniture, as portrayed on the monuments, might challenge competition with any produced by workmen of the present day. But we shall have occasion to examine this subject more at length in the section on Egyptian trade and commerce.

Gymnastic exercises and music were the favourite amusements of the ancient Egyptians. At their meals, instead of squatting, like the generality of Orientals, or reclining on couches, like the Romans, they used chairs and tables not very unlike our own. Women were treated more respectfully than in other countries of the East; but the law invested husbands with power over life and limb in case of delinquency.

The stick was the common instrument of punishment for all minor offences; but only a stated number of stripes could be inflicted. Great respect was paid to old age and to rank. It seems plain from the monuments, that the different degrees of reverence, from a simple bow to complete prostration, were accurately settled, according to the station of the parties.

The principal trees of ancient Egypt were the sycamore, the fig, the pomegranate, the peach, the locust-tree, and the vine. Great care was taken of the vines: they were frequently trained over rafters, supported by low columns, affording shady arbours, and facility for gathering the ripened clusters. Wine was used in great quantities by the nobles and wealthy merchants.

Of esculent vegetables growing wild, the most remarkable were the lotus, a kind of lily, and the papyrus: the leaves of the latter, dried and prepared, were used for writing upon; and it is still used for mats and similar purposes. The cultivated vegetables were corn and pulse of various kinds, flax, cotton, melons, cucumbers, onions, &c. So abundant was the produce of these herbs, that four thousand persons were found to subsist by the sale of vegetables in Alexandria, when it was taken by the Saracens.

The domestic animals of the Egyptians were the same as those of most civilised countries. The cat was held in particular honour; and there is reason to believe that this useful animal was first brought under the dominion of man in Egypt. Dogs existed in several varieties: the race of hounds seems to have been very distinctly marked; whence we may conclude, that great attention was paid to the purity of their breed, on account of their value in hunting. Huntsmen, indeed, are said to have formed a separate caste, or rather subdivision of a caste, in Egypt; but the higher classes were fond of the sports of the field, and frequently enjoyed the chase of the wild beasts of the desert and the mountains. Not only hounds, but lions were trained to the chase of the deer and antelopes; but we find no trace of the leopard being employed for that purpose, as is now common in the East. The animals of the mountain and desert were chiefly the wild ox, goat and sheep, the gazelle or antelope, the hare, and the ostrich: the most common beasts of prey were the leopard, wolf, hyena, and jackal.

From the Ethiopian states, or from countries farther south, the monarchs of Egypt, in its proudest days, received as presents or tribute elephants, giraffes, monkeys, and other rare animals. They seem also to have obtained camels from some foreign country.

Among the amphibious animals of the Nile, the crocodile and the hippopotamus deserve especially to be noticed. The chase of the hippopotamus was not a mere amusement, the skin being regarded as the best covering for shields. It was rather a dangerous sport; the animal was first entangled in a running noose, at the extremity of a long line wound upon a reel, and then struck with the hunting spear. This weapon had a flat broad head, sharply barbed; a string was attached to the shaft, which was movable, and was drawn back when the blade entered the animal's body. The hippopotamus, on receiving a wound, plunged into the deep water, and was allowed to exhaust itself by violent struggles before it was again drawn to the surface. Then the same process was repeated, until the exhausted animal fell an easy prey to its assailants.

Wild and tame fowl abounded; the vulpanser goose of the Nile, bustards, partridges, quails, and widgeons, frequented the skirts of the desert, and the valley of the Nile. The poultry-yard was stocked not merely by the natural process of rearing chickens, but also by artificial means: the eggs of geese, and other poultry, were hatched in ovens heated to the requisite temperature; and this ingenious process is still used by the modern Copts.

SECTION III.—*History of Egypt from the earliest period to the Accession of Psammetichus.*

FROM B.C. 1900 TO B.C. 650.

IN the preceding section it has been stated that Egypt was originally composed of several small states, which, according to Manetho's catalogues, were first founded in Upper Egypt:* the principal states were Thebes, Elephantine, Theis, and Heracleia; to which may be added Memphis, in Middle Egypt. It is only in the last part of his enumeration that we find the dynasties of Lower Egypt, such as Tanis, Mendes, and Bubastis. Though Thebes was the most ancient of the powerful states, Memphis is that of which we have the earliest accounts. It was visited by Abraham and his great-grandson Joseph, who became the prime minister of its sovereign. At this time Egypt possessed a regular government, a brilliant court, and an organised priesthood and army. Agriculture was in a flourishing condition; and many of its institutions displayed a great advance in civilisation. Joseph brought his father and brethren into Egypt, and obtained for them from the Pharaoh, or king, then reigning, a grant of a fruitful district, called Goshen, near the city of Heliopolis, between the Red Sea and the Nile. During his administration the class of free proprietors was destroyed, and the property of all the soil in Egypt assigned to the king and the priests. This measure was perfectly in accordance with the principles of the Egyptian constitution, and was, in fact, only a union of the nomes into one system of government.

After the death of Joseph, the Bedouín Arabs, or Hyksos, invaded Lower Egypt: their incursions, at first undertaken merely for plunder, became expeditions for permanent conquest: they settled in the country, fortified Avaris or Pelusium; and, having become masters of Memphis, they made that metropolis the seat of their government. Like other bar-

* Manetho's original work is lost, but fragments have been preserved by several writers, especially Josephus and Eusebius. A more detailed examination of these catalogues will be found in the Appendix, No. I.

barian conquerors, they adopted much of the manners and civilisation of the vanquished, though they were tyrannical oppressors. The Israelites settled on the eastern bank of the Nile were regarded with great jealousy by the Hyksos: they were the natural allies of the Theban kings, who maintained their independence; and they occupied a position whence they could make an important diversion in favour of these monarchs, or intercept the retreat and the reinforcements of the Hyksos. On this account they were persecuted by the Pharaoh of the invaders,* and an attempt made for their extirpation by commanding their male children to be destroyed as soon as born. This savage expedient failed; and God, in his own good time, raised up Moses to deliver his chosen people. The Pharaoh, terrified by divine judgments, consented to the departure of the Israelites; but soon after, repenting of his extorted permission, he pursued them with a mighty host, and perished in the waters of the Red Sea.

This calamity (B.C. 1491) greatly weakened the power of the Hyksos, already menaced by the increasing strength of the Theban monarchy. Previous to this, we have scarcely any probable account of the names and ages of the Egyptian kings, except that Menes appears to have been the founder of the monarchy, and Osirtesen I. the Pharaoh who received Joseph. But henceforth we are able to determine with probability some general epochs, by comparing the evidence of the monuments with that of the historians. To this period belong the eighteenth and nineteenth dynasties of Manetho, the founders of the most important monuments of Upper Egypt. In the reign of Amenoph I. the Thebans extended their conquests to the south, and seized on part of Nubia. Crude brick arches were constructed at this period (B.C. 1540), and glass was soon after brought into use. Under the fourth king of this dynasty, Thutmosis, or Thothmes III., the children of Israel departed from Egypt, and the Theban monarch succeeded in expelling the Hyksos from the greater part of the country, and shutting

* Many of the statements in this chapter are founded on theory rather than certain evidence: the proofs of the view we have here taken will be found in the Appendix, No. I.

them up in their fortress. This stronghold was taken by his son and successor, Thothmes IV.; and the shepherd-kings surrendered on condition of being allowed to withdraw into Syria. The intimate connexion between these two events—the exodus of the Israelites, and the expulsion of the Hyksos—have led to their being confounded together. The next remarkable monarch was Amenoph III., who reigned conjointly with his brother; but, soon becoming weary of divided empire, he expelled his partner. The dethroned brother was probably the Danaus* of the Greeks, who, leaving Egypt with his partisans, settled in Argos, of which he became king (B.C. 1430). The pretended vocal statue of Memnon was erected in honour of Amenoph; and in his reign the building of the great temples seems to have been commenced. He annexed the greater part of Nubia to his dominions. Among his successors the name of Rameses is the most distinguished. It was borne by four sovereigns; two in the eighteenth, and two in the nineteenth dynasty. The first was expelled by his brother, and is by some identified with Danaus: the second, called Mi-Ammon, "he who loves Ammon," was the founder of the palace of Medínet Abú at Thebes; and from the sculptures on its walls, he appears to have been a warrior and conqueror.

Amenoph IV. was the last of the eighteenth dynasty. In his unfortunate reign the Hyksos renewed their invasions; and Amenophis, confiding his son, a child of five years old, to the care of a friend, fled into Ethiopia, where he remained thirteen years an exile. During this period the Hyksos were guilty of the most wanton excesses; for "they not only set fire to the cities and villages, but committed every kind of sacrilege, and destroyed the images of the gods, and roasted and fed upon those sacred animals that were worshipped; and, having compelled the priests and prophets to kill and sacrifice them, they cast them naked out of the country."† Amenophis at length, aided by an Ethiopian army, and sup-

* Others assign Danaus to a later period.

† Manetho, as quoted by Josephus.

ported by his gallant son, expelled the shepherd-kings, and restored the prosperity of his country.

Rameses the Great, called also Sethos or Sesostris,* is the most celebrated of the Egyptian monarchs. The conquests attributed to him are so mighty, that he has been by some regarded as merely a symbolical being; but, from the evidence of the monuments, he appears to be undoubtedly a historical personage. It is indeed doubtful whether the Rameses who founded Medínet Abú, or the son of Amenoph, be the great conqueror who carried his arms into Bactria in the east, and Thrace in the west, and before whose throne captives from the frozen Caucasus mingled with the sable tribes from the extreme south of Ethiopia: but the existence of this conqueror, his daring hunts of the lion in the desert while a youth, his aid in the expulsion of the Hyksos, his extensive conquests, and the vast treasures he collected from the vanquished nations, are satisfactorily proved by the sculptured history of his exploits on the walls of the buildings he erected or enlarged.

Having subdued the mountainous districts east of Egypt, and part of the Arabian peninsula, he fitted out a fleet of war-galleys to scour the Indian seas. The naval engagements sculptured on the walls of Medínet Abú and Karnac fully support the account of these expeditions given by the historians, and shew that they were extended to the western coasts of Hindústan. Ethiopia was subdued, and compelled to pay a tribute of ebony, gold, and elephants' teeth. The battle, the victory, the offering of the booty and tribute, are represented on the monuments at Kalabshè, in Lower Nubia. In one compartment, the captive king is seen falling beneath the sword of his ruthless conqueror; in the next, the widowed queen, accompanied by her two sons, supplicates for mercy. Another shews the tribute, consisting of wild and tame animals, apes, and birds of prey: even the giraffe, from the heart of Africa, forms part of the procession. His campaigns in Asia

* Wilkinson identifies Rameses II. with Sesostris.

and Europe were equally remarkable. Northwards he subdued Syria, Anatolia, and part of Thrace; eastwards he is said to have advanced as far as Bactria and India. There can, however, be no doubt of his exploits in the neighbourhood of Assyria and the Euphrates; for they are represented on the sculptures of the building called the tomb of Osymandyas, but which should rather be called the temple-palace of King Rameses.

" On the north face of the eastern pyramidal tower or propylon is represented the capture of several towns from an Asiatic enemy, whose chiefs are led in bonds by the victorious Egyptians towards the camp of their army. Several of these towns are introduced into the picture, each bearing its name in hieroglyphic characters." . . . . These sculptures prove the barbarity of ancient warfare. " In the scene here represented, an insolent soldier pulls the beard of his helpless captive; while others wantonly beat the suppliant, or satiate their fury with the sword. Beyond these is a corps of infantry in close array, flanked by a strong body of chariots; and a camp, indicated by a rampart of Egyptian shields, with a wicker gateway, guarded by four companies of sentries, who are on duty on the inner side, forms the most interesting object in this picture. Here the booty taken from the enemy is collected; oxen, chariots, waggons, horses, asses, sacks of gold, represent the confusion incident after a battle; and the richness of the spoil is expressed by the weight of a bag of money, under which an ass is about to fall. One chief is receiving the salutation of a foot soldier; another, seated amidst the spoil, strings his bow, and a sutler suspends a water-skin on a pole he has fixed in the ground. Below this a body of infantry marches homewards; and beyond them, the king, attended by his fan-bearers, holds forth his hand to receive the homage of the priests and principal persons, who approach his throne to congratulate his return. His charioteer is also in attendance; and the high-spirited horses of his car are with difficulty restrained by three grooms, who hold them. Two captives below this are doomed to be beaten, probably to death, by four Egyptian soldiers; while they in vain, with outstretched hands, implore the clemency of their heedless conqueror." .... "Upon the west tower is represented a battle, in which the king discharges his arrows upon the broken lines and flying chariots of the enemy; and his figure and car are again introduced, on the upper part, over the smaller sculptures. In a small compartment beyond these, which is formed by the end of the corridor of the area, he stands, armed with a battle-axe, about to slay the captives he holds beneath him, and who, in the hieroglyphics above, are described as the chiefs of the foreign courtiers." .... "On the north face of the south-east wall of the next area, the king is represented pursuing an enemy, whose numerous chariots, flying over the plain, endeavour to regain the river, and seek shelter under the fortified walls of their city. In order to check the approach of the Egyptians, the enemy had crossed the river, whose stream, divided into a double fosse, surrounded the towered walls of their fortified city, and opposed their advance by a considerable body of chariots; while a large reserve of infantry, having crossed the bridges, was posted on the other bank to cover their retreat, or second their advance; but, routed by the Egyptian invaders, they are forced to throw themselves back upon the town; and many, in recrossing the river, are either carried away by the stream, or fall under the arrows of the advancing conqueror. Those who have succeeded in reaching the opposite bank are rescued by their friends, who, drawn up in three phalanxes, witness the defeat of their comrades, and the flight of the remainder of their chariots. Some carry to the sea the lifeless corpse of their chief, who was drowned in the river, and in vain endeavour to restore life, by holding the head downwards to expel the water; and others implore the clemency of the victor, and acknowledge him their conqueror and lord." .... "On the south wall of the great hall is a small but interesting battle, in which the use of the ladder and the testudo throw considerable light on the mode of warfare at this early period. The town, situated on a lofty rock, is obstinately defended, and many are hurled headlong from its walls by the spears, arrows, and stones of the besieged. They, however, on the nearer approach of the Egyptian king, are obliged to sue for peace, and send heralds, with presents, to deprecate his fury; while his infantry, commanded by his sons, are putting to the sword the routed enemy they have overtaken beneath the walls, where they had in vain looked for refuge, the gates being already beset by the Egyptian troops."*

The successors of Sesostris seem to have sunk into the usual indolence of Oriental monarchs. Their history, for nearly three hundred years, presents little more than a catalogue of names, until we come to Sesonchis, the Shishak of the Holy Scriptures, who was the first monarch of the twenty-second dynasty. In the fifth year of the reign of Rehoboam, the foolish and wicked son of Solomon (B.C. 970), Shishak made war against Palestine, and pillaged Jerusalem. His army consisted of twelve hundred chariots, sixty thousand horsemen, and an innumerable body of infantry, consisting not only of Egyptians, but also of Libyans, Ethiopians, and Troglodytes. His empire consequently extended beyond the bounds of Egypt, and included a large portion of southern and western Africa.

In the next century the Egyptian monarchy declined rapidly, and the country was subjugated by Sabaco, a foreign conqueror from Ethiopia. The history of the Ethiopian dynasty will be found in the next chapter.

After some time, a priest, named Sethos, usurped the government, contrary to all precedent. He not only neglected the caste of warriors, but deprived them of their privileges and lands; at which they were so incensed, that they refused to bear arms in his defence. Sennacherib, king of Assyria, prepared to invade Egypt with a very powerful army, and advanced to Pelusium (B.C. 713). Sethos, deserted by the military caste, armed the labourers and artificers, and with this undisciplined host marched to meet the invader. A pestilence in the Assyrian camp saved Egypt from ruin, and Sennacherib returned to meet fresh misfortunes at Jerusalem. When Sethos died, twelve princes, or heads of nomes, shared the

* Wilkinson's Thebes and its Monuments, pp. 15—22.

kingdom among them; but, soon quarrelling about the limits of their respective principalities, they engaged in mutual war, and drove one of their number, Psammetichus, prince of Sais, into exile. Psammetichus levied an army of Greek and Carian mercenaries, most of whom appear to have been pirates; and, having overcome all his rivals, once more united all Egypt into a single monarchy, of which Memphis ranked as the capital, though Sais was usually the seat of government. The intercourse with the nations in the eastern Mediterranean was greatly extended during the reign of Psammetichus: many Greeks settled in the Egyptian sea-ports; and a new caste of interpreters and brokers was formed to facilitate commerce. But the patronage of foreigners, and the preference that Psammetichus shewed for the mercenaries to whom he owed his crown, so disgusted the caste of warriors, that the whole body emigrated from their country, and settled in Ethiopia (B.C. 650).

Section IV.—*History of Egypt from the Reign of Psammetichus to its Subjugation by Cambyses.*

FROM B.C. 650 TO B.C. 525.

The accession of Psammetichus was followed by a complete revolution in the ancient policy of Egypt: foreign auxiliaries performed the duties of the warrior caste; plans of permanent conquests in Syria succeeded to the predatory expeditions of the ancient Pharaohs; and the political influence of the priesthood rapidly declined, as new opinions were imported from abroad, and new institutions rendered necessary by increasing commerce. For several reigns, the great object of Egyptian policy was to obtain possession of the commercial cities of Syria and Phœnicia, not merely on account of the vast wealth that had been accumulated in them during the course of centuries, but from a desire to monopolise the carrying trade between Europe and Asia, by securing all the routes between the Indian Ocean and the Mediterranean. Psammetichus led the way by laying siege to Azotus, a frontier town of Syria,—persevering in successive attacks for twenty-nine years, until he accomplished his object.

Nechus, called in Scripture Pharaoh-Necho, succeeded his father Psammetichus (B.C. 616), and became a powerful prince both by land and sea. He built a fleet in the Mediterranean and the Red Sea, and attempted to unite them by cutting a canal across the isthmus of Suez; an enterprise subsequently completed by Darius Hystaspes.* The increasing strength of the Medes and Babylonians, who had overthrown the ancient empire of Assyria, justly alarmed Necho. He led an army against the king of Assyria, directing his march towards the Euphrates, but was checked by the interference of Josiah, king of Judah, who tried to prevent him from besieging Charchemish or Circesium. Necho remonstrated with Josiah, declaring, "What have I to do with thee, thou king of Judah? I come not against thee this day, but against the house wherewith I have war: for God commanded me to make haste: forbear thee from meddling with God, who is with me, that he destroy thee not."† Josiah disregarded this friendly remonstrance; and, encountering the Egyptians in the valley of Magdolus or Megiddo, was defeated and slain. Necho, having reached the Euphrates, captured the important city of Charchemish or Circesium, which he garrisoned. On his return to Egypt he became master of Jerusalem, led its monarch, Jehoahaz, away captive, and placed Jehoiakim upon the throne.

The Chaldean dynasty in Babylon rose into power on the ruins of the Assyrian empire. Nebuchadnezzar, its mightiest monarch, resolved on the conquest of western Asia; and one of his earliest efforts was the expulsion of the Egyptians from Charchemish. Necho tried to check the progress of this formidable opponent; but he was defeated with great slaughter, and stripped of all his possessions in Syria and Judæa, to the very walls of Pelusium.

* The navigation of the northern part of the Red Sea is so very dangerous, that this canal was never of much use. Vessels usually stopped at Myos Hormos, now Cosseir, whence there was a good caravan-road to the Nile.

† 2 Chron. xxxv. 21.

During his wars in Syria, Necho did not neglect the improvement of navigation. A Phœnician fleet, equipped at his expense, sailed down the Red Sea, passed the straits of Babel-Mandel, and, coasting the African continent, discovered the passage round the Cape of Good Hope, two thousand years before the re-discovery of it by Diaz and Vasco de Gama. The expedition returned to Egypt through the Atlantic Ocean, the Straits of Gibraltar, and the Mediterranean, after an absence of three years.

During the reign of Psammis, the son of Necho, a remarkable circumstance occurred (B.C. 600), tending to prove the ancient connexion between the institutions of Greece and Egypt, which has been denied by the modern historians of the German school. An embassy was sent from the city of Elis to obtain directions for the management of the Olympic games; and the regulations suggested by the Egyptian priests were implicitly obeyed.

Apries, the Pharaoh-Hophra of Scripture, immediately after his accession (B.C. 594), attacked the Phœnician states, and conquered Sidon. He entered into a close alliance with Zedekiah, king of Judah, promising to aid him in his revolt against Nebuchadnezzar. Apries, in fulfilment of his engagement, led an army into Judæa; and Nebuchadnezzar, on receiving intelligence of his approach, broke up the siege of Jerusalem, and hastened to meet him: but the Egyptians were afraid to encounter the Babylonian forces, and retired, without striking a blow, to their own country, leaving their allies to bear the brunt of Nebuchadnezzar's vengeance. For this act of perfidy, God, by the mouth of his prophet Ezekiel, denounced severe vengeance on the Egyptians and their sovereign, declaring, "Behold, I will bring a sword upon thee, and cut off man and beast out of thee. And the land of Egypt shall be desolate and waste; and they shall know that I am the Lord: because he hath said, The river is mine, and I have made it. Behold, therefore, I am against thee; and I will make the land of Egypt utterly waste and desolate, from Migdol to Syene,* even

* Migdol was a city on the north-eastern frontier of Egypt, and Syene the last city to the south.

unto the border of Ethiopia . . . And I will bring again the captivity of Egypt, and will cause them to return to the land of Pathros,* into the land of their habitation; and they shall be there a base kingdom. It shall be the basest of the kingdoms; neither shall it exalt itself any more above the nations: for I will diminish them, that they shall no more rule over the nations."† Not less distinct is the prophecy of Jeremiah: "Behold, I will give Pharaoh-Hophra, king of Egypt, into the hand of his enemies, and into the hand of them that seek his life; as I gave Zedekiah, king of Judah, into the hand of Nebuchadnezzar, his enemy, and that sought his life."‡

The accomplishment followed close upon the latter prediction. A Grecian colony established at Cyrene, being strengthened by fresh bodies of their countrymen, under their third king, Pattus the Happy, attacked the neighbouring Libyans, and seized their land. Andican, one of the dispossessed princes, applied for aid to Pharaoh-Hophra, who sent a large army to his relief. The Egyptians were routed with great slaughter by the Cyreneans; and the fugitives, to excuse their defeat, averred that they had been designedly betrayed by their monarch. This calumny was the pretext for a universal revolt. After a long civil war, of which Nebuchadnezzar took advantage to devastate Lower Egypt, Apries was dethroned by Amasis, and strangled in prison (B.C. 569).

The usurper was a man of mean birth; but his great abilities enabled him to overcome the Egyptian prejudice of caste, especially as he had the wisdom to conciliate the affection of the priesthood. He entered into close alliance with the Greeks, and made a Cyrenean princess the partner of his throne. To secure the commerce of the Mediterranean, he conquered the island of Cyprus, and exacted a tribute from the inhabitants. Following the policy of his predecessors, he tried to establish his supremacy in western Asia, on the decline of the Babylonian power, and entered into close alliance with Crœsus against Cyrus. He was defeated, and compelled to become tributary to the conqueror. On the death of Cyrus, he attempted to

* The Thebaïd, or Upper Egypt. † Ezekiel, xxix. 8—15.

‡ Jeremiah, xliv. 30.

assert his independence, and thus provoked the rage of Cambyses, that monarch's successor. At the very moment that the Persian invaders were approaching, Amasis quarrelled with Phanes, the commander of the Greek mercenaries, and his ally Polycrates, the king of Samos, both of whom tendered their aid to Cambyses. But before the evil hour of the Persian invasion arrived, Amasis died (B.C. 525), bequeathing to his son Psammenitus a kingdom torn by internal dissensions, and menaced by a formidable enemy.

Scarcely had Psammenitus ascended the throne, when Cambyses appeared on the frontiers of Egypt, and laid siege to Pelusium. This important garrison was taken, after a very weak resistance; and the Persians advanced into the open country. Psammenitus led an army, chiefly composed of mercenaries, against them; but was so completely overthrown, that he was no longer able to save his capital. Cambyses, provoked by the murder of one of his ambassadors, put to death the chief of the Egyptian nobles, and reduced their wives and children to slavery. He was at first inclined to spare the life of the unfortunate king; but subsequently learning that he had incautiously expressed a desire for revenge, the cruel conqueror condemned him to drink poison.

Cambyses was the deadly enemy of the religion and the priestly caste of the Egyptians: he slew their sacred animals, destroyed their idols, and pillaged their temples. A national animosity existed between the Persians and Egyptians during the whole time that Egypt remained subject to the Persian empire, producing oppression on the one side, and frequent rebellions on the other. It is probable that the Persians, recently delivered from the yoke of the Medes, who appear to have been a priestly and warrior caste rather than a nation, considered every ecclesiastical aristocracy as their natural enemy, and that their persecutions were directed rather against the political influence of the priests than their religious opinions and usages. It is certain that the priests were the principal instigators of the several attempts made to throw off the Persian yoke, and that they were the principal sufferers when these insurrections were suppressed.

SECTION V.—*Egyptian Manufactures and Commerce.*

Having already mentioned the capabilities of Egypt for agriculture and pasturage, and the principal natural productions of the soil, it is unnecessary to repeat the statement of the great fertility and richness of the valley of the Nile. The monuments shew us that the progress of the Egyptians in the mechanical arts was much greater than had usually been supposed, and that an accurate examination of their machinery might suggest useful hints to the mechanist of the present day. It will not be possible, in our limited space, to do more than glance at the principal branches of their industry; and in many cases the raw materials of native growth cannot be distinguished from those imported.

Weaving was the most important branch of the national industry, the cotton and the flax being indigenous. It is uncertain whether silk was used; but the fibres of many river-plants appear to have furnished materials for nets and coarse canvass. Hence the prophet Isaiah, describing the miseries that were to befall Egypt and its labouring classes, joins the weavers and the fishermen together: "They shall turn the rivers far away; and the brooks of defence shall be emptied and dried up: the reeds and flags shall wither. The paper-reeds by the brooks, by the mouth of the brooks, and every thing sown by the brooks, shall wither, be driven away, and be no more. The fishers also shall mourn, and all they that cast angle into the brooks shall lament, and they that spread nets upon the waters shall languish. Moreover, they that work in fine flax (or cotton), and they that weave networks (more correctly, white stuffs), shall be confounded. And they shall be broken in the purposes thereof, all that make sluices and ponds for fish."* These stuffs were woven in large manufactories, under the superintendence of the priests, who had a monopoly of all the cloths used for sacred purposes, especially for the mummies.

* Isaiah, xix. 6—10, and Gesenius's Commentary.

These stuffs were generally dyed in the wool, and many of them were embroidered with threads of gold and silver wire; some are striped, others stained or flowered, and the colours of all exhibit those dazzling hues of the East which we are unable to rival in Europe. Some of the garments appear to be of the finest muslin, and shew the limbs beneath them; and this is especially the case with the robes of the kings and priests. The several colours, white, yellow, green, blue, red, and black, are met with in great perfection; but they are never found mixed, the Egyptians not having discovered the art of producing a variety of shades.

The manufactures in metal rank next in importance. Iron appears to have been but little known: nearly all the implements not made of gold or silver depicted on the monuments seem to be either copper or brass. It would seem that the Egyptians had some means of giving hardness and temper to copper now unknown; for we find not only swords, but bows and quivers made of this metal. Their workmanship, both in metal and wood, was superior to that of any other ancient nation. The forms of their beds and couches may even now be taken as models; their harps far surpassed ours in the elegance of their shapes; the spindles and work-baskets of the ladies inspire a high notion of the refinement of their domestic life.

Egypt produced excellent clay for pottery; and earthenware was used not only for domestic purposes, but for preserving the mummies of the sacred animals. No words could adequately describe the variety and beauty of the shapes into which their vases were moulded, and the rich colours with which some of them are painted: they rival the choicest specimens of Grecian or Etruscan art.

Ship-building did not become common in Egypt until its rulers became masters of the Phœnician forests; but they manufactured vessels of burden for navigating the Nile. "Their boats were of various kinds: the larger ones were built of acacia planks, fastened by bolts and nails upon strong piles, and were furnished with spacious cabins, one mast, and a large square sail. Their long rudder was suspended on a sort of mast or wooden pillar; and, according to the direction of a rope held by the steersman, it slided to the right and left along the edge of a broad squared recess at the stern, the pillar being the centre on which it turned. They were also furnished with large oars, supported and moving on tollpins; and, except in galleys of war, the men generally pulled standing, or rose to the stroke. Other boats of smaller size had a rudder on either side, which, like the former, consisted of a long, broad blade, and still longer handle, the rope serving for a tiller." *

The Thebaïd was the central point of trade between southern Asia and the western regions, and between Ethiopia and northern Africa. Besides the advantages arising from its geographical position, the most ancient and productive gold-mines in the world were in its immediate neighbourhood: thus it possessed at once the commodities most in request, and the greatest facilities for disposing of them. From Ethiopia and the Negro countries caravans brought gold, ivory, ebony, skins, and slaves, to Syene; incense was imported from Arabia, and spices from India; and these were sold to the Greek and Phœnician merchants at the northern ports; for the Egyptians seem to have neglected the carrying trade of the Mediterranean. The principal native commodities exported were corn and the varied produce of the Egyptian looms. The corn-trade must have been particularly valuable; for Egypt was generally regarded as the granary of the adjacent countries, especially Syria and Arabia.

Commerce was fettered by many restrictions, arising from the prejudices of caste and the national jealousy of strangers, until the accession of Psammetichus, when the services of the Greek mercenaries opened the ports to their countrymen. It was checked, but not destroyed, by the Persian invasion, and suffered many interruptions during the various rebellions that followed; but it was revived again in all its ancient greatness under the Ptolemies, whose history we shall have to consider in a future chapter.

* Wilkinson's Thebes, p. 254.

CHAPTER II.

THE ETHIOPIANS.

SECTION I.—*Geographical Outline. Natural History.*

THE northern part of Africa, west of Egypt, was inhabited by the semi-barbarous Libyan nation, whose tribes were different from those of the Moors and Arabs that now possess the country. Their descendants are recognised in the Berbers, who have been driven from the plains by successive invaders to the fastnesses of Mount Atlas. The eastern districts above the Nile, now called Nubia and Sennaar, have been possessed from a remote age by two different races, the Ethiopian and the Arabian, which are even now but partially blended. The country is full of historical monuments, chiefly erected on the banks of the Nile. Several tribes are mentioned by ancient authors as tenanting this vast district, of which the most remarkable is the Troglodytes, who dwelt in caves formed by nature and improved by art, along the mountain-ridge that forms the eastern coast of Africa. The Macrobians, or long-lived people, appear to have possessed the best part of the Abyssinian territories, and to have carried on an extensive trade in gums, myrrh, frankincense, and slaves. The Icthyophagi, or fish-eaters, lived along the coasts of the Red Sea, and were the lowest in the scale of civilisation. There were, in these countries above Egypt, all the gradations from the complete savage to the hunting and fishing tribes, and from them to the wandering herdsman and shepherd; but there was also a civilised Ethiopian people, dwelling in cities, possessing a government and laws, acquainted with the use of hieroglyphics, the fame of whose progress in knowledge and the social arts had, in the earliest ages, spread over a considerable portion of the earth.

The Nile, before its confluence with the Astaboras (Mugrúm), runs through a very irregular valley formed by two chains of hills, which sometimes retire back, and sometimes advance to the very margin of the river. The soil of this valley was once as fertile as the richest part of Egypt, and, where protected, it still continues so; but the hills on both sides are bordered by sandy deserts, against which they afford but a scanty protection; and this destructive enemy has not only forced its way into the valley, but has frequently partially or wholly buried the monuments. Traces of canals are still manifest, sufficiently proving the sad change effected by the moving sand. The Nubian valley below the junction of the Nile and the Astaboras appears to have been sometimes subject to the Ethiopians of Meroë, and sometimes to the Egyptians. The navigation of the Nile is here impeded by the windings of the river and by the intervention of cataracts and rapids; so that intercourse is more generally maintained by caravans than by boats. At the southern extremity of the valley, the river spreads itself, and encloses a number of fertile islands. Along the whole course of the Nubian valley is a succession of stupendous monuments, rivalling those of Thebes in beauty, and exceeding them in sublimity.

The productions of the Ethiopian and Nubian valleys do not differ materially from those of Egypt, except that beasts of prey are more ferocious and abundant, and that venomous animals, more especially scorpions and a species of gad-fly, are so numerous as to render particular districts all but uninhabitable. The island of Meroë, as it was called from being nearly surrounded with rivers, possessed an abundance of camels, which, as we have seen, were little used in Egypt; but the ivory, ebony, and spices, which the Ethiopians sent down the river, were probably procured by traffic with the interior of Africa. Meroë had better harbours for Indian commerce than Egypt: not only were her ports on the Red Sea superior, but the caravan-routes to them were shorter, and the dangerous part of the navigation of that sea was wholly avoided.

The wild tracts in the neighbourhood of Meroë are tenanted by animals whose chase afforded employment to the ancient, as it does now to the modern, hunting tribes; especially that singular creature the giraffe, or camelopard, so recently known in Europe. In the same tracts are found the species of antelope commonly called the cow of the desert, with straight and twisted horns, and gazelles in abundance. The elephant is found in Abyssinia, not far from the southern confines of the state of Meroë.

Section II.—*History of the Ethiopians.*

The early history of Meroë is involved in impenetrable obscurity. Its monuments bear evident marks of being the models for the wondrous edifices of Egypt; but, shut out from all intercourse with civilised nations by the intervention of the Egyptians, it is only when they were invaded, or became invaders, that we can trace the history of the Ethiopians. It has been already mentioned, that several of the Egyptian monarchs carried their arms into Ethiopia, and became for a time masters of the country. In the eleventh century before the Christian era, the Assyrian heroine Semiramis is reported to have attempted its conquest; but there is some doubt of the truth of this, as indeed of many other exploits attributed to this wonderful queen. But we have certain information of the Ethiopians being a powerful nation (B.C. 971), when they assisted Shishak in his war against Judæa "with very many chariots and horsemen." Sixteen years after this, we have an account of Judæa being again invaded by the Ethiopians, unaccompanied by any Egyptian force. The Scripture informs us—"Asa had an army of men that bare targets and spears, out of Judah three hundred thousand; and out of Benjamin, that bare shields and drew bows, two hundred and fourscore thousand: all these were mighty men of valour. And there came out against them Zerah the Ethiopian with an host of a thousand thousand, and three hundred chariots, and came unto Mareshah. Then Asa went out against him, and they set the battle in array in the valley of Zephathah, at Mareshah. And Asa cried unto the Lord his God, and said, Lord, it is nothing with thee to help, whether with many, or with them that have no power; help us, O Lord our God! for we rest on thee, and in thy name we go against this multitude. O Lord, thou art our God; let not man prevail against thee. So the Lord smote the Ethiopians before Asa, and before Judah; and the Ethiopians fled. And Asa and the people that were with him pursued them unto Gerar: and the Ethiopians were overthrown, that they could not recover themselves; for they were destroyed before the Lord, and before his host: and they carried away very much spoil."* From this narrative it appears that the Ethiopians had made considerable progress in the art of war, and were masters of the navigation of the Red Sea, and at least a part of the Arabian peninsula. The kingdom must have been also in a very flourishing condition, when it was able to bear the cost of so vast and distant an expedition.

The Ethiopian power gradually increased until its monarchs were enabled to conquer Egypt, where three of them reigned in succession, Sabbakon, Sevechus, and Tarakus, the Tirhakah of Scripture.† Sevechus, called So in Scripture, was so powerful a monarch, that Hoshea, king of Israel, revolted against the Assyrians, relying on his assistance;‡ but was not supported by his ally. Tirhakah was a more warlike prince: he led an army against Sennacherib, king of Assyria, § then besieging Jerusalem; and the Egyptian traditions preserved in the age of Herodotus give an accurate account of the providential interposition by which the pride of the Assyrians was humbled.

In the reign of Psammetichus the entire warrior-caste of the Egyptians migrated to Ethiopia, and were located in a tract of country sixty days' journey from Meroë, and consequently at the extreme southern frontier of the kingdom. These colonists instructed the Ethiopians in the recent improvements made in the art of war, and prepared them for resisting the formidable invasion of Cambyses.

Scarcely had the Persian dynasty been established in Egypt, when Cambyses determined to make war on the Carthaginians, the Ammonians, and the Egyptian Macrobians; that is, the mixed race of Ethiopians and exiled warriors. He first sent

* 2 Chron. xiv. 8—13.

† Mr. Hawkins, in his recent work on Meroë, identifies Tirhakah with the priest Sethos, on what we deem very insufficient grounds.

‡ 2 Kings, xvii. 4.

§ 2 Kings, xix. 9.

an embassy to the Ethiopian monarch; but receiving a scornful answer, he instantly resolved to invade the country. Cambyses set out without preparing any store of provisions, apparently ignorant of the deserts through which it was necessary for him to pass. Before he had gone over a fifth part of the route from Thebes, the want of provisions was felt; yet he madly determined to proceed. The soldiers fed on grass, as long as any could be found; but at length, when they reached the deserts, so dreadful was the famine, that they were obliged to cast lots, that one out of every ten might be eaten by his comrades. The march and misfortunes of the Egyptian army have been admirably described by the poet Darwin:—

"Slow as they pass'd, the indignant temples frown'd,
Low curses muttering from the vaulted ground;
Long ailes of cypress waved their deepen'd glooms,
And quivering spectres grinn'd amid the tombs;
Prophetic whispers breathed from Sphinx's tongue,
And Memnon's lyre with hollow murmurs rung;
Burst from each pyramid expiring groans,
And darker shadows stretch'd their lengthen'd cones;
Day after day their deathful route they steer,
Lust in the van, and rapine in the rear.
Gnomes,* as they march'd, you hid the gather'd fruits,
The bladed grass, sweet grains, and mealy roots;
Scared the tired quails that journey'd o'er their heads,
Retain'd the locusts in their earthy beds;
Bade on your sands no night-born dews distil,
Stay'd with vindictive hands the scanty rill.
Loud o'er the camp the fiend of Famine shrieks,
Calls all her brood, and champs her hundred beaks;
O'er ten square leagues her pennons broad expand,
And twilight swims upon the shuddering sand;
Perch'd on her crest the griffin Discord clings,
And giant Murder rides between her wings;
Blood from each clotted hair and horny quill,
And showers of tears in blended streams distil;
High poised in air, her spiry neck she bends,
Rolls her keen eye, her dragon-claws extends,
Darts from above, and tears at each fell swoop,
With iron fangs, the decimated troop."

* Elementary spirits, that form the machinery of Darwin's poem, the "Botanic Garden."

It is said that the king of Ethiopia was always elected from the priestly caste; and there was a strange custom for the electors, when weary of their sovereign, to send him a courier with orders to die. Ergamenes was the first monarch who ventured to resist this absurd custom: he lived in the reign of the second Ptolemy, and was instructed in Grecian philosophy. So far from yielding, he marched against the fortress of the priests, massacred most of them, and instituted a new religion.

Queens frequently ruled in Ethiopia: one named Candace made war on Augustus Cæsar about twenty years before the birth of Christ, and though defeated by the superior discipline of the Romans, obtained peace on very favourable conditions. During the reign of another of the same name, we find that the Jewish religion was prevalent in Meroë, probably in consequence of the change made by Ergamenes; for the queen's confidential adviser went to worship at Jerusalem, and on his return (A.D. 53) was converted by St. Philip,* and became the means of introducing Christianity into Ethiopia.

These are the principal historical facts that can now be ascertained respecting the ancient and once-powerful state of Meroë, which has now sunk into the general mass of African barbarism.

Section III.—*Arts, Commerce, and Manufactures of Meroë.*

The pyramids of Meroë, though inferior in size to those of Middle Egypt, are said to surpass them in architectural beauty, and the sepulchres evince the greatest purity of taste. But the most important and striking proof of the progress of the Ethiopians in the art of building, is their knowledge and employment of the arch. "In describing the pyramids of Meroë," says Mr. Hoskins, "I mentioned that the arch I there found was the segment of a circle; but here (at Gibel-el-Birkel) it is very important to observe, that there are not only specimens of that, but of the pointed arch. The latter, consisting of six stones, is accurately drawn in the section. The stones are slightly hollowed out to the shape of the arch, but do not ad-

* Acts, vii. 33.

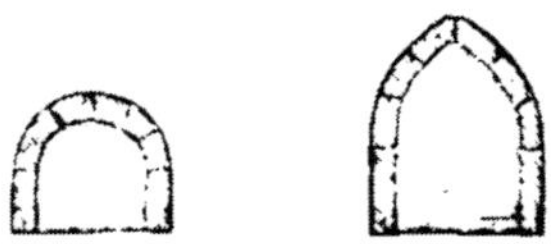

vance beyond each other, like the arch near the temple excavated out of the rock at Thebes, but are supported only by lateral pressure . . . The reader will observe also a specimen of a semicircular arch. They are drawn very small, as belonging to the pyramids, but they are not on that account less accurate. The arch, then, not only the circular, but the pointed, had its origin in Ethiopia."* The author has elsewhere stated that these pyramids are of superior antiquity to those of Egypt.

The Ethiopian vases depicted on the monuments, though not richly ornamented, display a taste and elegance of form that has never been surpassed. In sculpture and colouring, the edifices of Meroë, though not so profusely adorned, rival the choicest specimens of Egyptian art.

We have already noticed the favourable position of Meroë for commercial intercourse with India and the interior of Africa: it was the entrepôt of trade between the north and south, between the east and west, while its fertile soil enabled the Ethiopians to purchase foreign luxuries with native productions. It does not appear that textile fabrics were woven in Meroë so extensively as in Egypt; but the manufactures of metal must have been at least as flourishing; for the Ethiopians were early acquainted with the use of iron; and the war-chariots on the Ethiopian monuments appear to be more gracefully built than those on the Egyptian. But Meroë owed its greatness less to the produce of its soil or its factories, than to its position on the intersection of the leading caravan-routes of ancient commerce. The great changes in these lines of trade, the devastations of successive conquerors and revolutions, the fanaticism of the Saracens, and the destruction of the fertile soil by the encroachments of the moving sands from the desert, are causes sufficient for the ruin of such a powerful empire. Its decline, however, was probably accelerated by the pressure of the nomad hordes, who took advantage of its weakness to plunder its defenceless citizens.

* Hoskins's Ethiopia, p. 156.

CHAPTER III.

BABYLONIA AND ASSYRIA.

Section I.—*Geographical Outline. Natural History.*

Babylonia, or Chaldæa, was situated between two great rivers, the Euphrates on the west, and the Tigris on the east. Both of these rise in the great chain of the Armenian mountains, and, flowing from north to south, finally unite their waters, and fall into the Persian Gulf. It was almost as dependent on these rivers as Egypt was upon the Nile; and an account of them is an essential part of the description of the nature of the country. The plain between the rivers slopes considerably from west to east, so that the bed of the Tigris is much lower than that of the Euphrates, its channel much deeper, and the banks so precipitous that it very rarely overflows them. On the other hand, the Euphrates has in a great part of its course level banks filled to the brink by the mass of waters; and when these are swelled by the melting of the snows in the Armenian mountains, the river overflows its banks, and inundates the surrounding country. The ill effects of this inundation were but partially averted by the natural ditches and marshes that were gradually formed; but they probably suggested the construction of canals and lakes, by which the whole of Babylonia was intersected.

Babylonia was properly the country on the lower Euphrates; north of it were the extensive plains of Mesopotamia; and beyond these the mountainous districts of Armenia, supposed by many writers to have been the first habitation of the posterity of Noah after the flood. Between Mesopotamia and Babylonia, where the two rivers make a near approach to each other, the Median wall was constructed, to control the Medes and other nomad tribes; and this object was further secured by cutting four canals, about three miles apart, sufficiently deep to be navigable for ships of burden. Besides canals, huge dams and embankments were erected, to check the power of the current, and regulate its velocity; and enormous lakes were dug as a reservoir for the waters. It followed from these great works, that the Euphrates was drained of the greater part of its waters before it reached the sea, so that its proper mouth was never navigable. The river at present loses itself in the Tigris, about sixty miles from the sea; but we are assured that its ancient channel had not disappeared in the time of the Persian empire.

Beyond the Tigris was the region properly called Assyria, a table-land bounded on the north and east by chains of mountains, which have afforded shelter to plundering nomad tribes from the remotest antiquity. The soil, though not so rich as that of Babylonia, was generally fruitful. Rabshakeh, the Assyrian general sent by Sennacherib against Hezekiah, describes Assyria as "a land of corn and wine, a land of bread and vineyards, a land of olive oil and of honey;"* but almost ever since the fall of the Assyrian empire, the country has been devastated by wars between powerful monarchies and nations; and it is now little better than a wilderness, save that some patches of land are cultivated in the neighbourhood of the few inconsiderable towns within its precincts.

Babylonia, in the neighbourhood of the Euphrates, rivalled the fertility of the valley of the Nile: the soil was so peculiarly suited for corn, that the husbandman's returns were sometimes three hundred fold, and rarely less than two hundred fold. The rich oily grains of the *panicum* and *sesamum* were produced in luxuriant abundance, and their stalks grew to an almost incredible height. But this richness was counterbalanced by the deficiency of wood: the fig-tree, the olive, and the vine, were wholly wanting; but there were large groves of palm-trees on the banks of the Euphrates. The Babylonians were the first to discover the distinction between the male and female palm-trees, and to introduce the artificial culture of dates. From the palms they obtained not only fruit, but wine, sugar, and molasses, as the Arabs do at the present time. Dwarf cypress-trees were scattered over the plains; but these were a

* 2 Kings, xviii. 32.

poor substitute for other species of wood. To this deficiency of timber must be attributed the neglect of the river navigation, and the abandonment of the commerce of the Indian seas, by the Babylonians.

Stone and marble were even more rare in this country than wood, but the clay was well adapted for the manufacture of bricks. These, whether dried in the sun, or burned in kilns, became so hard and durable, that now, after the lapse of so many centuries, the remains of ancient walls preserve the bricks uninjured by their long exposure to the atmosphere, and retaining the impression of the inscriptions in the arrow-headed character as perfectly as if they had only just been manufactured. Naphtha and bitumen, or earthy oil and pitch, were produced in great abundance above Babylon, near the modern town of Hit: these served as substitutes for mortar or cement; and so lasting were they, that the layers of rushes and palm-leaves laid between the courses of bricks as a binding material, are found at this day in the ruins of Babylon as perfect as if a year had not elapsed since they were put together.

Section II.—*Political and Social Condition of the Assyrians and Babylonians.*

Despotism, in its most severe form, was established in the Assyrian monarchy, and in those by which it was succeeded. The king's will was the law; no code existed to restrict his judgments; and even ancient customs were set aside at his pleasure. He was the head of the church as well as the state, and claimed divine worship, as if he were an incarnation of the Deity. His palace was crowded with as many wives and concubines as he chose to collect, and these were placed under the guardianship of eunuchs, an unfortunate race, first brought into use in Assyria. The principal officers of the royal household were the captain of the guards, whose duty it was to execute the king's edicts against criminals; the chief of the eunuchs, who, in addition to watching the royal seraglio, superintended the education of the young nobles employed as pages; the master of the soothsayers, who appears to have presided over a college of priests, that pretended to interpret dreams and discover future events by astrology; and a prime minister, like the viziers of modern times, who sat in the king's gate to hear complaints and administer justice.

It is impossible to determine whether the priests, usually called Chaldæans, were a caste or an order; but it is most probable that, like the Egyptians, the Jews, and the Persians, the Babylonians had an hereditary priesthood. Their religion was the kind of idolatry usually called Sabian; that is, they worshipped the sun, the moon, and the starry host. In a later age they added to this the worship of deified mortals, whom they supposed to be in some way connected with the celestial luminaries, just as Eastern monarchs of the present day call themselves "brothers of the sun and moon." Their supreme deity was named Baal, or Bel, which signifies Lord: the mixture of the astronomical with the historical character of the idol, has rendered the Assyrian mythology complicated and obscure; for Baal at one time is spoken of as the sun, and at another as the founder of the empire. Next to Baal ranked a female deity, or rather a deity in which the male and female attributes were united, called Mylitta by the Babylonians, and Astarte by the Syrians. The worship of this deity was licentious and obscene; but, from its gratifying the impure passions, it was very popular throughout central and western Asia; and this led to the great variety of names by which the idol was known. In Scripture the idol, or rather its temple, is called Succoth Benoth, "the dwellings of the daughters," because brothels were a part of the temple. This deity had both an astronomical and historical character: in the former respect it was supposed to represent the moon, and also the productive power of the earth, which was supposed to depend on lunar influences; in the latter respect Mylitta was identified with the celebrated queen Semiramis. This double character of the deities has brought confusion not only into mythology but history; for many of the fabulous legends respecting Ninus and Semiramis are manifestly imperfect astronomical theories. Cruelty and obscenity were the most marked attributes of the

Babylonian and Assyrian idolatry; human victims were sacrificed, prostitution was enjoined as a religious duty. It had also much of the absurdity that belongs to the Brahminism of the present day: monstrous combinations of forms were attributed to the gods; their idols had many heads, and jumbled the limbs of men and the members of animals together; these had probably at first a symbolic meaning, which the priests preserved by tradition, but which was carefully concealed from the vulgar herd.

The condition of women was more degraded in Babylon than in any other Eastern country. No man had a right to dispose of his daughters in marriage; when girls attained mature age, they were exposed for sale in the public markets, and delivered to the highest bidder. The money thus obtained for beauty was applied to portioning ugliness; husbands from the poorer class being purchased for those to whom nature had not been lavish of exterior gifts. Debauchery and gross sensuality were the natural results of such a system, and these evils were aggravated by the habitual intoxication of every class of society. It would be an offence to decency to dwell any longer on the gross licentiousness of this dissolute people: it must be added, that they were as superstitious as they were depraved, and were the slaves of the Chaldæan priests and jugglers.

The Babylonians had made considerable progress in the mechanical arts, and in mathematical science; their astronomical knowledge was very extensive, but it was so disfigured by astrological absurdities as to be nearly useless. The arts of weaving and working in metal were practised in Babylon; the naphtha and petroleum furnished excellent fuel for furnaces; and the accounts given of their skill in metal-founding shew that they had made many ingenious contrivances, which supplied their natural wants of stone and wood.

The Babylonian language belongs to that class called Semitic, of which the Hebrew, Arabic, and Syriac, are branches. They possessed an alphabetic character, and wrote on bricks and earthen cylinders. It is not certain that they possessed books, their country producing no materials from which paper could be manufactured. It will be seen in the next section that the Chaldeans were a different nation from the Babylonians; and it is probable that they, having become the ruling caste, attributed to themselves the fame of the knowledge that properly belonged to the Babylonians.

Section III.—*History of the Assyrians and Babylonians.*

FROM B.C. 2204 TO B.C. 538.

The history of the origin of a nation, however powerful, is always obscure, because at first the traditions are neglected; and when they are collected at a later period, national vanity is interested in disfiguring them with a cloud of fables. But in the East, the habitual exaggeration of the historians renders the discovery of truth almost impossible. A handful of men becomes an army of myriads; the prince of a territory not so large as an English county, is called the lord of the world; a slight skirmish is described as a battle that decides the fate of empires; and the meanest upstart that attains power can easily procure a fabricated genealogy of emperors and deities. Hence arises the inconsistency in the different accounts given of the Assyrian and Persian empires,—accounts which, professedly treating of the same period, have scarcely a common name or event. Hence also arises the difficulty of extracting any reasonable narrative from the vast mass of fictions. Assyrian history, according to Grecian authorities, particularly Ctesias and Diodorus, is nothing more than traditions of the heroes and heroines, who, at some early period, founded a kingdom in the countries bordering on the Euphrates — traditions without any chronological data, and in the ordinary style of Eastern exaggeration. The Assyrian history contained in the Holy Scriptures is that of a distinct nation of conquerors that founded an empire. This history is, however, confined to incidental notices of the wars between the Assyrians and the Israelites and Jews. Herodotus briefly touches on the Assyrian empire; but his narrative, so far as it goes, confirms the narrative given in the Old Testament. We shall endeavour to deduce from all these sources the most authentic account of the Assyrian monarchy, carefully distinguishing tradition from history.

The miraculous interruption of the building of Babel led to the abandonment of that spot by the followers of Nimrod, who appears to have been the first nomad chief that founded a permanent monarchy. "He began," says the book of Genesis, "to be a mighty one in the earth. He was a mighty hunter before the Lord. . . . . And the beginning of his kingdom was Babel, and Erech, and Accad, and Calneh, in the land of Shinar. *He went out of that land into Assyria*,* and builded Nineveh," and several other cities. Nimrod, therefore, appears to be the Ninus of profane history, — a warrior, a conqueror, the builder of cities, and the founder of an empire. Tradition has based a long romance on these few facts, which it is not necessary to detail. The Assyrian empire appears to have been founded B.C. 1237, and Nineveh was its metropolis. Ninus chose for his principal queen Semiramis, the wife of one of his officers, to whose prudent councils he is said to have been indebted for many of his victories.

On the death of Ninus, Semiramis assumed the administration of the empire as regent. Tradition absurdly adds, that she personated her son, — as if it was possible that a woman could pass herself for a boy as yet in the age of childhood. She is said to have founded the city of Babylon; but this is clearly erroneous. The additions, however, that she made to the city, and the stupendous edifices with which she adorned it, in some degree justified the tradition. Her wars were waged in the most remote countries; she is said to have conquered Egypt, and invaded Ethiopia on one side, and to have attacked India on the other. These traditions are not very improbable, if we regard the Assyrian armies as plundering nomad hordes similar to the Calmucks and Moguls of more modern times; but even thus, they must be regarded as exaggerated. Semiramis was succeeded by her son Ninyas, who gave himself up to indolence and debauchery, keeping

* This is the translation in the margin of our Bibles, and in this, as in many instances, the margin is more correct than the text. Genesis, x. 8—11.

himself secluded in his palace, and entrusting the entire care of the administration to his ministers. His successors for several generations followed his base example; and the Assyrian monarchy gradually decayed.

Leaving the traditions respecting Ninus and Semiramis, in which a few historical facts are quite obscured under a cloud of fables and astronomical allegories, we come to the portion of Assyrian history founded on the authentic records of the Old Testament. The Assyrians began to extend their empire westwards beyond the Euphrates in the reign of Pul (B.C. 771). He approached the confines of the kingdom of Israel, then ruled by the usurper Menahem, and inspired so much terror, that his forbearance was purchased by a thousand talents of silver.*

Tiglath-pul-assur succeeded to the throne (B.C. 747), and prepared to pursue the plans of conquest that Pul had sketched. He conquered the kingdom of Israel, and transplanted a great number of the inhabitants to the remote parts of his empire.† Invited by Ahaz, king of Judah, he made war against the ancient kingdom of Syria, stormed its celebrated metropolis, Damascus, and removed the vanquished people beyond the Euphrates.

Shalman-assur was the next monarch (B.C. 728). He invaded the kingdom of Israel, took Samaria after a siege of three years, and led the greater part of the ten tribes into captivity, supplying their place with colonies from other states. It seems to have been a fixed maxim of the Assyrian government to garrison one conquered country with colonies from another; and this policy greatly tended to secure the permanence of their empire. After the conquest of Israel, Shalman-assur invaded Phœnicia, and subdued all the principal cities except Tyre. He laid siege to this great metropolis; but was baffled by the naval power of the Tyrians, with which the Assyrians, ignorant of navigation, could not pretend to cope.

San-herib, or Sennacherib, was the next monarch. He led an army against Hezekiah, king of Judah (B.C. 724), and also

* 2 Kings, xv. 19. † 2 Kings, xv. 29.

attacked Egypt. His impious blasphemies against the God of the Jews were punished by the miraculous destruction of his army; and he returned home mortified and disgraced. A conspiracy was formed against him, and he was slain by his own sons.

Assar-haddon-pul, the Esarhaddon of Scripture, and Sardanapalus of profane history, was the third son of Sanherib, and was chosen his successor, in preference to the parricides, Adram-melek and Shar-ezer. The accounts given of this prince are so very inconsistent, that many have supposed that there were two of the name; but it is more probable that he was in the early part of his reign an active conqueror, and that he subsequently sunk into sensuality and sloth. The native traditions of the Assyrians would preserve the memory only of his glories; the accounts of the people that succeeded to sovereignty would naturally exaggerate his vices, to excuse their rebellion. He conquered the kingdom of Judah, and made some impression on Egypt; but, returning to Nineveh, he became the slave of intemperance, and thus disgusted the hardy warriors whom he had so often led to victory. The satraps of Media and Babylonia revolting besieged Sardanapalus in his capital; and he, finding himself deserted by his subjects, and unable to protract his defence, made a huge pile, on which he placed his wives and his treasures; then, setting it on fire, he threw himself into the midst of the flames (B.C. 717). Thus ended the Assyrian monarchy; and the supremacy of central and western Asia was transferred to the Babylonians.

The Kasdím, a northern nomad tribe from the mountain-chains of Taurus and the Caucasus, appear to have been employed as mercenaries by the Assyrian monarchs, and to have been stationed in Babylonia, whose inhabitants were impatient of the yoke imposed upon them by the people of Nineveh. As is not unusual in the East, these soldiers revolted against their masters, and prepared to carve out an empire for themselves. Whether they were called Chaldeans from a corruption of their ancient name Kasdím; or whether, as is more probable, to sanctify their power, they took the name of the dominant caste in Babylonia, it is difficult to determine; but that they were a conquering horde which settled in the country, is proved by the express testimony of Isaiah. "Behold the land of the Chaldeans (Kasdím); this people was not, until the Assyrian founded it for them that dwell in the wilderness: they set up the towers thereof, they raised up the palaces thereof."* The chronology of the Babylonian Chaldeans commences with the reign of Nabonassar (B.C. 747) — a remarkable era in history, because the introduction of the Egyptian solar year during the reign of that prince first supplied the Chaldeans with an accurate mode of measuring time. There is nothing worthy of note in the history of Nabonassar, and his twelve immediate successors. During their reigns, indeed, Babylonia appears again to have become dependent upon Assyria, and not to have recovered its freedom until the general insurrection against Sardanapalus.

Nabopolassar, or Nebo-pul-assur, became king of Babylon soon after the overthrow of the Assyrian empire (B.C. 627). Pharaoh-Necho took advantage of the distracted state of central Asia to extend his dominions to the Euphrates. He gained possession of Carchemish (Circesium), and induced the governors of Cœle-Syria and Phœnicia to revolt against Nabopolassar. In the reduction of these provinces the Babylonian monarch was greatly assisted by his son, Nebuchadnezzar, or Nebo-kal-assur, who subsequently raised the empire to the summit of its greatness. Nebuchadnezzar obtained a brilliant victory over Pharaoh-Necho, at Carchemish (B.C. 604); and was about to follow up his success by invading Egypt, when he was recalled to Babylon in consequence of his father's death.

Nitocris was probably the queen of Nebuchadnezzar; for Herodotus attributes to her some of the most splendid edifices of the city of Babylon, which were certainly erected during his reign. She seems to have acted as regent while the king was employed in foreign wars, and her name would therefore be more naturally associated with the buildings than that of her husband.

* Isaiah, xxiii. 13.

Before invading Egypt, Nebuchadnezzar had conquered the kingdom of Judah, and brought several of its princes to Babylon as captives or hostages. Among these was the prophet Daniel,* who, aided by divine inspiration, revealed and interpreted a dream which the Chaldean soothsayers were unable to expound, and was rewarded with the government of Babylon. Soon afterwards the Scythians, probably some Tartar horde, invaded the Assyrian provinces, and the Jews embraced this opportunity of asserting their independence. Nebuchadnezzar was prevented from immediately punishing this revolt, by the obstinate resistance of Nineveh, which he was besieging in conjunction with Cyaxares the Mede; but having taken and destroyed this ancient rival of Babylon, he marched against Jerusalem with a resistless force. The holy city was taken and plundered, its monarch slain, his son sent prisoner to Babylon, and a new king appointed as deputy to the conqueror. So many captives were forced to cross the Euphrates, that there were scarcely enough of inhabitants left in Judah to till the lands. Undismayed by this calamity, the Jews again revolted, relying on the promised aid of the Egyptians, but were once more subdued, and treated with barbarous cruelty. Their city was laid desolate, their lands wasted, and the bulk of the nation led into captivity. The conqueror then proceeded into Phœnicia, which he completely subdued; whence he advanced to Egypt, and plundered the lower valley of the Nile. It was after his return from this expedition that Nebuchadnezzar erected the golden image in the plains of Dura;† for refusing to worship which, Shadrach, Meshach, and Abed-nego, were thrown into the fiery furnace, from which they were miraculously delivered. Towards the close of his reign the impiety of Nebuchadnezzar was punished by a fit of lunacy; during which "he was driven from men, and did eat grass as oxen, and his body was wet with the dew of heaven, till his hairs were grown like eagles' feathers, and his nails like birds' claws."‡

* Dan. ii. 1, &c.

† Id. iii. 1, &c.

‡ Id. iv. 33.

Evil-Merodach succeeded, and after a short reign was murdered by his sister's husband, Neriglissar. But the young prince, Belshazzar, was saved from the conspirators, and conveyed to a place of security by Nitocris, whom some writers describe as his mother, others as his wife. He continued several years in obscurity, but did not profit by the stern lessons of adversity. At this time the power of the Medes had reached a formidable height, and the Babylonians summoned the kings of western Asia to aid in preventing its further extension. The allied army marched northwards, and soon encountered the Medes, who were commanded by Cyaxares and his nephew Cyrus. After a fierce engagement, the Babylonians were totally defeated, and their sovereign slain.

Labosoarchad succeeded his father Neriglissar (B.C. 555); but on account of his tyranny was dethroned after a reign of only a few months, and the legitimate line restored in the person of Nebo-an-dal, called also Nabonadius and Labynetus, who took the surname of Belshazzar, that is, "the mighty prince of Bel." As he was a youth, the regency was entrusted to Queen Nitocris, who made the most diligent exertions to improve and extend the defences of the city. She completed the works which Nebuchadnezzar had commenced, and is said to have connected the eastern and western banks of the Euphrates both by a bridge and a tunnel. To complete the last work it was necessary to turn the river for a time into a new channel; and for this purpose a lake and canal were constructed to the north of Babylon. When Belshazzar assumed the reins of government, he deserted the prudent line of policy by which Nitocris had delayed the fate of the tottering empire; not only abandoning himself to licentious pleasures, but provoking the hostility of the warlike Medes. Cyaxares, the "Darawesh" (Darius), that is, king of the Medes, accompanied by his nephew Cyrus, invaded Babylonia, and soon laid siege to the metropolis. Confiding in the strength of the walls, Belshazzar laughed his enemies to scorn; and while the enemy was still before the walls, gave a great feast in honour of his expected success. Cyrus, on the same evening, sent a detachment to open the canal leading to the lake that had been dug by Nitocris, ordering his soldiers, as soon as the water should be drawn from the bed of the river, to enter the city through the deserted channel.

Meantime in Babylon all was feasting, and revelry, and joy. "Belshazzar the king made a great feast to a thousand of his lords, and drank wine before the thousand."* To add to the splendour of the ceremony, he commanded that the sacred vessels of gold and silver which his father had taken from the Temple of Jerusalem should be brought forth for the use of the intemperate guests. But while they were thus profaning the sacred vessels by their debauchery, "there came forth fingers of a man's hand, and wrote over against the candlestick upon the plaster of the wall of the king's palace; and the king saw the part of the hand that wrote." The Chaldean priests and soothsayers, hastily summoned, were unable to read the mysterious characters traced by the awful hand; but the prophet Daniel explained them to the astonished king. "This is the writing that was written: MENE, MENE, TEKEL, UPHARSIN. This is the interpretation of the thing: MENE; God hath numbered thy kingdom, and finished it. TEKEL; thou art weighed in the balances, and art found wanting. PERES; thy kingdom is divided and given to the Medes and Persians."

The accomplishment followed close on the prediction. Hidden by the shades of night, and guided by the lights that gleamed from the chambers of revelry, the Medes penetrated into the very heart of the city, and attacked the guards before the palace. The guests within, startled by the clash of arms, flung the gates open to ascertain the cause of the tumult, and thus gave admission to the enemy. Belshazzar, in this hour of despair, behaved in a manner worthy of his illustrious descent: he drew his sword, and at the head of a few friends attempted to drive back the enemy; but, "flushed with success, and drunk with gore, whole multitudes poured in," he fell in his own hall; and with him fell the empire of Babylon (B.C. 538).

* Dan. v. 1, &c.

SECTION IV.—*Description of Nineveh and Babylon.*

THE city of Nineveh, probably so named from Ninus its founder, stood on the east bank of the Tigris, nearly three hundred miles north of Babylon. Like all the ancient cities of Asia, it was of a rectangular form, and retained the traces of the nomad encampment in which it originated. It was of enormous dimensions, being fifteen miles in length, nine in breadth, and forty-eight in circumference. Nor will this great extent seem incredible, when we reflect that the houses were not built in continuous streets, but stood apart, as the tents formerly did, each surrounded by gardens, parks, and farms, whose size varied according to the rank and wealth of the respective proprietors. Nineveh, in short, was less a city, according to the modern European notions, than a collection of villages, hamlets, and noblemen's seats, enclosed within one wall as a common defence. The prophet Jonah describes Nineveh as "an exceeding great city of three days' journey (round the walls) . . . wherein are more than six score thousand persons that cannot discern between their right hand and left hand; *and also much cattle.*"* The fortifications, according to the historians, were constructed on a stupendous scale; and this is not improbable, for the country supplied abundance of excellent clay for the manufacture of sunburnt bricks, and bitumen, which, as we have said, forms an excellent cement. There are besides sufficiently wonderful remains of antiquity, such as the Egyptian pyramids, to prove that it is difficult to fix boundaries to the capabilities of the united strength of congregated nations. The walls were two hundred feet in height, and so wide that three chariots might drive on them abreast, and they were further secured by fifteen hundred lofty towers. The prophet Nahum, who predicted the destruction of the city, describes the nature of its brick defences, its canals, its traffic, and the multitude of Assyrian nobles that had residences within its walls: "Draw thee water, for the siege, fortify thy strong-

* Jonah, iii. 3; and iv. 11.

holds: go into clay, and tread the mortar, make strong the brick-kiln. There shall the fire devour thee; the sword shall cut thee off, it shall eat thee up like the canker-worm: make thyself many as the locusts. Thou hast multiplied thy merchants above the stars of heaven: the canker-worm spoileth, and fleeth away. Thy crowned are as the locusts, and thy captains as the great grasshoppers, which camp in the hedges in the cold day, but when the sun ariseth they flee away, and their place is not known where they are."* He also describes very accurately the equestrian nation of the Medes, whose strength, like that of their successors, the Turkish tribes, consisted chiefly in cavalry. "The noise of a whip, and the noise of the rattling of wheels, and of the prancing horses, and of the jumping chariots. The horseman lifteth up both the bright sword and the glittering spear; and there is a multitude of slain, and a great number of carcasses; and there is none end of their corpses; they stumble upon their corpses."† After the destruction of the city by the Medes, Nineveh appears to have long remained desolate; several villages were subsequently erected from its ruins, the largest of which preserved the name of the ancient metropolis. It is now a desert waste: even the wild vegetation that usually veils the ruins of fallen greatness has disappeared, and desolation is spread over the entire landscape.‡

* Nahum, iii. 14—17. † Id. iii. 2, 3.

‡ The American poet Eckhard has written some beautiful lines on the ruined city, an extract from which we subjoin:—

"Two thousand years have roll'd along,
And blasted empires in their pride;
And witness'd scenes of crime and wrong,
Till men by nations died;
Two thousand summer suns have shone,
Till earth grew bright beneath their sway,—
Since thou, untenanted and lone,
Wert render'd to decay.

The moss-tuft and the ivy-wreath
For ages clad thy fallen mould,
And gladden'd in the spring's soft breath;
But they grew wan and old.

Babylon was built on both sides of the Euphrates; but the first edifices were constructed on the western bank of the river, where stood the tower of Belus, which was probably built on the foundations of Babel. When completed by Nebuchadnezzar, it formed an exact square, each of whose sides was about fifteen miles in length, and consequently the whole circumference was sixty miles. The eastern division of the city was the most recent: it was built by the Kasdím, or Chaldeans; and there Nebuchadnezzar erected the great palace whose circuit was equal to that of a moderate-sized city.

The walls of Babylon were made of brick, cemented by bitumen, eighty-seven feet thick; and more than three hundred high: they were surrounded by a deep ditch, and pierced by a hundred gates, all made of solid brass. Towers were erected for the defence of the gates and the corners of the walls, except where a morass protected the walls, and prevented the approach of an enemy. Wide, straight streets, or rather roads, from each of the gates, crossed each other at right angles, which, with the four half-streets that fronted to the walls, divided the city into six hundred and seventy-six squares, each

Now desolation hath denied
  That even these shall veil thy gloom;
And nature's mantling beauty died,
  In token of thy doom.

Alas! for the far years, when, clad
  With the bright vesture of thy prime,
The proud towers made each wanderer glad
  Who hail'd thy sunny clime.
Alas! for the fond hope and dream,
  And all that won thy children's trust;
God cursed—and none may now redeem,
  Pale city of the dust!

But a stern moral may be read
  By those who view thy lonely gloom;
Oblivion's pall alike is spread
  O'er slave and lordly tomb.
The sad, the gay, the old and young,
  The warrior's strength and beauty's glow,
Resolved to that from which they sprung,
  Compose the dust below."

of four furlongs and a half on each side, or two miles and a quarter in circumference. These squares were, in fact, separate villages, and many of them were wholly untenanted, being used as parks or pleasure-grounds by the king and his nobles.

A bridge passed over the Euphrates between the two palaces on the opposite banks, which we are assured were further connected by means of a tunnel. The length of the bridge was about a furlong, but its breadth only thirty feet: a long causeway on both sides of the river made the bridge appear of much greater extent than it really was.

The temple of Belus was the most wondrous structure of the city: it is generally identified with the vast mass of ruins five miles west of the modern town of Hillah, usually called Birs Nimrod (the tower of Nimrod), and consequently must have stood on the western bank of the river. It was at its foundation a furlong in length, and about the same in breadth: its height is said to have exceeded six hundred feet, which is more than that of the Egyptian pyramids.

It was built in eight stories, gradually diminishing in size as they ascended. Instead of stairs there was a sloping terrace on the outside, sufficiently wide for carriages and beasts of burden to ascend. Nebuchadnezzar made great additions to this tower, and surrounded it with smaller edifices, enclosed by a wall somewhat more than two miles in circumference. The whole was sacred to Bel or Belus, whose temple was adorned with idols of gold, and all the wealth that the Babylonians had acquired by the plunder of the East. Next to the temple was the old palace, strongly fortified; and on the opposite side of the river was the new palace, whose enclosures and pleasure-grounds covered a space of eight miles round. Within its precincts were the celebrated hanging gardens, consisting of terraces one above another, raised upon pillars higher than the walls of the city, well floored with cement and lead, and covered with earth, in which the most beautiful trees and shrubs were planted.

From the time of its conquest, Babylon gradually declined. The Persians were severe masters to a people that had once enjoyed the supremacy of central Asia, and who never quite resigned the hope of recovering their former ascendancy. Alexander the Great designed Babylon to be the capital of his empire, and was preparing to restore its ancient splendour when he was prematurely cut off. Thenceforward its decay was rapid; and it is now a vast heap of ruins, tenanted only by the beasts and birds that love to haunt solitary places. Thus literally has the prediction of the prophet been fulfilled: "Babylon, the glory of kingdoms, the beauty of the Chaldees' excellency, shall be as when God overthrew Sodom and Gomorrah. It shall never be inhabited, neither shall it be dwelt in from generation to generation: but wild beasts of the desert shall lie there; and ostriches shall fill their houses, and the daughters of the owl shall dwell there, and satyrs shall dance there. And the howlers (jackals) shall cry in their desolate houses, and wild hounds in their pleasant palaces."*

SECTION V.—*Commerce and Manufactures of the Babylonians.*

WEAVING of cotton, woollen stuffs, and carpets, were the principal manufactures established in Babylon; and the cotton robes called surdones, probably a species of muslins, were so highly esteemed for their delicacy of texture and brilliancy of colour, that they were appropriated to royal use. The cotton was chiefly procured from Carmania and Syria; and factories were established not only in Babylon, but in all the trading marts on the lower Euphrates. Articles of luxury, such as perfumed waters, carved walking-canes, engraved stones, and seal-rings, were made in the city; and the art of cutting precious stones was carried to a perfection not exceeded by our modern lapidaries.

The Babylonians had an extensive commerce eastwards with Persia and northern India, whence they obtained gold, precious stones, rich dye-stuffs, and the best hounds. From Kandahar and Kashmír they procured fine wool, and the shawls which are still so highly valued. This trade appears to

* Isaiah, xiii. 19—22. (Gesenius's translation.)

have been carried on by caravans through Bactra, the modern Balkh, which, from the remotest ages, has been the great commercial staple of eastern Asia. It is uncertain whether any commerce was opened with China before the later ages of the Persian empire; but the Babylonians had certainly intercourse with Tibet and the countries round the Hindú Kúsh.

The road from Babylon to the Mediterranean took a northern direction by the foot of the Armenian mountains, where it divided into two branches; one entering Syria, and the other passing into Asia Minor. From Armenia, boats, or rather rafts, were sent down the river laden with wine, and sold together with their cargoes, on account of the difficulty of navigating against the stream. It was chiefly through their commercial allies, the Phœnicians, that the Babylonians had any trade in the Indian seas, though Isaiah plainly states that they had a navy of their own; for he mentions "the Chaldeans, whose cry (exultation) is in their ships."* The trade by sea was between the mouths of the Tigris and Euphrates, and the western coasts of India and the island of Ceylon. From these countries they imported timber of various kinds, sugar-canes, spices, cinnamon, and pearls. This trade was completely destroyed by the Persians, through fear of the pirates who infested those seas, and who, by a sudden dash up the great rivers, like the Normans and Danes of Europe, might surprise and plunder the chief cities of the empire. To prevent this misfortune, they blocked up the Tigris with immense dams, which effectually put an end to all navigation on the river, and to the intercourse between Babylon and southern India.

* Isaiah, xlii. 14.

CHAPTER IV.

WESTERN ASIA:

INCLUDING

ASIA MINOR, SYRIA, AND PALESTINE.

Section I.—*Asia Minor. Geographical Outline.*

Asia Minor is a term not used by classical writers: it was invented in the middle ages, to describe the peninsula between the Ægean, the Black Sea, the Caspian, and the Levant, which by more recent authors is called Anatolia. It included a great number of petty states, whose boundaries varied at different periods. In the northern part of the peninsula, beginning from the western side, the chief countries were Mysia, Bithynia, Paphlagonia, and Pontus. In the centre, Lydia, Phrygia, Galatia, Lycaonia, Isauria, Cappadocia, and Armenia. In the south were Caria, Lycia, Pisidia, Pamphylia, and Cilicia.

The western part of Mysia, on the sea-coast, was called Lesser Phrygia, or Troas. It was celebrated for the Trojan plains and the city of Troy, immortalised by Homer. The lapse of ages has produced such changes in the Troad, that it is now difficult, if not impossible, to recognise the different localities mentioned by the poet; but, from his minute descriptions, it is easy to collect the ancient topography. A large roadstead, protected by the island of Tenedos, lay between the promontories of Rhæteum on the north, and Sigeium on the south. From this a level plain extended to the hills that skirt Mount Ida, watered by the rivers, or rather streams, Xanthus or Scamander, and Simois, which, descending from the mountain, intersect the plain, and fall into the Hellespont. Troy, or Ilium, was built on these hills; and on the loftiest, enclosed within its walls, was the citadel called Pergamus. The next most remarkable city was Cyzicus, on an island in the Propontis, joined to the mainland by two bridges: it was the seat of a flourishing Greek colony at a very early age.

Bithynia, Paphlagonia, and Pontus, skirt the Black Sea, and were studded with Greek colonies during the flourishing age of Grecian commerce. The Halys and Sangaris, the principal rivers of Asia Minor, fall into the Black Sea.

The entire west coast of Asia Minor was colonised by the Greeks, whose commercial cities in Ionia, Æolia, and Caria, were the most flourishing free states of antiquity, before they were conquered by the Persians.

Lydia, called also Mæonia, besides the Greek cities on its coasts, contained the celebrated metropolis Sardis, which stood on the banks of the Pactolus, at the foot of Mount Tmolus. It was the capital of the Lydian kingdom, and, after its conquest by the Persians, was regarded as one of the chief cities of their empire.

The boundaries of Phrygia were almost constantly varying: its chief cities were Gordium and Celænæ in ancient times; but many others were erected when the Macedonians became masters of the country; of which the chief were Apamea, Laodicea, and Colosse.

Galatia received its name from a body of Gauls who entered that country in the third century before the Christian era. Isauria and Lycaonia were intersected by the chain of Mount Taurus. Cappadocia lay between the Halys and Euphrates: its chief town was Mazaca. Armenia was the name of the mountainous districts bordering on the Caspian Sea: its chief rivers were the Cyrus and Araxes, both of considerable magnitude. For a long time it was without cities; but at length Tigranes, one of its monarchs, erected Tigranocerta.

Caria was chiefly remarkable for the Greek colonies on the coast. Lycia, Pisidia, and Pamphylia, were mountainous districts. Cilicia bordered upon Syria, from which it was separated by Mount Amanus: its chief cities were Tarsus and Anchiale, both founded by Sardanapalus.

Section II.—*Ancient History of Asia Minor.*

The three kingdoms of Asia Minor that best deserve notice were the Trojan, the Phrygian, and the Lydian. The history of Troy consists of mere traditions preserved by the Greek epic and dramatic poets: its chronology is very uncertain, and the entire narrative very doubtful. Troy is said to have been originally founded by Dardanus, a native of Samothrace, who, when exiled from his native country, was hospitably received by Teucer, king of western Mysia. Dardanus married the daughter of his host, and received a grant of land, which, as well as the city, he named Dardania (about B.C. 1400). To him succeeded Erichthonius, celebrated for his splendid herds of horses; Tros, who named the city Troy; Ilus, who changed the name to Ilium; Laomedon, during whose reign the city was sacked by Hercules; and Podarkes, who was also called Priam. Alexander, or Paris, the son of Priam, being sent as ambassador into southern Greece, carried off Helen, the wife of Menelaüs, king of Sparta. The Grecian kings espoused the cause of the injured husband, and with their united forces warred against Troy. The city was taken after a siege that lasted ten years, and was pillaged and burned by the conquerors.

Phrygian history is also composed of obscure traditions; but that the Phrygians were originally a very powerful people, appears from the great diffusion of their national worship throughout Europe. Their chief deity was Cybele, who seems to have been a personification of the prolific powers of the earth: her priests were named Corybantes; and their frantic dances, in which they beat and cut themselves, rendered them, when civilisation advanced, objects of contempt and disgust. Most of the Phrygian kings were named either Midas or Gordius; but the order of their succession cannot be ascertained. Gordius I., the founder of the city of Gordium, was originally a peasant: when raised to the throne, he consecrated his cart to the gods. The beam was fastened to the yoke by a complicated knot; and a traditional oracle declared, that whoever untied the knot should be king of Asia. When this was told to Alexander the Great, he cut it through with his sword. In the reign of Midas V., Phrygia became a province of the Lydian empire.

The Lydians, called also Mæonians, were a branch of the Carians. Three dynasties reigned over them successively. That of the Atyadæ terminated (B.C. 1232) in the person of Omphale, who was said to be the wife of Hercules. The race of the Heraclidæ terminated with Candaules, who was murdered at the instigation of his queen, by Gyges, a Lydian nobleman (B.C. 727). Gyges founded the dynasty of the Mermnadæ, under whose sway Lydia rose to great power. Gyges commenced a war against the Greek colonies, and made himself master of several important cities. He was repulsed by the citizens of Miletus, and bequeathed his vengeance as a legacy to his successors. During the reign of Ardys, the second of the dynasty, Asia Minor was devastated by hordes of northern barbarians, called Cimmerians, who had been expelled from their original seats by the Scythians. Their ravages were continued for about half a century; but they were finally driven out by Alyattes, the grandson of Ardys. Encouraged by his success against the Cimmerians, Alyattes endeavoured to check the growing power of the Medes, and for six years waged war against Cyaxares. The contest was at length about to be decided by a great battle, when a total eclipse of the sun so terrified both armies in the midst of the fight, that they separated in consternation (B.C. 601). This remarkable eclipse was predicted by Thales of Miletus, and is the first recorded to have been calculated by astronomers. Alyattes also made war on the Milesians, annually invading their territories, and destroying the harvests. During one of these incursions, a temple of Minerva was burned; and when the Lydian monarch sent to consult the oracle of Delphi on some difficult point, he was informed that no response would be given until the temple was repaired. When the Lydian ambassadors went to Miletus on this business, the tyrant or king of the city ordered the inhabitants to display all the corn that they possessed in the market-place. The ambassadors, misled by the apparent abundance, informed Alyattes, on their return, that Miletus had scarcely suffered by the war ; and he, deceived by this intelligence, readily consented to make peace.

Crœsus, the son and successor of Alyattes, subdued all the Grecian states in Asia Minor, and extended his empire on the eastern side to the river Halys. The magnificence of his court at Sardis attracted visitors from different countries; but Crœsus was most anxious to entertain philosophers and men of learning from Greece. The illustrious Solon was once his guest, and with honourable freedom refused to declare Crœsus perfectly happy until he knew the termination of his career. The Lydian monarch was deeply offended; but ere long he had reason to admire the wisdom of the Athenian sage. Seduced by the pretended oracles of Delphi, he waged war against the rising Persian empire; but was defeated by Cyrus, and taken prisoner. Being sentenced to death by the barbarous victor, he exclaimed, when placed on the funeral pile, "O Solon, Solon!" Cyrus asked the meaning of this invocation; and was so struck by the impressive example of the philosopher's wisdom, that he not only spared the life of Crœsus, but made him his friend and counsellor (B.C. 549).

Lydia, and the rest of Asia Minor, remained subject to the Persian empire until the time of Alexander the Great.

SECTION III.—*Syria. Geographical Outline.*

THE name of Syria was loosely given by the Greeks, as that of Aram was by the Hebrews, not only to the country now called by that name, but also to Mesopotamia and part of Asia Minor; but it is properly restricted to the regions between Mount Amanus on the north, the Euphrates on the east, Arabia on the south, and Phœnicia on the west. It has been variously divided, but the most convenient division is into three unequal portions,—Syria Proper, which includes the provinces of Commagene, Seleucis, and Cœle-Syria; Phœnicia and the country of the Philistines; and Palestine, of which we shall treat in a separate chapter.

The principal city of Commagene was Samosata on the Euphrates: there were several trading towns of minor importance, all in the vicinity. Seleucis was adorned with many splendid cities during the reigns of the successors of Alexander, of which the most remarkable were Antioch and Seleucia. It contained also Hierapolis, dedicated to the Syrian goddess Berœa, the modern Aleppo, and Heliopolis (Baalbec), whose magnificent ruins still attract admiration. Cœle-Syria, or Hollow Syria, was so called because it lies between two parallel chains of mountains, Libanus and Antilibanus: it contained Damascus, the ancient metropolis of Syria, which existed as a city in the days of Abraham, Abila, and Laodicea. The Syrian desert adjoins this division, in the midst of which is a fertile oasis, on which the city of Tadmor, or Palmyra, was founded by Solomon. Its ruins rival those of Baálbec in magnitude and beauty. South-east of this was Thapsacus, opposite to which the Euphrates was fordable.

Phœnicia, or Phœnice, skirted the eastern coasts of the Mediterranean, but its boundaries were almost perpetually varying. It contained Sidon, the most ancient commercial city in the world; Tyre, commonly called "the daughter of Sidon," which was properly two cities; New Tyre, on a small island, and Old Tyre, on the mainland; Aradus, also an insular city; Tripolis, so called because it was colonised by the three preceding cities conjointly; Byblus and Berytus, the modern Benoot, which is still a good harbour. The southern and midland portions of Phœnicia contained several seaports, which rose into importance after the destruction of Tyre.

The elder Tyre was originally a Sidonian colony, but rose rapidly above the parent state, and became a flourishing commercial city. It was besieged, or rather blockaded, by Nebuchadnezzar during thirteen years; but he appears not to have become master of the city. While the Babylonians were urging the siege, a great body of the inhabitants sought shelter upon a neighbouring island, where they already had large commercial establishments, and thus laid the foundation of New Tyre. Hiram, the contemporary of David and Solomon, resolved to make the island-city the metropolis of the kingdom, and erected there the temple of Melcarth (city-king), called by the Greeks the Tyrian Hercules, who was regarded as the tutelary deity of the nation. The city was of limited extent, and the houses were therefore built several stories high: it was protected by lofty walls of cut stone, and had two harbours; one on the north, towards Sidon; the other on the south, towards Egypt. The entrance to the latter was narrow, and could be closed by a boom or chains. After its capture by Alexander the Great, Tyre gradually declined, less in consequence of the conqueror's vengeance than of the founding of Alexandria in Egypt, which soon became the seat of the commerce that had previously centred in Tyre.

Section IV.—*Social and Political Condition of the Syrians and Phœnicians.*

Syria contained but one large river, the Orontes, a turbid and rapid stream, whose navigation is impeded by rapids, and whose waters cannot be used for domestic purposes. But there are several minor rivers, especially the Chrysorrhoas (Bárrady), in the neighbourhood of Damascus, which, as well as its tributary streams, is remarkable for its limpid waters and abundance of fish. The soil is generally better suited to pasturage than agriculture; and we shall hereafter see that Tyre derived its chief supply of corn from Egypt. Two large valleys of mineral salt added greatly to the natural wealth of the country; and the mountains of Lebanon supplied abundance of excellent timber both for house and ship-building. Syria was consequently partly suited to a nomad, and partly to a commercial people; and this mixture of the two opposite characters, with scarcely any trace of the intermediate agricultural class, led to many revolutions in the Syrian government: the cities were more or less republican, while the rural districts were subject to petty despots. The Syrian religion appears to have been elementary; that is, the objects of worship were the personifications of some powers of nature: their most celebrated deity, Astarte, or the Syrian goddess, represented both the moon and the prolific power of the earth, and was worshipped with the same licentious ceremonies as the Babylonian Mylitta.

The Phœnicians, like the Syrians, belonged to the great Aramean, or Semitic family of nations; but it is uncertain whether they came from Arabia, or from the interior of the country, to the shores of the Mediterranean. Their narrow and short line of coast, indented with excellent bays and harbours, was covered with lofty and wooded mountains, that jut out into the sea, and form bold promontories. Several islands stud the coast, on which cities and commercial establishments were founded, as well as on the mainland. Each of these cities was an independent state; but they were generally united by a federative league, under the presidency of Sidon, and afterwards of Tyre. But this alliance was frequently interrupted by clashing interests and commercial jealousy. Royal government, more or less modified by republican institutions, prevailed in these cities; the priests also possessed a considerable share of power, but they seem never to have formed a hereditary caste. The religion of the Phœnicians appears to have been more sanguinary than that of most other nations; human sacrifices were offered to Moloch, and the worshippers of Baal lacerated themselves with knives to propitiate the idol. Thammuz, or Adonis, was worshipped with very licentious rites, which were supposed to have a mystic signification.

SECTION V.—*History of the Syrians and Phœnicians.*

SYRIA was divided into a number of petty states, most of which were subdued by the Jewish king, David (B.C. 1044). Towards the close of Solomon's reign, Rezon, who had been originally a slave, threw off the yoke, and founded the Syrian kingdom of Damascus. Ben-hadad, the most powerful of his successors, waged a long and sanguinary war against the kingdom of Israel, during the reigns of Ahab and Jehoram. He was finally murdered by Hazael, one of his servants (B.C. 884), who usurped the vacant throne. Hazael was a warlike prince;

he gained several brilliant victories over the forces of Israel and Judah, compelling the monarchs of both to resign several important provinces, and pay him tribute. He also made himself master of Elath on the Red Sea, and greatly increased the commercial prosperity of his dominions. But these advantages were lost under the reign of his inglorious son, Benhadad II.

The Syrians recovered some of their power under Rezin; towards the close of his reign he entered into alliance with Pekah, king of Israel, against Ahaz, king of Judah. The Syrians and Israelites gained so many advantages, that Ahaz sought the protection of Tiglath-pileser, king of Assyria, who marched against Damascus, captured the city, dragged the inhabitants away captive, and put an end to the kingdom (B.C. 740).

It has been already mentioned that most of the Phœnician cities were independent states. Tyre is, however, the only one whose history can be satisfactorily traced. Its first sovereign was Abical (about B.C. 1050), who was contemporary with David. His son and successor, Hiram, was united by the strictest bonds of friendship to the great Jewish king, and also to his son Solomon, whom he supplied with timber for building the Temple. He joined with Solomon in establishing fleets on the Red Sea at the ports of Elath and Ezion-geber, whence an active commerce was maintained with Ophir, the general name of the rich countries round the Indian seas. During the reign of Hiram, Tyre acquired the supremacy of Phœnicia, and became the most flourishing emporium of commerce in the ancient world.

The most remarkable successors of Hiram were Ethbaal I., the father of the wicked Jezebel, wife of Ahab, in whose reign some important colonies were planted in Africa; and Pygmalion, whose murder of Sichæus led to the foundation of Carthage (about B.C. 900). Pygmalion, coveting the immense riches of Sichæus, his uncle and also the husband of his sister Elisa, or Dido, had him secretly assassinated. Dido, aided by numerous Tyrians weary of Pygmalion's tyranny, escaped by sea with her husband's treasures, and sought a new country on the northern shores of Africa. Here she erected the city of

Carthage, which soon rivalled Tyre itself in commercial prosperity.

The Tyrians exercised their supremacy over the surrounding cities with so much cruelty, that the Phœnicians applied for protection to the Assyrians, and afterwards to the Babylonians. The Assyrians, unable to cope with the Tyrians by sea, retired, leaving the city uninjured. But Nebuchadnezzar so exhausted Tyre by a constant blockade, that it was almost wholly abandoned by its inhabitants, who erected the city of New Tyre upon a neighbouring island. Soon after this event, a change was made in the form of government; annual magistrates, called Shophetím,* or, according to the Greek orthography, Suffetes, being chosen instead of kings. After Cyrus had conquered Babylon, the Phœnician cities submitted of their own accord (B.C. 538); but though they became dependencies of the Persian empire, they were permitted to retain their native governments. Tyre again became subject to kings, and supplied the strength of the Persian naval power. It was taken by Alexander the Great (B.C. 332), and from that time it sunk into hopeless decay.

SECTION VI.—*The Phœnician Colonies and Foreign Possessions.*

THE system of colonisation in commercial states has been always the greatest aid to the progress of civilisation: colonies are founded by trading nations, not for the sake of securing frontier provinces, as those of Macedon and Rome in ancient times, and those of Russia in our own days, but for the purpose of securing a lucrative commerce, by establishing a market for the manufactured produce of the parent state, and a carrying-trade for its merchants and seamen. Such colonies, unlike the military establishments of despotic states, require to be placed under the guidance of persons advanced in political knowledge, who know how to vary the institutions derived from the government at home, so as to suit the altered cir-

* *Shophetím*, translated *judges*, was the name of the chief governors of Israel before Saul was chosen the first king.

cumstances of their position and foreign relations: hence civil liberty has always advanced more rapidly in commercial colonies than in the states from which they were derived, and the science of legislation has attained greater perfection than in more ancient establishments. But this system has also many disadvantages: it leads to a thirst for conquest; it inspires a spirit of commercial jealousy; and these combine to make both the parent states and the colonists trample on the rights of the native inhabitants of the countries where settlements are established, and even to treat them with profligate cruelty, as the Carthaginians did the native Africans, and the Spaniards the Indians of South America.

In commercial states the distinction between the citizen and the soldier is very strongly marked: the latter is for the most part regarded as a mere hireling, the paid servant of the merchants; and hence most commercial states in ancient times employed foreign mercenaries. The prophet Ezekiel, whose account of Tyre is the most perfect record of its ancient condition, enumerates the countries that supplied the Tyrian armies and navies with warriors: it will be seen that the other cities of Phœnicia were forced to send contingents to the land and sea forces of the metropolis: "The inhabitants of Sidon and Arvad (the island-city Aradus) were thy mariners; thy wise men, O Tyre, that were in thee, were thy pilots. The ancients of Gebal (the Phœnician city Byblus) and the wise men thereof were in thee thy calkers: all the ships of the sea with their mariners were in thee to occupy thy merchandise. They of Persia, and of Lud (Lydia), and of Phut (north-western Africa) were in thine army, thy men of war; they hanged the shield and helmet in thee, they set forth thy comeliness. The men of Arvad were with thine army upon thy walls round about, and the Gammadims (brave mountaineers, probably from Lebanon) were in thy towers; they hanged their shields upon thy walls round about; they have made thy beauty perfect."*

The Phœnician colonies were sent out under the special

* Ezekiel, xxvii. 8—11.

protection of the national tutelary deity, Melcarth, or the Tyrian Hercules: to his guidance they attributed their success; and hence, when the Greeks identified Melcarth with their own Hercules, they represented the progress of the Phœnician colonies as exploits of their favourite hero. These colonies proceeded from east to west along the coasts of the Mediterranean, occupying the principal islands. Cyprus, called in Scripture Kittím, or Chittím, from its capital city Citium, was not only a colony but a province of Tyre, and vestiges of their establishment on the island still exist. From Cyprus they extended their settlements to Crete and some of the islands in the Archipelago. Thence they proceeded to Africa, Sicily, and Sardinia, spreading their cities unequally along the coasts, and very rarely attempting the conquest of the interior. Their establishments in Sicily and Sardinia, indeed, appear to have been only naval stations for the vessels employed in the trade with western Europe, especially with Spain, which was the Mexico or Peru of the ancient world. The Spanish peninsula, called in Scripture Tarshish, from the city Tartessus, was the country with which the Tyrians had the most lucrative trade; and the colonies they established there soon became independent states. It would seem that the Tyrians were by no means anxious to retain supremacy over their colonies, wisely preferring a close alliance, cemented by common descent, language, and religion, to a hollow dependence. Colonies were also planted beyond the straits of Gibraltar, or, as they were called by the ancients, the Pillars of Hercules. Trade was extended to the British islands and the coasts of the North Sea, which must have led to the establishment of colonies and naval stations along the western and northern coasts of Spain.

The colonies in northern Africa, Leptis, Carthage, Utica, &c. attained greater splendour than any of the other Phœnician cities, and rivalled Tyre itself in wealth and magnificence. It is exceedingly probable that they had also settlements in western Africa, and that they had even reached the island of Madeira. But to prevent any interference with their lucrative commerce, they designedly cast a veil of mystery over their intercourse with the western regions, of which the Greek poets took advantage to embellish their narratives of fictitious voyages and travels with the most fanciful inventions.

It is known that the Phœnicians preceded the Greeks in forming commercial establishments along the coast of Asia Minor and the shores of the Black Sea; but we have no account of the mode in which they were deprived of these possessions by the Greeks. It is probable that the Phœnicians resigned this branch of commerce to attend more closely to their lucrative trade with the western regions.

In the eastern seas they had establishments on the Persian and Arabian Gulfs; but their settlements on the latter were probably not made until David had conquered their commercial rivals the Edomites or Idumeans. From that time they paid great attention to their southern trade, and seem to have become close allies of the Egyptians.

Section VII.—*Phœnician Manufactures and Commerce.*

The textile fabrics of the Sidonians, and the purple cloths of the Tyrians, were celebrated from the earliest antiquity. The Tyrian purple was not a single colour, but was a generic name for all the shades of purple and scarlet. The dye was obtained from a shell-fish found in great abundance on the shores of the Mediterranean. Vegetable dyes of great beauty and variety were also used; the dying was always performed in the raw materials; and the Phœnicians alone understood the art of producing shot colours by using threads of different tints. Glass was very anciently manufactured both at Sidon and Sarepta: tradition, indeed, ascribes the invention of glass to the Phœnicians; but the Egyptians seem to have a claim at least as good to the discovery. Carvings in wood and ivory, manufactures of jewellery and toys, complete all that has been recorded of the products of Tyrian industry; and it seems probable that their commerce consisted more in the interchange of foreign commodities than in the export of their own wrought goods.

The land-trade of the Phœnicians may be divided into three great branches: the Arabian, which included the Egyptian and that with the Indian seas; the Babylonian, to which is referred the commerce with central Asia and north India; and the Armenian, including the overland trade with Scythia and the Caucasian countries.

From Yemen, called Arabia the Happy, the southern division of the Arabian peninsula, caravans brought through the desert frankincense, myrrh, cassia, gold, and precious stones, the gold being probably obtained from the opposite shores of Africa. But before the Phœnicians had a port on the Red Sea, they obtained, through Arabia, the produce of southern India and Africa, more especially cinnamon, ivory, and ebony. This trade is fully described by Ezekiel, to whose account of Tyre we shall more than once have occasion to refer: it will be seen that some of the cities mentioned retain their names at the present day. "Wedan and Javan (probably cities near the straits of Bab-el-Mandel) brought thee from Uzal (the district of Sanaa) wrought iron, cassia, and cinnamon, in exchange for thy wares. Dedan (one of the Baharein islands in the Persian Gulf) was thy merchant in precious clothes for chariots. Arabia and all the princes of Kedar (the nomad tribes of northern Arabia) were the merchants of thy hand in lambs, and rams, and goats: in these were they thy merchants. The merchants of Sheba (Saba or Mariaba) and Raamah (an Arabian city on the Persian Gulf), they were thy merchants: they occupied in thy fairs with chief of all spices, and with all precious stones and gold. Haran, Cannah, Aden, and the merchants of Sheba (Saba), Ashur, and Chilmad (Arabian tribes), were thy traffickers."* The traffic in the Persian Gulf is still more emphatically noticed in another verse: "The sons of Dedan were thy merchants; many distant lands were the merchandise of thine hand: they brought thee for a requital horns, ivory, and ebony."† The distant lands spoken of in connexion with Daden must have been the western coasts of India; and the Phœnician settle-

* Ezekiel, xxvii. 19—23, according to Michaelis and Gesenius.

† Ib. xxvii. 15.

ment on the island has left traces of its establishment that may still be seen near the town of Gerra.

From the description we have quoted of the Arabian trade, it appears to have been principally carried on by caravans. The northern Arabs, especially the princes of Kedar and the Midianites, were in ancient times great travelling merchants; and the kingdom of Edom, or Idumæa, in the north of the Arabian peninsula, attained a very high degree of commercial prosperity. On the sea-coast the Idumeans possessed the ports of Elath and Ezion-geber (Akaba); in the interior, they had for their metropolis Petra, whose magnificent remains have been but recently discovered. Ezekiel unites Edom with Syria, because the route of the caravans lay through the latter country: "Syria trafficked with thee by reason of the multitude of the wares of thy making; they gave for thy merchandise emeralds, purple and broidered work, and fine linen and agate."* The articles thus enumerated are Indian and Egyptian, brought by caravans from the shores of the Red Sea. The greater part of the Phœnician trade with Egypt was overland, at least so long as the seat of government was at Thebes, in Upper Egypt: when Memphis rose into power, an entire quarter of the city was assigned to the Phœnician merchants, and the trade by sea to the mouths of the Nile grew into importance. The first branch of the eastern Phœnician trade was with Judæa and Syria Proper: "Judah, and the land of Israel, they were thy merchants; they traded in thy market corn of Minnith, and sweetmeats, and honey, and oil, and balm. Damascus was thy merchant in the multitude of the wares of thy making, for the multitude of all thy riches; in the wine of Chalybon (Aleppo), and wool of the wilderness."† The dependence of the Phœnicians on Palestine for grain fully explains the cause of their close alliance with the Jewish kingdom in the reigns of David and Solomon.

But the most important branch of eastern trade was that through Babylon with the interior of Asia. A great part of

* Ezekiel, xxvii. 16, according to Gesenius.

† Ib. xxvii. 17, 18.

the route lay through the Syrian desert; and to facilitate the passage of the caravans, two of the most remarkable cities of the ancient world, Baalbec and Palmyra, were founded. They were both built by Solomon: "he founded," says the Scripture, "Baalath (Baalbec) and Tadmor (Palmyra) in the desert."* They were erected by that wise monarch to procure for his subjects a share in this lucrative traffic; but this object was frustrated by the subsequent revolt of the ten tribes, and the wars between Israel and Judah.

The northern land-trade of the Phœnicians is described by no ancient writer but the prophet Ezekiel: "Javan (Ionia and the Greek colonies), Tubal, and Meshech (the countries around the Black and north Caspian Seas), they were thy merchants: they traded the persons of men and vessels of brass in thy markets. They of the house of Togarmah (Armenia and Cappadocia) traded in thy fairs with horses and horsemen and mules."†

But the Mediterranean Sea was the great high road of Phœnician commerce: it probably commenced with piracy; for in the infancy of Grecian civilisation, we find frequent mention of the kidnapping practised by corsairs from Tyre and Sidon. But when Greece advanced in power, and Athens and Corinth had fleets of their own, the Greeks became the rivals and political enemies of the Phœnicians, purchasing from them only such articles as could not be procured from their own colonies in Asia Minor. Spain was the richest country of the ancient world in the precious metals. The Phœnician colonies enslaved the natives, and compelled them to work in the mines: these metallic productions are enumerated by Ezekiel. "Tarshish (Tartessus, or south-western Spain,) was thy merchant by reason of the multitude of all kind of riches; with silver, iron, tin, and lead, they traded in thy fairs."‡ From Spain the Phœnicians entered the Atlantic Ocean, and proceeded to the south of the British Islands, where they procured the tin of Cornwall; and probably to the coasts of Prussia for amber,

* 1 Kings, ix. 18. † Ezekiel, xxvii. 13, 14.

‡ Ezekiel, xxvii. 12.

which in the ancient world was deemed more precious than gold. In the eastern seas, the Phœnicians had establishments on the Arabian and Persian Gulf, whence they traded with the coasts of India and Africa, and the island of Ceylon. During the reign of Pharaoh-Necho, king of Egypt, they discovered the passage round the Cape of Good Hope; but this led to no important results, on account of the calamities that Tyre endured from the invasion of Nebuchadnezzar. Though their voyages did not equal in daring those of modern times; yet, when we consider that they were ignorant of the mariner's compass, and of the art of taking accurate astronomical observations, it is wonderful to reflect on the commercial enterprise of a people whose ships were to be seen in the harbours of Britain and Ceylon.

CHAPTER V.

PALESTINE.

SECTION I.—*Geographical Outline.*

PALESTINE, or the Holy Land, lies between Phœnicia on the north, and Idumæa on the south, separated from both by chains of lofty mountains; to the east its boundaries were the Asphaltic Lake, the river Jordan, and the Sea of Galilee; on the west it extended to the Mediterranean. It was variously divided at different periods of its history; at first it was partitioned by lot among the twelve tribes of Israel, then into the two kingdoms of Israel and Judah, and finally into small provinces, or toparchies, by its Persian, Grecian, and Roman conquerors.

The mountains are the most remarkable features in the geography of Palestine. Lebanon (the white mountain) derives its name from the perpetual snow that crowns its summits—it consists of four ridges of mountains, rising successively above each other, on the highest of which were the celebrated forests of cedars; Hermon, another lofty range, supplied the snow used in the Phœnician cities to cool their liquors; Tabor, more to the south, was the scene of Christ's transfiguration; Carmel (the vine of God), a lofty range on the sea-coast, remarkable for its blooming vineyards; the mounts of Olives and Moriah, or Calvary, join the city of Jerusalem; Engadi (the goat-fountain) was famed for its abundant brooks and palm-groves; and, finally, Ebal and Gerizim, near the city of Shechem, where the Law was ordered to be solemnly proclaimed. These mountains, and many others of less note, divided Palestine into a series of valleys and table-lands, leaving two great plains, that called "the region about Jordan," and the plain of Esdraelon, or Jezreel. These valleys and plains were of very unequal value; some were so unproductive as to be called deserts, others were the most fertile spots in western Asia.

Jordan was the only great river of Palestine: it falls into

the Asphaltic Lake, or Dead Sea, which occupies the site of the ancient cities Sodom and Gomorrah. There is no outlet from the Asphaltic Lake, and its waters are bitter and unwholesome. The Sea of Galilee, through which the Jordan flows, is a beautiful fresh-water lake, abounding in fish.

The principal cities were, Jerusalem, the metropolis of the kingdom of Judah, and Samaria, the capital of Israel. Jerusalem, in its most flourishing state, was divided into four parts, each enclosed within its own walls: 1. the old city of Jebus, which stood on Mount Zion, where David built a magnificent palace—whence this division is frequently called "the city of David;" 2. the lower city, called also "the daughter of Zion," first raised into importance by the exertions of King Solomon; 3. the new city, principally inhabited by merchants, tradesmen, and artificers; and, 4. Mount Moriah, on which the Temple was erected.

Idumæa lay south of Palestine, beyond the chain of Mount Seir: it was in general a rocky and barren country; but being the high road of Arabian traffic, its natural capabilities were improved to the utmost, and it contained the great city of Petra, whose commercial wealth was deservedly celebrated. Idumæa, or Edom, was annexed to the kingdom of Israel in the reign of David.

The valleys of Palestine were in general very fruitful; and the varied elevations of the country, causing so many different climates, gave the country a greater variety of natural productions than is usually found in so confined a space. The hills afforded excellent pasturage for cattle; the valleys produced abundant crops of corn. Olives and vines grew in great abundance; and the oil and wine extracted from their fruits were the chief articles of export, next to corn. The balsam-shrub, that yields the celebrated balm of Gilead, abounded in the plains of Jericho, which were also remarkable for their groves of palm-trees. Honey was also very plentiful, and was found deposited wild in the rocks, by the bees which used the natural caverns for hives. Fish abounded in the Sea of Galilee and the Jordan. The Asphaltic Lake, though it produced no living thing, contributed to the wealth of the country by yielding large quantities of excellent salt, which was said to be superior to that of any other locality.

A series of calamities, unparalleled in any other portion of the globe, has now reduced Palestine almost to sterility; but even now there are spots to be found whose luxuriance revives the memory of the verdure and beauty that once covered the entire country.

SECTION II.—*History of Palestine.*

FROM B.C. 1920 TO B.C. 975.

GOD in his wisdom called Abram from the land of the Chaldees to Palestine, then named Canaan, to be the founder of a nation that should be his peculiar people (B.C. 1920), and preserve the true religion amid the idolatrous corruptions of other nations. Abraham, at his death (B.C. 1821), transmitted the inheritance of the divine promise to his son Isaac; and he was deceived into making his second son Jacob, or Israel, the heir of this glorious privilege. The twelve sons of Jacob, envying their brother Joseph, sold him as a slave to some Arabian merchants, by whom he was carried into Egypt. Protected by Providence, Joseph escaped from the snares of a wicked woman, and became the chief minister of the Pharaoh of Egypt; his brethren having come into that country to purchase corn, he made himself known to them, and invited his father, with his whole family, to dwell in the rich district of Goshen (B.C. 1705). In process of time, the Israelites became so numerous as to excite the envious alarm of the Egyptians: they were in consequence cruelly persecuted, until God raised up Moses as their deliverer. The miraculous plagues he inflicted on the land of Egypt induced the reigning Pharaoh to consent to the departure of the Israelites (B.C. 1491). Repenting of his permission, he pursued them with a mighty host; but he and all his followers perished in the Red Sea. After wandering forty years in the wilderness, during which time Moses died, the Israelites, having received a code of laws from God on Mount Sinai, entered the promised land under the guidance of Joshua (B.C. 1451), and exterminated the greater part of the ancient inhabitants.

During three hundred years, the tribes of Israel formed a kind of federative republic, the worship of Jehovah being their great bond of union. In consequence of their lapses into idolatry, they were permitted to be subjected by the neighbouring nations; but on their repentance, God raised up for them a succession of deliverers, especially Othniel, Gideon, Deborah, and Samson. The governors during this period, whether chosen by God or elected by the tribes, were named Shophetím, or judges. Samuel was the last of the Shophetím. Urged by the people, he chose Saul for the king of Israel, under the divine direction (B.C. 1150).

The new king was a brave warrior, but he wanted almost every other qualification for power: contrary to the law, he usurped the priestly office, and Samuel was commanded by God to anoint David, the son of Jesse, his successor. Saul and all his sons but one fell in a fatal battle with the Philistines (B.C. 1055).

Eleven of the tribes adhered to Ishbosheth, the son of Saul; but David's right was supported by the tribe of Judah; and after a desultory war of nine years' continuance, he became sole monarch, Ishbosheth having been murdered by his own servants. During this reign the nation was regularly formed. Jerusalem, the mountain-fortress of the Jebusites, supposed to have been descended from the Hyksos, was subdued, and made the capital of the kingdom. Externally, the empire was enlarged by the conquest of Syria and Idumæa, and enriched by the opening of an extensive commerce with Tyre.

Solomon succeeded his father David (B.C. 1015), and applied himself to improving the internal state of the kingdom, in preference to foreign conquests. He erected the Temple at Jerusalem, and adorned his capital with many magnificent structures. The lapse of the king into idolatry weakened the unity of the state, at the same time that heavy taxes alienated the northern tribes; and he left to his son Rehoboam a kingdom of great splendour, but of little real strength (B.C. 975).

The northern tribes applied to the new monarch for a remission of some of the onerous burdens imposed upon them; but receiving a harsh answer, they threw off their allegiance to the house of David, and chose Jeroboam for their king.

SECTION III.—*The Kingdom of Israel.*

FROM B.C. 975 TO B.C. 722.

JEROBOAM, immediately after his elevation to the throne, hasted to destroy the great bond of union between all the descendants of Jacob—community of religious worship; and, to prevent his subjects from going to Jerusalem, erected golden calves at Dan and Bethel as religious sanctuaries, appointing some of his unworthy favourites to the priesthood. He was almost constantly engaged in war with the kingdom of Judah, as likewise was his son and successor Nadab. But while Nadab was besieging a city of the Levites, he was murdered by Baasha, one of his generals, who usurped the throne, and extirpated the entire family of Jeroboam (B.C. 952).

Baasha, having entered into alliance with Benhadad, king of Syria, greatly weakened the kingdom of Judah, but was afterwards exposed to the enmity of his ally. On his death (B.C. 929), he was succeeded by his son Elah, who, after a brief reign, was murdered by Zimri, and he in his turn was slain by Omri, who, after a brief struggle, obtained possession of the throne.

Omri built the city of Samaria, which became the capital of the kingdom of Israel. He was succeeded (B.C. 918) by his son Ahab, who was one of the most wicked princes that ever disgraced a throne, and was fitly matched with his queen Jezebel, a Sidonian princess, whose iniquity has become proverbial. Ahab was slain in a war with the Syrians (B.C. 897), and his crown descended successively to his sons Ahaziah and Jehoram.

Jehoram was dethroned by Jehu (B.C. 883), who extirpated the family of Ahab, and abolished the Sidonian rites introduced by Jezebel. He and his son Jehoahaz waged an unsuccessful war with the Syrian kings, and lost the provinces east of the Jordan: but Jehoash, the next king, gained several advantages over the monarchs of Jerusalem and Damascus; and in the reign of Jeroboam II. (B.C. 773), the kingdom of Israel was restored to its ancient extent. After a turbulent interregnum of twelve years, Zechariah ascended the throne; but was immediately murdered by Shallum, who, after a brief usurpation, fell a victim to the ambition of Menahem (B.C. 761).

Menahem was engaged in endeavouring to restore some order to the distracted kingdom, when he was alarmed by the invasion of the Assyrians under Pul, the first of the Assyrians that crossed the Euphrates. Menahem purchased an inglorious security by paying a large tribute, and soon after died, leaving the kingdom to his son Pekahiah. The young monarch was dethroned and murdered by Pekah (B.C. 759), who held the usurped throne for twenty years, during which the country suffered severely from the ravages of the Assyrians under Tiglath-Pileser. Pekah was at length slain by Hoshea, one of his generals, who did not obtain the throne without a severe struggle, that kept the kingdom of Israel in anarchy for nearly nine years. He was forced to become tributary to Shalmanezer, king of Assyria; but trusting to the promised support of the Egyptians, he subsequently threw off the yoke, and was punished for the revolt by the loss of his liberty and kingdom. Shalmaneser carried the ten tribes into captivity beyond the Euphrates (B.C. 721), and thus put an end to the kingdom of Israel, which, under nineteen sovereigns, had lasted two hundred and fifty-four years.

SECTION IV.—*Kingdom of Judah.*

FROM B.C. 975 TO B.C. 588.

REHOBOAM made some efforts to recover his hereditary dominion over the northern tribes, but he possessed neither the abilities of a warrior nor a statesman. Though Jerusalem continued to be the national sanctuary, and the worship of Jehovah was maintained in the Temple, yet this wicked and foolish king sanctioned the introduction of foreign idolatry. He was punished by the invasion of Shishak, king of Egypt, who captured and plundered Jerusalem. Rehoboam was succeeded by his son Abijah (B.C. 958), who gained a brilliant victory over the Israelites, and destroyed their national sanctuary at Bethel.

Asa was the next king (B.C. 955): he began his reign by strenuous exertions to extirpate idolatry, and deposed his own mother from her royal state for patronising the worship of false gods. He was rewarded by the divine protection, when Zerah, the Ethiopian, came against him with an enormous army; the invaders were routed with great slaughter, and Asa returned to Jerusalem with immense spoil. Many of the Israelites were induced by his fame to transfer their allegiance to the crown of Judah; Baasha, in revenge, induced Benhadad, king of Syria, to join him in a war against the Jewish kingdom; but Asa, by a large bribe, prevailed upon him to turn his arms against Israel.

Jehoshaphat succeeded his father Asa (B.C. 914), and carried into full effect the reformation of religion that had been commenced in the preceding reign; rooting up all the idolatrous groves, altars, and monuments, and severely prohibiting the worship of false gods. He entered into close alliance with the king of Israel, and, in conjunction with Ahaziah, attempted to revive the Jewish trade in the Red Sea; but their efforts were frustrated by the wreck of their united navy, owing to the inexperience of the sailors. Jehoshaphat made his son Jehoram a partner in his government, and, by divine assistance, gained a decisive victory over the Ammonites and Moabites.

On the death of Jehoshaphat (B.C. 889), his son and successor Jehoram, who had married Athaliah, the daughter of Ahab, introduced all the idolatries and abominations that his father had removed, and drew closer the alliance between the kingdoms of Judah and Israel. He was punished by the revolt of the Edomites, who had remained subject to the Jewish crown from the time of their conquest by David; they were defeated in a general engagement, but could not again be reduced to obedience. Soon afterwards the Philistines and Arabians invaded Judæa, took and plundered Jerusalem, and carried away all the king's sons as captives, except Ahaziah. A severe disease, aggravated by grief, soon rendered Jehoram incapable of government; and he resigned his power to Ahaziah a short time before his death (B.C. 885). Ahaziah was killed, after a brief reign, by Jehu, who had usurped the crown of Israel; and the government of Judah was usurped by the queen-mother Athaliah, who, to secure her power, attempted to murder the whole royal family.

Joash, only a year old, was rescued from the malice of Athaliah by Jehoiada, the high priest; and, having been secreted for six years, was placed on the throne by his protector; and the usurper, Athaliah, fell a victim to the popular rage. Jehoiada, as guardian of the young prince, restored the worship of Jehovah, and destroyed the priests and worshippers of Baal. But after his death (B.C. 840), Joash sunk into idolatry, and murdered Zechariah, the son of his benefactor, for reproving his apostacy. His dominions were soon afterwards invaded by the Syrians, whose forbearance he was forced to purchase by the sacrifice of all the royal treasures; and scarcely had the invaders departed, when he was murdered by his servants.

Amaziah waged war against the Edomites, and gained a signal victory over them, which he followed up by storming their capital, and putting the garrison to the sword. Elated by success, he attacked Joash, king of Israel; but was defeated with great loss, and taken prisoner. He was liberated on the payment of a large ransom, and returned to Jerusalem. His subjects at length became weary of his incapacity, and he fell a victim to a conspiracy in the twenty-ninth year of his reign (B.C. 810). Uzziah, a prudent and religious prince, succeeded to the throne: he exerted himself to root out idolatry, and was rewarded by the divine protection, which rendered him victorious over his hostile neighbours. At length he usurped the priestly office, and was stricken with leprosy, which compelled him to entrust the government to his son Jotham (B.C. 761). He died about two years afterwards, and was succeeded by his son.

Jotham's reign was peaceful and prosperous: it was followed by that of the wicked Ahaz (B.C. 742), who lapsed into idolatry.

His kingdom was attacked by the joint forces of Israel and Syria, nor could he defend himself without the protection of the Assyrian monarchs, to whom he became tributary. Hezekiah, the son of Ahaz, was a prince of a very different character: immediately after his accession, he purified the Temple, prohibited idolatry, and restored the national worship in its former splendour. Many of the Israelites, still mindful of their fathers' God, migrated into the kingdom of Judah, and Hezekiah found himself sufficiently powerful to throw off the Assyrian yoke. Sennacherib, enraged at this revolt, sent an immense host to besiege Jerusalem; but the greater part of his army was destroyed by the angel of the Lord in a single night.

To Hezekiah succeeded Manasseh (B.C. 698), one of the most wicked princes that ever reigned in Judah. His territories were subdued by the Assyrians, and he himself carried away captive; but, on his repentance, God restored him to his throne; and the close of his reign was spent in virtue and tranquillity. Ammon, his son and successor (B.C. 643), restored idolatry, and was soon murdered by his officers, leaving the throne to Josiah, a child only eight years old.

No sooner had Josiah arrived at mature age, than he commenced a thorough reformation of his kingdom, destroying all the monuments of idolatry, and repairing the holy Temple. In executing this work, a copy of the Book of the Law, which had been lost, was discovered, and it was publicly read to the people; after which a solemn fast and national humiliation was held for the recent transgressions of Judah. After a glorious reign, Josiah was slain in a battle against Pharaoh-Necho, king of Egypt, and was buried amid the general lamentations of his subjects (B.C. 610).

Jehoahaz succeeded, but was deposed by the Egyptian victor, and the crown bestowed on his brother Jehoiakim. The Babylonian empire was now fast rising into importance under Nebuchadnezzar, who marched against Jerusalem, captured the city, and took away the sons of the nobility as hostages; but he permitted Jehoiakim to retain nominal sovereignty as his viceroy. Unfortunately Jehoiakim, relying on his Egyptian allies, revolted, and was conquered and put to death by the Assyrians.

His son, who was also called Jehoiakim, after a reign of three months, was led captive to Babylon, and the name of king given to Zedekiah. Not warned by the example of his predecessor, Zedekiah also revolted, but was soon beseiged in his capital. Jerusalem, after an obstinate defence, was taken by storm, the Temple was destroyed, the city plundered and burned, and Zedekiah, after having seen his children murdered before his face, was deprived of sight, and sent a prisoner to Babylon (B.C. 588). Thus ended the kingdom of Judah, which, under twenty monarchs of the house of David, had lasted more than three hundred and eighty years.

The Jews were neither a manufacturing nor commercial people: their principal trade was the export of their agricultural produce to the Phœnician cities, and also to Idumæa and Egypt. Their peculiar laws and social customs were intimately blended with their religion, and may be best understood by the study of the Mosaic institutions, as recorded in the Holy Bible.

CHAPTER VI.

THE EMPIRE OF THE MEDES AND PERSIANS.

SECTION I.—*Geographical Outline.*

THE boundaries of Irân, which Europeans call Persia, have undergone many changes: in its most prosperous periods, its limits were the Persian Gulf and Indian Ocean on the south, the rivers Indus and Oxus on the east, the Caspian Sea and Caucasian mountains on the north, and the Euphrates on the west. The most striking features of this extensive country are numerous chains of mountains, and extensive tracts of desert, interspersed with fertile valleys and rich pasture-lands. The southern coast along the Persian Gulf has a considerable resemblance to Arabia; it is a sandy plain, desolated by pestilential winds from the desert of Kerman, and scarcely possessing any indentation or navigable river which could serve as a harbour. From thence to the Caspian Sea and the Oxus there is a succession of mountains and valleys of different elevation and extent. Few of the mountains are of extraordinary height, though some of the ranges are capped with perpetual snow; none of the valleys are wide, but some of them extend to the length of one hundred miles. The largest tracts of country are the salt deserts, the most remarkable of which extends from the banks of the Etymander (Heirmund) to the modern province of Mekran, which skirts the Indian Ocean.

Persia Proper, the modern province of Phars, contained the sacred metropolis of the empire, known to us only by its Greek name, Persepolis. This celebrated city was destroyed by Alexander; but its ruins, called Chehl-Menaî, or the forty pillars, testify that it must have rivalled the most splendid cities of antiquity. Pasargada was a royal mausoleum and treasury dependent on Persepolis, and appears to have been regarded as the sanctuary of the monarchy.

The province of Susiana (Khuzistan) separated Persia Proper from Babylonia; between the two provinces was a range of mountains, inhabited by warlike pastoral tribes, who compelled the Persian kings to pay them tribute when they went from Susa to Persepolis. Susiana was a fertile province, watered by several small streams, that supplied a vast number of canals and water-courses. Susa, the capital of this district, once the favourite residence of the Persian monarchs, is now a vast desert, where the ruins of a city can with difficulty be traced. North of these provinces were wild mountainous districts, extending to the confines of Media, whose inhabitants could with difficulty be brought to submit to a settled government. Media was divided into two provinces; Atropatene or Media Minor (Azerbiján), and Media Major (Irák agemí). The former contained the city of Tauris (Tabríz), but was only partially cultivated. Media Major abounded in rich pasturages, especially near the city of Nysa; and hence it was rich in flocks and herds. The Nysean horses were regarded as the best in Asia; and the breed, not yet wholly extinct, still maintains a very high character. Ecbatana (Hamadan) was the capital of Media, and rivalled Susa and Persepolis in magnificence, while it exceeded them in extent and the strength of its fortifications. The eastern districts of Media, named Aria, formed an extensive steppe, which merged in the desert of Carmania (Kerman): it was separated from Media by a fortified defile, called the Pylæ Caspiæ (Caspian Gates). The capital was named Aria, or Arlacoana, and occupied the site of the modern Herat.

North of Media lay Parthia and Hyrcania (Taberistán and Mazenderan); mountainous regions, with some fertile valleys. The capital of Hyrcania was Zandracarta, which was occasionally a royal residence. North-east of these were the sandy deserts now called Khwan, tenanted by nomad tribes, who then and now practised alternately the arts of merchants, herdsmen, and robbers. East of Aria was Bactriana, divided by the Oxus from Sogdiana: its capital city was Bactra, which is usually identified with the modern city of Balkh. The metropolis of Sogdiana was Maracanda, now called Samarcand, one of the most ancient commercial cities in the world.

East of the province of Phars were Carmania (Kerman) and Gedrosia (Mekran); flat and sandy, but interspersed with some very fertile tracts. The people of Gedrosia were among the most uncivilised subject to Persia; they have always been destitute of corn and cattle, and were for the most part compelled to subsist upon fish. The other eastern districts of Persia were known only by name to the ancients before the time of Alexander.

The hills in the interior of Persia are but thinly clad with vegetation, and none but those of Mazenderan and Georgia possess forests; a few, however, have groups of large trees mingled with the shrubs and underwood that cover those which are not entirely barren. There are but few rivers of sufficient magnitude to be navigable: the most remarkable are the Ulai or Eulæus (Karún), the Arras or Araxes, and the Etymander (Heirmund).

The valleys of the centre of Persia abound in the rarest and most valuable vegetable productions, and under a good system of government might be cultivated almost to any extent. The orchards produce all the fruits of the temperate zone, and the most beautiful flowers of our gardens grow wild in the fields. The horses and dogs are of uncommon size, strength, and beauty; and no country possesses a more robust, active, and well-shaped race of men; probably in consequence of the great variety of climate, which inures them to the vicissitudes of heat and cold from earliest infancy. In short, Persia possesses every natural advantage for becoming a powerful and prosperous empire; but from the remotest ages it has been subjected to a blighting despotism, by which its resources have been not merely neglected, but wasted and destroyed.

Section II.—*The Sources and Extent of our Knowledge respecting the ancient Persians.*

The history of the ancient Persians is involved in great obscurity, though no nation took more pains to transmit correct accounts to posterity. The records that have come down to us are for the most part so inconsistent, that their narratives have as little similarity in the most important details as the histories of England and Japan. It is necessary, therefore, to state the sources from which the following account has been derived, and to shew how much of the narrative depends on plausible conjecture, and how much on probable evidence. The sources of Persian history are either native or foreign; the latter including the accounts both of the Greek historians and the Jewish prophets.

The first native authority is the Zend-a-vesta, a collection of the sacred books of the ancient Persians; parts of which are undoubtedly very ancient, though other portions have been corrupted by the lapse of ages. In this work are contained the early traditions of the nation, the religious system and moral code ascribed to Zerdusht, or Zoroaster, the great Persian legislator, and the liturgy still used by "the worshippers of fire." Connected with this is the Dabistán, a work describing twelve religions, written by a Mohammedan traveller about two centuries ago, in which the author treats very fully of the ancient religion of Persia, professedly deriving his information from original sources. To these must be added some minor Parsí works, collected by Orientalists in India.

Next in importance to these ranks the Sháh Námeh, or Book of Kings, an immense epic poem, containing sixty thousand verses, written by Ferdousí, the greatest poet of Persia, about the middle of the tenth century. This historical poem was compiled from vague traditions, and from the few fragments of ancient Persian literature that survived the fanaticism of the first Mohammedan conquerors; and, consequently, facts are so disguised by a multitude of fictions, that it is always difficult, and frequently impossible, to arrive at the truth of his representations. Mirkhond and his son Khondemír both wrote histories of Persia, about the close of the fifteenth century; they have, however, in general followed the narrative of Ferdousí; but in some places Mirkhond undoubtedly has used the same authorities as the compiler of the Dabistán. It will readily be believed that these works are not entitled to the same credit as the national histories with which we are familiar in Europe: history, as a science, has never been cultivated in the East; truth has never been the main object of Oriental writers, and a critical estimate of rival authorities never has been practised in Asia. The traditional legends that survived the Macedonian conquest, the wars of the Seleucidæ, and the Parthian dynasty, appear to have been collected by the Sassanides; but they were again dispersed when the Saracens subverted the ancient empire of Persia. After more than twelve hundred years had elapsed since the fall of Darius, Ferdousí was able to collect but scanty materials; and he chiefly paid attention to the legends that related to eastern Persia, and the Asiatic wars of the empire. Mirkhond equally neglected the European relations of the ancient Persians; and hence arises one great cause of the discrepancy between his statements and those of western writers.

Herodotus, Xenophon, and the fragments of Ctesias, are the principal Greek authorities for the history of ancient Persia: of these the first is by far the most valuable, and his account of the Persian wars with Greece is entitled to our confidence. It must also be added, that many parts of his narrative are singularly confirmed by the legends preserved in the works of Mirkhond and Ferdousí. The writings of Xenophon are, a life of Cyrus, a philosophical romance founded on history, and an account of his own campaigns in Persia. Ctesias has given us catalogues of kings, professedly derived from the Persian archives; but, from his fragments, he appears to have exercised little discretion in selecting his authorities.

In the Bible, the book of Esther is altogether a Persian history, and much important information is given incidentally in the books of Daniel, Ezra, and Nehemiah.

Finally, much light has been thrown on ancient Persian history by the writings of modern Oriental scholars; especially the philological researches of Bopp, Burnouf, and Schlegel, which have shewn how closely allied the ruling people of Hindustán was with the ruling nation of Irán, by pointing out the close resemblance between the original languages of both, the Sanscrit and the Zend.

From authorities so very different in nature and value, all confessedly more or less imperfect, a complete view of the history and condition of ancient Persia cannot reasonably be expected; but by combining all these together, we may hope to obtain at least a more correct account than has yet been deduced from them taken separately.

SECTION III.—*Social and Political Condition of ancient Persia.*

CENTRAL ASIA from the most remote ages has been exposed to the invasions of nomad hordes from the north and east, most of which, according to their native legends, descended from the mountainous tracts extending from the great Altaian chain to the Paropamisian range on the borders of India. Recent investigations have rendered it probable that this was also the native country of the Brahmins and Hindús, at least of the higher castes; but it is impossible to discover at what period migrations commenced to the south and west. The colonists who came into Media called themselves Arii, manifestly the same word as the Sanscrit Arya, which signifies *pure men*, in opposition to the Mlêchas, or barbarians. They were a mixed priestly and warrior caste, who treated their subjects as beings of an inferior nature. A cognate race, the Persians, having nearly the same institutions, proceeded farther to the south-west, and formed a nation of herdsmen and shepherds. A monarch named Jemshíd, the Achæmenes of the Greeks, first instructed his subjects in agriculture, and they gratefully made royalty the inheritance of his family. The Medes, having long held dominion as the ruling caste, were overthrown in an insurrection of the agricultural and shepherd tribes: this political revolution was effected by Cyrus; and it was followed necessarily by a religious change, consequent on the altered position of the priestly caste.

Under the Medes, or rather the Magi, as their priests were called, a species of the Sabian superstition seems to have prevailed: the sun, moon, and planets, received divine worship, while the more ancient belief in one supreme God, though obscured, was not wholly lost. When the Persians triumphed, the priestly caste lost much of its influence, and seems to have been regarded as naturally hostile to the new dynasty: hence we find the Persian monarchs bitter persecutors of the priests wherever they established their sway, destroying the Chaldeans in Babylon, and the sacerdotal caste in Egypt. The nature of the religious changes made by Cyrus cannot now be determined; but the revolution was completed by Zoroaster, whose system is the most perfect devised by unassisted human reason. "God, he taught, existed from all eternity, and was like infinity of time and space. There were, he averred, two principles in the universe,—good and evil: the one was named Hormuzd, which denoted the presiding agent of all that was good; and the other Ahrimán, the lord of evil. Each of these had the power of creation, but that power was exercised with opposite designs; and it was from their co-action that an admixture of good and evil was found in every created thing. The angels of Hormuzd, or the good principle, sought to preserve the elements, the seasons, and the human race, which the infernal agents of Ahrimán desired to destroy; but the source of good alone, the great Hormuzd, was eternal, and must therefore ultimately prevail. Light was the type of the good, darkness of the evil spirit; and God had said unto Zoroaster, 'My light is concealed under all that shines.' Hence the disciple of that prophet, when he performs his devotions in a temple, turns towards the sacred fire that burns upon its altar; and when in the open air, towards the sun, as the noblest of all lights, and that by which God sheds his divine influence over the whole earth, and perpetuates the work of his creation."*

With these speculative tenets was combined a system of castes, which are thus described by Ferdousí, who attributes their introduction to Jemshíd:—

"This done, for fifty years his active mind
Combined and class'd the grades of human kind.
The sage's class, the *Amuzban*, he chose,
And named a mount of hallow'd rites for those;
They, with a chief devote to prayer alone,
Guardians of fire, stand next the royal throne.
Next those, *Nisari* call'd, who weapons wield,
The lion-guard, the glory of the field;

* Sir John Malcolm's Persia, vol. i. p. 194. The Jews have a tradition that Zoroaster was instructed in the true religion by one of the prophets.

Pride of the brave, they found and fix the throne,
As *Merdipai*, or martial succour, known.
From all mankind a meed of thanks is claim'd
For the next class, 'The Full of Wisdom' fram'd:
Remote from haughtier sway, from lust of fame,
Tillage and harvest-toils their simple aim;
No cries of hunger rise, nor famines come
To stint their meals, or scare their humble home;
From cold, from want secure, their peaceful ear
Rings not of doom, nor sounds of death and fear.
Yes! these are blest; but mark this maxim grave—
'Tis sloth that turns the freeman to a slave.
The fourth, the *Ahmenshushi* class, combined
Those of ingenious hand and active mind;
Laborious, staid, who crafts of skill espouse,
While care and want deep grave their wrinkled brows.
In fifty years the monarch fix'd the place
Of this, the artist and mechanic race;
Selecting one from each, the task to guide
By rules of art, himself the rules applied." *

The conservation of the ordinances that regulated public morals was entrusted to the Magi, who were, as we have said, originally a caste or tribe of the Medes. Zoroaster reformed the institutions of this body, and appears to have opened the priestly dignity to persons of every caste, though few entered on the functions of public worship who were not of Magian descent. Thus the sacerdotal rank in Persia partook of the nature both of a caste and an order. It was high in power: the court was principally composed of sages and soothsayers; and it was deemed one of the highest royal privileges to be initiated in the mysteries of the Magian religion. The priests also were judges in civil cases, because religion was the basis of their legislation; but they were strictly bound by the ancient code. No circumstances were deemed sufficiently strong to warrant a departure from ancient usages; and hence "the laws of the Medes and Persians" were proverbial for their strictness of execution.

The king was as much bound by the national code as his meanest subject; but in every other respect his power was

* Poatt's Specimens. (Unpublished.)

without control; and the satraps, or provincial governors under him, were equally despotic in their respective provinces. The court scarcely differed in any material point from the Oriental courts of the present day. The king had his harem of wives, and a crowd of intriguing eunuchs. The succession was always open to dispute; and rival mothers poisoned or murdered those whom they deemed competitors for the crown. It was a heavy tax on the national resources to support the barbarous splendour with which the kings and satraps deemed it necessary to surround their dignity; and the exactions wrung from the cultivators of the soil always made the Persian peasantry the most miserable even in Asia. The army was another source of wretchedness to the country: a vast amount of standing forces was always maintained, and hordes of the wandering tribes on the borders of Persia kept in pay: besides this, in case of any emergency, every man capable of bearing arms was enrolled in his own district, and forced to become a soldier on the first summons. This constitution enabled the Persians to make rapid conquests, but it prevented their empire from becoming permanent: the soldiers fought for pay or plunder, and were held together by no common principle save attachment to their leader; hence the fall or flight of the commander-in-chief instantly decided the fate of a Persian army, however great its numbers; and when the army was defeated, the kingdom was subdued. With a despotic king, an army drawn together more like a herd of slaves than warriors, a grinding system of taxation, and a deliberate disregard of popular rights, the great Oriental monarchies were liable to vicissitudes scarcely known in European states. There was no patriotic spirit in the people, no love of independence in the nation; if the invader prevailed in the battle-field, he had no further enemies to dread; the mass of the population cared little for a change of rule, which left unaltered the miseries of their situation.

SECTION IV.—*History of the Medes and Persians under the Kaianian Dynasty.*

FROM B.C. 710 TO B.C. 522.

MEDIA and Persia were provinces of the great Assyrian empire; and their native legends preserve the memory of the cruelty with which they were treated by the monarchs of Nineveh, though sadly disguised by fiction, in the history of the tyrant Zahak. When that empire was broken to pieces after the death of Sardanapalus, Media fell into a state of anarchy, from which it was delivered by Deioces (B.C. 710), the Kai Kobad of Oriental writers: he built the city of Ecbatana, and greatly strengthened his new kingdom by inducing his subjects to form permanent settlements; but in the midst of his useful career, he was summoned to check the rising power of the Babylonians, and fell in battle. The Median power was restored by Phraortes, who succeeded his father; but it attained its highest glory under Cyaxares, the third monarch of this dynasty.

In the early part of his reign, Cyaxares had to encounter many formidable difficulties. While he was engaged besieging Nineveh, the Scythian hordes from the north entered Media, and overran the greater part of central and western Asia. Their ravages were continued for twenty-eight years, when they were simultaneously destroyed by a conspiracy of their hosts, which Cyaxares had organised. A party that had escaped the general massacre entered into the service of the Median monarch; but finding reason to dread the fate of their countrymen, they transferred their allegiance to the king of Lydia, and thus caused a war between the two monarchs. The most memorable event of this war, which lasted five years, was the total eclipse of the sun, that took place in the midst of a battle, and so alarmed the contending parties, that both the Medes and Lydians fled in confusion from the field. A peace was soon after concluded between the two crowns, and Cyaxares renewed his war against the Assyrians. Aided by the king of Babylon, he besieged and took Nineveh, and totally destroyed that ancient city (B.C. 601). The allies next attacked the districts that the Egyptians possessed in Syria, defeated Pharaoh-Necho at Carchemish, and subdued the principal part of western Asia. It seems probable that the supremacy of the Medes over the Persian principalities was first established during the reign of Cyaxares, who is generally identified with the Kai Kaoos of Mirkhond and Ferdousí. The cruelty of the Median conquerors, and the sufferings of the unhappy Persians, are powerfully described by the prophet Ezekiel. "There is Elam (Persia) and all her multitude round about her grave, all of them slain, fallen by the sword, which are gone down uncircumcised into the nether parts of the earth, which caused their terror in the land of the living; yet have they borne their shame with them that go down to the pit."*

Astyages, called in the book of Daniel Ahasuerus,† that is, "the mighty hero," (Achash Zwerosh), an epithet given to several Oriental monarchs, was the next king. To reconcile the Persians to his authority, he gave his daughter in marriage to Cambyses, of the family of the Achæmenidæ, and the royal tribe of the Pasargadæ. The issue of this union was Agradates, subsequently named Cyrus, Khorésh, or Khosrau, different forms of a Persian word which signifies the sun.

The main facts of the romantic legend that Herodotus has preserved respecting the early years of Cyrus are confirmed by the Oriental historians; and, when stripped of some embellishments, can scarcely be deemed incredible. The following are the facts in which the Greek and Persian historians confirm each other's testimony; the Persian names of the principal actors are enclosed in brackets. Cambyses (Siyáwesh) is said to have sought refuge at the court of Astyages (Afrasiáb), king of a country north of Persia (Turán), to avoid the effects of his father's jealousy. He obtained the hand of his host's daughter Mandane (Ferangíz) in marriage. Envious courtiers prejudiced the Median king against his son-in-law; he resolved to destroy him, and the child of which his own daughter was pregnant. The Persian prince, according to the Oriental historians, was

* Ezekiel, xxxii. 24. † Dan. ix. 1.

murdered; but the princess and her unborn child were saved by Harpagus (Pirán Wisah), the tyrant's prime minister. The posthumous child of Cambyses was the celebrated Cyrus: he was brought up in obscurity until he approached the age of manhood, when he learned the secret of his birth. With all the courage of enthusiastic youth, he went among his countrymen, who revered the memory of his father, and were weary of the tyranny of Astyages; they flocked to his standard; and the young prince entering Media, dethroned Astyages, and threw him into prison. Instead, however, of seizing the crown for himself, he submitted to the rule of Cyaxares II. (Kai Kaoos), his maternal uncle, whom the Persians describe as his paternal grandfather.

Cyaxares, immediately after his accession to the dignity of Darawesh, or king of Media (B.C. 560), sent his nephew to invade the Babylonian empire, which had now fallen from its high estate. Cyrus invested the city of Babylon, and, after a long siege, took it, in the manner that has been already related (see page 54). Cyaxares, whose title of Darawesh, or Darius, is frequently mistaken for a proper name, removed the seat of his government to the newly acquired city, where, becoming acquainted with the merits of the prophet Daniel, he took him into his service, and appointed him his chief vizier. Some envious courtiers attempted to ruin him by means of his well-known piety, and procured an edict from the Darawesh, forbidding any one, for thirty days, to offer up prayers to any one but the king, under penalty of being exposed to lions. Daniel disobeyed the impious command, and was thrown into the lions' den; but God closed the mouths of the ferocious animals, and he was taken out uninjured. He was immediately restored to his office, which he retained to the end of his life; and it deserves to be added, that, in consequence of his fidelity to the Median and Persian kings, he is described as a renegade in some ancient Jewish traditions.

Cyrus succeeded Cyaxares in the kingdom; and thus the supremacy was transferred from the Medes to the Persians (B.C. 534). But long before he reigned alone, he had been associated with his uncle in the government, and had the sole command of the army that subdued Lydia, Assyria, Babylonia, and western Asia, to the confines of Egypt. Immediately after his accession, he issued an edict permitting the Jews to return to their native land, and rebuild the walls and Temple of Jerusalem, as the prophet Isaiah had predicted a hundred years before his birth. For seven years he ruled his empire in peace and prosperity, directing his attention to establishing a stable government in his extensive dominions, and endeavouring, as we have good reason to believe, to restrict the extravagant privileges claimed by the Magi, or priestly caste. There is some doubt about the manner of his death. Xenophon, in his philosophical romance, declares that he died in his bed; Herodotus, on the contrary, asserts that he perished, with a great part of his army, in a war against the Scythians; that having invaded their country, he incautiously advanced into the deserts, where he was surrounded, attacked at a disadvantage, and slain. The latter account seems to be confirmed by the native Persian legends. Ferdousí and Mirkhond declare, that he proceeded to some spot which he had selected for retirement, where he suddenly disappeared; and his train, among whom were some of the most renowned warriors of Persia, perished in a dreadful tempest. We need scarcely add, that the Oriental writers frequently use storms to typify any great or wide-spreading calamity, such as an invasion of barbarians, or the destruction of an army.

Cambyses (Lohorásp) succeeded to the throne (B.C. 529), and immediately prepared to invade Egypt. He soon made himself master of Pelusium, and, being aided by the local information of Phanes, a Greek deserter, he overthrew Psammenitus, the last Egyptian monarch, and subdued the entire country. His fierce hostility to the sacerdotal caste, which he inherited from his father, made him a persecutor of the Egyptian priests, who, in revenge, have portrayed him as the worst of tyrants. After the conquest of Egypt, he resolved to annex Ethiopia to his dominions, and, at the same time, to plunder the Ammonium, or great temple of Jupiter Ammon, built on an oasis in the midst of the desert. The dreadful sufferings of the Persians in Ethiopia have been already described (p. 38); but the fate of the Ammonian expedition was still more unfortunate. There was no road or track through the sandy waste that the invaders had to traverse; no hill or tree which might serve to guide their course. The army was placed at the mercy of the Egyptian guides, whose minds were soured by recent defeat, and who felt a fraternal affection for the Ammonians. In the midst of the desert their perfidious guides deserted the Persians; they wandered about in indescribable confusion; and the greater part of them were finally overwhelmed by the moving sands that winds sometimes raise in the desert. This fearful catastrophe is thus powerfully described by Darwin:

"Now o'er their heads the whizzing whirlwinds breathe,
And the lone desert pants and heaves beneath;
Tinged by the crimson sun, vast columns rise
Of eddying sand, and war amid the skies,
In red arcades the billowy plain surround,
And whirling turrets stalk along the ground.
Long ranks in vain their shining blades extend,
To demon gods their knees unhallow'd bend,
Wheel in wide circles, form in hollow square,
And now they fly, and now they front the air,
Pierce the deaf tempest with lamenting cries,
Press their parch'd lips, and close their blood-shot eyes.
Gnomes! o'er the waste you led your myriad powers,
Climb'd on the whirls, and arm'd the flinty showers!
Onward resistless rolls the infuriate surge,
Clouds follow clouds, and mountains mountains urge;
Wave over wave the driving desert swims,
Bursts o'er their head, inhumes their struggling limbs;
Man mounts on man; on camels camels rush;
Hosts march o'er hosts; and nations nations crush;—
Wheeling in air, the winged islands fall,
And one great earthy ocean covers all.
Then ceas'd the storm.—Night bow'd her Ethiop brow
To earth, and listen'd to the groves below;
Grim Horror shook:—awhile the living hill
Heav'd with convulsive throes, and all was still.

Cambyses intended to have carried his arms into western Africa; but his designs were frustrated by the refusal of the Phœnician mariners to serve against their Carthaginian brethren. To secure his throne, he, with the cruel precaution so common in Asia, put his brother Smerdis to death; but was soon alarmed by hearing that a usurper, under his brother's name, had seized the Persian crown. On his return home, Cambyses died of an accidental wound from his own sword, having first solemnly assured his officers of the falsehood practised by the pretended Smerdis. As Cambyses died without heirs, the Kaianian dynasty, which, as we have seen, included both Medes and Persians, became extinct (B.C. 522).

SECTION V.—*History of the Persians under the Hystaspid Dynasty.*

FROM B.C. 522 TO B.C. 330.

THE real history of the false Smerdis appears to be slightly disguised in the narratives of the Grecian writers: he was manifestly raised to the throne by a conspiracy of the priestly caste, who were desirous of restoring their own supremacy, and that of their allies the Medes. The Persian nobles combined to prevent such a calamity, destroyed the usurper, and chose for their sovereign, or darawesh, Hystaspes (Gushtásp), who appears to have been a member of the family of the Achæmenidæ. Darius Hystaspes appears to have been the first who used the old title of royalty (Darawesh or Darius) as a proper name. When fixed upon the throne, he persecuted the Magi with great severity, and patronised the religious system ascribed to Zerdusht, or Zoroaster. The Persian legends describe this philosopher as his contemporary; and this is rendered exceedingly probable by a comparison of the various accounts given of this great reformer.* We have already examined the leading points of his religious system, which was finally established in Persia, after Hystaspes had triumphed over the Magi.

To secure his title, Darius, for henceforth he will be best known by this name, united himself in marriage with the two surviving daughters of Cyrus, and then prepared to punish the Babylonians, who, in consequence probably of the ancient con-

* See Professor Shea's admirable translation of Mirkhond, p. 274.

nexion between the Chaldeans and the sacerdotal caste of the Medes, had not only revolted, but murdered all whom they regarded as useless mouths, to prove their determined obstinacy. Babylon sustained a siege of twenty months; and might have baffled its besiegers, had not a Persian noble mutilated himself, and gone over to the citizens as a deserter who had escaped from the inhuman cruelty of his sovereign. His wounds gave credit to his words: he was entrusted with the command of an important post, which he betrayed to Darius, and thus enabled that monarch to become master of the rebellious city. The attention of the conqueror was next directed to western Asia, where the Greek commercial cities that had been subjugated successively by Crœsus and Cyrus had never resigned the hope of recovering their former freedom. All thoughts of insurrection were laid aside at the approach of the victorious monarch: he added Thrace to his dominions; and, perhaps anxious to revenge the fate of Cyrus, or eager to eclipse his fame, he undertook an invasion of Scythia. The Danube was passed on a bridge of boats; and the Persians advanced without opposition through a difficult and barren country, until they had advanced beyond the reach of their supplies. Then difficulties began to thicken around them: no forage was to be found in the fields; the irregular cavalry of the Scythians hovered round the camp, intercepted convoys, cut off stragglers, and kept the army on the alert by incessant skirmishes, without running the hazard of a general engagement. Darius was forced to retreat, and his safety was purchased by the loss of the greater part of his followers. He narrowly escaped a greater danger: Miltiades, the king, or, as sovereigns were then called, the tyrant of the Thracian Chersonese, proposed to the Greeks of Asia Minor to intercept the king's return by breaking down the bridge over the Danube, and then forming a league for the maintenance of their mutual freedom. This was prevented by Hystiæus, the tyrant of Miletus, who was badly rewarded for his eminent services.

Aristagoras, the nephew of Hystiæus, was justly indignant at the treatment of his uncle: he went into Greece, to rouse the principal cities to support the cause of freedom in Asia, but found little sympathy in Sparta and the Peloponnesian states. The Athenians had recently expelled their tyrant Hippias, who had sought refuge among the Persians, and obtained from them promises of aid: they gladly promised assistance to Aristagoras, and their example was imitated by the Eretrians. With such weak support, Aristagoras raised the standard of revolt: his bold efforts were at first crowned with success, and he burned the important city of Sardis to the ground (B.C. 500); but subsequently meeting with some reverses, he was deserted by his disheartened allies; and the insurrection, after a protracted struggle, was completely suppressed. Having severely punished the revolters, Darius resolved to extend his vengeance to their Grecian allies, and collected a large naval and military force, which he entrusted to the command of his son-in-law Mardonius. Mardonius crossed the Hellespont into Thrace, whence he passed into Macedonia, at that time a Persian province. All the neighbouring countries submitted; but his fleet was shattered in a storm while doubling Mount Athos, and his army soon afterwards was attacked unexpectedly by the barbarous Thracian tribes, who slew a great many of the soldiers, and severely wounded Mardonius himself. A second expedition was sent to Greece, under the command of Datis and Artaphernes, who forced a passage into the northern parts of that country, stormed Eretria, and were menacing Athens, when they were totally routed by the Athenians under Miltiades, at the memorable battle of Marathon (B.C. 490). To avenge these losses, Darius resolved to invade Greece in person; but an insurrection of the Egyptians, and disputes among his children respecting the succession, frustrated his designs. He had scarcely put an end to these domestic quarrels, when he was seized by mortal disease, and died, leaving behind him the character of a warlike and prudent sovereign, whose failures in the West were amply compensated by his conquests in the East, where his empire was extended beyond the confines of India.

Xerxes, immediately after his accession (B.C. 485), marched against the Egyptian rebels, whom he completely subdued. Elated by this success, he prepared to invade Greece, and collected the largest army that had ever been assembled. His naval preparations were on an equally extensive scale; and he entered into alliance with the Carthaginians, who agreed to attack the Greek colonies in Sicily and southern Italy, while the Persians were engaged with the parent states. Three years were consumed in preparations before Xerxes and his immense host appeared on the shores of the Hellespont. The Persians passed over the straits on a huge bridge of boats, and a canal is said to have been cut through the isthmus of Mount Athos, to facilitate the passage of his fleet; but on the very threshold of Greece, at the mountain-pass of Thermopylæ, his countless hordes were checked and repulsed by a handful of men under the command of Leonidas, king of Sparta. Treachery enabled him to turn the flank of the gallant warriors; but Leonidas and three hundred Spartans, disdaining to fly, burst into the Persian camp, and had almost reached the royal tent, when they fell, overpowered by numbers. Xerxes now entered Greece; but the account of his campaigns belongs properly to Grecian history. It is sufficient to say, that, after having suffered unparalleled losses by sea and land, he returned to Persia covered with disgrace. The forces that he left behind him under Mardonius were annihilated at the battle of Platææ; and the Greeks, following up their success, destroyed the power of the Persians in the Mediterranean, and made them tremble for the security of their provinces in Asia Minor.

Xerxes is unknown by name to the Oriental historians; they name the son of Darius Hystaspes (Gushtásp), Esfendíar, and ascribe to him the most eminent qualities of a general and soldier. It is probable that the memory of Xerxes' exploits in youth were alone preserved in eastern Persia, and that the compilers of these legends omitted the account of his western campaigns, as disgraceful to the national honour; or, perhaps, no one east of the Euphrates deemed western wars worthy of being recorded. It is generally thought that Xerxes was the Ahasuerus (Achash Zwerosh, that is, "brave hero") mentioned in the book of Esther. After his return from Greece his attention was occupied by the intrigues of his harem; and he was just such a weak prince as would have ordered a ruthless massacre to gratify a profligate favourite like Haman. Esther, it is known, procured a counter edict, by which the Jews were delivered from their enemies, and the wicked minister put to death. It seems not improbable that the Persians should have taken the part of their countryman Haman against the Jewish favourites, and circulated a false and prejudiced account of the transaction.

Xerxes was murdered by a captain of his guards, named Artabanus (B.C. 470), and his eldest son shared his fate. The assassin conferred the crown on Artaxerxes, the third son of the deceased monarch, hoping to reign in the name of the young prince; but the new king embraced the earliest opportunity of revenging the death of his father and brother, and Artabanus with his accomplices were put to death by torture.

Artaxerxes, surnamed Makrocheir, or "the long-handed," is called by the native historians Ardeshír Bahman,* and is celebrated for his just and beneficent administration. He sent Ezra and Nehemiah to rebuild Jerusalem; for the envy of neighbouring nations had prevented the Jews from profiting by the beneficent decree of Cyrus. But his virtues were insufficient to check the decline of the empire, which began to exhibit signs of weakness in every quarter. The war with Greece continued; and after the Persians had suffered countless humiliations, Artaxerxes was forced to sign a disgraceful peace, by which he recognised the independence of the Asiatic Greeks; consented that his fleet should be wholly excluded from the Ægean; and that the Persian army should not come within three days' march of the coast (B. C. 449).

Internal wars and rebellions were of frequent occurrence; Hystaspes, the elder brother of Artaxerxes, took up arms in Bactria, and was with great difficulty subdued. The Egyptians, instigated by Amyrtæus, a native chief, and Inarus, king of Libya, made an effort to recover their independence, and were supported by an Athenian fleet (B. C. 463). The confederates defeated the Persian army, and slew the king's

* Ardeshír (in Sanscrit, of which the Zend, or old Persian, was a dialect, *Urdhha Siras*,) signifies "of exalted head;" and Bahman (in the same language) means "possessing arms."—SIR J. MALCOLM's *Persia*, vol. i.

brother; but they were in turn overthrown by Megabyzus, the satrap or provincial governor of Syria, who at last shut them up in the city of Byblus, to which he laid close siege. Inarus surrendered on favourable terms (B.C. 456); but Amyrtæus, escaping with some devoted followers to the morasses of the Delta, continued to harass the Persians by a guerilla war. The queen-mother, a haughty and cruel princess, enraged at the loss of her son in the Egyptian revolt, entreated Artaxerxes to violate the capitulation granted to Inarus by Megabyzus, and deliver the prisoners taken at Byblus to her revenge. After resisting this infamous proposal for five years, he was at length wearied into compliance, and the unhappy captives perished by cruel tortures. Megabyzus, justly indignant, revolted (B.C. 447), and being zealously supported by the Syrians, repeatedly defeated the royal forces. He was at length allowed to dictate his own terms; but no sooner was he in the king's power, than he was perfidiously seized, and kept a close prisoner during the rest of his life. But this cruelty provoked afresh the hostility of the sons and friends of Megabyzus, whose turbulence kept the state for many years in a state of distraction and confusion.

On the death of Artaxerxes (B.C. 424), his only legitimate son, Xerxes, ascended the throne; but within forty-five days was murdered by his natural brother, Sogdianus; and he again was deposed by another illegitimate prince, Ochus, who, on his accession, took the name of Darius II.

Under the administration of Darius II., surnamed Nothus, that is, "illegitimate," the empire declined rapidly, chiefly owing to the increased power and consequent turbulence of the provincial satraps. Amyrtæus took advantage of these circumstances, and issuing from his fastnesses re-established the Egyptian kingdom; but he seems to have consented to own the nominal supremacy of the Persian monarchs. Fortunately for Darius, the Greeks were too deeply engaged in the Peloponnesian wars to profit by the weak state of their ancient enemies; on the contrary, the Persians acquired a paramount influence in the affairs of Greece; and Prince Cyrus, whom his father had entrusted with the government of western

Asia, by allying himself with the Spartan interest, largely contributed to the overthrow of the Athenian power.

On the death of Darius, his son Artaxerxes, surnamed Mnemon from the strength of his memory, ascended the throne (B.C. 405); but was opposed by his brother Cyrus, who had the support of the queen-mother, Parysatis, and of an army of Greek mercenaries, which he was enabled to levy through his connexion with Sparta. Cyrus, at first successful, was slain at the battle of Cunaxa (B. C. 401); but his ten thousand Greek auxiliaries, under the guidance of Xenophon, a renegade Athenian, though a delightful historian, succeeded in forcing a safe passage to their native land. During the remainder of his reign, the weak Artaxerxes was the mere puppet of his mother, Parysatis, whose inveterate hatred against queen Statira, and all whom she suspected of having contributed to the overthrow of her favourite son, Cyrus, filled the palace with murders, treasons, and assassinations. While the court was thus disgraced, Agesilaus, king of Sparta, joined with the Asiatic Greeks, was making rapid conquests in western Persia; and he would probably have dismembered the empire, had not the troubles excited in Greece by a lavish distribution of Persian gold, compelled him to return home.

The remainder of the reign of Artaxerxes was singularly unfortunate: he attempted to reduce Egypt, but his efforts failed, owing to a disagreement between the Athenian auxiliaries and the Persian commanders; Cyprus regained its independence; and the spirit of revolt spread through all western Asia. His domestic calamities were still more afflicting: he was obliged to punish his eldest son Darius with death for conspiring against him; Ochus, his youngest son, murdered his brother, to open a path to the succession; and Artaxerxes, overcome by such a complication of miseries, died of a broken heart.

Ochus, on his accession (B.C. 360), took the name of Artaxerxes III.; and, to secure himself on the throne, put to death no fewer than eighty of the royal family. Artabazus, the satrap of Asia Minor, attempted to take advantage of the unpopularity which those crimes brought on the monarch; and, aided by the

Thebans and Athenians, made a vigorous effort to seize the throne. Ochus, however, was as conspicuous for his military prowess as for his crimes; he defeated Artabazus, and forced him to seek refuge in Greece. He next marched against the Phœnician insurgents, who were supported by the Cypriots and Egyptians: the treason of the general of the confederates gave Ochus an easier victory than he had expected, and he levelled the city of Sidon with the ground. Being joined by a powerful body of Greek auxiliaries, he recovered the island of Cyprus, and once more reduced it to a Persian province. But the king's cruelties were not compensated by his victories; and he was at length poisoned by the eunuch Bagoas, who placed Arces, the youngest son of Ochus, on the throne.

Arces, after a brief reign, suffered the fate of his father; and the treacherous Bagoas transferred the crown to Darius Codomannus, a descendant of Darius Nothus (B.C. 336). The eunuch hoped that by raising so remote a branch to the throne, he would be permitted to retain royal power in his hands; but Darius soon asserted his independence, and Bagoas prepared to remove him by poison. The treachery was discovered; and Darius compelled the baffled eunuch to drink the medicated potion that he had prepared. But the fate of the Persian empire was now at hand; Alexander the Great of Macedon appeared in Asia, and his brave little army scattered the myriads of Persia like chaff before the wind. After the loss of the two battles of Issus and Arbela, Darius, while seeking refuge in a remote part of his empire, was murdered by the eunuch Bessus; and Asia received a new master.*

The Persians inherited the commercial power of the Babylonians and Phœnicians; but they opened no new branch of trade, and scarcely maintained those they found already established. It is not, therefore, necessary to repeat here what has been said in the preceding chapters on the commerce of central Asia.

* See the history of Macedon in a following chapter.

CHAPTER VII.

PHŒNICIAN COLONIES IN NORTHERN AFRICA.

ESPECIALLY

CARTHAGE.

Section I.—*Geographical Outline of Northern Africa.*

Although Africa was circumnavigated at a period of very remote antiquity, the interior of the country remained unexplored, and the southern part, on account of the difficulty of navigation in the ocean, was neglected until the knowledge of its discovery was forgotten. But the northern coast bordering on the Mediterranean became the seat of flourishing Greek and Phœnician colonies, which were enriched by an extensive commerce with the states in the south of Europe, and the wild tribes in the interior of Africa. This extensive district was divided by nature into three regions, or bands, of unequal breadth, nearly parallel with the sea-line: 1. the maritime country, consisting generally of very fertile districts, whence it was called Inhabited Africa; it is now named Barbary: 2. a rugged mountainous country, whose loftiest peaks form the chain of Mount Atlas, abounding in wild beasts and palm-groves, whence it was called by the ancients the Land of Lions, and by the moderns Beledulgerid, or the Land of Dates; the Romans usually named it Gætulia: 3. a vast sandy desert, which the Arabs call Sahara.

From the chain of Mount Atlas several small rivers flow into the Mediterranean by a short northern course; but there are no streams of importance on the south side of these mountains, and no great river in the interior until we reach the remote Niger, concerning which the ancients had very imperfect information; indeed, nothing was known with certainty of its true course until the recent discovery of its mouth by the Landers.

Proceeding westwards along the shore from Egypt, Africa

presented the following political divisions: 1. Marmarica, a sandy tract tenanted by nomad tribes; 2. Cyrenaica, a fertile territory occupied by Greek colonies, extending to the greater Syrtis—its chief cities were Cyrene and Barca; 3. Regio Syrtica, the modern kingdom of Tripoli, a sandy tract subject to the Carthaginians, but almost wholly occupied by nomad hordes; 4. the domestic territory of Carthage, which forms the modern kingdom of Tunis; 5. a very fruitful country subject to the Carthaginians, the northern part of which was named Byzacena, and the southern Zeugitana; and, 6. Numidia and Mauritania, occupied during the Carthaginian age by nomad hordes, but having some Carthaginian colonies along the coasts.

Carthage was built on a peninsula in the interior of a large bay, now called the Gulf of Tunis, formed by the projection of the Hermæan promontory (now Cape Bon) on the east, and the promontory of Apollo (now Cape Zebid) on the west. The peninsula was about midway between Utica and Tunis, both of which could be seen from the walls of Carthage; the former being about nine, and the latter only six miles distant: it was joined to the land by an isthmus averaging three miles in length; and on the sea side there was a narrow neck of land projecting westwards, which formed a double harbour, and served as a mole or breakwater for the protection of shipping. Towards the sea the city was fortified only by a single wall; but the isthmus was guarded by the citadel Byrsa, and a triple wall eighty feet high and about thirty wide.

The African territory of Carthage extended westwards along the coast to the Pillars of Hercules, and eastwards to the Altars of the Philæni. These altars were erected to the memory of two brothers who had sacrificed themselves for their country on the following occasion:—The boundary line between the Cyrenean and Carthaginian territories, falling in the midst of sandy deserts, could not be determined by any natural landmarks; and this circumstance occasioned frequent wars between the rival states. It was at length agreed, that on the same day ambassadors should set out from both cities, and that the boundary should be fixed at the place of their meeting. The

Philæni were chosen as deputies for the Carthaginians; and they travelled with such extraordinary diligence, that their rivals found that Carthage, according to the terms of the agreement, would receive full three-fourths of the disputed territory. After much controversy, it was agreed that either the Carthaginians should submit to be buried alive at the limit they claimed, or that the Cyrenians should choose another boundary line, and submit to the same fate. The Philæni cheerfully offered their lives to secure the additional land for Carthage; and the altars or sepulchres erected to their memory long continued to mark the frontier between the territories of Cyrene and Carthage. Southwards, the dominions of Carthage extended to the Tritonian Lake; but many of the nomad tribes beyond these limits paid nominal obedience to the republic.

The foreign possessions of Carthage included the Balearic islands, Corsica, Sardinia, and the smaller islands in the Mediterranean, the southern part of Sicily and Spain, some settlements on the western coast of Africa, and the Fortunate Islands in the Atlantic, which are probably the Canaries, and the fertile Madeira.

SECTION II.—*Social and Political Condition of Carthage.*

THE government of Carthage was formed by circumstances; it was originally monarchical, like Tyre, its parent state; but at a very early period it assumed a republican form, in which aristocracy was the prevailing element, though the power of the people was not wholly excluded. There were two kings, or chief magistrates, called suffetes (the shophetím, or judges, of the Hebrews), who appear to have been nominated by the senate, and then presented for confirmation to the general assembly of the people. There was a double senate; a synedrium, or house of assembly, called also synklétos; and a select council, denominated gerusia, which was composed of a hundred of the principal members of the synedrium, and formed the high court of judicature. The members of the gerusia were chosen by the pentarchies, or committees of five, into which the house of assembly and the gerusia itself were divided.

There are no means of ascertaining the qualifications required for a senator, or the mode of election; but it is probable that the senate itself had the privilege of supplying vacancies.

Public affairs were not submitted to the assembly of the people, except when there was a difference of opinion between the suffetes and the senate, when the decision of the general assembly was final. But the best political institution at Carthage, and that which preserved the state from the convulsions that distracted the other republics of antiquity, was the separation of civil from military power. The generals were chosen by the gerusia, and entrusted with more or less authority, according to circumstances; but they were always accompanied by a committee of the senate, and were subject to a rigid examination on their return from the expedition that had been confided to their charge.

Little is known of the administration of justice at Carthage: we have already mentioned that the gerusia was the high court of justice for state offences; but there was a separate tribunal, consisting of one hundred and four members, that seems to have been a court of appeal in civil matters, and a court of original jurisdiction in suits of great importance.

The religion of the Carthaginians was the same as that of their ancestors the Phœnicians, and was consequently polluted by sanguinary rites and human sacrifices. Melcart or the Tyrian Hercules, Moloch or Bel (whom the Latins identified with their own Saturn), and Astarte or Venus, were the principal divinities: but the Carthaginians were not averse to the introduction of foreign gods; they adopted the worship of Ceres from the Sicilians, and sent ambassadors to the oracle of Delphi. It does not appear that there was a distinct sacerdotal caste, or even order, in Carthage; the priestly functions were united with the magisterial; and the temples were not only used for the worship of the gods, but also for preserving the archives of government, and monumental records of important events.

A species of national banking was established at Carthage which was very curious. Pieces of a compound metal, the secret of whose composition was strictly preserved, in order to prevent forgery, were sewed up in leather covering, and marked with a government seal, which declared their nominal value. This money was, of course, current only in Carthage itself; but we are not acquainted with the laws by which its issue was regulated. The public revenues of Carthage were derived from the tribute imposed on the dependent cities and African tribes, from the custom-house duties collected in the port, and from the Spanish mines, the richest of which were in the neighbourhood of Carthago Nova, the modern city of Carthagena.

Carthage maintained a very powerful navy, and supported numerous land armies; but, unlike most other ancient states, its forces were chiefly composed of mercenaries and slaves; the citizens themselves, engrossed by commercial pursuits, were unwilling to encounter the hardships and perils of a campaign. There was, however, always one Carthaginian corps, which was regarded as the pride of the army. Their African subjects, or Libyans, constituted the principal part of their forces, both horse and foot; in addition to these, they employed bodies of Gauls, Spaniards, and even Greeks and Italians. They had also the celebrated slingers from the Balearic islands, and very formidable troops of light cavalry furnished by the nomad hordes of northern Africa. There was, however, little sympathy between the army and the state: when Carthage could no longer afford a high rate of pay, the mercenaries abandoned her standards, and sold their services to the highest bidder.

Section III.—*History of Carthage from the Foundation of the City to the Commencement of the Syracusan Wars.*

FROM B.C. 880 TO B.C. 416.

Dido, after having escaped from the tyranny of her brother Pygmalion, traversed the greater part of the Mediterranean, and at length chose for her new country the Carthaginian peninsula. She is said to have acquired, by a fraudulent purchase, the ground on which the city was built; but this legend is unworthy of serious notice. At first the Carthaginians were compelled to pay tribute to the neighbouring barbarian princes; but when their riches and strength increased, they shook off this degrading yoke, and extended their dominion by the subjection of the nearest native tribes in the interior, and by new establishments along the coasts. The more ancient Phœnician colonies, such at Utica and Leptis, far from feeling jealous of the rising power of Carthage, joined in a federation, of which the new city was recognised as the head. The Greek settlers at Cyrene, whose state had attained great commercial prosperity, viewed the Carthaginians with more jealousy, and war soon broke out between the rival cities. The territory between these states was inhabited by the Lotophagi and Nasamones; nomad tribes, whose caravans carried on the greater part of the trade with the interior of Africa. After frequent struggles for obtaining exclusive supremacy over this district, the rival states agreed to share it between them; but by the patriotism of the Philæni the greater portion was assigned to Carthage.

While the Persian empire was rising into importance in the east, Carthage was fast acquiring supremacy over the western world, chiefly by means of the family of Mago,—a family that held the chief power of the state for more than a century. But just as they were rising into eminence, they had to encounter a formidable enemy in the western Mediterranean, whose proved skill and courage threatened dangerous rivalry. This led to the first naval engagement recorded in history, and arose from the following circumstances:—

After Cyrus had overthrown Crœsus, he entrusted the subjugation of the Greek colonies in Asia Minor to Harpagus, one of his generals, and returned to complete the conquest of Babylonia. One of the first places against which Harpagus directed his efforts was Phocæa, the most northern city of Ionia (B.C. 589). Its inhabitants were celebrated for their commercial enterprise and skill in navigation; they had frequently visited the coast of Spain, and ventured beyond the Pillars of Hercules. But they had not strength to resist the myriads of Persia; and when summoned by Harpagus, they begged for a short interval to deliberate on his proposals. During this period, they embarked their wives, children, and movable property on board their galleys, and abandoned the naked walls of their city to the Persians. The brave exiles steered first to

Chios, hoping to purchase some islets in its vicinity; but their offers being refused, they resolved to found a new settlement in the western Mediterranean. The course of their voyage brought them within view of their ancient city; the sight roused them to fury, and, suddenly landing, they surprised and massacred the Persian garrison. Embarking again after this memorable act of vengeance, they flung into the sea a ball of burning iron, and swore never to return until it should emerge again unextinguished. They then proceeded to the island of Corsica, part of which was already occupied by the Carthaginians, and prepared to establish themselves on its coasts. The Carthaginians and the Tyrrhenians, or Tuscans, dreading the rivalry of the enterprising Phocæans, entered into an alliance for their destruction, and sent a fleet of one hundred and twenty sail to drive them from Corsica. The Phocæans, with half the number of vessels, gained a brilliant victory; but conscious that their numbers were too weak to sustain repeated attacks, they abandoned Corsica for the shores of Gaul, where they founded the city of Marseilles.

Cambyses, after the conquest of Egypt, was eager to seize on Carthage, whose wealth was celebrated even in Asia; but the Phœnician mariners, by whom his fleet was principally manned, refused to bear arms against their brethren; and the design was laid aside. Soon after this, in the very year that the Tarquins were expelled, a treaty was concluded between the republics of Rome and Carthage (B.C. 509); from the terms of which it appears that the Carthaginians were already supreme masters of the northern coast of Africa and the island of Sardinia, and that they possessed the Balearic islands, and a considerable portion of Sicily and Spain.

Ever since the sea-fight off Corsica, the Carthaginians had a jealous dread of Grecian valour and enterprise, which was naturally aggravated by the increasing wealth and power of the Greek colonies in Sicily and southern Italy. When Xerxes, therefore, was preparing to invade Hellas, they readily entered into alliance with the Persian monarch, and agreed to attack the colonies, while he waged war against the parent state. An armament was accordingly prepared, whose magnitude shews the extensive power and resources of Carthage. It consisted of two thousand ships of war, three thousand transports and vessels of burden, and a land army amounting to three hundred thousand men. The command of the whole was entrusted to Hamilcar, the head of the illustrious family of Mago.

A landing was effected without loss at Panormus (the modern Palermo); and when the troops were refreshed, Hamilcar advanced and laid close siege to Himera. The town was but ill prepared for resistance; but the governor Theron, and his gallant garrison, made a vigorous defence, though pressed not only by the overwhelming forces of the enemy, but by the still more grievous pressure of famine. Foreseeing, however, that the town, unless speedily relieved, must be forced to surrender, he sent an urgent request for assistance to Syracuse.

Gelon, king of Syracuse, had taken up arms on the first news of the invasion; but his utmost efforts could only collect about five thousand horse and fifteen thousand foot. With this very disproportionate force he marched against the Carthaginians, to take advantage of any opportunity that fortune might offer. On his road he fortunately captured a messenger from the Selinuntines to Hamilcar, promising on a certain day to join him with the auxiliary force of cavalry that he had demanded. Gelon sent the letter forward to Hamilcar; and having taken measures to intercept the treacherous Selinuntines, he despatched a chosen body of his own troops to the Carthaginian camp in their stead at the specified time. The Syracusans being admitted without any suspicion, suddenly galloped to the general's tent, slew Hamilcar and his principal officers, and then hurrying to the harbour set fire to the fleet. The blaze of the burning vessels, the cries of Hamilcar's servants, and the shouts of the Syracusans, threw the whole Carthaginian army into confusion; in the midst of which they were attacked by Gelon with the rest of his forces. Without leaders and without command, the Carthaginians could make no effective resistance; more than half of the invaders fell in the field; the remainder, without arms and without provisions, sought shelter in the interior of the country, where most of them perished. It is remarkable that this great victory was won on the same day that the battle of Thermopylæ was fought, and the Persian fleet defeated at Artemisium; three of the noblest triumphs obtained in the struggle for Grecian freedom (B.C. 480).

The miserable remnant of the Carthaginian troops rallied under Gisgon, the son of Hamilcar; but the new general found it impossible to remedy the disorganisation occasioned by the late defeat, and was forced to surrender at discretion. Gelon offered favourable terms of peace to the Carthaginian senate, which were ungraciously accepted; and Gisgon was banished by his discontented countrymen for having yielded to imperious necessity in surrendering his troops.

For seventy years after this defeat little is known of the history of Carthage, except that during that period the state greatly extended its power over the native tribes of Africa, and gained important acquisitions of territory from the Cyrenians. Sicily was, in the meantime, the scene of a war which threatened total annihilation to Syracuse, the Athenians having invaded the island, and laid siege to that city. But when the Athenians were totally defeated (B.C. 416), the Carthaginians had their attention once more directed to Sicilian politics by an embassy from the Segestans, seeking their protection against the Syracusans, whose wrath they had provoked by their alliance with the Athenians.

SECTION IV.—*History of Carthage during the Sicilian Wars.*

FROM B.C. 416 to B.C. 264.

THE Carthaginians gladly seized the pretext afforded them by the Segestan embassy; and a new expedition was sent against Sicily, under the command of Hannibal, the son of Gisgon. This new invasion was crowned with success; Selinuntum and Himera were taken by storm, their inhabitants put to the sword, and all their buildings, public or private, levelled to the ground. The Sicilians, unable to meet the enemy in the field, solicited a truce, which was granted on terms extremely favourable to the Carthaginians.

Hannibal was received with the highest honours on his return to Carthage; and so elated was the state at his success, that nothing less than the entire subjugation of Sicily was contemplated. Inules, the son of Hanno, and Hannibal, were placed at the head of a powerful armament, with which, after having effected a landing at Lilybæum, they proceeded to besiege Agrigentum, the second city of the island. During the siege, which lasted eight months, the assailants suffered severely from pestilential disease, and the garrison from famine. The Carthaginians had destroyed several sepulchres to obtain materials for their works, and the effluvia from the disinterred corpses probably produced the pestilence; but they attributed it to Divine wrath, and in order to appease the supposed anger of the gods, offered a child of noble birth to Neptune. After having endured with wonderful patience the severest extremities of famine, the Agrigentines forced their way through the enemies' lines by night, and retreated to Gela, abandoning the aged, the sick, and the wounded, to the mercy of the Carthaginians. Himilco, who had succeeded to the chief command on the death of his father Hannibal, ordered these helpless victims to be massacred, and his cruel edict was strictly executed. Gela soon shared the fate of Agrigentum; and Dionysius I., king of Syracuse, who had taken the command of the confederated Sicilians, deemed it prudent to open negotiations for peace. A treaty was concluded (B.C. 405), which neither party intended to observe longer than the necessary preparations for a more decisive contest would require. Scarcely were the Carthaginians withdrawn, when Dionysius sent deputies to all the Greek states in Sicily, exhorting them by a simultaneous effort to expel all intruders, and secure their future independence. His machinations were successful; the Carthaginian merchants who, on the faith of the late treaty, had settled in the principal commercial town, were perfidiously massacred; while Dionysius, at the head of a powerful army, captured several of the most important Carthaginian fortresses.

All the forces that the wealth of Carthage could procure

were speedily collected to punish this treachery; and Himilco returned to Sicily with an army which the confederates could not venture to encounter in the field. Having captured several places of minor importance, Himilco advanced against Syracuse itself, and laid siege to it with the fairest prospects of success. He blockaded the harbour, destroyed the outworks, and established his head-quarters in the fortified suburb of Acradina, which he captured by assault. But just as every thing seemed to promise a favourable result, a plague of such uncommon virulence broke out in the Carthaginian camp, that the living were unable to bury the dead, and the putrescent bodies loaded the atmosphere with fresh sources of disease and death. Information of this state of things being conveyed to Syracuse, Dionysius sallied forth with all his forces, and assaulted the Carthaginian camp. Scarce any attempt was made at resistance: night alone put an end to the slaughter; and when morning dawned, Himilco found that nothing but a speedy surrender could save him and his followers from total ruin. He stipulated only for the lives of himself and the Carthaginians, abandoning all his auxiliaries to the vengeance of the exasperated Syracusans.

To escape the reproaches of his countrymen, Himilco committed suicide; but his death did not close the fatal results of his conduct at Syracuse. The African nomads, justly indignant at the sacrifice of their brethren to save the lives of the Carthaginians, flew to arms, captured several important towns, and at length ventured to besiege Carthage itself; but there was no leader of sufficient weight to unite these barbarous tribes: when their prospects of success seemed fairest, they began to dispute for supremacy, and their army was finally dispersed without striking a blow.

When this danger was averted, the Carthaginians sent another armament, commanded by Mago, a nobleman of high rank, to retrieve their losses in Sicily; but their forces were routed with great slaughter, and the leader slain. The younger Mago, son of the late general, having received a strong reinforcement from Africa, hazarded a second engagement, in which the Syracusans were totally defeated. Dionysius was induced by this overthrow to solicit a peace, which was concluded on terms honourable to both parties.

The conclusion of the Sicilian war was followed by a plague, which destroyed multitudes of the citizens of Carthage (B.C. 347); and scarcely had this visitation passed away, when insurrections broke out in the African provinces, and in the colonies of Sicily and Sardinia. But the Carthaginian senate shewed itself equal to the crisis; by a course of policy in which firmness was tempered by conciliation, these dangers were averted, and the state restored to its former vigour and prosperity.

In the meantime, Syracuse was weakened by the death of Dionysius I., who, though stigmatised as a tyrant by the Greek historians, appears to have been a wise and prudent sovereign. "No one," said Scipio Africanus, "ever concerted his schemes with more wisdom, or executed them with greater energy, than the elder Dionysius." His son, Dionysius II., was a profligate prince, whose excesses filled the state with tumult and distraction. The Carthaginians eagerly embraced the opportunity that his tyranny afforded them of accomplishing the favourite object of their policy, the conquest of Sicily; and a great armament was prepared, of which Mago was appointed the chief commander.

Mago, at the very first attack, made himself master of the harbour of Syracuse. While he possessed the port and its fortifications, Icetes the Leontine was master of the city, Dionysius with a strong garrison held possession of the citadel, and the Syracusans themselves were destitute of money, of arms, and almost of hope. In this extremity they solicited the aid of the Corinthians; and Timoleon, one of the greatest generals and purest patriots of antiquity, was sent to their assistance. Timoleon's first effort was to gain possession of the citadel, in which he succeeded with little difficulty; for when Dionysius shut himself up in that fortress, he had neglected to supply himself with provisions. Timoleon thus obtained the immense magazines which the elder Dionysius had collected; and, having armed the citizens, he compelled the Leontines to place their forces at his disposal. A great portion of the Carthaginian army had been levied in the Greek colonies; Timoleon, hoping to work on their patriotic feelings, addressed letters to the leaders of these mercenaries, expostulating with them on the disgrace of bearing arms against their countrymen: and though he did not prevail on any to desert, yet Mago having heard of these intrigues, felt such distrust of his followers, that he at once abandoned Syracuse, and returned home.

Great was the indignation of the Carthaginians at this unexpected termination of the campaign: Mago committed suicide, to escape their wrath; but so violent was the hatred of the people, that they refused his dead body the rites of sepulture, and exposed it on a gibbet. New forces were raised, to retrieve their losses in Sicily; two generals, Hannibal and Hamilcar, were appointed to the command, and were entrusted with an army of seventy thousand men, and a fleet consisting of two hundred war-galleys and a thousand ships of burden.

The news of the approach of so formidable an armament filled the Syracusans with terror; Timoleon alone remained unmoved, and hasted to meet the invaders, though his forces barely amounted to seven thousand men. Notwithstanding this vast disproportion of strength, Timoleon unexpectedly attacked the Carthaginian army on its march, near the river Crimisus; and the confusion produced by the surprise terminated in a total rout. Three thousand citizens of Carthage and seven thousand auxiliaries fell on the field, while the survivors were so dispirited that they could not be brought again to encounter Timoleon. The Syracusans captured town after town, until at length the senate of Carthage was forced to solicit peace, and accept the terms dictated by the conqueror.

While Carthage was thus unfortunate abroad, her liberties at home narrowly escaped destruction. Hanno, one of the principal leaders of the state, resolved to make himself master of his country by poisoning the leaders of the senate at a banquet. This diabolical plot was frustrated by a timely discovery, and the exasperated traitor resolved to hazard an open rebellion. Having armed his slaves, to the number of twenty thousand, he took the field, and invited the native African tribes to join his standard. This appeal was disregarded; and before Hanno could levy fresh forces, he was surrounded by an army hastily raised, his followers routed, and himself made prisoner. He was put to death with the most cruel tortures; and, according to the barbarous custom of Carthage, his children and nearest relatives shared the same fate.

New dissensions in Syracuse afforded the Carthaginians a fresh pretext for meddling in the affairs of Sicily. Agathocles, an intriguing demagogue of mean birth, had acquired great influence among his countrymen, and finally, by the secret aid of the Carthaginians, became master of the state. But he soon shewed little regard for the ties of gratitude, and declared his resolution to expel his benefactors from the island. The Carthaginian senate immediately sent Hamilcar with a powerful army against this new enemy. Agathocles was completely defeated, and forced to shut himself up within the walls of Syracuse. The city was soon closely invested, and every thing seemed to promise Hamilcar complete success at no distant day; when Agathocles suddenly baffled all his calculations, by adopting one of the most extraordinary measures recorded in history. Having assembled the Syracusans, he declared that he could liberate them from all dangers, if an army and a small sum of money were placed at his disposal; adding, that his plan would be instantly defeated, if its nature was divulged. An army of liberated slaves was hastily levied, the sum of fifty talents entrusted to his discretion, and a fleet prepared in secret; when all was ready, Agathocles announced his design of transporting his forces into Africa, and compelling the Carthaginians, by the dread of a nearer danger, to abandon Sicily.

Having eluded the vigilance of the blockading squadron, Agathocles arrived safely in Africa before the Carthaginians had received the slightest notice of his intentions (B.C. 309). An eclipse of the sun, immediately after his landing, at first terrified his superstitious followers; but he quieted their fears by assuring them that this prodigy always portended a change of fortune, and consequently was ominous to the Carthaginians, who had hitherto been successful. To inspire his soldiers with a resolution to conquer or die, he cut off all chance of retreat by burning his transports; then fearlessly advancing, he stormed Tunis and several other cities, the plunder of which he divided among his soldiers, and instigated the African princes to throw off the yoke of Carthage. Hanno and Bomilcar were sent to check the progress of this daring invader, with forces nearly four times as great as the Sicilian army; but Agathocles, knowing that most of the enemies were raw and mercenary levies, who felt no deep interest in the cause for which they fought, did not decline the engagement. His valour was rewarded by a decisive victory; Hanno fell in the very commencement of the battle, and Bomilcar, whose misconduct exposed him to the suspicion of treachery, made no effort to remedy the disorder occasioned by the death of his colleague. Following up his success, Agathocles stormed the enemies' camp, where were found heaps of fetters and chains, which the Carthaginians, confident of success, had prepared for the invading army.

Dreadful consternation was produced in Carthage by the news of this unexpected defeat; the soothsayers were consulted, to know what had occasioned the anger of the gods; and these miscreants replied, that the deities were offended because the human sacrifices recently offered were the children of slaves and aliens, instead of being, as of old, the offspring of the highest nobility. In consequence of this cruel response, a number of youths of the highest rank were cruelly sacrificed on the altar of Moloch or Saturn. While the national distress was thus aggravated by superstitious cruelty, vessels arrived from Tyre, conveying the old men, women, and children, who had been sent away when Alexander advanced against that city. Notwithstanding their own dangerous situation, the Carthaginians received these helpless exiles with the greatest kindness, and exerted themselves to relieve their distress.

Hamilcar was vigorously pressing forward the siege of Syracuse, when he was surprised by the unexpected order to return home and defend his own country. Before commencing his retreat he resolved to attempt an assault; and in order to dispirit the garrison, he spread a report that Agathocles had been defeated and slain; but just as he was about to begin the attack, he had the mortification to see a Sicilian vessel arrive from Africa under the walls of Syracuse, after baffling the blockading squadron. Hopeless of success, he broke up the siege, and sent home five thousand of his best troops. Having supplied their place by hiring fresh mercenaries, he again invaded the Syracusan territories; but was unexpectedly attacked, defeated, and slain.

A new danger menaced Carthage from the treason of Bomilcar, who attempted to take advantage of the national calamities to make himself absolute sovereign. His efforts, however, were unsuccessful; and he was induced to surrender by a promise that his life should be spared. But the promise was treacherously violated; and Bomilcar, after having endured the most shocking indignities, was put to death by torture.

Ophellas, king of Cyrene, had joined Agathocles with all his forces; but the Syracusan monarch, jealous of his influence, had him privately poisoned. Having thus removed his rival, he thought he might safely revisit Sicily, and entrust the command of the African army to his son. But during his absence the fruits of all his former labours were lost; the army, under a young and inexperienced general, threw aside the restraints of discipline; the Greek estates, indignant at the murder of Ophellas, withheld their contingents; and the African princes renewed their allegiance to Carthage. Agathocles hearing of these disorders, hasted to remedy them; but finding all his efforts vain, he fled back to Sicily, abandoning both his sons and his soldiers. The army, exasperated by his desertion, slew their leaders, and surrendered themselves to the Carthaginians; and Agathocles died soon after, either from grief or poison.

After the death of this formidable enemy, the Carthaginians renewed their intrigues in Sicily, and soon acquired a predominant influence in the island. Finding themselves in danger of utter ruin, the Greek colonists solicited the aid of Pyrrhus, king of Epirus, who had married a daughter of Agathocles, and was then in Italy endeavouring to protect the colonies of Magna Græcia from the increasing power of the

Romans (B.C. 277). Pyrrhus made a very successful campaign in Sicily, every Carthaginian town except Lilybæum submitting to his arms. But he was soon induced to return to Italy; and the fruits of his victories were lost almost as rapidly as they had been acquired, notwithstanding the heroic exertions of Hiero, king of Syracuse.

SECTION V.—*From the Commencement of the Roman Wars to the Destruction of Carthage.*

FROM B.C. 264 TO B.C. 146.

WHEN Pyrrhus was leaving Sicily, he exclaimed to his attendants, "What a fine field of battle we are leaving to the Carthaginians and Romans!" His prediction was soon verified, though the circumstances that precipitated the contest were apparently of little importance. A body of mercenaries in the pay of Agathocles, after the death of that monarch, treacherously got possession of Messina, and put all the inhabitants to the sword. Inspired by their example, and supported by their assistance, a Roman legion perpetrated a similar crime at Rhegium, on the opposite side of the Sicilian strait. The Roman senate, with great promptitude, sent a consular army to punish the revolters at Rhegium, and they were all mercilessly destroyed. At the same time Hiero, king of Syracuse, marched against the Mamertines, as the independent companies that had seized Messina were called, and defeated them in the field. Dreading the fate that had befallen their allies at Rhegium, half of the Mamertines invoked the aid of the Carthaginians, and placed them in immediate possession of the citadel; while the others sought the powerful protection of Rome. After much hesitation, the Romans consented to grant the required aid; and an army commanded by Appius Claudius crossed the strait of Sicily, eluding the vigilance of the Carthaginian fleet. The citadel of Messina was taken after a brief siege; and the Carthaginians, aided by Hiero, attempting to recover it, were routed with great slaughter. Hiero immediately deserted the Carthaginians, and entered into alliance with the

Romans. Thus commenced the first Punic war, which lasted twenty-three years, the details of which will be found in the chapters on Roman history.

In this war Carthage lost Sicily, and its supremacy in the western Mediterranean, which involved the fate of all its other insular possessions. The treasury was exhausted, the finances had fallen into complete disorder, and money was wanting to pay the arrears due to the soldiers. The mercenaries who had been transported from Sicily to Africa, pursuant to the terms of the treaty, being refused immediate payment, mutinied, and advancing in a body laid siege to Tunis. Thence, after some time had been wasted in fruitless negotiations, they marched against Utica, while the light African cavalry that had joined in the rebellion ravaged the country up to the very gates of Carthage. Hanno, one of the suffetes, was sent with what forces could be mustered against the insurgents; but through his incapacity the insurrection acquired fresh strength, and the Carthaginian senate resolved to give him as a colleague his great political rival Hamilcar, of the house of Barca, whose abilities had already been proved in the war against the Romans in Sicily. Under the new general the Carthaginian fortune prevailed, and the revolters were subdued; but not until they had reduced the fairest provinces of the republic to a desert. The mercenaries in Sardinia had also thrown off their allegiance; and the Romans, in violation of the recent peace, took possession of the island; an injury which Carthage was unable to resent.

Hamilcar Barca,* grieved to see his country sinking, formed a project for raising it once more to an equality with its imperious rival, by completely subduing the Spanish peninsula. His son Hannibal, then a boy only nine years of age, earnestly besought leave to accompany his father on this expedition; but before granting the request, Hamilcar led the boy to the altar, and made him swear eternal hostility to Rome. During nine years Hamilcar held the command in Spain, and found means,

* Barca signifies "thunder" in the Phœnician language, and also in Hebrew, which is closely allied to Phœnician. The Hebrew root is ברק to thunder.

either by force or negotiation, to subdue almost the entire country. He used the treasures he acquired to strengthen the influence of the Barcine family in the state, relying chiefly on the democracy for support against his great rival Hanno, who had the chief influence among the nobility.

Hasdrubal, the son-in-law of Hamilcar, succeeded to his power and his projects. He is suspected of having designed to establish an independent kingdom in Spain, after having failed to make himself absolute in Carthage. But the Romans, alarmed by his success, compelled him to sign a treaty, by which he was bound to abstain from passing the Iberus (Ebro), or attacking the territory of the Saguntines.

When Hasdrubal fell by the dagger of an assassin, the Barcine family had sufficient influence to have Hannibal appointed his successor, though he had barely attained his legal majority (B.C. 221). The youthful general having gained several victories over the Spaniards, boldly laid siege to Saguntum, and thus caused the second war with the Romans, for the details of which we must refer to the chapters on Roman history.

During the course of this war, the Carthaginian navy, the source of its greatness and the security of its strength, was neglected. The spirit of party also raged violently in Carthage itself, and the Barcine faction usurped a kind of despotic power, which was supported by appeals to the passions and prejudices of the people. At the conclusion of the war, Carthage was deprived of all her possessions out of Africa, and her fleet was delivered into the hands of the Romans. Thenceforward Carthage was to be nothing more than a commercial city under the protection of Rome. A powerful rival also was raised against the republic in Africa itself by the alliance of the Numidian king Massinissa with the Romans; and that monarch took possession of most of the western Carthaginian colonies.

Hannibal, notwithstanding his late reverses, continued at the head of the Carthaginian state, and reformed several abuses that had crept into the management of the finances and the administration of justice. But these judicious reforms provoked the enmity of the factious nobles that had hitherto been permitted to fatten on public plunder; they joined with the old rivals of the Barcine family, and even degraded themselves so far as to act as spies for the Romans, who still dreaded the abilities of Hannibal. In consequence of their machinations the old general was forced to fly from the country he had so long laboured to serve; and, after several vicissitudes, died of poison, to escape the mean and malignant persecution of the Romans.

But the Carthaginians had soon reason to lament the loss of their champion: the Romans were not conciliated by the expulsion of Hannibal; and Massinissa, relying upon their support, made frequent incursions into the territories of the republic. Both parties complained of each other as aggressors before the Roman senate (B. C. 162); but though they received an equal hearing, the decision was long previously settled in favour of Massinissa. While these negotiations were pending, Carthage was harassed by political dissension; the popular party believing, and not without reason, that the low estate of the republic was chiefly owing to the animosity that the aristocratic faction had shewn to the Barca family, and especially to Hannibal, on account of his financial and judicial reform—convened a tumultuous assembly, and sent forty of the principal senators into banishment, exacting an oath from the citizens that they would never permit their return. The exiles sought refuge with Massinissa, who sent his sons to intercede with the Carthaginian populace in their favour. The Numidian princes were not only refused admittance to the city, but ignominiously chased from their territory. Such an insult naturally provoked a fresh war, in which the Carthaginians were defeated, and forced to submit to the most onerous conditions.

The Roman senate, continually solicited by the elder Cato, at length came to the resolution of totally destroying Carthage; but it was difficult to discover a pretext for war against a state which, conscious of its weakness, had resolved to obey every command. The Carthaginians gave up three hundred of their noblest youths as hostages, surrendered their ships of war and their magazines of arms; but when, after all these concessions, they were ordered to abandon their city, they took courage from despair, and absolutely refused obedience. War was instantly proclaimed; the Romans met with almost uninterrupted success; and at the close of the four years that the war lasted, Carthage was taken by storm, and its magnificent edifices levelled with the ground.

Section VI.—*Navigation, Trade, and Commerce of Carthage.*

The colonial and commercial policy of the Carthaginians was far less generous than that of their ancestors the Phœnicians; the harbours of the capital were open to the ships and merchants of foreign nations, but admission was either wholly refused to all the remaining ports in the territory of the republic, or subjected to the most onerous restrictions. This selfish system, which has been imitated by too many modern commercial states, was forced upon the Carthaginians by peculiar circumstances. Their trade with the barbarous tribes of Africa was carried on principally by barter; the ignorant savages exchanged valuable commodities for showy trifles; and the admission of competition would at once have shewn them how much they lost in the exchange. Had the Carthaginians, under such circumstances, permitted free trade, they would, in fact, have destroyed their own market. A free exportation of corn would certainly have been beneficial to Carthage and her dependencies; but restriction was justified by the necessity of keeping a large supply at home to furnish provisions to the numerous armies of mercenaries. A very few words will suffice to shew the fallacy of this excuse, which has found favour with too many modern historians, among whom, with surprise and sorrow, we must reckon Professor Heeren. It is evident that prohibiting the export of corn limited the demand, and consequently prevented farmers from devoting their attention to the growth of grain; the more strictly the prohibition was enforced, the less would be the quantity of ground used for tillage: and consequently this policy, instead of insuring to the

Carthaginians a plentiful supply, exposed them every year more and more to the danger of a scarcity. In fact, we know that such was the result; we read of seasons of dearth in northern Africa under the restrictive system of Carthage; but we meet no account of a similar calamity when the corn-trade was set free under the Romans.

The principal commerce of the Carthaginians in the western Mediterranean was with the Greek colonies in Sicily and the south of Italy, from which they obtained wine and oil, in exchange for negro slaves, precious stones, and gold procured from the interior of Africa, and also for cotton cloths manufactured at Carthage and in the island of Malta. Corsica supplied honey, wax, and slaves; Sardinia yielded abundance of corn; the Balearic islands produced the best breed of mules; resin and volcanic products, such as sulphur and pumice-stone, were obtained from the Lipari islands; and southern Spain was, as we have already said, the chief source whence the nations of antiquity procured the precious metals.

Beyond the Pillars of Hercules the Carthaginians succeeded the Phœnicians in the tin and amber trade with the south British islands and the nations at the entrance of the Baltic. After the destruction of Carthage, this trade fell into the hands of their earliest rivals, the Phocæans of Marseilles, who changed its route; they made their purchases on the north shore of Gaul, and conveyed their goods overland to the mouth of the Rhone, — in that age a journey of thirty days.

On the west coast of Africa the Carthaginian colonies studded the shores of Morocco and Fez; but their great mart was the island of Cerne, now Suana, in the Atlantic Ocean (29° 10′ N. lat. 10° 40′ W. long.). On this island was the great depôt of merchandise; and goods were transported from it in light barks to the opposite coast, where they were bartered with the native inhabitants. From the description given of these African tribes, they appear to have been the same as the Tuaricks of modern times. The Carthaginian exports were trinkets, saddlery, linen, or, more probably, cotton webs, pottery, and arms; for which they received undressed hides and elephants' teeth. To this trade was added a very lucrative fishery: the tunny fish (*Thynnus scomber*), which is still plentiful on the north-western coast of Africa, was deemed a great luxury by the Carthaginians; it was salted and dried on the shores near which it was caught, and then sent to Carthage, where it was so highly valued that its exportation was prohibited. There is every reason to believe that these enterprising merchants had some intercourse with the coast of Guinea, and that their navigators advanced beyond the mouths of the Senegal and Gambia; but the secrecy with which every thing respecting this trade was concealed, renders it impossible to determine its nature and extent with accuracy.

It is at least equally difficult to discover any particulars respecting the caravan-trade with the interior of Africa. From the districts bordering on the desert the chief articles obtained were dates and salt; but from beyond the desert, the imports were negro slaves and gold dust. The nature of this lucrative commerce was the more easily concealed, as the caravans were found not at Carthage, but at remote towns in the interior, and all the chief staples were situated on the confines of the Great Desert.

CHAPTER VIII.

THE FOUNDATION OF

THE GRECIAN STATES.

SECTION I.—*Geographical Outline of Hellas.*

GREECE was bounded on the north by the Cambunian mountains, which separated it from Macedonia; on the east by the Ægean, on the south by the Mediterranean, and on the west by the Ionian Seas. Its extent from north to south was about two hundred and twenty geographical miles, from east to west one hundred and sixty miles, and consequently its area was about 34,000 square miles; making a small, indeed too small a reduction for the irregularity of its outline. No European country was so advantageously situated; on the eastern side, the Ægean Sea, studded with islands, brought it into close contact with Asia Minor and the Phœnician frontiers; the voyage to Egypt was neither long nor difficult, though it afforded not so many resting-places to the mariners; and from the west there was a short and easy passage to Italy. The entire line of this extensive coast was indented with bays and harbours, offering every facility for navigation; while the two great gulfs that divided Hellas, or northern Greece, from the Peloponnesus, or southern Greece, must have, in the very earliest ages, forced naval affairs on the attention of the inhabitants.

Nature herself has formed three great divisions of this very remarkable country. The Saronic and Corinthian Gulfs sever the Peloponnesus from Hellas; and this latter is divided into two nearly equal portions, northern and southern, by the chain of Mount Œta, which traverses it obliquely. This great mountain-chain, which on the west receives the name Othrys, and afterwards Pindus, turns off in a northerly direction about twenty miles before it reaches the Ambracian Gulf, and joins the Cambunian mountains, thus severing Thessaly and Epirus from central Hellas.

Thessaly, the largest of all the Grecian provinces, may be generally described as an extensive table-land, enclosed on three sides by the mountains just mentioned, and on the eastern side by the Ægean Sea, close to whose shores rise the lofty peaks of Ossa and Olympus. Its principal, indeed almost its only river, is the Peneus, which rises in Mount Pindus, and, flowing in an easterly direction, after having received many tributary streams from the north and south, falls into the Ægean Sea. Ancient traditions relate that, at a very remote age, this river terminated in a stagnant marsh, until some great convulsion separated Ossa from Olympus, and opened a free passage for its waters, forming at the same time the beautiful vale of Tempe. The great luxuriance of the Thessalian soil, and the high place it held in the mythological age of Greece, render these traditions far from improbable, especially when they are taken in connexion with the well-authenticated account that the Thessalians were the first of the Greeks who applied themselves to agriculture, and that their country was the original parent of the tribes that became the ruling races in the south.

The most celebrated cities of Thessaly were Larissa and Pheræ in the interior; Iolchos, whence the Argonauts sailed; and Magnesia, on the sea-coast. Thessaly was ruined by its natural wealth; the inhabitants rioted in sensual enjoyments; anarchy and tyranny followed each other in regular succession; and thus Thessaly, prepared for the yoke of a master, was the first to submit to the Persian invaders, and afterwards to the Macedonian Philip.

Epirus was, next to Thessaly, the largest of the Grecian provinces; but it was also the least cultivated. It was divided into two provinces; Molossis, of which Ambracia was the capital, and Thesprotia, containing the commercial port Buthrotum, and Dodona, the most ancient of the Grecian oracles, consecrated to Jupiter. Central Greece, or Hellas, contained nine countries: 1. Attica; 2. Megaris; 3. Bœotia; 4. Phocis; 5. eastern Locris; 6. western Locris; 7. Doris; 8. Ætolia; 9. Acarnania.

Attica is a headland extending in a south-easterly direction about sixty-three miles into the Ægean Sea. It is about twenty-five miles broad at its base, whence it gradually tapers towards a point, until it ends in the rocky promontory of Sunium (*Cape Colonna*), on the summit of which stood a celebrated temple of Minerva. It was not a fertile country, never being able to produce sufficient corn for the support of its inhabitants; but it had rich silver-mines in Mount Larium, excellent marble-quarries in Mount Pentelicus, and the ranges of hills by which it is intersected in every direction produced abundance of aromatic plants, from which swarms of industrious bees formed the most celebrated honey. The small plains between the mountainous ranges were covered with olive-groves, and fig-trees grew on the lower hills. The country was watered by the Ilissus, the Cephissus, and a multitude of other smaller streams; the climate was salubrious; and the natural prospects among the most beautiful in the world. Its chief city was Athens, which shall be described in a subsequent page; with this were connected three sea-ports on the Saronic Gulf, which washed the southern shores of Attica. The province was divided into more than one hundred and seventy cantons (δῆμοι), most of which possessed a town or small village. The most remarkable of these north of Athens were Marathon, Rhamnus, Acharnæ, Decelea, and Oropus, a good port on the Euripus, opposite the island of Eubœa. East of Athens were Brauron and Sunium; and to the west Eleusis, where the mysteries in honour of Ceres were celebrated. Besides the mountains already mentioned, Attica contained Hymettus, famous for the picturesque appearance of its double peak, and its excellent honey.

Megaris, the smallest of the Grecian territories, lay west of Attica, close to the Corinthian isthmus. Its capital was Megara, a town of considerable strength, joined by long walls to the sea-port Nicæa, taken and destroyed by Pericles in the Peloponnesian war. The only other place of note was Crommyon, near the Scironian rocks: these are said to have been very dangerous, and to have derived their name from Sciron, a notorious pirate slain by Theseus.

Bœotia was a large plain, almost wholly surrounded by

mountains: it was divided by Cithæron from Attica, a mountain celebrated by the poets for the mystic orgies of Bacchus, the metamorphosis of Actæon, the death of Pentheus, and the exposure of Œdipus. On the west were the chains of Parnassus and Helicon, sacred to the Muses, separating it from Phocis; and on the north it was divided from eastern Locris by a prolongation of the chain of Mount Cnemis. On the east was Mount Ptoüs, extending to the Euripus, a narrow strait that divides the island of Eubœa from the mainland. The climate was cloudy, and the soil marshy, as might be conjectured from the position of the country; but it was a fertile and well-watered district, and the most densely populated in Greece. Its chief rivers were the Asopus, the Ismenus, and the Cephissus, which must not be confounded with the stream of the same name in Attica. These rivers, descending from the heights, had stagnated in several places and formed lakes, of which Copais, now merely a swamp, was the largest. Thebes, renowned for its seven gates and its citadel Cadmeia, was the chief of the Bœotian cities; but the names of almost all frequently occur in history, for the fate of Greece was often decided in Bœotia. Its freedom was won at Platææ by the overthrow of the Persians, and lost at Chæroneia by the triumph of the Macedonians. The supremacy of the Spartans was established by the battle of Tanagra,—and their power for ever destroyed on the field of Leuctra. The other places of note were Aulis on the Euripus, the rendezvous of the Grecian fleet in the Trojan war; Lebadeia (*Livadia*), celebrated for the oracle of Trophonius; and Orchomenus, near which was the Acidalian fountain sacred to Venus.

Phocis, a district of moderate size and unequal shape, extended from the mountain-chains of Œta and Cnemis, southward to the Corinthian Gulf. It contained several important mountain-passes between northern and southern Greece, the chief of which, near the capital city Elateia, was early occupied by Philip in his second invasion of Hellas. Mounts Helicon and Parnassus, and the fountains of Aganippé and Hippocrené, are names familiar to every reader of poetry; and these, with the temple and oracle of Delphi, render the soil of Phocis sacred. Delphi was situated on the south side of Mount Parnassus, overshadowed by its double peak; and above the city was the magnificent temple of Apollo. Here, under the patronage of the god, were collected all the masterpieces of Grecian art in countless abundance; together with costly offerings from nations, cities, and kings. Here the Amphictyonic council promulgated the first maxims of the law of nations; here the Pythian games, scarcely inferior to those of Olympia, exercised the Grecian youth in athletic contests; while the poets, assembled round the Castalian fountain, chanted their rival odes in noble emulation. All now is perished; time has effaced the very ruins. One monument alone survives—it is said to mark the spot where Œdipus slew Laïus; and thus, while every trace of greatness and glory has vanished, nothing is perpetuated but the memory of a crime. Phocis possessed two harbours, Cirrha, on the river Plistus, where the pilgrims to Delphi generally landed; and Crissa, whose name is sometimes given to the whole Corinthian Gulf, though it should probably be confined to the inlet near which the city stood.

East Locris extends along the Euripus: it was inhabited by two tribes, the Opuntii and Epicnemidii, deriving their names from Mounts Opus and Cnemis. The most remarkable place in the province is the pass of Thermopylæ, so memorable for the gallant stand made there by Leonidas against the Persian myriads. It derived its name from the hot springs (θερμαὶ) in its neighbourhood, and the gates (πύλαι) erected at the narrowest part of the pass. Thermopylæ was long regarded as the only road by which an army could pass from Thessaly into Hellas, for nothing more than a footpath ran across the mountains; and consequently this pass, whose narrowness rendered it easily defensible, was long considered the key of Greece.

Western Locris, separated by Phocis from the eastern province, joined the bay of Corinth; its inhabitants were called Ozolæ. The chief city was Naupactus (*the ship-building town*), deriving its name from the circumstance of the Heracleidæ having there constructed the fleet in which they crossed over to the Peloponnesus. It is now called Lepanto, and is celebrated in modern times for the great naval victory obtained by the confederate Christians over the Turks A.D. 1571.

The mountainous district of Doris, though a small territory, was the parent of many powerful states: it was named Tetrapolis from its four cities, Pindus Dryopis, Erineum, Citium, and Boium; none of which were of any note. The province was enclosed between the southern ridge of Œta and the northern extremity of Mount Parnassus.

Acarnania, the most western country of Hellas, lay west of the river Acheloüs, from which it extended to the Ambracian Gulf. It was very thickly covered with wood; and the inhabitants remained barbarians after other branches of the Hellenic race had become the instructors of the world. Its chief cities were the Amphilochian Argos and Stratus. It contained also the town and promontory of Actium, off which the battle was fought that gave Augustus the empire of the world.

Ætolia extended from Mount Œta to the Ionian Sea, having the Locrian territory on the east, and the river Acheloüs on the west. Its chief cities were Calydon and Thermus. The Ætolians were deemed a warlike people in the heroic ages, but their fame soon declined; and it was not until after the overthrow of the Macedonian empire, that they again occupied a conspicuous place in history by their wars with the Romans.

SECTION II.—*Geographical Outline of the Peloponnesus.*

SOUTHERN Greece, anciently called the Apian land, was named the Peloponnesus in honour of Pelops, who is said to have introduced the arts of peace into that peninsula from Asia Minor. It consists of a mountainous range in the centre, whence hills branch out in various directions, several of which extend to the sea. Its modern name, the Morea, is derived from its resemblance to a mulberry leaf, which that word signifies. It was divided into eight countries: 1. Arcadia; 2. Laconia; 3. Messenia; 4. Elis; 5. Argolis; 6. Achaia; 7. Sicyonia; and 8. the Corinthian territory.

Arcadia, so renowned in poetical traditions, occupied the

central mountainous district of the Peloponnesus, no where bordering on the sea. It resembles Switzerland in appearance; and this similarity may be extended to the character of the inhabitants, both being remarkable for their love of freedom and their love of money. The country is covered with the richest vegetation, and abounds in brooks and waterfalls; hence it has always been celebrated for its pastures, and was consecrated by the ancients to Pan, the god of shepherds. The inhabitants of Arcadia, devoted to a pastoral life, were disinclined to erect cities; and when they began to have considerable towns, the contests between them destroyed the peace and liberties of the people. Arcadia is supposed by many writers to have been the cradle of the Pelasgic race; but though this is doubtful, it certainly was retained by that people long after the Hellenes had occupied every other part of Greece. The principal Arcadian mountains were Cyllene and Erymanthus; the chief rivers were the Alpheus and Erymanthus; but there were many smaller streams. Arcadia contained the only lake in the Peloponnesus, Stymphalus (*Zaracca*), from which the rivulet Erasinus, in Argolis, was supposed to derive its waters by a subterranean channel. The chief cities were Mantineia, Tegæa, Orchomenus, Psophis, and in a late age Megalopolis, erected as a common capital.

Laconia occupied the south-eastern division of the Peloponnesus: it was rugged and mountainous, but was nevertheless so densely inhabited, that it is said to have contained nearly a hundred towns and villages. It was separated from the south-western province, Messenia, by the chain of Mount Taygetus, which also separated it on the north from Arcadia and Argolis; it contained, besides, the lofty promontories of Malea and Tænarum. The chief city was Sparta, on the river Eurotas, the most clear and limpid of the Grecian streams. Sparta remained for many ages without walls or gates, its defence being entrusted to the valour of its citizens; but fortifications were erected when it fell under the sway of despotic rulers. Though a very large city, it was far from splendid; and it is now difficult to ascertain the precise spot where it stood. The monuments erected along the banks of the Eurotas to the memory of fallen heroes have disappeared; but the laurel-groves still flourish in their ancient beauty:

> "Art, glory, freedom fail; but nature still is fair."

The other places of note were Gythium, the port of Sparta, Amyclæ, and Sellasia.

Messenia lay to the west of Laconia, and was more level and fruitful than that province. Messene, the capital, was a strongly fortified town; and when the country was subjugated by Sparta, its citizens escaping to Sicily gave the name of their old metropolis to the principal town of the colony they formed, which it still retains with very slight alteration. On the frontiers were the strong fortresses of Ira and Ithome, memorable for their obstinate defence in the wars with Sparta. The other places of note were Pylos (*Navarino*), the capital of Nestor's kingdom, remarkable in ancient and modern times for important naval engagements, Methone, and Œchalia.

Argolis was a foreland on the south side of the Saronic Gulf, opposite Attica and not unlike it in shape, extending southwards from Arcadia fifty-four miles into the Ægean Sea, and terminating in the Scyllæan promontory. The chief city was Argos, on the river Inachus, a stream that had disappeared even in ancient times. During the reign of Perseus the seat of government was transferred to Mycenæ, the celebrated city of Agamemnon; but soon after the Trojan war, it was besieged by the Argives, and levelled to the ground. The other most remarkable towns were Tiryns, whence Hercules set forth to commence his labours; Epidaurus; Nemæa, where the games in honour of Neptune were celebrated; Trœzene; and Nauplia (now *Napoli di Romania*), in ancient and modern times the principal harbour of eastern Greece.

Elis, in the west of the Peloponnesus, was the holy land of ancient Greece. It was safe from the din of arms; and when bands of warriors traversed the sacred soil, they laid aside their weapons. It was a fertile country, being well watered by the Alpheus, the Peneus, and several other streams, all whose sources were in the Arcadian mountains. It was subdivided into three districts: the northern, named Elis Proper, from the chief city of the province, was a plain enclosed by the mountains of Pholoë and Scollis, both branches of the Arcadian Erymanthus. The city Elis stood on the banks of the Elean Peneus, and was more celebrated in the heroic than in the historic ages. The central district, Pisatis, was named from the city of Pisa, in the neighbourhood of which the Olympic games were celebrated every five years. Olympia, the name of the country round Pisa, was the most splendid sanctuary of the arts that the world ever beheld. The great temple stood in a sacred grove of olives and plane-trees, called Altis, on the banks of the Alpheus. It was built by the Eleans in the age of Pericles: but as it was a national sanctuary, all the Greek states contributed to the expense. It rivalled the Pantheon in extent, and surpassed it in grandeur: within it was placed the colossal statue of the Olympian Jupiter, sixty feet high, carved by Phidias, and universally acknowledged to be the most perfect piece of sculpture that ever existed. There were several minor temples; but the whole grove was filled with monuments and statues erected in honour of deities, heroes, and victors at the games. There were also several treasure-houses, founded by the patriotism, the piety, or the vanity of the principal Grecian cities and colonies, to preserve their votive offerings. "It was with a just pride," says Heeren, "that the Grecian departed from Olympia. He could say to himself with truth, that he had seen the noblest objects on earth, and that these were not the work of foreigners, but the creation and the property of his own nation."

The maritime district occupying the north-western portion of the Peloponnesus was originally called Ægialus, or Ægialeia, either from some hero, or from its situation on the coast. Its inhabitants were afterwards blended with a colony of Ionians from Attica, when it took the name of Ionia; but these being subsequently expelled by the Achæans, it received and retained the denomination of Achaia, by which it is best known in history. It was a narrow strip of country, watered by a multitude of mountain-streams, which descended from the lofty Arcadian ridges; but it was not eminent either for fertility or population. The inhabitants were a peaceful, industrious people, aspiring neither to eminence in war nor literature, but attached to liberty, and governed by wise laws. Twelve cities, of which the chief were Dymé, Patræ, and Ægium, ruling a small independent territory, were united by a confederation called the Achæan league; and this wise system preserved Achaia tranquil, while the rest of Greece was convulsed by the Peloponnesian wars. After the destruction of Grecian liberty, and the decline of the Macedonian empire, the Achæan league was renewed and enlarged; and it was the best security for Grecian independence against the ambition of the Macedonians and Romans.

The territory of Sicyonia, frequently regarded as a part of Achaia, was remarkable only for the city of Sicyon, the most ancient in Greece, having been founded more than two thousand years before the Christian era.

The Peloponnesus was connected with Hellas by the Corinthian isthmus, having the Saronic Gulf on the eastern side, and the Corinthian on the western. Several attempts were made to join these seas by a canal; but the nature of the ground to be cut through presented insuperable difficulties; and hence "to cut the Corinthian isthmus" was a proverbial expression for aiming at impossibilities. On this narrow pass the Isthmian games were celebrated in honour of Neptune, near the national temple of that deity, which stood in the midst of a grove of fir-trees. Here also a stand has frequently been made in defence of the liberties of Greece; the narrowness of the isthmus easily admitting of fortification. At the south of the isthmus stood the wealthy city of Corinth, anciently called Ephyre, more than four miles in extent: it was erected at the foot of a lofty hill, called the Acro-Corinthus, on which the citadel was built. This was the strongest fortress in Greece, and perhaps no other spot in the world afforded so brilliant a prospect. Beneath it might be seen the bustling commercial city, whose trade was more extensive than that of any other in Greece, with its temples, its theatres, and its aqueducts, built on a grand and extensive scale, such as could not be paralleled in eastern Europe; beyond lay the two harbours, Cenchreæ on the Saronic, and Lechæum on the Corinthian Gulf, always crowded with shipping. The peaks of Helicon and Parnassus were visible in the distance, and a strong eye could even discover the Acropolis of Athens. The Corinthian territory was one of the smallest in Greece; but commerce, not dominion, secured the strength of Corinth, and trade rendered it rich and powerful; like Venice, whose prosperity was never greater than when the republic possessed not a single square mile on the continent.

SECTION III.—*The Grecian Islands in the Ægean and Mediterranean Seas.*

THE Thracian islands occupy the north of the Ægean Sea: the principal were, Thasos, Samothrace, and Imbrus. Thasos (*Tasse*) in the earlier ages of Grecian history was named Æthria. It produced wine and marble, and had some productive gold-mines. The inhabitants were daring navigators, and at one time contended for the mastery of the sea with the Athenians; but after a struggle of two years, they were forced to surrender at discretion.

Samothrace (*Samandrachi*) derived its name from the island of Samos, having been at an early age occupied by a Samian colony. It was celebrated for the mysterious worship of certain deities called Cabiri; and from this island Dardanus introduced the worship of Cybele into Troy, as most mythologists say; though the reverse process is at least equally probable, for Cybele was a native Phrygian deity.

Imbrus (*Embro*) lay to the south of Samothrace. Opposite to it, on the Asiatic coast, at the entrance of the Hellespont, was the island of Tenedos, remarkable for a temple dedicated to Apollo, under the name of Smintheus. The deity is said to have derived this name from Sminthæ, which in the Phrygian language signifies "mice," because he destroyed a vast multitude of these animals that at one time infested the island.

South-west of Tenedos was Lemnos (*Stalimene*), dedicated to Hephæstus or Vulcan, because the poets asserted that Vulcan, when flung from heaven by Jupiter, had fallen in this island: it contained two cities, Hephæstia and Mucina. Still farther west, on the Macedonian coast, was Halonnesus (*Dromo*), which is said at one time to have defeated an invasion by the valour of the women alone, after all the men were slain. South of these were Sciathus (*Sciatea*), Scopelos (*Skopelo*), and Scyros (*Skiro*), where Achilles was concealed by Thetis.

South of Tenedos, and opposite the city of Ephesus, on the Asiatic coast, was Lesbos (*Metelin*), the birth-place of many celebrated writers: its chief towns were Methymna, in whose neighbourhood were the rich vineyards from which the celebrated Lesbian wine was produced, and Mitylene, whence the island derives its modern name. Farther to the south was Chios (*Scio*), whose wines were deemed the best in the ancient world.

The largest island in the Ægean was Eubœa (*Egripo*), separated from the Bœotian coast by a narrow strait called the Eurípus, which is now choked up: its chief towns were Chalcis, Eretria, and Oreus, near the last of which was the remarkable headland of Artemisium.

In the Saronic Gulf were the islands of Salamis and Ægina. Salamis (*Elimi*) is remarkable in the heroic ages for having been the kingdom of Telamon, father of Ajax and Teucer; but it is still more memorable in the historic period for the complete overthrow of the Persian navy. Ægina (*Engia*), anciently called Ænone, was strongly fortified by nature: its inhabitants were excellent sailors; they disputed the empire of the sea with the Athenians; and to them the prize of valour was assigned at the battle of Salamis.

South-east of Eubœa were the Cyclades, a cluster of islands deriving their name from their nearly forming a circle round the island of Delos. Ortygia, or Delos, is celebrated in mythology as the birth-place of Apollo and Diana: the poets declare that the jealous Juno having discovered that Latona was pregnant by Jupiter, swore that Earth should not afford her a resting-place, and that Neptune caused the floating island of Delos to rise out of the sea as an asylum for her. They add, that Apollo, through respect for his birth-place, rendered the island stationary, by binding it to the adjacent islands of Mycone and Gyarus. In history, Delos is remarkable as one of the places consecrated by Grecian religion. The temple of the Delian Apollo on Mount Cynthius was a shrine to which pilgrimages were made from all parts of Greece. A sacred galley, called *Paralus*, was annually sent thither from Athens with a solemn sacrifice; and during its absence it was unlawful to inflict any punishment on a criminal.

The other remarkable islands in this group were Andros; Ceos; Paros, celebrated for its white marble; Melos; Naxos, sacred to Bacchus; and Ios, said to have been the burial-place of Homer.

East of the Cyclades, and close along the Asiatic coast, was another cluster of islands called the Sporades, from their being irregularly scattered over the sea. The chief of these were, Samos, sacred to Juno, and the birth-place of the philosopher Pythagoras; Icaria, which gave name to the Icarian Sea; Patmos, where St. John wrote the Revelations; Cos, the native country of the celebrated physician Hippocrates, where a venerable plane-tree is still exhibited, under which he is said to have lectured;* Carpathus (*Scarpanto*), which gave name to the Carpathian sea; and Rhodes.

Rhodes is still one of the most beautiful islands in the world; but, unfortunately, it is the spot where Turkish despotism has most effectually counteracted the bounties of Providence. It was celebrated for its large raisins, but still more for its oranges and roses, which in ancient times were the em-

* This tree, so celebrated by the geographers of the sixteenth and seventeenth centuries, still exists, and has been thus described by a modern traveller:—"About half a century ago its branches extended over the largest open space in Cos. One of the largest fell some years ago; but still this patriarch of the vegetable kingdom preserves an air of grandeur and majesty. The branches that remain, pressed down by the weight of years, extend horizontally over a wide space; several of them are propped by the marble columns which once supported a temple of Æsculapius or Apollo: these props have been in this position so long, that the stone has penetrated the bark, and seems to form part of the tree whose boughs it sustains. The plane-tree of Cos is revered both by Turks and Greeks, who extol it above all the antiquities of the island, and never fail to tell travellers that Hippocrates (who was a native of Cos) lectured his pupils and advised his patients beneath its shade."—MICHAUD's *Correspondence d'Orient.*

blems of the isle, and shared with the sun the glory of having given it a name. Traces of its former prosperity might have been discovered in the last century ; but the Turkish governors have come with their fiscal barbarity: they have not only overwhelmed the people with taxes, but have established monopolies of silk, wax, honey, oil, oranges, raisins, indeed of all the productions of the island. Gardens have disappeared; harvests no longer cover the earth ; and in places once renowned for their fertility, nothing is left but the simple soil. What a contrast is this to its ancient glory! Rhodes, the chief city, was one of the most flourishing and beautiful commercial staples of antiquity. At the entrance of its harbour stood the celebrated Colossus, a huge brazen statue erected in honour of the sun, having its feet at the opposite side of the harbour; and so lofty, that large vessels could pass between its legs without striking their topsails. It was thrown down by an earthquake, and subsequently broken up for the sake of its brass by the Saracens. The other most remarkable cities in the island were Lindus and Camyrus.

Creté (Candia), the largest of the Grecian islands except Eubœa, lies at the entrance of the Ægean. In ancient times it was celebrated for its hundred cities, of which the chief were Gnossus, Cydonia, and Gortyna. Mythology has invested Creté with the fabled honour of having given birth to many of the gods of Greece; Jupiter himself was supposed to have been born on its chief mountain, Ida: but it had the superior, because real, merit of having given to Greece its most useful institutions. The Cretans, protected by their insular situation from the fierce incursions that so often devastated Hellas, and within a short sail of Egypt, the cradle of civilisation, were early distinguished by their wise institutions. The code established by the elder Minos is said to have been the chief source of the legislation of Lycurgus; and the mechanical inventions of Dædalus gave the first great stimulus to the cultivation of the useful arts. During the earlier ages of Grecian history the Cretans were a leading people, but they subsequently degenerated; and we find them in the Peloponnesian wars serving as mercenaries to the Athenians.

North-east of Creté is Cyprus, the favourite island of Venus, whose Paphian bower is not yet forgotten in song, and whose loveliness has been celebrated by poets of every age and nation, from the days of King Solomon to those of the lion-hearted Richard. Cyprus, however, is now scarcely less miserable than Rhodes; the present capital, Lamaca, built over the ruins of the ancient Citium, may be regarded as the type of its fortunes; every thing great or glorious moulders in the grave; nothing exhibits signs of life but tyranny and hopeless servitude. Nature, however, has bestowed her blessings so lavishly, that even Turkish oppression has failed to blight all its fertility. In addition to the metropolis, Cyprus contained the celebrated city of Salamis (*Famagusta*), founded by Teucer, the brother of Ajax Telamon, after the Trojan war.

SECTION IV.—*The Ionian Islands.*

CORCYRA (*Corfu*) is celebrated by Homer, under the name of Phæacia, for its amazing riches and fertility. It was opposite that part of Epirus named Thesprotia, from which it was separated by a narrow strait called the Corcyrean. The chief city was and is of the same name as the island: it has been celebrated both in ancient and modern times for the excellence of its harbour, and the strength of its fortifications. It was, in an early age, much improved by a Corinthian colony; and the natural abundance of its productions, the convenience of its harbours, and the adventurous spirit of its new inhabitants, gave them an undisputed advantage over their neighbours in industry and commerce.

Leucadia (*Santa Maura*) was originally a peninsula; but the isthmus that joined it to the mainland was cut through to facilitate navigation. The most remarkable place in the island was the town and headland of Leucas: from the summit of the Leucadian promontory unfortunate lovers used to precipitate themselves into the sea.

The Echinades (*Curzolari*) were a small cluster of islands near the mouth of the river Achelous, of which the most celebrated was Dulichium, part of the kingdom of Ulysses. Near it was the little island of Ithaca (*Theaki*), immortalised by Homer. The capital, of the same name as the island, stood at the foot of Mount Neritus.

Cephalonia, anciently called Scheria, was the largest of the western Grecian islands, and the least noted in history. Its chief town was Same, which sometimes gave its name to the whole island.

South of this was Zacynthus (*Zante*), with a capital of the same name, celebrated for its fertile meads, its luxuriant woods, and its abundant fountains of bitumen : the oily matter exuding from these sometimes reached the sea, and, spreading over its surface, adorned the waves with prismatic hues.

West of the Peloponnessus are the Strophades (*Strivoli*), more anciently called *Plotæ*, because they were supposed to have been floating islands ; and south of them is the island of Sphacteria (*Sphagiæ*), which guards the entrance of Pylos (*Navarino*).

South of the Peloponnesus is the island of Cytherea (*Cerigo*), sacred to Venus, and celebrated in ancient times for its fertility and beauty. It contained two large cities, Cythera and Scanda, provided with excellent harbours, and long enriched by the commerce of Egypt and Libya. But the island, having been taken by the Athenians in the Peloponnesian wars, was treated with the cruelty and injustice which most commercial states have displayed towards their colonies and dependencies ; and it never recovered its former prosperity.

Section V.—*Social and Political Condition of Greece.*

It is useless to investigate the social condition of the Greeks in what are called the heroic ages, because we have no credible account of that period. But when the certain history of Greece commences, we find the country divided between two races, the Ionian and the Dorian ; distinguished from each other by striking characteristics, which were never wholly obliterated. We know, also, that two other races, the Æolian and Achæan, existed ; but they seem to have become in a great degree identified with one or other of the two former.

The Ionians were remarkable for their democratic spirit, and consequent hostility to hereditary privileges. They were vivacious, prone to excitement, easily induced to make important changes in their institutions, and proud of their country and themselves. Their love of refined enjoyments made them diligent cultivators of the fine arts, but without being destitute of martial vigour. They were favourably disposed towards commerce; but, like too many other free states, they encumbered it with short-sighted restrictions; and they were cruel masters to their colonial dependencies.

The Dorian race, on the contrary, was remarkable for the severe simplicity of its manners, and its strict adherence to ancient usages. It preferred an aristocratic form of government, and required age as a qualification for magistracy, because the old are usually opposed to innovation. They were ambitious of supremacy, and the chief object of their institutions was to maintain the warlike and almost savage spirit of the nation. Slavery in its worst form prevailed in every Dorian state; and the slaves were almost deprived of hope,—for the Dorian legislation was directed chiefly to fix every man in his hereditary condition. Commerce was discouraged, on account of its tendency to change the ranks of society; and the fine arts all but prohibited, because they were supposed to lead to effeminacy. The great advantage that the Dorian possessed over the Ionian institutions was their permanence; but even this is a doubtful gain; for the progress of improvement was checked, and no means supplied for reforming those parts of ancient institutions that became unsuited to the changes necessarily wrought in the condition of the state by time and circumstance.

The differences between these two races is the chief characteristic of Grecian politics; it runs, indeed, through the entire history, and was the principal cause of the deep-rooted hatred between Athens and Sparta. Next to this, the most marked feature in the political aspect of Greece is, that it contained as many free states as cities. Attica, Megaris, and Laconia, were civic rather than territorial states; but there are few of the other divisions of the country that were united under a single government. The cities of Achaia, Arcadia, and

Bœotia, were independent of each other, though the Achæan cities were united by a federative league; and Thebes generally exercised a precarious dominion over the other cities of Bœotia. This parcelling out of a small country,—added to the frequent revolutions, facilitated by the narrow limits of each state,—necessarily led to a more rapid development of political science in Greece than in any other country.

Divided as the Greeks were, there were many circumstances that united the whole Hellenic race by a common bond of nationality. Of these the chief was unity of religion, connected with which were the national festivals and games, at which all the Hellenes, and none others, were allowed to take a share. If, as is commonly supposed, the Greeks derived the elements of their religion from Asia or Egypt, they soon made it so peculiarly their own, that it retained no features of its original source. All Asiatic deities are more or less of an elementary character; that is, they symbolise some natural object, such as the sun, the earth, an important river; or some power of nature, such as the creative, the preserving, and the destroying power. In many instances both were combined, and the visible object was associated with the latent power. On the other hand, the gods of Greece were human personages, possessing the forms and the attributes of men, though in a highly exalted degree. The paganism of Asia was consequently a religion of fear; for it was impossible to conceive deities of monstrous forms sympathising with man: hence, also, the priesthood formed a peculiar caste; for the mystery which veiled the god was necessarily extended to the mode in which he should be worshipped. Instead of this gloomy system, the Greeks had a religion of love; they regarded their gods as a kind of personal friends, and hence their worship was cheerful and joyous. The priesthood was open to all; the office was commonly filled for a limited time only, and was not deemed inconsistent with other occupations. There is no doubt that the Grecian religion received its peculiar form from the beautiful fictions of the poets, especially Homer and Hesiod; for in all its features it is essentially poetical. We need scarcely dwell on the beneficial effects produced by this system on the fine arts, or its facilitating the progress of knowledge, by separating religion from philosophy.

The oracles of Dodona and Delphi, the temples of Olympia and Delos, were national; they belonged to the whole Hellenic race. The responses of the oracles were more reverenced by the Dorian than the Ionian race, for the latter early emancipated itself from the trammels of superstition. The worship in all was voluntary, and the large gifts emulously sent to them were the spontaneous offers of patriotic affection. Delphi was under the government of the Amphictyonic council; but this body did not limit its attention to the government of the temple: by its influence over the oracle, it acquired no small share in the affairs of different states; and it superintended the administration of the law of nations, even when the states represented in it were engaged in war.

The great public games were the Olympian, the Pythian, the Nemean, and the Isthmian. Foreigners might be spectators at these games, but Hellenes alone could contend for the prize. This right belonged to the colonies as well as to the states in the mother country: and, as it was deemed a privilege of the highest value, it preserved the unity even of the most distant branches of the Hellenic race.

All the constitutions of the Grecian states were republican; but they varied so much in the different cities, that hardly any two were alike. In general, however, it may be stated, that in all the most severe public and private labours were entrusted to slaves; and in many, as Laconia, agriculture was managed by them exclusively. This degraded manufacturing industry, and led to an undue depression not only of artisans and retailers, but even of master manufacturers. Foreign merchants were treated with unwise jealousy, and could never obtain the privileges of citizens. The right of coinage was reserved to the state; but it was not until a very late period that the Greeks began to pay attention to finance. Little or no taxation was necessary while the citizens served as voluntary soldiers; and the magistrates were rewarded with honour, not money. But when mercenary armies were employed, and ambassadors sent into distant lands; when the importance of a navy induced cities to outbid each other in the pay of their sailors; heavy taxes became necessary, and these brought many of the cities into great pecuniary embarrassment.

Another source of expense was the provision for public festivals and theatrical shows; to which was added, in Athens and other places, the payment of the dicasts, or persons analogous to our jurymen; though, instead of their number being limited to twelve, they frequently amounted to several hundreds, and had no presiding judges. This was doubly injurious; the multitude of the dicasts not only entailed a heavy expense upon the state, but the sum paid being small, few save those of the lower classes attended, whose decisions were not unfrequently guided by prejudice and passion, instead of law and justice.

The poetical nature of its religion, and the free constitution of its states, not only rendered Greece peculiarly favourable to the progress of literature, philosophy, and the fine arts, but gave these, in turn, a decided influence on the government. The tragic and lyric poets produced their pieces in honour of the gods; the comic poets at Athens discussed public affairs on the stage with a freedom, or rather licentiousness, which the wildest excesses of the modern press have never equalled; and the influence of the orators at Athens rendered them the leaders of the state.

The seeds of dissolution were thickly sown in the social system of the Greeks. The rivalry between the Dorian and Ionian races; the turbulence and sedition natural to small republics; and the gradual decline of religion, followed by a consequent corruption of morals,—rendered the duration of the constitution as brief as it was glorious. Beautiful as the poetical religion of Greece appears to the fancy, it could have no permanence; for its influence depended on feeling, not on faith, and its support was left to voluntary offerings, that is, to all the variations of human whim and caprice.

SECTION VI.—*The traditional History of Greece from the earliest Ages to the Commencement of the Trojan War.*

From an unknown period to about 1200 B.C.

SACRED history, confirmed by uniform tradition, informs us that Thrace, Macedon, and Greece, were peopled at an earlier period than the other portions of the western world. The first inhabitants were tribes of hunters and shepherds, whose earliest approaches to civilisation were associations for mutual defence against robber-tribes, and the Phœnician corsairs that swept the coasts of the Ægean to kidnap slaves. The Pelasgi were the first tribe that acquired supremacy in Greece: they were probably of Asiatic origin; and the first place in which they appear to have made a permanent settlement was the Peloponnesus, where they erected Sicyon (* B.C. 2000), and Argos (* B.C. 1800). Inachus was regarded by the Pelasgi as their founder: he was probably contemporary with Abraham; but nothing certain is known of his history. To the Pelasgi are attributed the remains of those most ancient monuments generally called Cyclopian. They are usually composed of enormous rude masses piled upon one another, with small stones fitted in between the intervals to complete the work. Several of these stones are from ten to twelve feet in length, and of proportionate breadth and thickness. The Cyclopic fortresses are, for the most part, remarkable for the various contrivances to protract the defence of the interior after the enemy had conquered the outer wall; and for a deficiency of flank defences, which could only belong to the infancy of fortification. These circumstances are found in some of the most ancient hill-forts of India, and in the first efforts towards the erection of works for protection which were made by the South Sea islanders that had most advanced in civilisation when first they were discovered by Europeans. The rudeness of the Cyclopian work, the magnitude of the masses, and the firmness with which their weight keeps them together, have preserved the ruins from the destructive effects of time, and of the succeeding generations, who so frequently pull to pieces the venerable relics of antiquity for the sake of the materials.† From the Peloponnesus the Pelasgi extended themselves northwards to Attica, Bœotia, and Thessaly, which they are said to have entered under three leaders, Achæus, Phthius, and Pelasgus; though by these names we ought probably to understand separate tribes rather than individuals. Here they learned to apply themselves to agriculture, and continued to flourish for nearly two centuries. (From *B.C. 1700 to *B.C. 1500.)

The Hellenes, a more mild and humane race, first appeared on Mount Parnassus in Phocis under Deucalion, whom they venerated as their founder (*B.C. 1433). Being driven thence by a flood, they migrated into Thessaly, and expelled the Pelasgi from that territory. From this time forward the Hellenes rapidly increased, and extended their dominion over the greater part of Greece, dispossessing the more ancient race, which only retained the mountainous parts of Arcadia and the land of Dodona. Numbers of the Pelasgi emigrated to Italy, Crete, and some of the other islands. At the distance of twelve centuries from this revolution, traces of the Pelasgi were to be discovered in several of the Arcadian and Epirote cities; a district of Thessaly retained their name; their colonies continued to inhabit the southern coast of Italy and the shores of the Hellespont; and in these widely separated countries their ancient affinity was recognised in the uniformity of their rude dialect and barbarous manners, so very dissimilar to the refined customs and polished language of their Grecian neighbours.

The Hellenic race was subdivided into four great branches, the Æolians, Ionians, Dorians, and Achæans, which, in the historic age of Greece, were characterised by many strong and marked peculiarities of dialect, customs, and political government; we may perhaps add, religious, or, at least, heroic traditions, only that these appear to be connected rather with the localities in which they settled than with the stock from which they sprung. There were many smaller ramifications of the Hellenic race; but all united themselves to one or other of the

† Colonel Leake's Travels in the Morea contain the best account of the Cyclopian remains at Tiryns, Argos, and Mycenæ.

four great tribes, whose names are derived from Deucalion's immediate posterity. It is the common attribute of ancient traditions to describe the achievements of a tribe or army as personal exploits of the leader; and hence we find the history of the tribes and their migrations interwoven with the personal history of Deucalion's descendants.

Hellen, the son of Deucalion, gave his name to the whole Hellenic race: he had three sons, Æolus, Dorus, and Xuthus; of whom the first settled in the district of Thessaly called Phthiotis, and became the founder of the Æolian tribe; the second settled in Estiæotis, and there established the Dorian tribe; the third, expelled by his brethren, migrated to Athens, where he married Creusa the daughter of king Erectheus, by whom he had two sons, Ion and Achæus. After the death of Erectheus, Xuthus was forced to remove to Ægialeia (the province of the Peloponnesus afterwards called Achaia), where he died. His son Ion, the founder of the Ionian race, became general of the Athenian forces, and lord of Ægialeia, to which he gave the name of Ionia. Achæus, the founder of the Achæan race, obtained possession of the greater part of the Peloponnesus, especially Argolis and Laconia.

The Æolian tribe spread itself over western Greece, Acarnania, Ætolia, Phocis, Locris, Elis in the Peloponnesus, and the western islands. The Dorians, driven from Estiæotis by the Perrhæbians, spread themselves over Macedonia and Crete; a part of them subsequently returning, crossed Mount Œta, and settled in Doris on the Doric Tetrapolis, where they remained until they migrated into the Peloponnesus under the guidance of the Heracleidæ; an important revolution, which will soon engage our attention.

The Ionians inhabited Attica and Ægialeia; but they were expelled from the latter by the Achæans at the time of the great Dorian migration, and the name of the country changed to Achaia. The Achæans retained Argolis and Laconia until they were expelled by the Dorians, when, as we have just said, they established themselves in Ægialeia.

From the middle of the sixteenth to the middle of the fourteenth century before Christ, several colonies from Egypt,

Phœnicia, and Phrygia, settled in different parts of Greece, bringing with them the improvements in the arts and sciences that had been made in their respective countries, and thus greatly advancing the progress of civilisation in Greece. There have been some modern theorists who have denied the fact of these migrations, though supported by the unanimous testimony of ancient writers; but it is a sufficient answer to the objections of such sceptics, that these colonists, few in number, never formed a separate caste, but were soon blended with the mass of the native population; and that all the improvements and inventions the Greeks derived from abroad, they so modified and suited to their national character as to make them completely their own. The chief of these colonies were,—

An Egyptian colony led from Sais in the Delta to Attica by Cecrops (*B.C. 1550): he is said to have introduced the institution of marriage and the first elements of civilisation.

A second colony from lower Egypt led by Danaus, who fled from a brother's enmity, and settled in Argos (* B.C. 1500). The fable of his fifty daughters is well known; but its historical foundation is altogether uncertain.

A Phœnician colony, under Cadmus, settled in Bœotia, and founded Thebes, nearly at the same time that Cecrops established himself in Africa. He was the first who introduced the use of letters into Greece. Those who deny the fact of these colonies dwell strongly on the improbability of a Phœnician prince establishing himself in an inland city; forgetting that a political exile would naturally secure himself from the persecutions of his countrymen, and that the Phœnicians were at that period the undisputed masters of the Ægean.

Pelops led a colony from Phrygia into the Peloponnesus (*B.C. 1400): he did not acquire so large a kingdom as the settlers mentioned before; but his descendants, by intermarriages with the royal families of Argos and Lacedæmon, acquired such paramount influence, that they became supreme over the peninsula, and gave it the name of their great ancestor.

Several circumstances, however, impeded the progress of

civilisation. The coasts of Greece were temptingly exposed to the Phœnicians, Carians, and islanders of the Ægean, who at first made the art of navigation subservient to piracy rather than commerce; and the Thracians, the Amazons, and other barbarous tribes from the north, made frequent incursions into the exposed Hellenic provinces. To resist these incursions the celebrated Amphictyonic league was founded by Amphictyon, a descendant of Deucalion: the federation was constantly receiving fresh accessions, until it included the greater part of the Grecian states; deputies from which met alternately at Delphi and Thermopylæ.

Like Europe in the middle ages, Greece at this period was infested by bands of robbers, who deemed plunder an honourable profession, and some of whom exercised the most atrocious cruelties on the hapless passengers. As there was no paramount authority to control these banditti, their excesses became intolerable, until a species of knight-errantry was established, which, in its most prominent features, resembled that which, from similar causes, became, at a long-subsequent period, prevalent in western Europe. The adventurers who acquired most fame by their exertions in destroying the freebooters, were Perseus, Hercules, Bellerophon, Theseus, and the Dioskouroi Castor and Pollux, whose romantic histories form a very large portion of Grecian mythology.

The most celebrated events in this period of uncertain history are, the Argonautic expedition, the two Theban wars, the siege of Troy, the return of the Heracleidæ, and the migration of the Ionian and Æolian colonies to Asia Minor. It is not easy to discover the real nature and objects of the Argonautic expedition: it appears certain that in the thirteenth century before the Christian era, a Thessalian prince, named Jason, collected the young chivalry of Greece, and sailed on an expedition, partly commercial and partly piratical, in a ship named Argo, to the eastern shores of the Euxine sea. The Argonauts fought, conquered, and plundered; they planted a colony in Colchis, and their chief brought a princess of that country home to Thessaly. But though impenetrable darkness veils the nature of this expedition, there can be no doubt of its results. From the era of the Argonauts, we may discover among the Greeks not only a more daring and more enlarged spirit of enterprise, but a more decisive and rapid progress towards civilisation and humanity. The chiefs, who had hitherto been the isolated leaders of barbarous hordes, and owed their pre-eminence principally to their physical strength and ferocious courage when combined in a joint expedition, practically learned the value of the political virtues; and found that to retain their superiority, it was necessary to brighten the lustre of martial spirit by the milder virtues of justice and humanity.

Soon after the close of the Argonautic expedition, most of the Grecian heroes joined in an Æolian war, called by the poets "the hunt of the Calydonian boar;" and northern Greece was disturbed by religious feuds, occasioned by the introduction of the Dionysiac or Bacchanalian rites from Asia. The worship of Dionysus or Bacchus was established at Thebes by Cadmus; and the Phœnician mythology is full of the miseries and crimes that debased and ruined the family of Cadmus. Œdipus, the most remarkable of his descendants, having been removed from the throne for an involuntary series of crimes, his sons, Eteocles and Polynices, seized the kingdom, and agreed to reign in turn. Eteocles refused to perform the agreement; and Polynices being joined by six of the most eminent generals in Greece, commenced the memorable war of "the Seven against Thebes" (*B.C. 1225). The result was fatal to the allies; Eteocles and Polynices fell by mutual wounds; and Creon, who succeeded to the Theban throne, routed the confederate forces, five of whose leaders were left dead on the field. After the lapse of about ten years, the sons of the allied princes, called the Epigoni, marched against Thebes to avenge the death of their fathers. After a sanguinary conflict, the Thebans were routed with great slaughter, their leader slain, and their city captured. In consequence of these wars the Thebans were long odious to the rest of the Greeks, and they repaid this hatred by infidelity to the Hellenic cause during the Persian war.

When the family of Pelops became powerful in southern

Greece, they appear to have attempted to retaliate the injuries that had driven their ancestor into exile. In one of their plundering expeditions to the Phrygian coast, a young prince named Podarkes was carried away captive, and detained until a large ransom had been paid for his liberation. From this circumstance, he was afterwards named Priam, or "the purchased." At a subsequent period, Priam having become king of Troy, sent his son Paris, or Alexander, as an ambassador to the Peloponnesian princes, probably to negotiate a peace. He seduced Helen, the beautiful wife of Menelaus, king of Sparta, and conveyed her, with some valuable treasures, to Troy. The injured husband applied to his countrymen for redress. A large army, raised by the confederate kings, was placed under the command of Agamemnon, the brother of Menelaus. After a war of ten years, Troy was taken (*B.C. 1183), and razed to the ground. The victors, however, suffered nearly as much as the vanquished. During the protracted absence of the chiefs, usurpers had seized many of their thrones, aided by faithless wives and the rising ambition of young men. These circumstances necessarily led to fierce wars and intestine commotions, which greatly retarded the progress of Grecian civilisation.

SECTION VII.—*Grecian History from the Trojan War to the Establishment of the Greek Colonies in Asia.*

FROM B.C. * 1183 TO B.C. 994.

WE have seen how the posterity of Pelops, by various means, obtained possession of the entire Peloponnesus, to the exclusion of the more ancient dynasties. Their rivals were the Perseidæ, who claimed through their ancestor Perseus the honours of a divine descent, and who could boast of having in their family such heroes as Perseus, Bellerophon, and Hercules. From the last-named hero a powerful branch of the Perseid family received the name of the Heracleidæ: they were persecuted by the Pelopid sovereigns, and driven into exile. After having been hospitably received by the Athenians, and protected from the vindictive pursuit of their enemies, they retired to the mountainous district of Doris, where their leader Hyllus was adopted by Epalius, monarch of that country; and after the death of their benefactor, the Heracleidæ became masters of that wild and barren province. The Dorian mountains were ill calculated to satisfy men whose ancestors had inherited the fertile plains of the Peloponnesus; but the growing greatness of the rival house, and especially the extensive power obtained by Agamemnon and Menelaus, checked their natural ambition. When the consequences of the Trojan war filled Greece with confusion, the Heracleidæ were encouraged to make an effort to regain their ancient rights: twice they attempted to break through the Corinthian isthmus, but were each time repulsed with considerable loss. Warned by these misfortunes, they abandoned the design of entering the Peloponnesus by land, and resolved to try their fortune in a naval expedition.

Their rendezvous was Naupactus (*Lepanto*), on the Corinthian Gulf, where they were joined by a body of Ætolians, and by several of the Dorian tribes, anxious to exchange their savage rocks and gloomy forests for a more fertile and civilised country. By secret intrigues, a party was gained in Lacedæmon; and before setting sail, they prudently detached a body of light-armed troops, whose appearance at the isthmus drew the strength of the enemy towards that quarter. A favourable gale in the meantime wafted their armament to the eastern coast of the Peloponessus. Laconia was betrayed to the invaders; Argolis, Messenia, Elis, and Corinth, submitted to their authority; the mountainous districts of Arcadia, and the coast province, Ægialeia (afterwards Achaia), were the only parts of the peninsula that remained unsubdued. The revolution was effected with little bloodshed; but not without great oppression of the ancient inhabitants, many of whom emigrated, while those who remained were reduced to slavery.

The associated victors divided the conquered provinces among themselves by lot. Aristodemus, who obtained Laconia, happening to die, the kingdom was secured for his twin children, Eurysthenes and Procles, and from that time forth Sparta was governed by two kings. The commander of the Pelopid forces at the isthmus, instead of attempting to recover his kingdom, invaded Ægialeia, expelled the Ionians, and gave that province the name of Achaia, which it ever after retained (B.C. 1104). Many of the fugitives sought refuge in Attica, where they were hospitably entertained by the Athenians, who were alarmed by the success and ambition of the Dorians. A still greater number passed over into Asia Minor, and founded the colonies of Ionia, Æolia, and Caria.

The jealousy of the Athenians was soon proved to be derived from reasonable fears. In the reign of Codrus the Dorians passed the boundaries of Attica, and seized the territory of Megara, on the northern coast of the Saronic Gulf. A cruel war ensued. Codrus in vain attempted to drive the intruders from their stronghold: at length, hearing that a superstitious rumour prevailed among them, that they would be successful as long as they refrained from injuring the Athenian king, he entered their camp in disguise, provoked a quarrel with a Dorian soldier, and suffered himself to be slain. On recognising the body, the superstitious Peloponnesians, despairing of success, abandoned their hostilities; and the Athenians, out of respect for his memory, declared that none of the human race was worthy to succeed Codrus, and therefore abolished royalty altogether (B.C. 1068).

Two of the Pelopidæ, having unsuccessfully traversed the northern part of Greece in search of new settlements, finally yielded to the dictates of their enterprising spirit, crossed the Hellespont eighty-eight years after the taking of Troy, and established themselves along the coast of the ancient kingdom of Priam. Their colonies gradually extended from the peninsula of Cyzicus on the Propontis to the mouth of the river Hermus, which delightful country, together with the island of Lesbos, received the name of Æolia. The younger sons of Codrus, dissatisfied with the abolition of royalty, collected a numerous band of Athenians and Ionian exiles, with which they crossed the sea, and established themselves along the coast from the river Hermus to the promontory of Posideion, expelling the ancient inhabitants. The islands of Chios and

Samos were subsequently seized, and all these countries were united by the common name of Ionia, or, as it was sometimes called, the Pan-Ionian confederacy.

The renewal of hostilities between the Athenians and Dorians led to the establishment of a third series of Greek colonies in Asia (B.C. 994). The Dorians having been driven from their stronghold in Megara, were ashamed to return to the Peloponessus; part of them sailed to the islands of Crete and Rhodes, already peopled by Doric tribes; the rest settled in the peninsula of Caria, to which, in honour of their mother country, they gave the name of Doris.

CHAPTER IX.

THE HISTORY OF THE

GRECIAN STATES AND COLONIES

BEFORE THE PERSIAN WAR.

Section I.—*Topography of Sparta.*

The city of Sparta, called also Lacedæmon, a name properly belonging to the suburbs, was built on a series of hills, whose outlines are varied and romantic, along the right bank of the Eurotas, within sight of the chain of Mount Taygetum. We have already mentioned, that it was not originally surrounded by walls; but the highest of its eminences served as a citadel, and round this hill were ranged five towns, separated by considerable intervals, occupied by the five Spartan tribes. The great square or forum, in which the principal streets of these towns terminated, was embellished with temples and statues: it contained also the edifices in which the senate, the ephori, and other bodies of Spartan magistrates, were accustomed to assemble: there was besides a splendid portico, erected by the Spartans from their share of the spoils taken at the battle of Platææ, where the Persians were finally overthrown. Instead of being supported by pillars, the roof rested on gigantic statues, representing Persians habited in flowing robes.

On the highest of the eminences stood a temple of Minerva, which, as well as the grove that surrounded it, had the privileges of an asylum. It was built of brass, as that at Delphi had formerly been, and was profusely adorned with bas-reliefs, representing the achievements of Hercules, the Dioskouroi, and other heroes. To the right of the edifice was a statue of Jupiter, supposed to be the most ancient in Greece: it was composed of pieces of brass fastened together with nails. There were many monuments erected to fabulous heroes, to conquerors at the Olympic, and the great legislator Lycurgus was honoured with a temple; but only four or five of the most eminent warriors in the historic period received funeral honours, and even these appear to have been reluctantly conceded. Forty years had elapsed before the bones of Leonidas were conveyed to Sparta, and deposited in a tomb near the theatre; and it was at the same time that the names of the three hundred Spartans who had fallen with him at the pass of Thermopylæ were inscribed on a monumental column.

The greater part of these edifices had no pretensions to architectural beauty; they were of rude workmanship, and destitute of ornament. Private houses were small and unadorned; for the Spartans spent the greater part of their time in porticos and public halls. On the south side of the city was the Hippodromos, or course for horse and foot races; and at a little distance from that, the Platanistæ, or place of exercise for youth, shaded by beautiful plane-trees, and enclosed by the Eurotas on one side, a small river that falls into it on the other, and on the third by a narrow canal which united the two streams. It was entered by two bridges, on one of which stood the statue of Hercules, emblematic of all-subduing valour; on the other the statue of Lycurgus, the symbol of all-regulating law.

It was justly observed by Thucydides, that "if Lacedæmon were demolished, and nothing remained but its sacred buildings and foundations, men of a distant age would find a difficulty in believing the existence of its former power, or that it had possessed two of the five divisions of the Peloponnesus, or that it had commanded the whole country, as well as so many allies beyond the peninsula,—so inferior was the appearance of the city to its fame, being neither adorned with temples and splendid edifices, nor built in contiguity, but in separate quarters in the ancient method; whereas if Athens," adds the historian, "were reduced to a similar state, it would be supposed that her power had been twice as great as the reality."

Some idea may be formed, from the ancient authorities, of the position of the five Spartan tribes. 1. The Pitanetæ inhabited all the part of Sparta adjacent to the Agora or forum, the most desirable and fashionable part of the city, and extended to the river about the centre of its course in front of

Sparta, where probably was in all times the most frequented ford. 2. The Limnatæ inhabited the northern part of the city, near the Eurotas, deriving their name from the marshes which formerly existed there. 3. The Messoatæ occupied the south-eastern part of the town, not far from the race-course and exercise-ground. 4. The Ægeidæ possessed the north-western part of the city, near the tomb of the hero Ægeus, from whom they derived their name. And 5. the Cynosurenses inhabited the part adjacent to the branch of Taygetum, which overlooks Sparta, its rocky projections having been anciently called Cynosuræ (dogs' tails).

Section II.—*Legislation of Lycurgus, and Messenian Wars.*

FROM *B.C. 880 TO B.C. 500.

The Dorian conquerors of Laconia formed themselves into a permanent ruling caste, and reduced the greater part of the inhabitants of the country to a state of vassalage, or rather perfect slavery. During two centuries the Spartans were engaged in tedious wars with the Argives, and their state was agitated by domestic broils, resulting from the unequal division of property, the ambition of rival nobles, and the diminished power of the kings. At length Lycurgus having obtained the supreme authority, as guardian of his nephew Charilaus, directed his attention to establishing a system of law, which might prevent the recurrence of such disorders. The legislation of Lycurgus was not a written code; it consisted of Rhetrai, or short sentences like proverbs, containing directions for civil life, all of which were confirmed by the oracle of Delphi: hence many ancient usages of the Doric race, many customs borrowed from the Cretans and the institutions of Minos, and many things of later origin, have been erroneously attributed to this lawgiver. His great object was to insure the continuance of the Spartans as a dominant military caste, by perpetuating a race of athletic and warlike men; and hence his laws referred rather to domestic life and physical education than to the constitution of the state, or the form of its government.

He continued the relation of caste between the Spartans and Laconians, and the double line of kings as leaders in war and first magistrates in peace. He is said to have instituted the gerousia, or senate, of which no one could be a member who had not passed the age of sixty; but it is uncertain whether he founded the college of the five ephori, or inspectors, chosen annually, with powers somewhat similar to those of the Roman tribunes; he certainly did not invest them with the power they assumed in later ages. There were also popular assemblies; but they could originate no law, nor make any alteration in the resolutions submitted to them by the kings and the senate, their power being confined to a simple approbation or rejection.

The chief regulations in private life were, the equal distribution of lands, the removal of every species of luxury, the arrangement of domestic relations so as to insure a race of hardy citizens, and the complete establishment of slavery. Thus a military commonwealth was established in Greece, which for ever banished a chance of tranquillity; since the Spartan citizens must have been impelled to war by the restlessness common to man, when all the occupations of household life and of agriculture were entrusted to the care of the Helots, as their slaves were usually called.

The first great war in which the Spartans engaged was with their neighbours the Messenians, whose smiling fields were too tempting to those who inhabited the rugged mountains of Laconia. Complaints of mutual provocation, as is usual in such cases, were made on both sides; but it is confessed that the Spartans, without publishing a declaration of war, attacked the small town of Ampheia in the dead of night, and murdered the greater part of the inhabitants in their beds (B.C. 743). After a long series of sanguinary engagements, whose horrors were aggravated by cruel superstitions, the Messenians were totally subdued, and forced to give up half the revenue of their lands to the Spartans (B.C. 722). During this war, the Spartan army, consisting of the greater part of the citizens who had attained the military age, bound themselves by a voluntary oath not to return home until they had subdued their enemies. The war being protracted beyond expectation, the senate, fearing that the Spartan race would become extinct, invited the young men, who had not taken the obligation, to return home, and permitted them to have promiscuous intercourse with the women. The offspring of these irregular connexions were called Partheniæ; they had no certain father, nor were they, though citizens of Sparta, entitled to any inheritance. Finding themselves despised by the other Spartans, they entered into a conspiracy with the Helots, which was fortunately detected at the moment it was about to explode. The senate, however, was afraid to punish so powerful a body; sufficient means of transport, arms, and munitions, were supplied to the Partheniæ, who, under the guidance of Phalantus, proceeded to southern Italy, where they founded the city of Tarentum.

The oppression of the Spartans drove the Messenians to revolt, and they found a worthy leader in Aristomenes, a youth descended from the ancient line of Messenian kings. So rapid and decisive were his successes, that the Spartans sought the advice of the oracle, and received the mortifying response, that they should solicit a general from the Athenians. Ambassadors were sent to urge this request; and the Athenians sent back the poet Tyrtæus, who had, indeed, borne arms, but was never distinguished as a warrior. His patriotic odes roused the spirit of the Spartan soldiers, and they renewed the war with more zeal and greater success than ever. Notwithstanding these advantages acquired by the Spartans, Aristomenes protracted the defence of his country more than eleven years; but at length Messene was taken by treachery, and its heroic defenders forced to seek refuge in Arcadia. Here Aristomenes planned an expedition against Sparta, whose citizens were engaged in plundering Messenia; but he was betrayed by the Arcadian monarch, and his last plan for the redemption of his country frustrated (B.C. 671). While the Messenian exiles were in doubt whither to direct their course, they received an invitation from the prince of Rhegium, who was one of their own princely line, entreating them to aid him against the Zancleans, an Æolian colony on the opposite side of the Sicilian strait, by whose piratical incursions his subjects were cruelly harassed. They obeyed the summons, and took Zanclè by storm; but they had learned mercy from their own sufferings, and spared the lives of the citizens. Both united into one people, and the name of the city was changed to Messene, which, after the lapse of twenty-five centuries, it still retains with little alteration. Aristomenes did not accompany his countrymen; he travelled to Rhodes, and thence to Lydia, hoping probably to engage its monarch in some enterprise that might finally restore Messene. But upon his arrival at Sardis, he was seized with a disease which put an end to his life.

Sparta had conquered, but the struggle had greatly weakened the strength of the state; and in her subsequent wars with the Tegeans and Argives, she was far from maintaining her ancient superiority in arms. The important island of Cythera was, however, wrested from the Argives about B.C. 550.

Section III.—*Topography of Athens.*

Athens was situated in a plain, which, on the south-west, extended for about four miles towards the sea and the harbours, but on the other side was enclosed by mountains. Several rocky hills arose in the plain itself; the largest and highest of which was fortified by Cecrops as the citadel, or Acropolis, and was sometimes called Cecropia. Around this the city was built, most of the buildings, however, spreading towards the sea. The summit of the hill was nearly level for a space of about eight hundred feet in length and four hundred in breadth; as if Nature herself had prepared a fit locality for those master-pieces of architecture which announced at a distance the splendour of Athens. The only road that led to the Acropolis passed through the Propylæa, a magnificent gateway adorned with two wings, and two temples full of the finest pieces of sculpture and painting. It was erected under the administration of Pericles, by the architect Mnesicles, and was decorated with the admirable sculptures of Phidias. Through these splendid portals was an ascent by marble steps to the summit of the hill on which were erected the temples of the guardian deities of Athens. On the left was the temple of Pallas Athenè (Minerva), the protectress of cities, containing a column fabled to have fallen from heaven, and an olive-tree believed to have sprung spontaneously from the earth at the mandate of the goddess. Beyond this was a temple of Neptune. On the right side arose the Parthenon, sacred to the virgin Minerva, the glory of Athens, the noblest triumph of Grecian architecture. From whatever quarter the traveller arrived, whether by land or sea, the first thing he saw was the Parthenon rearing up its lofty head above the city and the citadel. Its ruins, sublime in decay, are still the first object that strikes the eye of a stranger. It was of the Doric order, built of that beautiful white marble found in the quarries of Mount Pentelicus. It was about one hundred feet wide, two hundred and twenty-six feet deep, and seventy feet high. There was a double portico of columns at the two fronts, and single rows along each side. There was an architrave, or frieze, along the exterior of the nave, beautifully sculptured with the representation of a procession in honour of Minerva. Within the temple was the statue of Minerva carved by Phidias, so celebrated for its size, the richness of its materials, and the exquisite beauty of the workmanship. It was made of gold and ivory, and was nearly forty feet in height. She was represented erect, covered with her ægis or buckler, holding in one hand a lance, and in the other a figure of Victory six feet high.

Behind the temple was the public treasury, in which individuals deposited such sums of money as they did not think it prudent to keep at home; there likewise were preserved the offerings made to the goddess, which usually consisted of splendid coronals, vases, and little figures of the divinities either of gold or silver. The Athenian ladies frequently presented their ornaments and trinkets at the shrine of the goddess. These treasures were entrusted to annual officers, who accounted annually to their successors for their charge, by delivering to them a list specifying the weight of each article and the name of the donor. The inventory, which was immediately cut in marble, was both a testimonial of the fidelity of the keeper, and an incentive to further liberality.

The prospect from the Acropolis and the Parthenon commanded, on the right, the two peaks of Hymettus; on the north, Pentelicus, with its marble quarries; to the north-west, Mount Cithæron was discernible at a great distance, raising its lofty summit above the smaller mountains; and Mount Laurium, with its rich mines of silver, lay to the south-east, almost at the end of the peninsula. But the most delightful prospect was towards the south-west, where the eye could range freely over the three harbours and the Saronic Bay, with the islands of Salamis and Ægina, as far as the Corinthian Acropolis. Many of the chief places of the cantons, or démoi, into which Attica was divided, might also be seen; and even the towns and villages on the mountains were distinctly perceptible. No one of these was important as a city, and yet there were few which had not something worthy of observation, either statues, altars, or temples; for to whatever part of his country the Athenian strayed, he always beheld something to remind him that he was in Attica.

At the foot of the Acropolis, on one side, was the Odeum, or music-hall, and the Theatre of Bacchus, where the tragic contests were celebrated on the festival of that deity; on the other side was the Prytaneum, where the chief magistrates and most meritorious citizens were honourably entertained at a table furnished at the public expense. A small valley called Cœle (*the hollow*) lay between the Acropolis and the hill on which the court of Areopagus held its sessions; and it also separated the Areopagus from the Pnyx, a small rocky hill on which the general assemblies of the people were held. It was remarkable only for the meanness and simplicity of its furniture, which formed a striking contrast to the grandeur of the neighbouring buildings. Here the spot from which the eminent orators addressed the people may still be seen; for it is imperishable, being cut in the natural rock, and it has been recently cleared from rubbish, as well as the four steps by which it was ascended. As the harbour of the Peiræeus may be distinctly seen from the top of the hill, the orators, while the democracy and commercial interest maintained their ascendency, always turned their faces towards the harbour, in order to remind the people that the strength of the state consisted in its navy and its trade. The aristocracy and landed interest were greatly offended by this custom, asserting that the first legislators only favoured agriculture, and that Themistocles, by uniting the city to the harbour, and thus, as it were, connecting sea and land, had given an undue preponderance to the mercantile interest and the multitude: accordingly, the first measure adopted by the thirty tyrants was to change the direction of the béma, or pulpit, and compel the orators to turn their back upon the sea.

Beyond the Pnyx lay the Ceramícus, or pottery-ground, containing the market-place. This was a large square, surrounded on all sides with statues and public buildings; at the south was the senate-house, and the statues of the Eponymi, ten heroes from whom the tribes of Athens received their respective names. At the east were erected two splendid *stoai*, or porticoes; that of the Hermæ, or statues of Mercury, on which were inscribed the names of the citizens, allies, and slaves, who had distinguished themselves in the Persian war; and that called Pœcile, ornamented with many splendid paintings, particularly one representing Miltiades at the battle of Marathon. Under this *stoa* the philosopher Zeno used to lecture his pupils, whence his followers are called Stoics.

There were three principal gymnasia, or places of public exercise, near the city, where philosophers and rhetoricians delivered their lectures. The most celebrated of these was the Academy, deriving its name from having been the country-seat of the wealthy Academus, who spent the greater part of a large fortune in ornamenting this delightful spot. Here Plato delivered his eloquent lectures, and hence his followers are called Academics. The Lyceum, on the opposite side of the city, near the Ilyssus, was chosen by Aristotle for his school after his return from Macedon, the Academy having been pre-occupied by Xenocrates. He generally instructed his pupils while walking about the groves and avenues of this highly cultivated place, and on this account his followers were called Peripatetics. Cynosarges was about a mile from the Lyceum, and was the residence of Antisthenes, the founder of the Cynic sect.

The whole country round Athens, particularly the long road

to the Peiræeus, was ornamented with monuments of all kinds, especially with tombs of great poets, statesmen, and warriors. This road was enclosed by a double wall, called the northern and southern, erected under the administration of Themistocles: it was nearly five miles in length on both sides, and enclosed the two harbours, Peiræeus and Phalereus. It was rather more than eighty feet high, built entirely of freestone, and so broad that two baggage-waggons could pass each other. The Peiræeus and Phalereus, but especially the former, might be regarded as little cities, with public squares, temples, market-places, &c.; and the commercial crowd that enlivened the quays gave the chief harbour a more animated appearance than Athens itself. The Munychian port lay east of Athens, and, like the others, was formed naturally by the bays of the coast. It was a place of considerable natural strength, and was garrisoned by the Lacedæmonians after they had subdued Athens. We cannot better conclude this sketch of the most beautiful city of ancient times than by quoting a fragment of the lost comedies of Lysippus: "Whoever does not desire to see Athens is a fool; whoever sees it without being delighted is a greater fool; but he is the greatest fool of all, who sees it, admires it, and leaves it."

SECTION IV.—*The History of Athens to the Beginning of the Persian War.*

FROM B.C. * 1300 TO B.C. 500.

THE political history of Athens begins properly with the reign of Theseus, who succeeded his father Ægeus about B.C. 1300. Certain institutions, such as the court of Areopagus, and the division of the people into eupatridæ (*nobles*), geórgoi (*husbandmen*), and demiurgi (*mechanics*), are so manifestly derived from the Egyptian system of caste, that we may without hesitation assign them to Cecrops. Theseus, however, deserves to be regarded as the founder of the state, since, instead of the four independent districts, or démoi, into which Attica was divided, he established one body politic, and made

Athens the seat of government. Among his successors, the most remarkable were Mnestheus, who fell before Troy, and Codrus, whose generous devotion, as has been already related, led to the total abolition of royalty. After the abolition of royalty (B.C. 1068), thirteen archons of his family ruled in succession, differing from kings only in being accountable for their administration. The first was Medon, the last Alcmæon; after his death (B.C. 752), archons were chosen every ten years from the family of Codrus. There were seven of these, the last of whom ceased to rule B.C. 682. Nine annual archons were then appointed by the powerful class of nobility, consisting not only of the descendants of such foreign princes as had taken refuge in Athens, but of those Athenian families which time and accident had raised to opulence and distinction. The powers of these magistrates were not equal; their rank and offices were so arranged, that the prerogatives of the former kings and the preceding archons were divided among the three first of the nine. Nothing was gained by the great body of the people during these revolutions. The equestrian order, so called from their fighting on horseback, which before the improvement of tactics rendered them superior in every rencounter with the disorderly rabble, enjoyed all authority, religious, civil, and military. The Athenian populace were reduced to a condition of miserable servitude, nor did they recover even the semblance of freedom until the institutions of Theseus were revived and reformed by Solon. An inconsiderable number of laws, almost as ancient as the state, usually called the Royal Laws, were insufficient to regulate the new interests, necessities, and vices, created by the progress of society; the lives and fortunes of individuals were consequently left at the discretion of magistrates, who were too much disposed to decide according to party prejudices or their own private interests.

In this confusion, which threatened instant destruction to the state, Draco was chosen to prepare a code of laws (B.C. 622) by which the administration of justice might be regulated. He was a man of unswerving integrity, pure patriotism, and rigid morals, but of unexampled severity. His laws bore the impress of his character; the punishment of death was denounced against all crimes, small as well as great; and this indiscriminate cruelty rendered the whole code inoperative. Human nature revolted against such legal butchery; and Draco, to avoid the public indignation, fled to Ægina, where he died an exile.

This ineffectual effort only augmented the divisions of the state; the excesses of the aristocratic factions produced such violent indignation, that a citizen named Cylon formed the project of seizing the sovereign power by the aid of the people (B.C. 598). He was besieged in the citadel, where he long defended himself; but at length, wanting provisions, and destitute of every hope of succour, he eluded punishment by flight. His followers took refuge in the temple of Minerva; but they were induced to quit the asylum by a promise of mercy, and then treacherously massacred. The Alcmæonidæ were the leaders in this act of perfidy, which proved fatal to the power of its authors; for it long afforded a pretence for restraining aristocratic influence.

The indignation excited by this butchery was universal; treachery had been aggravated by impiety, for many of the victims fell at the altar of the awful Eumenides. Amidst the general consternation, news arrived that the city of Nisæa and the island of Salamis had been taken by the Dorians of Megara; and this melancholy intelligence being followed by the appearance of a pestilence, convinced the Athenians that they had provoked the righteous indignation of heaven. The oracles being consulted, declared that the holy places, having been polluted by blood-guiltiness, should be purified by peculiar circumstances of expiation. The Athenians sent to Crete for Epimenides, a fanatic or impostor, who was supposed, in that superstitious age, to have a direct communication with the divinities, and who had acquired such a reputation for wisdom and sanctity, that nations suffering under any calamity supplicated him to teach them the means of averting the anger of the gods. On his arrival at Athens, he first tranquillised the minds of the people by his extraordinary eloquence, and then directed them to build new temples and altars for immolating the victims he specified (B.C. 594). When public confidence was restored, he returned home, refusing any reward but a branch of Minerva's sacred olive, and the friendship of the Athenians for Gnossus, his native city.

Soon after the departure of Epimenides, the factions were again revived with fresh fury, and the state was reduced to perfect anarchy. To remedy these disorders, Solon, who had already won the confidence of his countrymen by planning and accomplishing an enterprise for the recovery of Salamis, was unanimously raised to the dignity of first magistrate, legislator, and sovereign arbiter (B.C. 594). He was eminently qualified for this important station. Descended from the ancient kings of Athens, he applied himself in early life to commercial pursuits, and, having secured a competency by honourable industry, he travelled to distant lands in search of knowledge. Such was his success, that he was reckoned the chief of the sages commonly called the Seven Wise Men of Greece, who in his age laid the foundation of Grecian philosophy. The other six were, Thales of Miletus, Pittacus of Mitylene, Bias of Priene, Cleobulus of Lindus, Myson of Chena, and Chilo of Lacedæmon. To these is sometimes added Anacharsis, whom the celebrity of these Greeks brought from the uncivilised regions of Scythia to enjoy the delights of their conversation.

The chief object of Solon's legislation was to restrain the excessive power of the aristocracy, without, however, introducing a pure democracy. To remedy the pressure of immediate difficulties, he abolished all the laws of Draco, except those against murder. The state of debtors calling loudly for relief, he made an equitable adjustment of the claims of creditors; but at the same time conciliated capitalists by raising the value of money. He abolished slavery and imprisonment for debt, which had led to great abuses and cruelties.

His laws for the constitution of the state evince a thorough knowledge of republican governments, and their effect on human nature. Instead of regarding morals as subordinate to polity, the fatal error made by Lycurgus, he regarded polity as of less importance than morals; and he left the constitution free to receive such reforms and improvements as might be rendered necessary by the progress of society.

Without abolishing the ancient local divisions into four phylæ (wards), and more than one hundred and seventy districts (demoi), he arranged the citizens in four classes, according to their property, measured in agricultural produce. 1. the first class were the pentacosi-medimni, whose annual income exceeded five hundred bushels (medimni); 2. the knights (hippéis), whose revenue was equal to four hundred; 3. the zeugitæ, who had three hundred; and 4. the thetes, whose yearly revenue fell short of that sum. Citizens of all classes had a right of attending and voting at the popular assemblies and in the courts of judicature; but magisterial offices were limited to the three first classes. The archonship was left unaltered; but it was ordained that none of these magistrates should hold military command during his year of office. A council of four hundred was chosen from the three first classes, possessing senatorial authority: the members were selected by lot; but they were obliged to undergo a very strict examination into their past lives and characters before they were permitted to enter upon office. The archons were bound to consult the council in every important public matter; and no subject could be discussed in the general assembly of the people which had not previously received the sanction of the four hundred.

The popular assemblies consisted of all the four classes, and usually met on the rocky hill called the Pnyx, described in the preceding section. They had the right of confirming or rejecting new laws, of electing the magistrates, of discussing all public affairs referred to them by the council, and of judging in all state trials.

According to Solon's plan, the court of Areopagus should have been the chief pillar of the Athenian constitution. Before his time it was a mere engine of aristocratic oppression; but Solon modified its constitution, and enlarged its powers. It was composed of persons who had held the office of archon, and was made the supreme tribunal in all capital cases. It was likewise entrusted with the superintendence of morals, with the censorship upon the conduct of the archons at the expiration of their office; and it had besides the privilege of amending or rescinding the measures that had passed the general assemblies of the people.

Soon after this constitution was established, Solon was sent as a deputy to the Amphictyonic council at Delphi, and had no small share in stimulating that body to undertake the first sacred war. This event is recommended to our attention both from the cause in which it originated, and the consequences by which it was attended,—consequences which, after the lapse of nearly three centuries, tended in no small degree to hasten the downfal of Grecian liberty. The Crisseans, possessing the best sea-port on the Corinthian Gulf, and the most convenient to persons going on pilgrimage to Delphi, levied a heavy tax on all who passed through their city, and thus greatly diminished the emoluments of the Delphians. Mutual reproaches and accusations soon engendered a fierce spirit of hostility: the Crisseans took up arms, entered the sacred territories, and not only ravaged the country, but even plundered the shrine of Apollo. The Amphictyonic council, dismayed rather than enraged by such a daring outrage, were slow to punish the transgressors; but Solon roused them to avenge this gross violation of religion and national law. The war was protracted ten years; but it terminated in the final destruction of the Crissean community, and the dedication of their territory to the deity whose temple they had sacrilegiously plundered (B.C. 590). The termination of the war was celebrated by the revival of the Pythian games, which had been discontinued during the contest.

Scarcely had the liberties of Athens been established, when they were again subverted by the usurpation of Peisistratus. Like Solon, the usurper was descended from the ancient kings of Athens. He was also possessor of an enormous fortune, which he distributed to the poor with lavish munificence. His generosity, his eloquence, and his courteous manners, won for him universal favour; but he had the art to persuade the lower ranks of his countrymen, that his popularity had rendered him odious to the nobles, and that the protection of a body-guard was necessary to the safety of his life. Scarcely had this been granted, when he seized on the Acropolis, and made himself absolute master of Athens (B.C. 561). Solon refused the usurper's offers of favour and protection: he went into voluntary exile, and died, or at least was buried, at Salamis. Megacles, the chief of the powerful family of the Alcmæonidæ, retired, with all his attendants and political friends, beyond the boundaries of Attica; but he entered into a secret intrigue with Lycurgus, the chief of another faction, and by their joint efforts Peisistratus was driven into exile about twelve months after he had obtained the sovereignty.

Megacles soon quarreled with Lycurgus, and opened a negotiation with Peisistratus, offering to restore him, if he would become his son-in-law. The terms were accepted, and Peisistratus was again summoned to assume sovereign power, amid the general exultation of the people. A quarrel with Megacles drove him a second time into banishment; but he returned again at the head of an army, and having recovered the reins of power, held them without interruption to the day of his death. The power, thus illegally acquired, was administered with equity and mildness. Peisistratus ceased not to exert himself to extend the glory of Athens, and secure the happiness of the Athenians. His court was the resort of all the learned men of the age; and to his patronage we owe the first revised edition of the works of Homer. So conscious were the Alcmæonidæ, who had gone into exile after his third usurpation, of the merits of his government, that they made no attempt to disturb its stability, but remained quiet in Macedonia.

On the death of Peisistratus (B.C. 528), his sons Hipparchus and Hippias succeeded to his power, but not to his prudence and abilities. After a joint reign of fourteen years, Hipparchus was murdered by two young Athenians, Harmodius and Aristogeiton, whose resentment he had provoked by an atrocious insult (B.C. 514). The cruelty with which Hippias punished all whom he suspected of having had a share in his brother's death alienated the affections of the people, and encouraged the Alcmæonidæ to make an effort for his expulsion. By large bribes to the Delphian priesthood, they obtained a response from the oracle commanding the Spartans to expel the Peisistratidæ; and that superstitious people immediately sent an army for that purpose (B.C. 510). After a brief struggle, Hippias was forced to abandon Athens, and thenceforward lived in perpetual exile.

Scarcely was the tyrant expelled, when the state was rent in sunder by the rivalry of contending factions. Clisthenes, the son of Megacles, headed one; the other, chiefly composed of the aristocracy, was led by Isagoras. Clisthenes depended for success principally on the aid of the people; and to enlarge their power, he increased the number of tribes from four to ten, and added a hundred new members to the council. Isagoras applied for aid to foreign states, and received armies to support his cause from the Spartans, the Corinthians, the Bœotians, the Chalcidians, and the Æginetans. But the confederates could not agree; Demaratus, one of the Lacedæmonian kings, espoused the cause of the Athenians, in opposition to his colleague Cleomenes, who was the patron of Isagoras; and these dissensions broke up the alliance. After some time, the Spartans, having discovered the trick played upon them by the Delphian oracle, wished to restore Hippias; but, finding their allies universally opposed to the project, they abandoned him to his fate, and he fled to the court of Persia, where his exertions greatly contributed to the forcing Darius into a war against Greece.

SECTION V.—*Historical Notices of the minor Grecian States previous to the Persian War.*

FROM B.C. 1100 TO B.C. 500.

AFTER the capture of Thebes by the Epigoni, the Bœotians were expelled by Thracian hordes, and retired to Arne in Thessaly; but about the time of the great Dorian migration they returned to the land of their forefathers, and became united with some Æolian tribes.

Royalty was abolished upon the death of Xuthus (B.C. 1126), and the Bœotians formed a confederation of as many states as there were cities in the province: at the head of which was Thebes, but with very indefinite privileges. The constitutions of the states were unfixed; and they continually fluctuated between a licentious democracy and a tyrannical oligarchy. This great evil, combined with the unsettled nature of the confederation, prevented the Bœotians from taking a leading share in the affairs of Greece. General affairs were decided in councils, held in each of the four districts into which the province was divided; and these assemblies united to elect seven Bœotarchs, who were supreme magistrates in peace, and generals in war.

Acarnania, Ætolia, and Locris, offer nothing remarkable; and the most important event in the history of Phocis was the sacred war, which has been described in the last section. The states of Thessaly were for the most part governed by arbitrary individuals, of whom the most memorable were the tyrants of Larissa, belonging to the family of the Aleuadæ, which claimed to be descended from Hercules. In Epirus the most powerful tribe was that of the Molossi, governed by a family of kings called Æacidæ, which claimed for its founder Pyrrhus or Neoptolemus, the son of Achilles.

In the Peloponnesus, Corinth was the most remarkable state next to Sparta. At the time of the Dorian conquest of southern Greece, its throne was seized by Aletes, whose descendants retained the power and title of royalty for five generations. On the death of Telessus, the last of the Aletian race, Bacchis usurped the throne (B.C. 777), and his descendants, called Bacchiadæ, held the regal authority for five generations more. Telestes, the last of these kings, having been murdered, the kingly office was abolished, and a species of oligarchy established in its stead, under yearly magistrates, called prytanes, chosen exclusively from the house of Bacchis. It would have been scarcely possible for such a narrow oligarchy to maintain its ground, even if it had used its power with moderation and wisdom; but the Bacchiads, proud of their race and great commercial wealth, insulted their subjects; and Cypselus, an opulent citizen of Æolian descent, aided by the commonalty, usurped the government (B.C. 657), and held the supreme power for thirty years. On his death, he was succeeded by his son Periander, who is sometimes ranked among the Seven Wise Men of Greece, though he is described by many writers as a rapacious, oppressive, and cruel despot. His reign lasted forty years, and yet is supposed to have been shortened either by violence or grief for the loss of his son. He was succeeded by his nephew Psammetichus, whose reign lasted only three years, when he was expelled by his subjects, assisted by a Spartan army (B.C. 584). Nearly at the same time, another branch of the Cypselids lost their throne in Ambracia, a powerful Corinthian colony on the coast of Epirus. This revolution was followed by the establishment of a commercial aristocracy, whose exact constitution is unknown, but which long kept Corinth in close alliance with Sparta. The Corinthian trade consisted chiefly in the exchange of Asiatic and Italian merchandise, for which her position gave her many peculiar advantages. Like other commercial states, she planted several colonies, the chief of which were, in the west, Corcyra, Ambracia, Epidamnus, Leucas, and Syracuse; and in the east, Potidæa. The period of Corinth's highest prosperity closed with the government of the Cypselids; and the loss of Corcyra, which had been kept in subjection by Periander, but revolted after his death, proved a blow to her power which she never recovered. The naval engagement between the Corcyrians and Corinthians (B.C. 650) is the first sea-fight recorded in history.

The history of Sicyon and the other Achæan states presents a series of revolutions similar to those of Corinth. It is not precisely known at what period royalty was abolished; but, after various revolutions and usurpations, they all adopted republican institutions, about the time that the Cypselids were expelled from Corinth.

The constitution of Arcadia became republican when Aristodemus, its last king, was stoned by his subjects for having betrayed Aristomenes and the Messenians. Its chief states were Tegæa and Mantinea, the former of which long maintained a doubtful contest for supremacy with Sparta.

The regal dignity was abolished in Argos so early as B.C. 984; but nothing is known of the circumstances that led to the change, or the peculiar nature of the republic by which it was succeeded. The Argives at an early age conquered Mycenæ and Tiryns; but the Argolic states in the south, Epidaurus and Trœzene, maintained their independence.

Elis preserved its internal peace, owing to the wise laws of Iphitus, a contemporary of Lycurgus; while the sanctity of its soil ensured its external security. After the abolition of royal power, two supreme magistrates were chosen, called Hellanodicæ, to whose office was added the charge of superintending the Olympic games. Their number was subsequently increased to ten, one being chosen from each of the Elian tribes; and their power was limited by a senate of ninety, whose members were chosen for life.

SECTION VI.—*History of the principal Grecian Islands.*

THE revolutions in the Grecian islands were very similar to those on the continent, republican constitutions having succeeded to monarchy in most of them. After the Athenians had acquired the sovereignty of the sea, the insular states lost their independence; for though they were called confederates, they were treated as subjects; no change, however, was made in their internal constitutions. We shall only notice the islands that were most remarkable in history.

Corcyra was occupied by a Corinthian colony under Chersicrates (B.C. 753), who expelled or subdued the former inhabitants. As the leader and most of his companions had been driven into exile by political commotions, they retained but little affection for the parent state; while the rapid progress of the Corcyrean power excited the commercial jealousy of Corinth. These circumstances led to an open war, when Epidamnus, a Corcyrean colony founded on the western coast of Macedonia, known in later ages by the name of Dyracchium, sought the protection of Corinth. When the struggle commenced, Corcyra was at the summit of its greatness, being able, without foreign aid, to man a fleet of one hundred and twenty war-galleys. The Corcyrean constitution appears to have been originally aristocratic or oligarchical, like that of most Dorian states; but after the Persian wars a democratic faction arose, powerfully supported by the Athenians, which produced the most violent internal commotions, and ended in the total ruin of Corcyra.

Ægina, originally called Œnona, was first colonised by some Æolian Myrmidons from Thessaly (B.C. 1358). About two hundred years after, it was seized by a Dorian colony from Epidaurus; it, however, soon shook off the yoke of the mother city, and rapidly grew, by commerce and navigation, to be one of the first Grecian states. It even established colonies of its own in Crete and Pontus. Ægina was long the successful rival of Athens, and maintained its naval supremacy until near the commencement of the second Persian war, when it was subdued by Themistocles (B.C. 485).

The island of Eubœa received many different colonies from the mainland of Greece; but its cities were not united by any confederation, each possessing a separate constitution. Its chief towns, Chalcis and Eretria, were ruled by an aristocracy called hippobatæ, or knights; but their rule was frequently interrupted by the usurpation of tyrants. It was subdued by the Athenians after the Persian wars; but the islanders made several sanguinary struggles to regain their independence.

The Cyclades were originally peopled by some Carian tribes, but these were subsequently expelled by Ionian and Dorian colonies. They were all, except Delos, rendered tributary to Athens, when that state acquired the supremacy of the sea.

Crete was celebrated in the heroic ages for the laws of Minos (* B.C. 1300), from whose code Lycurgus is said to have borrowed several of his institutions. After the death of Cleanthus (* B.C. 800), republican constitutions were adopted in the principal cities, which thenceforth became independent states. The island was severely harassed by intestine commotions, arising chiefly from the jealousy between the two principal cities, Gortina and Gnossus: the disputes of these states, nearly equal in power, shook all Crete, until the state of Cydonia, by joining one side or the other, turned the balance. After the abolition of royalty, nearly the same form of constitution was established in all the Cretan states; the government was entrusted to a senate, called gerusia, and to ten magistrates, named cosmi, who united the powers of the Roman censors and consuls, having both the regulation of morals and the direction of all civil and military affairs. The Cretans rarely engaged in foreign wars, but they were almost incessantly involved in mutual hostilities; a circumstance that tended greatly to degrade the national character.

Cyprus was only partially colonised by the Greeks, whose principal settlement was at Salamis, founded by Teucer a little after the Trojan war (B.C. 1100). The island was successively subject to the Phœnicians, Egyptians, and Persians. The kings of Salamis frequently revolted against their Persian masters, and always maintained a qualified independence. When Alexander the Great beseiged Tyre (B.C. 332), he was voluntarily joined by the nine Cypriot kings, and thenceforth the island was annexed to the Macedonian monarchy.

The history of Rhodes belongs properly to the portion of this work that treats of the successors of Alexander, to which we refer our readers.

SECTION VII.—*History of the Greek Colonies in Asia Minor.*

FROM B.C. 1200 TO B.C. 500.

THE colonies founded by the Greeks were the most numerous and important established by any nation. They all acted a very conspicuous part in accelerating the progress of civilisation, developing the sources of trade, and facilitating the commercial intercourse of nations; and many of them attained such eminence as to acquire a commanding influence in political history. These remarks are especially applicable to the colonies founded by the Hellenic race between the period of the Dorian migration and the final subversion of Grecian liberty by the triumph of the Macedonians. There were colonies established in Italy by the Pelasgi previous to this period, but their history is obscure; and the little known of them belongs rather to the annals of western Europe than to those of Greece.

The military settlements founded by the Macedonians after the death of Alexander were as much garrisons as colonies; and the notice of them belongs to the history of the successors of that monarch.

The colonies that must first engage our attention are those that were established along the western coast of Asia Minor, from the Hellespont to the confines of Cilicia, in consequence of the revolutions produced by the Dorian migration and conquest of the Peloponnesus. They were established by the Æolians, Ionians, and Carians; their commerce soon exceeded that of the parent states; and in them were produced the first of Grecian poets, Homer and Alcæus; and the first of Grecian philosophers, Thales and Pythagoras.

The Æolians, after the conquest of the Peloponnesus, quitted their native land in small bands, headed by different princes of the house of Pelops, advancing slowly through northern Greece in search of a new residence. On their route, some of the emigrants stopped in Attica; but their place was supplied by recruits from Bœotia and Phocis. They settled for a time in Thrace, whence they passed over, after the lapse of a generation, to Asia (* B.C. 1124), and occupied the coasts of Mysia and Caria, giving to the strip of land they colonised the name of Æolis. They acquired possession, also, of the islands of Lesbos, Tenedos, and the cluster called the Hecatonnesi (hundred islands). Twelve cities were erected on the mainland by the Æolians, of which the chief were Cymê and Smyrna. The latter city was destroyed by the Lydians (* B.C. 600), and was not restored until four hundred years later, when it became a flourishing Macedonian colony. The Æolian cities maintained their independence until the age of Cyrus, when those on the mainland were subdued by the Persians. When Athens acquired supremacy by sea, the insular states were forced to submit to her authority, and were in general ruled with great severity. Though the Æolian cities were not united by any formal confederation, Mitylene, in the island of Lesbos, was usually regarded as the common metropolis of the nation; and in that city were chosen the æsymnetæ, magistrates occasionally elected with absolute power to remedy the disorders produced by faction and civil commotions. The most celebrated of these æsymnetæ was Pittacus of Mitylene, the contemporary of Sappho and Alcæus, who flourished about B.C. 600, and was deservedly ranked amongst the most eminent sages of Greece.

The Ionian migration took place some years after the Æolian, about B.C. 1044. It was the largest that ever left Greece; and fortunately it is that with whose details we are best acquainted. It originated in the abolition of royalty at Athens: the sons of Codrus were naturally reluctant to live as private individuals in a country where they deemed that they had a right to rule as princes; and when they declared their design of leading a colony into Asia, they were readily joined by the Ionian exiles from the northern Peloponnesus, who were straitened for room in Attica, and by large bands of emigrants from the neighbouring states, actuated by political discontent, or the mere love of change. They assembled in the Prytaneum at Athens, the metropolis of the Ionian states, and were supplied liberally with ships and munitions of war. Their voyage, nevertheless, was tedious, and interrupted by several disasters. They delayed for some time at the Cyclades, both to refresh themselves after their toils, and to establish colonies in some of the islands. Thence they pursued their voyage to Asia Minor, and landed on the coast south of Æolis, at that time inhabited by a mixed race of Carians, Leleges, and Mygdonians. It was not until after a long series of sanguinary wars that these barbarians resigned their lands to the intruders; but they were finally subdued, and the Ionians acquired possession of the whole of the valuable district between Miletus and Mount Sipylus.

Scarcely was the war terminated, when the Ionians began to erect cities: they established twelve, united by an Amphictyonic confederacy, viz. Ephesus, Erythræ, Clazomenæ, Colophon, Myus, Miletus, Priène, Phocæa, Lebédos, Samos, Teos, and Chios, of which the three last were insular stations.

Miletus was the chief of the Ionian colonies: it had been successively occupied by the Leleges, the Carians, and the Cretans; the latter of whom were its masters when it was besieged by the Ionians. The town was obstinately defended, which so exasperated the victors, that they put all the male inhabitants to the sword, and only spared the women because they were in want of wives.

Ephesus, though not the metropolis, was the most renowned of the Ionian cities. Its original foundation is attributed to the Amazons, a fabulous nation of female warriors. Its temple and shrine of Diana were held in the highest reverence by the nations both of Europe and Asia. The worship of the goddess is said to have been introduced by a Crètan colony, though it may perhaps be attributed with more probability to the Phrygians. When captured by the Ionians, the lives of the inhabitants were spared, and the sacred precincts of the temple assigned to them as a residence.

Phocæa was one of the latest cities founded by the Ionians. It derived its name from a later immigration of Phocæans, whom the fame of the success of the former adventurers had invited into Asia. It had the most extensive trade by sea of any of the Grecian states, and was particularly remarkable for its commerce with the remote parts of western Europe. It was commercially connected with Miletus, which engrossed the chief part of the trade to the Euxine and Black Seas; and both, in the days of their prosperity, from the eighth to the sixth century before the Christian era, were no unworthy rivals of Tyre and Carthage. Phocæa founded several colonies, of which the most remarkable was Massiliæ (*Marseilles*), in Gaul, whither the Phocæans removed when their city was taken by the Persians.

Colophon was almost the only Ionian city the original inhabitants of which received the colonists without a struggle. In later ages this city became remarkable for its formidable cavalry, whose resistless charge was supposed sufficient to decide an engagement: whence "to add the colophon" became a proverbial phrase for completing any undertaking.

Samos was the most important of the insular cities for its trade and naval power. It had been originally colonised by another Ionian tribe, a little after the Persian war; and the descendants of these settlers were still in possession when they were forced to share their lands with the new adventurers. The most brilliant period of its history was under the administration of the tyrant Polycrates (B.C. 540), whose extraordinary good fortune during the greater part of his career is sadly contrasted with his miserable and disgraceful end. The island was for a brief space subject to the Persians; and during this period was almost depopulated by the desperate struggles made to regain its independence. It afterwards became subject to the Athenians, who established a democratic government in the island, and made it their chief naval depôt and magazine during the Peloponnesian wars.

Chios is said to have entered voluntarily into the Ionian confederation, probably because its possessors already belonged to that branch of the Hellenic race. It was scarcely inferior to Samos in power or wealth, and its inhabitants were more devotedly attached to freedom. Though it submitted to the Persians with the rest of the Ionian cities, it was the first to throw off the yoke, when the struggle for independence commenced; and it contributed ninety-eight war-galleys to the confederate fleet. After the close of the Persian war, it acknowledged the supremacy of Athens, but yielded only a reluctant and hollow obedience to that haughty republic. The Chians made an excellent use of their opulence, and did not, like their neighbours, risk their happiness for schemes of ambition.

All the Ionian cities were united by an Amphictyonic confederacy. Deputies from the different states met, at stated times, in a temple of Neptune, erected on the headland of Mycale, which they named Heliconean, from Helice, the chief of their ancient cities in the northern Peloponnesus. Here they deliberated on all matters that affected the Pan-Ionian league; but the council never interfered with the domestic government of the several cities. They also celebrated festivals and public games, which rivalled in magnificence those of Greece. In the midst of their prosperity, the Ionian cities became engaged in a long and arduous struggle with the Lydian kings, which continued almost without intermission until both were absorbed in the rising greatness of the Persian empire.

Neither the extent nor progress of the Dorian colonies could compare with those we have just described. Limited to a narrow and not very fruitful territory, their confederation always continued in a state of feebleness; and, with the exception of Halicarnassus, which, at a comparatively recent age, became the capital of an opulent monarchy; and the isle of Rhodes, whose daring navigators rivalled those of the most potent commercial states,—there is scarcely a Dorian state that rose above mediocrity.

The Dorians, after the conquest of the Peloponnesus, meditated new acquisitions; but, being checked by the Athenians at Megara, they proceeded in detached bands to the coast of Caria, and to the islands of Cos and Rhodes. It is impossible to assign the exact age of these migrations; but they were certainly later than the Ionian and Æolian: they appear also to have been conducted without any definite plan, and to have taken place at very different times. The six cities forming the Doric confederation, called Hexapolis, were Halicarnassus and Cnidus on the Carian peninsula, Cos in the island of the same name, and Ialyssus, Camirus, and Lindus, in the island of Rhodes, three cities that sunk into insignificance when the city of Rhodes was built, at the close of the Persian war. Halicarnassus, from some unknown cause, was excluded from the confederation some time before the Persian war, and became the capital of the Carian monarchy, whose most remarkable sovereigns were Mausolus and Artemisia.

Cnidus is supposed to have been originally built by the Pelasgians, and to have been the first Dorian colony established in Asia; and it had consequently some claim to be regarded as the head of the Hexapolis. It was at the temple of Apollo-Triopius, in the neighbourhood of Cnidus, that the six Dorian cities had their common sanctuary; and there the deputies of the confederation assembled to deliberate on public affairs. The constitution of Cnidus was subject to violent revolutions; the most important of which terminated in the subversion of the oligarchy, and the establishment of a turbulent democracy in its place.

The Dorians submitted without a struggle to the Persian

power, and seem to have made no effort to regain their independence.

SECTION VIII.—*The Greek Colonies on the Euxine Sea, the Coasts of Thrace, Macedon, &c.*

MOST of the Greek colonies on the shores of the Propontis, the Euxine Sea, and the Palus Mæotis, were founded by the citizens of Miletus between the eighth and sixth centuries before the Christian era. That city, whose commerce occupied four harbours, and whose naval power amounted to eighty or a hundred galleys of war, owed its greatness to its possession of the northern trade; and to secure this lucrative commerce, it planted several colonies, all of which became prosperous marts of trade. Their commerce was not confined to the sea-coasts: their merchants penetrated into southern Russia, and advanced even beyond the Caspian to the countries that now form the kingdoms of Khiva and Bokhara. The Phocæans shared the honour of founding these important colonies; but they were too much devoted to the western trade to waste their energies on the northern; and it may be generally stated, that the settlements on the Euxine depended chiefly on Miletus.

On the Propontis, adjoining the Hellespont, stood Lampsacus, originally founded by some Phocæans, who obtained a grant of the site of the city from one of the native princes whom they had assisted in war. It was afterwards occupied by the Milesians, under whom it became a place of great wealth and extensive commerce.

Cyzicus, erected on an island joined by bridges to the Asiatic coast, was a very ancient city; it is said to have been colonised in the earliest ages by the Tyrrhenian Pelasgi, and afterwards by the Argonauts. About B.C. 751 it was occupied by the Milesians, who at the same time took possession of the neighbouring island of Proconnesus (*Marmora*). Cyzicus, in a late age, under the dominion of the Romans, became one of the most beautiful and flourishing cities in Asia.

Opposite to Cyzicus, on the Thracian coast, was Perinthus, at a later age called Heracleia, founded by a Samian colony;

on the European side of the Thracian Bosphorus was Byzantium (*Constantinople*); and over against it, on the Asiatic coast, Chalcedon (*Scutari*), both colonised from Megara.

The first Greek city on the Black Sea was Heracleia, on the Bithynian coast, which appears to have been successively colonised from Megara and Miletus. It long enjoyed prosperity, until commercial jealousy impelled its citizens to wage war against the Byzantines; in this struggle the Heracleians were completely defeated, and forced to receive the conditions imposed by the conquerors. Internally the state was harassed by factious struggles between the oligarchy and democracy, until about * B.C. 370, when Clearchus made himself absolute monarch of the city. He was murdered by two disciples of Plato; but the supreme power remained in possession of his family.

Sinope, in Paphlagonia, was the most powerful of the Greek states on the Euxine Sea. It was said to have been originally built by the Argonauts, and to have been twice colonised from Miletus, the first settlers having fallen victims to the barbarous Cimmerians. Its great wealth was chiefly derived from the shoals of migratory fish that issued annually from the Palus Mæotis, and spread along the shore of the Black Sea. In a late age it fell under the power of the kings of Pontus, to whom it continued subject until the establishment of the Roman empire in western Asia.

Amisus, in Pontus, was, next to Sinope, the best harbour on the Euxine Sea. After having been long subject to Miletus, it was seized by the Athenians in the age of Pericles, and its name changed to Peirææus. During the days of its prosperity, Amisus is said to have become the parent of a colony that soon surpassed itself in importance, Trapezus (*Trebisonde*); though some writers attribute this honour to Sinope. The citizens of Trapezus were celebrated for their attachment to the language, literature, and customs of ancient Greece, even in the most degenerate days of the Eastern empire.

On the eastern coast of the Euxine were Phasis, Dioscurias, and Phanagoria. In the Macedonian age, Phanagoria became the capital of the Greek cities on the Asiatic side of the Bosphorus: its prosperity was owing to its being the chief mart for the slave-trade, which has always prevailed in the countries round the Caucasus, and also to its being the staple for the goods brought from central and southern Asia by the route of the Caspian Sea and the Oxus.

The Milesians formed several establishments in the Tauric Chersonese (*Crimea*), and wrested the greater part of that peninsula from its barbarous inhabitants. The city of Panticapæum was the most important, and probably the most ancient, of these settlements. It became the capital of the little Greek kingdom of the Bosphorus, and continued to maintain its independence until, in the Roman age, it was seized by Mithridates the Great, who laid there the foundations of his subsequent power. Tanais, at the mouth of the river of the same name, was another important port; but it was inferior to Olbi, at the mouth of the Borysthenes, which had acquired the greater part of the inland trade with southern Russia and central Asia.

The coasts of Thrace and Macedon were covered with Greek colonies, principally derived from Corinth and Athens. In Thrace we may notice Sestos, Ægos-potamos, Maronea, and Abdera. Those in Macedon were of more importance: the chief were Amphipolis on the Strymon, founded by the Athenians; Chalcis, established by the city of the same name in Eubœa; Olynthus, a Doric settlement, but which became tributary to Athens; and Potidæa, a colony of the Corinthians. The history of these colonies is blended with that of the Peloponnesian wars, and will be found in the next chapter.

On the coast of Africa was the celebrated Greek city of Cyrene, long the commercial rival of Carthage, founded by a Dorian colony from the island of Thera (B.C. 651), in obedience to the directions of the Delphic oracle. The government was at first monarchical, the crown being hereditary in the family of Battus the founder. About B.C. 450, royalty was abolished, and a republic formed; but the citizens of Cyrene never were able to form a permanent constitution; and their state continued to be rent by factions until it was annexed to the Egyptian kingdom, in the age of the Ptolemies.

The history of the Greek states in Sicily and southern Italy being closely connected with the Roman wars, will be found in the chapters on Italy.

CHAPTER X.

HISTORY OF GREECE,

FROM THE COMMENCEMENT OF THE PERSIAN WARS TO THE ACCESSION OF ALEXANDER THE GREAT.

FROM B.C. 500 TO B.C. 336.

SECTION I.—*The First Persian War.*

FROM B.C. 500 to B.C. 490.

WHEN Darius Hystaspes invaded Scythia, he entrusted the guard of the bridge of boats that he had constructed over the Danube to the Greeks of Asia and Thrace, who had been so recently brought under subjection to the Persians. Many of these were anxious to recover their freedom; and they deliberated seriously on the propriety of destroying the bridge, and leaving the Persians to perish without resource in an inhospitable desert. The proposal was strenuously advocated by Miltiades, the king or tyrant, as he was called, of the Thracian Chersonese; but he was opposed by Histiæus, the tyrant of Miletus, whose selfish councils finally prevailed. Miltiades retired to Athens, his native city, where he subsequently rose to the highest honours; Histiæus accompanied the monarch he had saved to the court of Persia. But the gratitude of absolute princes is not permanent; Histiæus soon found that the very magnitude of his services exposed him to danger; and he concerted, with his nephew Aristagoras, a revolt, which included all the Ionian colonies. In order that the insurrection should have any reasonable prospects of success, it was necessary that it should be supported by the Grecian states; and to engage this assistance, Aristagoras came to Lacedæmon.

Being harshly repulsed by the Spartans, he proceeded to Athens, where he was more generously received (B.C. 500). Twenty ships were prepared for him with all convenient speed; and these being reinforced by five more from the little state of

Eretria, in the island of Eubœa, sailed over to the harbour of Miletus, and commenced the war. The allies were at first very successful. Sardis, the wealthy capital of Lydia, was taken and plundered; but Aristagoras had not the talents of a general; the fruits of success were lost as soon as won; the several divisions of the army quarrelled and separated; and the Asiatic Greeks were left to bear the brunt of the vengeance of their merciless masters. Miletus was taken, its walls razed, and its citizens massacred; several minor cities suffered similar calamities. Aristagoras fled to Thrace, where he was murdered by the barbarians; and Histiæus, after a vain attempt to escape, was crucified at Sardis by command of the Persian satrap.

Darius next turned his resentment against the Greeks, who had aided this revolt; he sent ambassadors to demand homage from the Grecian states, especially requiring the Athenians to receive back Hippias, their exiled tyrant. All the states, insular and continental, except Athens and Sparta, proffered submission; but these noble republics sent back a haughty defiance, and fearlessly prepared to encounter the whole strength of the Persian empire.

Darius, having prepared a vast armament, entrusted its command to his son-in-law Mardonius, who soon subdued the island of Thasus and the kingdom of Macedon (B.C. 493). But his fleet, while doubling Mount Athos, was shattered by a violent storm; three hundred vessels were dashed against the rocks, and twenty thousand men are said to have perished in the waves. Mardonius returned home to excuse his disgrace, by exaggerating the cold of the climate and the dangers of the Ægean Sea.

A second and more powerful armament was prepared (B.C. 490), over which Darius placed his two best generals, Datis a Mede, and Artaphernes a Persian nobleman. The fleet passed safely through the Cyclades, receiving the ready homage of the insular states, and arrived at the island of Eubœa, where a landing was effected. Eretria was taken by storm, and its citizens sent in chains to Darius, who assigned them lands in the neighbourhood of Babylon, where their descendants were distinguishable for several centuries. From Eubœa the Persians crossed the Eurípus, and, by the advice of the exiled Hippias, encamped with an army said to exceed five hundred thousand men on the plains of Marathon, within thirty miles of Athens.

To resist this mighty force, the Athenians could only muster an army of ten thousand citizens, and about double that number of slaves, who were armed in this extremity. The little city of Platææ sent an auxiliary force of a thousand men; but the Spartans, yielding either to superstition or jealousy, refused to send their promised aid before the full of the moon. The Athenians entrusted their little army to ten generals with equal authority; but the superior abilities of Miltiades procured him the supreme command by the tacit consent of his colleagues. This was chiefly owing to the magnanimity of Aristides, who set the example of yielding up his power for the common good.

Miltiades formed his lines at the foot of a hill that protected his rear and right flank; his left was secured by an extensive marsh, and his front protected by trunks of trees, strewn for some distance, to break the force of the Persian cavalry. The Athenian citizens occupied the right wing, the Platæans the left, while the raw levies of slaves were stationed in the centre. Datis saw the advantages of this position; but confident in his superior numbers, he gave the signal for battle. The Greek centre was broken at the moment that the two wings had routed the divisions opposed to them: this had been foreseen; and Miltiades directed the victorious wings to attack the Persians rushing incautiously through the broken centre on both flanks. Surprise is fatal to an Oriental army; in a few minutes the Asiatics were wholly routed, and fled in confusion to their ships. The Greeks pursued them vigorously, and destroyed seven of their vessels; the rest sailed away with a favourable gale, and, after a vain attempt to surprise Athens, returned to Asia.

Miltiades subsequently obscured his glory, in a disgraceful expedition against the island of Paros: he was accused of having taken a bribe, convicted on rather doubtful evidence, and sentenced to pay a heavy fine, which not being able to pay, he was thrown into prison, where he died of his wounds.

Themistocles, the most able statesman, and Aristides, the most uncorrupt patriot of Greece, for a time shared the power that had been previously possessed by Miltiades. The former increased the wealth and extended the influence of Athens, by conquering the insular states that had submitted to the Persians; the latter won the respect of his fellow-citizens by the wisdom he displayed in the courts of law. Their struggle for power ended in the banishment of Aristides; but when his wise counsels were required in the hour of emergency, he was recalled on the motion of his successful rival. Themistocles directed all his efforts to improving the naval power of Athens, and he succeeded in securing for his country the complete supremacy of the Grecian seas.

In the interval between the two Persian wars nothing remarkable occurred in any of the other Grecian states, save that in Sparta, one of its kings, Demaratus, was deposed and driven into exile by the intrigues of the other, Cleomenes. Demaratus sought refuge in the court of Persia; Cleomenes perished by his own hand, a victim to remorse. Leotychides succeeded the former, Leonidas the latter.

Section II.—*The Second Persian War.*

FROM B.C. 480 TO B.C. 449.

Nine years after the battle of Marathon, Xerxes, the son and successor of Darius, resolved to attempt the conquest of Greece, and for this purpose collected an army, which, after making every allowance for the exaggerations of historians, appears to have been the most numerous ever assembled. He crossed the Hellespont on a bridge of boats, and directed his march southwards along the coasts of Thrace and Macedon, to be within reach of his fleet, which brought supplies of provision from Asia. On his road he received offers of submission from several of the Grecian states, especially the Thebans and

Thessalonians. He was thus led to expect an easy victory; but when he reached the pass of Thermopylæ, through which lay the road from Thessaly to Greece, he found a handful of men, commanded by the Spartan Leonidas, prepared to dispute the passage. The haughty Persian instantly sent a herald, commanding these warriors to surrender their arms, and was maddened by the contumelious reply, "Come and take them."

After many ineffectual efforts to break the Grecian lines, all of which were repulsed with great slaughter, Xerxes was on the point of retiring in despair, when the treachery of Ephialtes, a Trachinian deserter, revealed to him a path leading to the top of the mountain, that secured the Grecian flank. Leonidas, on hearing of this unexpected misfortune, advised his allies to retire, declaring that he and his Spartans were forbidden by law to abandon their posts. Retaining with him only a thousand men, he resolved to attack the Persian camp by night, hoping in the confusion and darkness to reach the royal tent, and, by the slaughter or capture of Xerxes, to put an end to the war. The plan had nearly succeeded when morning dawned on the assailants, wearied with slaughter: they were surrounded by multitudes; but they still fought with all the energies of despair, until they sunk, fatigued rather than vanquished.

About the same time the Greeks obtained a victory over the Persian fleet off the headland of Artemisium, in the island of Eubœa; but this triumph was rendered fruitless by the loss of the pass of Thermopylæ; and Themistocles persuaded the allies to remove the navy into the Saronic Gulf, where they anchored off the island of Salamis.

Xerxes, having entered Phocis, divided his army, sending a large detachment to plunder and destroy the temple of Delphi. A dreadful storm, which they attributed to supernatural causes, overtook the Persians in the tortuous defiles of Mount Parnassus; they were attacked by the Phocians in the midst of their confusion, and hewn down almost without resistance. A miserable remnant escaped to Xerxes, who, having destroyed Thespiæ and Platææ, was rapidly advancing against Athens. On his approach, the Athenians, by the persuasion of

Themistocles, abandoned their beloved city; those capable of bearing arms retired to the island of Salamis, while those whom age or sex rendered unfit for war found shelter in the hospitable city of Trœzene. Athens was burned to the ground; and Xerxes, in the pride of success, resolved to annihilate the last hopes of Greece in a naval engagement.

Eurybiades, the Spartan who commanded the allied fleet, was disposed to listen to the timid counsels of the Peloponnesians, who proposed that the entire Grecian navy and army should be employed solely in the defence of the Corinthian isthmus; but the firmness of Themistocles induced him to adopt the wiser and more generous plan of hazarding an engagement. Fearing, however, some change, the crafty Athenian sent a spy, as a pretended deserter, to Xerxes, informing him that the Greeks were preparing to disperse and escape; upon which the whole Persian navy was sent to blockade the harbour of Salamis. Themistocles learned the success of his stratagem from Aristides, who crossed over from Ægina in a small boat with the intelligence; a circumstance that at once put an end to the rivalry between these great men. The Peloponnesians now withdrew their opposition to the proposed engagement; they consented to fight, because to fly was impossible.

Xerxes witnessed the battle of Salamis from a rocky eminence on the coast of Attica:* he had the mortification to see his magnificent navy utterly annihilated, and to find that none of his followers but Artemisia, queen of Halicarnassus, displayed a particle of martial spirit. From that moment he resolved to return into Asia, leaving three hundred thousand men under Mardonius to prosecute the war. When he reached the Hellespont, he found his magnificent bridge broken down, and he was forced to cross the strait in a common fishing-boat.

* "A king sat on the rocky brow
  That looks o'er sea-girt Salamis,
And ships in thousands lay below,
  And men in nations—all were his.
He counted them at break of day,
And when the sun set—where were they?"

Mardonius having wintered in Thessaly, before opening the next campaign, sent the king of Macedon as an ambassador to the Athenians, offering them the rebuilding of their city, and the friendship of his master, on condition of their seceding from the alliance. Contrary to the fears of the Spartans, who judged of their rivals from their own system of selfish policy, these offers were rejected. Attica was once more desolated by fire and sword, while the Spartans obstinately refused to take the field. At length they were driven by very shame to levy an army, which they sent into Bœotia under the command of Pausanias. The confederates encamped at the foot of Mount Cithæron, in front of the Persian lines. Several skirmishes took place, in all of which the Greeks had the advantage; but being distressed for want of water, they broke up their camp to seek a better position. This movement being made with some appearance of confusion, Mardonius, believing that his enemies were in full retreat, ordered his soldiers to pursue the fugitives and complete the victory. A battle ensued not far from the city of Platææ, which ended in the total defeat of the Persians, and the annihilation of their army, with the exception of forty thousand that escaped to the Hellespont under Artabazus. Two hundred thousand of the barbarians are said to have fallen in this memorable battle, and the value of the plunder found in the Persian camp exceeds calculation. On the very same day (September 22d, B.C. 479), an equally important victory was gained by the confederate fleet, commanded by the Athenian Xanthippus and the Spartan Leotychides, at Mycale, on the coast of Asia Minor. Dreading the heroism of the Greeks, the Persians had drawn their ships on shore, surrounded them with fortifications, and protected them with an army of sixty thousand men. The allied Greeks, with far inferior numbers, landed their troops, stormed the works, destroyed the navy, and put the greater part of the Persians to the sword.

During the half century that followed the battle of Platææ, the Athenian republic attained the summit of its greatness, and became the first state, not only of Greece, but of the civilised world. The Spartans envied the glory of Athens, and, in the very outset, attempted to crush its prosperity by labouring to prevent the rebuilding of the city-walls. Themistocles met the hypocritical pretences of the Spartans with equal duplicity: he went as ambassador to Lacedæmon, but studiously delayed opening his commission to the senate, while his countrymen urged forward the completion of the fortifications with all possible speed. A vague rumour of the building of these walls having reached the Spartan senate, they were about to wreak their vengeance on Themistocles, but he persuaded them to send ambassadors to inquire into the real state of the case. These deputies were seized as hostages at Athens, and Themistocles then, throwing off the mask, declared that his native city could now defy the malice of false friends and open foes, and that Sparta's most eminent citizens were held as sureties for the safety of himself and his colleagues. The Spartans, completely baffled, dismissed the Athenian ambassadors; but thenceforward they pursued Themistocles with the most unrelenting hatred. On his return, Themistocles not only finished the defences of the city, but fortified the harbour of the Peirææus, and joined it to Athens by what were called "the long walls."

In the meantime the Spartan Pausanias, at the head of the confederate Greeks, continued to wage war against the dependencies of the Persian empire in the Ægean Sea and on the coast of Thrace. Byzantium, already regarded as a strong and flourishing city, was taken, after a long siege (B.C. 476), and its vast wealth became the prey of the conquerors. But this sudden influx of riches proved fatal to Pausanias; he resolved, by the aid of the Persians, to become supreme master of Greece; and, confident of success, he treated his colleagues with such insolence, and his allies with such tyranny, that most of the confederate states, especially the Ionians, seceded from the Spartan alliance, and placed themselves under the protection of Athens. Secret information of their general's treason was conveyed to the Spartan senate; he was recalled, and brought to trial; but escaped the first time, it is said, by bribing his judges. Fresh evidence being obtained against him, he was secretly warned of his danger, and fled for safety to the temple of Minerva. The Spartans did not dare to drag the traitor from the sanctuary; they blocked up the door of the temple with huge stones, stripped off its roof, strictly guarded all its avenues, and left the wretch to perish by cold and hunger.

Themistocles, by the artifice of the Spartans, was involved in the fate of Pausanias: he appears to have been acquainted with the plot; but he strenuously denied that it had ever received his sanction. He was banished by ostracism for ten years; but the malice of his enemies pursued him in his exile, and, to save his life, he was forced to seek refuge at the court of Persia. Artaxerxes, who had recently succeeded to the empire, received the banished statesman with joy, and assigned him the revenues of three cities for his support. He soon, however, ended his life by poison. Nearly at the same time Aristides died full of years and honours, having administered the public finances with so much integrity, that he did not leave behind him a sum sufficient to defray the expenses of his funeral. A sum was issued from the public treasury to pay for the last rites to his corpse, to complete his son's education, and to portion his daughters.

Cimon, the son of Miltiades, succeeded Aristides as leader of the Athenian republic: he continued the war against the Persians with equal vigour and skill, reducing all their cities and forts, not only in Europe and the islands, but even on the coast of Asia. At length he completely destroyed the whole Persian navy off the coast of Cyprus (B.C. 470), and then dressing his men in the vestures and arms of his prisoners, surprised the Persian camp at the mouth of the river Eurymedon on the very same day, and, before the barbarians could recover from their confusion, completed their destruction. The war continued twenty-one years, during which the naval power and commercial wealth of the Athenians were continually increasing; both sides at length began to entertain thoughts of peace. The Greeks were disheartened by the loss of an army sent to aid the insurrection of the Egyptians, and by the death of Cimon, who was mortally wounded at the siege of Citium. Artaxerxes was still more anxious for a treaty, to prevent the total ruin of the Persian commerce, and the loss of the island of Cyprus. The articles were soon arranged, and they were worthy of the valour that the Greeks had shewn in this great struggle (B.C. 449). It was stipulated that the independence of the Greek cities in Lower Asia should be restored; that no Persian vessel should appear between the Cyanean rocks and Chelidonian islands, that is, between the northern extremity of the Thracian Bosphorus and the southern promontory of Lycia; that no Persian army should come within three days' journey of the sea-coast; and that the Athenians should withdraw their fleets and armies from the island of Cyprus. Thus gloriously were terminated the Persian wars, which, reckoning from the burning of Sardis, had lasted, with little intermission, during fifty-one years.

Section III.—*The First Peloponnesian War.*

FROM B.C. 431 TO B.C. 422.

Whilst the Athenians were acquiring wealth and glory in the war against Persia, the Spartans, jealous of their rival's rising fame, were secretly preparing to weaken the Athenian power by a sudden war. But their animosity, before it broke into action, was diverted by a calamity equally great and unexpected. Laconia was laid waste by an earthquake, which destroyed one hundred and twenty thousand of its inhabitants, and overwhelmed the city of Sparta (B.C. 469). The oppressed Helots and the remnant of the Messenians took advantage of this calamity to make a vigorous effort for the recovery of their freedom: they failed in surprising Sparta; but they made themselves masters of their ancient fortress Ithome. Though aided by the Athenians, whose assistance they repaid with ingratitude, the Spartans had great difficulty in subduing the insurgents, and were finally forced to allow them to retire from the Peloponnesus with their families and properties. These exiles were hospitably received in the Athenian colony of Naupactus; and they repaid the kindness shewn to them by subsequently adhering, through every vicissitude of fortune, to the cause of Athens. The Argives had declined to support the general cause of Greece in the great struggle with the Persians;

and the dependent states, despising their treachery, had thrown off obedience to the capital. Mycenæ was the only city on which the Argives could wreak their vengeance; the rest, supported by Sparta, maintained their independence. From similar reasons, Thebes had lost her supremacy over the Bœotian cities; but here the Athenians embraced the cause of the minor states, while Sparta supported the sovereignty of the Bœotian metropolis.

Athens had now attained the summit of its greatness, under the brilliant administration of Pericles. That eminent statesman, though sprung from a noble house, had risen to power by warmly supporting the cause of the people, and procured the banishment of his rival Cimon, on account of his partiality to Sparta. To secure his influence, Pericles weakened the power of the great aristocratic court, the Areopagus, by removing various causes from its jurisdiction to that of the popular tribunals. He adorned the city with the most splendid monuments of architecture, sculpture, and painting; and in order to defray the necessary expenditure, he augmented the contributions imposed on the allied states, under the pretence of supporting the Persian war, and removed the treasury of the confederates from Delos to Athens. Finding that the Spartans were supporting the cause of Theban supremacy, he sent an army to maintain the independence of Bœotia, which, though at first worsted near Tanagra, won a decisive victory on the same ground in the following year (B. C. 457). A fleet at the same time ravaged the coasts of the Peloponnesus, and made the Spartans tremble for their own safety. The recall of Cimon, and the defeat of the Athenians in an enterprise against Thebes, through the rashness of their leader Tolmidas, led to a truce for five years (B. C. 450), which might probably have led to a permanent peace, but for the death of Cimon before the walls of Citium. The close of the truce led to a brief renewal of war; but a second truce was concluded for fifty years, which gave Pericles time to mature his favourite policy of making Athens mistress of the maritime and insular states. Some of the islands revolted, but they were successively subdued; and the subjugation of Samos, the chief city in the island of that name, gave Pericles the fame of a military leader as well as a statesman. About the same time he completed the overthrow of the aristocratic party, by procuring the banishment of its leader, the elder Thucydides; and secured the popular favour by his unrivalled shows and theatrical exhibitions. The brilliancy of Athens, however, provoked a host of secret enemies, especially in the Peloponnesus, who only waited an opportunity of combining for her destruction.

The circumstances that gave rise to the first Peloponnesian war originated in the unsettled state of colonial relations among the ancient Greeks. Corcyra, originally a Corinthian colony, had risen so rapidly in wealth and power, that it more than rivalled the parent state, and possessed many flourishing colonies of its own, among which one of the most important was Epidamnus, on the western coast of Macedonia. The people of Epidamnus, pressed by their barbarous neighbours, sought aid from the Corcyreans; but finding their request unheeded, they applied to the Corinthians, who readily sent an armament to their assistance (B.C. 436). Nothing could exceed the rage of the Corcyreans when they received this intelligence; a fleet was instantly sent to the harbour, and its citizens were haughtily commanded to dismiss the Corinthians, and receive a Corcyrean garrison. This mandate was spurned with contempt, and Epidamnus was immediately besieged. The Corinthians sent a powerful navy to raise the siege; but they were encountered by the Corcyreans in the Ambracian Gulf, and completely defeated. Epidamnus immediately surrendered; contrary, however, to the general expectation, its inhabitants were treated with great leniency. But the haughty islanders abused their victory by ravaging the territories of the states that had assisted Corinth, and provoked universal indignation by burning the city of Cyllene, on the coast of Elis. Both powers applied to Athens, as the head of the maritime states, to decide their quarrel. By the advice of Pericles, a defensive alliance was concluded with the Corcyreans, and a fleet sent to their aid, which fortunately arrived at the moment when the Corinthian navy, having obtained a decisive victory, seriously menaced the island. On the arrival of the Athenians, the Corinthians retired; but as they returned, they surprised the garrison of Anactorium, on the coast of Epirus, which enabled them to bring home twelve hundred and fifty Corcyrean prisoners. The fatal effects produced by this capture will soon demand our attention.

Potidæa, a Corinthian colony on the Macedonian coast, that had been for some time subject to Athens, revolted during the Corcyrean war, and was instantly besieged. The Potidæans sought aid from their ancient parent; and the Corinthians, too weak to afford efficient protection, besought the assistance of the Spartans. About the same time, ambassadors arrived from the city of Megara, complaining that they had been, by an unjust decree, excluded from the ports and harbours of Attica, soliciting the Spartans, as heads of the Dorian race, to procure a reversal of so unjust a law; and emissaries came from Ægina to represent the miserable condition to which that island had been reduced by Athenian oppression. After some affected delay, the Spartans resolved that the Athenians had violated the principles of justice, and should be coerced to redress the injuries they had inflicted; but to give their proceedings an appearance of moderation, it was resolved to send ambassadors to Athens with demands which they knew well would be refused. They required that the siege of Potidæa should be raised, the decree against Megara repealed, the island of Ægina abandoned, the independence of the maritime states respected, and the descendants of Cylon's murderers banished. This last demand was levelled at Pericles, whose maternal ancestor had headed the aristocratic party when that sacrilegious murder was committed; and it was urged at a favourable moment, when Pericles was suspected of impiety on account of his protecting the philosopher Anaxagoras.

But the haughtiness with which the Spartan ambassadors urged their injurious demands, roused the fiery spirit of the Athenian people, and it required all the influence of Pericles to induce them to couch their refusal in temperate and dignified language. While the declaration of war was yet withheld, intelligence arrived at Sparta of the Thebans having been foiled in an attempt to surprise Platææ, and that their defeat was owing to the instigation and aid of the Athenians (B.C. 431). War was instantly proclaimed, and the Spartan king Archidamus elected chief of the Peloponnesian confederates.

Athens, supported by the insular and maritime states, was supreme mistress of the sea; Sparta, on the other hand, was joined by the chief powers on the Grecian continent, and was consequently superior by land. Both began the war by displaying their strength on their own peculiar element: a Spartan army ravaged Attica, an Athenian fleet plundered the coasts of the Peloponnesus. The Spartans were thus forced to return home to the defence of their own country; and no sooner had they withdrawn than Pericles invaded Megaris, and laid the whole of its narrow territory desolate. Early in the next summer the Peloponnesians again invaded Attica; but the Athenians were assailed by a more dreadful calamity,—a plague of unparalleled virulence had been introduced into the Piræeus from Asia, and it raged fiercely in a city crowded by the peasants who had sought refuge within the walls on the approach of the Spartans. At length, two years and six months after the commencement of the war, Pericles himself fell a victim to the pestilence (B.C. 429). His death-bed was surrounded by his friends and admirers, who recited the many illustrious exploits of his glorious life. "You forget," said the dying patriot,—"you forget the only valuable part of my character; none of my fellow-citizens was ever compelled by any action of mine to assume a mourning robe."

The war was supported by mutual ravages, and the success of the contending parties nicely balanced. Potidæa surrendered to the Athenians, its inhabitants were banished, and their place supplied by fresh colonists; Platææ, after a brave and protracted defence of five years, was yielded to the Spartans, but the whole garrison was mercilessly butchered (B.C. 427). In the same year that the Spartans had stained their national character by the atrocious massacre of the Platæans, the Athenians narrowly escaped being disgraced by a similar atrocity. The Lesbians of Mitylene had revolted, and sought the assistance of the Peloponnesians, but the tardy and selfish policy of Lacedæmon delayed the succours until the insurgents were forced to surrender at discretion. When the fate of Mitylene was discussed in the Athenian assembly, the populace, instigated by Cleon, a vulgar demagogue, decreed that the city should be destroyed, and the male inhabitants put to the sword. But night brought better counsels; a general feeling of pity and regret spread among the people; and on the following day the sanguinary decree was revoked, and a fast-sailing vessel sent to prevent its execution. The messengers of mercy made such speed, that they entered the harbour of Mytilene a few hours after the preceding boat, and thus saved Lesbos from desolation.

The Spartan admiral having failed to succour Lesbos, sailed against Corcyra, then agitated by the tumults of a most dangerous sedition. It has been already mentioned, that many Corcyreans had been made prisoners by the Corinthians; these men were won by the kindness and bribes of their captors to aid the aristocratic party of their countrymen in an attempt to subvert the democratic constitution of Corcyra, and break off the alliance with Athens. On their return home, they made a vigorous effort to accomplish their designs, and very nearly succeeded. After a violent and sanguinary contest, in which both parties were disgraced by the most savage atrocities, the democratic faction prevailed by the aid of an Athenian fleet, but sullied its triumph by exterminating all its opponents, under circumstances of equal treachery and cruelty.

The presence of the Athenian fleet in the Ionian sea rendered western Greece the scene of war; and Demosthenes, its chief commander, subdued all the allies of the Peloponnesians in Ætolia and Epirus. The term of his command having expired (B.C. 425), he was returning home, when the Messenians who served in his fleet proposed to effect a landing in the harbour of Pylus (*Navarino*), and, fortifying themselves there, make the Spartans tremble in their own capital, which was only fifty miles distant. The bold design was accomplished; and the Spartans in alarm sent a fleet and army to besiege Pylus; they garrisoned the little island of Sphacteria; but their navy being defeated by the Athenians, this garrison, consisting of the noblest of the Spartan families, was brought to the brink of ruin, and would have been utterly destroyed, but for the inadequate resources which Demosthenes had at his command. Under these circumstances, the Spartans sent deputies to solicit peace; but the Athenian people, instigated by their unworthy favourite Cleon, rejected the proffer with disdain. This arrogant boaster, whose cowardice was notorious, offered, if he were made general, that he would make the Spartans in Sphacteria prisoners within twenty days. He had no notion that his offer would be accepted; but the Athenian populace, ready at all times to sacrifice every thing for a joke, took him at his word. Cleon sailed to the scene of war, and was enabled, by an accidental fire which destroyed the Spartan fortifications, to accomplish his promise. This success was followed by the capture of the island of Cythera, the destruction of the Megarean harbour Nicæa, and of several seaports on the coast of the Peloponnesus. But these triumphs were counterbalanced by the defeat of the Athenians at Delium, the revolt of their northern colonies, and the commencement of hostilities against them by Perdiccas king of Macedon. The Spartans, roused to vigour by this unexpected turn of events, sent an army under Brasidas, their ablest general, through northern Greece, to aid the revolted colonies; and this eminent leader soon deprived the Athenians of their principal cities in Thrace and Macedon. Cleon headed an Athenian army sent to retrieve these losses; he was defeated and slain; but the Spartan victory was deprived of all its fruits by the death of Brasidas, who incautiously exposed himself, and was mortally wounded (B.C. 422).

Sparta had no general fit to succeed Brasidas, and the senate was anxious to recover the prisoners taken in Sphacteria; the Athenians were equally eager to procure the restitution of their northern colonies; and Nicias, who had succeeded Cleon, was naturally of a pacific disposition. These favourable circumstances led to the conclusion of a peace, or rather truce, for fifty years, on the basis of mutual restitution, by which Sparta wantonly sacrificed the interests of her allies.

Section IV.—*The Second Peloponnesian War.*

FROM B.C. 421 TO B.C. 404.

Justly provoked by the neglect of their interests in the recent treaty, the Corinthians privately instigated the Argives against the Spartans; and a combination was formed by the principal democratic states, which was secretly encouraged by the Athenians. This sudden departure from pacific policy was owing to the influence of Alcibiades, the nephew of Pericles, who, to a large share of his uncle's abilities, added a boundless ambition, and a reckless disregard of the means he used to accomplish his ends. The Argives and Spartans, after having harassed each other by petty expeditions, at length prepared for open war; but just as the two armies were on the point of engaging, the remembrance that they were both descended from the Dorian race suspended their rage, and a truce was concluded between their respective leaders. Alcibiades, who was then ambassador at Argos, roused the populace to refuse their ratification of this agreement; a fresh attack was made on the Spartan allies, but it proved unsuccessful. Two years of mutual recrimination followed; during which the Argive republic was harassed by sanguinary revolutions, which ended in the complete establishment of a democracy. In the meantime, the Athenians, anxious to restore their naval supremacy, attacked the Dorian island of Melos, and punished the resistance of the inhabitants by a cruel massacre, which provoked universal indignation throughout Greece. But public attention was soon engrossed by a more important topic, the Athenian expedition to Sicily, undertaken at the instigation of Alcibiades (B.C. 415), nominally to deliver the Egestans from the tyranny of the Syracusans, but really to establish the Athenian supremacy in that island.

Notwithstanding the remonstrances of Nicias and Socrates, the most powerful armament that had ever left a Grecian port was speedily prepared, and entrusted to the joint command of Alcibiades, Nicias, and Lamachus. When reviewed at Corcyra, it was found to consist of a hundred and thirty-four ships of war, with a proportional number of transports and tenders. The army was composed of five thousand heavy-armed infantry, accompanied by a sufficient body of slingers and archers. Instead, however, of sailing directly to Syracuse, which probably would have fallen, the fleet was steered to Catana, whose inhabitants were induced to join the Athenians by the brilliant eloquence of Alcibiades. Scarcely, however, had he obtained this triumph, when he was summoned home to be tried for his life on a charge of impiety and sacrilege.

He was accused of having violated the Eleusinian mysteries, and wantonly defaced the Hermæ, or sacred statues of Mercury, which adorned the streets of Athens. Conscious of his guilt, or dreading the giddy populace, he refused to incur the hazard of a trial, but fled to Thurium, whence he removed to Argos, and afterwards, when a price was set on his head, to Sparta. Nicias, by the departure of Alcibiades, and death of Lamachus, remained sole commander of the Athenian forces : he was an able but cautious leader ; and after he had defeated the Syracusans, he wasted precious time in fortifying his camp and in useless negotiations. The Corinthians and Spartans profited by the delay to send succours to Syracuse, which they entrusted to Gylippus, the best general of his day. Under his command the fortune of the war soon changed ; and the Athenians, so far from making any impression on Syracuse, were severely defeated, and besieged in their camp. At the request of Nicias, a new armament was sent to Sicily, under the command of Demosthenes and Eurymedon ; but through the dilatory policy of the old general, and the rashness of his colleagues, this reinforcement was rendered unavailing, and the Athenians were defeated in a decisive engagement. Demosthenes now proposed to return ; but Nicias lingered in Sicily after all rational hopes of success were lost, and the Syracusans, in the meantime collecting a powerful navy, destroyed the Athenian fleet, and became masters of the sea. An attempt was made by the Athenians to retreat to some friendly city; but they were overtaken by the Syracusan army, and forced to surrender at discretion (B.C. 413). The generals were barbarously put to death, and the common soldiers sold as slaves.

This terrible calamity was fatal to the power of Athens; but it was not the only misfortune that befel the republic. Acting under the revengeful advice of Alcibiades, the Spartans fortified and garrisoned Deceleia, a town not fifteen miles from Athens, and commanding its richest lands; and thus, instead of harassing their enemies by annual incursions, they infested them by a continual war. Soon afterwards, they learned that the wealth of Persia was added to the formidable confederacy of the Spartans.

But under all these misfortunes the Athenians maintained their national courage, and prepared to meet the crisis with enthusiasm. Their most pressing danger arose from the discontent of the maritime states, whose desire of independence was stimulated by the presence of a superior Spartan fleet in the Ægean Sea. The ruin of the Athenians was, however, suspended by the intrigues of Alcibiades with the Persian satrap Tissaphernes; for this ambitious man, having provoked the resentment of the Spartans by his vices, was now eager to be reconciled to his native country. His intrigues procured the abolition of the Athenian democracy, and the substitution of an aristocratic government; but the new heads of the state justly dreaded the ambition of Alcibiades, and refused to repeal the sentence pronounced against him. The four hundred tyrants, as the aristocratic usurpers were justly called, alienated the minds even of their partisans by their cruelty and incapacity. At length the revolt of Eubœa, and the destruction of the Athenian fleet near Eretria, provoked a fierce insurrection: they were deposed, and thus, at the end of four months, the democracy was restored. Alcibiades was immediately recalled; but he resolved not to return home until his return should be gilded by the fame of some great exploit. He hastened, with a small squadron, to aid the Athenian fleet, at the moment it had joined battle with the Spartans; and this seasonable reinforcement decided the victory. But Alcibiades, eager for a more decisive blow, persuaded his countrymen to attack the Spartans in the harbour of Cyzicus, and by his prudent arrangements the whole hostile fleet was either taken or destroyed (B.C. 411). This great victory was followed by the re-establishment of the Athenian ascendancy in the Thracian Chersonesus. After having performed these essential services, Alcibiades returned home (B.C. 407), and was welcomed at Athens with great enthusiasm: he was appointed commander-in-chief by sea and land, and a large armament was placed at his disposal.

But when Alcibiades returned to the coast of Asia, he found the cause of Sparta retrieved by the crafty Lysander, who was more than his equal in the diplomatic arts of duplicity and cunning. The Spartan had the art to gain the confidence of the Persian prince Cyrus, to whom his father had just entrusted the government of Lower Asia; and by the simple expedient of raising the pay of the sailors on board the confederate fleets, he had at once deprived the Athenians of their most experienced mariners. Alcibiades went with a small squadron to raise contributions in Caria: during his absence, Antiochus, his lieutenant, contrary to orders, engaged Lysander, and was defeated with the loss of fifteen ships. Intelligence of this event being conveyed to Athens, the suspicions of the treachery of Alcibiades, which had been only partially lulled, returned in full force, and he was a second time deposed and banished. He fled to a fortress he possessed in Thrace, while ten admirals were appointed to command in his stead.

Lysander's year of office having expired, he was succeeded as admiral of the Peloponnesian fleet by Callicratidas, a man as inferior to him in ability as he was superior in rectitude and integrity. An engagement between the fleets, off the islands of Arginusæ, ended in the total defeat of the Spartans; but a violent storm prevented the Athenian admirals from improving their victory, and from recovering the bodies of their slain, to procure them the rites of sepulture. For these imaginary crimes, they were accused before the people by one of their colleagues, denied the benefit of a fair trial, condemned by clamour, and put to death.

The war for a time languished; but the re-appointment of Lysander to the command of the Peloponnesian fleet was fatal to Athens, whose best officers had been wantonly sacrificed to gratify the fury of a licentious populace. Profiting by the unskilfulness and presumption of the Athenian admirals, Lysander attacked them unawares at the mouth of the Ægos-potamos (Goat's river), and totally annihilated their navy, with the exception of eight galleys, which, by the prudent management of Conon, escaped to the island of Cyprus (B.C. 406). Lysander, having thus virtually put an end to the Peloponnesian war, mercilessly butchered his unfortunate prisoners, to the amount of three thousand.

Before sailing against Athens, Lysander reduced the principal maritime states, and thus prevented the import of grain into the devoted city. When he deemed that famine had sufficiently prepared the way for success, he appeared before the harbour with a fleet of one hundred and fifty sail, while Agis, king of Sparta, attacked the city by land. The Athenians made an obstinate defence; but they were at length forced to surrender, on the humiliating conditions of abolishing the democracy, and entrusting the chief power to thirty persons named by the Spartans, surrendering all their ships but twelve, resigning all claim to their colonies and foreign possessions, and consenting to follow the Spartan standard in war. Harsh as were these conditions, they were mercy compared to the sanguinary measures proposed by the Thebans and Corinthians. The Athenians submitted in bitter sorrow. On the sixteenth of May (B.C. 404), the anniversary of the memorable victory of Salamis, the harbours and forts of Athens were occupied by her enemies, and the demolition of her walls commenced amidst loud shouts and flourishes of martial music, while her citizens, broken-hearted, hid themselves from the light of day.

SECTION V.—*Tyrannical Rule of Sparta. Third Peloponnesian War.*

FROM B.C. 404 TO B.C. 361.

THE confederates had destroyed the supremacy of Athens, but soon found that they had thereby subjected themselves to the galling tyranny of the Spartans. Lysander proved to be the worst oppressor that had ever been raised to power; and the Greek cities in Asia would have gladly chosen the non-despotism of Persia, in preference to his avarice and cruelty. But, to secure her power, Sparta had established an oligarchy of her creatures in every state, and supported these domestic tyrannies with arms and money. The power of the thirty tyrants at Athens was secured and maintained by a Spartan garrison in the Acropolis: thus supported, these despots set no bounds to their cruelty and rapacity, putting to death all who possessed wealth or political influence, and enriching themselves by confiscations. They dreaded the influence of the exiled Alcibiades, and applied to Lysander to remove this dangerous enemy. The Spartan immediately informed the Persian satrap that the death of Alcibiades was necessary to the full success of their schemes, and that illustrious statesman was assassinated by a band of hired assassins in Phrygia.

Although the Thebans had been the most inveterate enemies of the Athenians, their hearts were affected by witnessing the evils brought upon their rivals by the cruelty of the tyrants, and they received with generous kindness those who fled from the persecution of the despots. A numerous band of exiles was soon assembled at Thebes, and at its head was placed Thrasybulus, whose daring valour was tempered by prudence and humanity. Under his guidance the exiles seized Phyle, a strong fortress on the frontiers of Attica and Bœotia, whence they opened a communication with the enemies of the tyrants in the city. Justly terrified, the thirty and their partisans flew to arms, but they suffered a shameful defeat; and Thrasybulus, strengthened by the accession of new partisans, seized the Peirææus. The aristocratic faction, in great alarm, deposed the thirty, and elected ten new magistrates in their stead, who emulated the wickedness of their predecessors, and, to secure their power, sought assistance from Sparta. Lysander quickly advanced to their aid, and blockaded the Peirææus; but his pride and ambition had given deep offence in Sparta; and Pausanias, the most popular of the Lacedæmonian princes, hastily marched with a second army to frustrate the plans of Lysander. Under the protection of Pausanias, the despots were stripped of power, the ancient constitution of Athens restored, and the Spartan garrison withdrawn from the citadel (B. C. 403). Some of the tyrants retired with their followers to Eleusis; but their unequal hostility was easily defeated by the vigour of the new republic. A few of the most obnoxious were put to death; the rest were pardoned by a general act of amnesty, which was ratified by the people on the motion of Thrasybulus.

Scarcely had the constitution been restored, when the Athenians shewed how greatly their national character had been deteriorated, by condemning the virtuous Socrates to death on a frivolous charge of impiety (B. C. 400). His death was worthy of his useful and honourable life; he submitted to the injustice of his countrymen without murmuring or repining, and spent his last moments in impressing on the minds of his friends those sublime lessons of philosophy which his eloquent disciple Plato has transmitted to posterity.

Another disciple of Socrates was at the same time less honourably engaged as a hireling soldier in Asia. Darius Nothus, at his death, bequeathed the crown of Persia to his eldest son Artaxerxes, surnamed Mnemon from the strength of his memory. Cyrus, his younger brother, was stimulated by the queen dowager Parysatis to claim the kingdom, on the ground of his having been born the son of a king, while the birth of Artaxerxes took place while Darius was as yet in a private station. Cyrus, while governor of Lower Asia, had earned the gratitude of Lysander and the Spartans, by supplying them with money to carry on the war against Athens, and in return he obtained their permission to raise an auxiliary force in Greece to aid his intended rebellion. Thirteen thousand adventurers soon enrolled themselves under his standard, consisting not only of the Spartans and their allies, but of some renegade Athenians, among whom was Xenophon, the celebrated historian. With these auxiliaries, and an army of one hundred thousand of his own provincials, Cyrus invaded Upper Asia, and advanced with little difficulty into Babylonia (B. C. 400). Here he encountered his brother's immense army, and rashly charging the centre of the royal guards, was slain on the field. His army, according to the usual custom of Asiatics, dispersed immediately; and the Greeks were left almost alone in the midst of a hostile country, to effect a difficult retreat of more than a thousand miles. Their leaders proposed terms of accommodation to the Persians. They were invited to a conference, under the pretence of arranging the preliminaries, and were mercilessly butchered. Undismayed, they chose new commanders; and, after enduring incredible hardships, succeeded in fighting their way to their native country. Thus gloriously ended "the retreat of the ten thousand;" but nothing can excuse the original guilt of the expedition.

The remnant of the ten thousand entered into the service of the Spartans, who had sent an army to protect the Greek cities of Asia from the threatened vengeance of Artaxerxes. A desultory war ensued, productive of no important result, until the command of the Greek forces was given to Agesilaus, who had been raised to the throne of Laconia by the influence and intrigues of Lysander. Agesilaus departed for Asia just as the Spartans had escaped from the peril of a plot formed for their destruction by the subject Lacedæmonians, at the instigation of the ambitious Cinadon (B.C. 396). His first action was to degrade Lysander, the author of his greatness, who returned home unpitied to bewail his friend's ingratitude. He then directed his entire attention to the war, and defeated the Persians in several battles. It is very probable that Agesilaus would have shaken the throne of Artaxerxes, had not the atrocious tyranny of his countrymen provoked the general enmity of all the Greek states, and kindled a new Peloponnesian war.

Under the most frivolous pretences, Lysander and the Spartan king Pausanias were sent to invade the Theban territories. The former laid siege to Haliartus, the latter encamped in the neighbourhood of Platææ. The garrison of Haliartus taking advantage of this division of the hostile forces, made a sudden sally, and defeated the Spartans with great slaughter, Lysander himself being slain (B.C. 394). Pausanias obtained leave to bury the dead, on condition of evacuating Bœotia; and he returned disgraced to the Peloponnesus, where he soon died of a broken heart.

The news of this event revived the courage of the enemies of Sparta; a league for mutual protection was formed by the republics of Argos, Thebes, Athens, and Corinth, to which most of the colonies in Thrace and Macedon acceded. Agesilaus was immediately recalled from Asia, and he obeyed the summons with great promptitude, leaving his fleet and a portion of the Asiatic army under the charge of his kinsman Pisander. Conon, one of the ten admirals who had been exposed to the anger of the Athenian populace after the sea-fight at Arginusæ, found a generous protector in Evagoras king of Cyprus, by whom he was introduced to the notice of Artaxerxes. The Persian monarch, alarmed at the progress of Agesilaus, gladly supplied Conon with the means of fitting out a fleet that might cope with that of Sparta. Knowing the vanity and inexperience of Pisander, Conon sailed in quest of the Lacedæmonians to the Dorian shore; and off the harbour of Cnidus gained a decisive victory, by which the Spartan navy was annihilated, and its empire over the maritime states irretrievably destroyed. With consummate skill Conon availed himself of this success to restore not only the independence of Athens, but her supremacy in the Ægean Sea. He conducted his victorious fleet to the principal islands and colonies, and, either by persuasion or menace, induced them to renew their allegiance to their ancient mistress.

Agesilaus received the intelligence of this unexpected reverse just as he was about to engage a Theban army at Coroneia (B.C. 394). He animated his soldiers by falsely reporting that the Spartan fleet had been victorious; but even this stratagem failed to gain him decisive success. He won the battle indeed, but at such a heavy cost that his victory was nearly as calamitous as a defeat. The best and bravest of the Spartan veterans fell, and Agesilaus himself was dangerously wounded. The battles of Cnidus and Coroneia were the only important engagements in this war, which lasted nearly eight years; both parties exhausted their strength by petty skirmishes in the neighbourhood of Corinth; and that wealthy city was almost wholly destroyed by the rivalry of the Argive and Spartan factions.

Conon having employed the Persian money to rebuild the walls of Athens, and the Persian fleet to restore its maritime supremacy, became suspected by Artaxerxes of designing to raise a revolt of the Greeks in Asia; and this suspicion was fostered by Spartan emissaries, who offered to abandon, in the name of their government, the cause of Grecian liberty, provided that the Persian monarch would grant favourable terms of peace. Artaxerxes listened to the treacherous proposals; Conon was seized and murdered in prison; articles of peace were arranged with the Spartan Antalcidas, by which the liberty of the Greek cities was sacrificed, and the independence of all the minor republics proclaimed. The Persian monarch and the Spartan republic took upon themselves to enforce the latter regulation, which was designed to prevent Athens from maintaining her superiority over the maritime states, and Thebes from becoming mistress of the Bœotian cities (B.C. 387). The disgraceful peace of Antalcidas, by which the Spartans resigned the free cities of Asia to a barbarian, in order to gratify their unworthy jealousies, sufficiently proves that the selfish policy inculcated by the laws of Lycurgus was as ruinous as it was scandalous.

The city of Olynthus, in the Macedonian peninsula, having incurred the resentment of the Spartans, an army was sent to reduce it; but this was found no easy task; and it was not until after a war of four years, in which the Spartans suffered many severe defeats, that the Olynthians were forced to accept a peace on very humiliating conditions. In the course of this war, Phœbidas, a Spartan general, in violation of the laws of nations, seized the Cadmeia, or citadel of Thebes, then enjoying a profound peace; and his crime was justified and rewarded by Agesilaus (B.C. 383). The chief of the Theban patriots fled to Athens, where they were kindly received; an oligarchy of traitors was established under the protection of the Spartan garrison; and Thebes was doomed to the misery that Athens had endured under the thirty tyrants.

Pelopidas, one of the Theban exiles, stimulated by the recent example of Thrasybulus, concerted, with a friend who had remained in Thebes, a bold plan for the liberation of his country. The most licentious of the tyrants were invited to a feast; and when they were hot with wine, the conspirators entered disguised as courtesans, and slew them in the midst of their debauchery (B.C. 378). The rest of the traitors met a similar fate; and the patriots being reinforced by an Athenian army, vigorously besieged the citadel, and soon forced the Lacedæmonian garrison to capitulate.

Cleombrotus was sent with a numerous army from Lacedæmon, in the depth of winter, to chastise the Thebans. The Athenians were beginning to repent of their having aided the revolters; but a perfidious attempt having been made by one of the Spartan generals to seize the Peirææus, as Phœbidas had the Cadmeia, the whole city of Athens was filled with just indignation, and the most vigorous preparations were made for war. Agesilaus himself repeatedly invaded Bœotia, without performing any thing worthy of his former fame. Pelopidas, who was chosen general by his grateful countrymen, won two splendid victories at Tanagra and Tegyra, though in the latter fight he had to encounter a vast disparity of force. The Athenians swept the Spartan navy from the seas, and infested the coasts of the Peloponnesus. Nothing, in short, could have saved Sparta from destruction, had not the Thebans, intoxicated with success, provoked hostility by their vaunting pride, and the cruelty with which they treated the cities of Bœotia.

A convention of all the Grecian states was summoned to Sparta, at the request of the Persian monarch, who wished to obtain aid from the chief republics in subduing an insurrection of the Egyptians (B.C. 372). The representative of the Thebans was Epaminondas, the best military commander that Greece had yet produced, and the wisest statesman it had seen since the days of Pericles. His eloquent denunciation of Spartan ambition produced a deep impression on the minds of the deputies, which all the ingenuity of Agesilaus could not remove; the assembly was dissolved without coming to any conclusion; but the influence of Sparta was destroyed for ever.

Early in the following spring, Cleombrotus, who, during the sickness of Agesilaus, had been appointed to the chief command, invaded Bœotià with a powerful army. Epaminondas met him on the memorable field of Leuctra, and by attacking the long lines of the Lacedæmonians with massy columns, won a decisive victory, in which Cleombrotus himself was slain. The consequences of this battle were more important than the triumph itself; for all the states previously under the yoke of Sparta began openly to aspire at independence.

The Athenians, though justly enraged with the Spartans, were by no means satisfied with the result of the battle of Leuctra. They withdrew their friendship from the Thebans, who soon, however, found a more powerful ally in Jason, the captain-general of Thessaly. This noble prince, who had planned the union of all the Grecian states into a single monarchy, of which he designed himself to be the head, joined the Thebans after the battle, and mediated a truce between them and the Spartans. He was planning further schemes of empire, when he was murdered by seven assassins in the presence of his army (B.C. 370). Two of the murderers were slain on the spot; five escaped by the fleetness of their horses, and were received in the Grecian republics as heroic asserters of liberty.

No danger more imminently threatened Sparta than the revolt of the Peloponnesian states that had hitherto tamely submitted to her authority; but it was dangerous to attempt their subjugation by force, lest they might combine together for mutual protection. These states were equally reluctant to encounter the hazards of war, until they had secured the support of a Theban army; and they sent pressing messages for aid to Bœotia. After some delay, Epaminondas and Pelopidas were sent into the Peloponnesus at the head of a powerful army, and they advanced without interruption into Laconia, where the face of an enemy had not been seen for five centuries (B.C. 369). The whole country was laid desolate; but what was more afflicting to the Spartans even than these ravages, Epaminondas rebuilt the ancient city of Messene, placed a Theban garrison in its citadel, and called back the wreck of the Messenian nation to their native land, where they watched every favourable occasion for wreaking their vengeance on their oppressors. Scarcely had this great enterprise been accomplished, when the Theban generals heard that the Athenians had not only entered into alliance with the Spartans, but had sent a large army to their aid, under the command of Iphicrates. They immediately evacuated Laconia, and returned home laden with plunder through the isthmus of Corinth, meeting no interruption from Iphicrates, who led his forces by a different road. The Thebans, instead of receiving their illustrious generals with gratitude, brought them to trial for having continued their command beyond the time limited by law. Pelopidas lost his presence of mind, and escaped with difficulty; but Epaminondas, proudly recounting his heroic deeds, awed his accusers into silence, and was conducted home in triumph.

The Peloponnesian war lingered during the six following years. The Spartans were engaged in punishing their revolted subjects in Laconia; the Thebans were involved in a difficult struggle against Alexander the tyrant of Pheræ, who had succeeded to the influence of Jason in Thessaly, and Ptolemy the usurper of the throne of Macedon. Pelopidas was entrusted with the command of the army sent to regulate these difficulties. He forced Alexander to submit to the terms of peace imposed by the Theban senate, and he restored Perdiccas, the legitimate heir, to the throne of Macedon. To secure the Theban interest in the north, he brought home with him several of the Macedonian princes and nobles as hostages, among whom was Philip, the younger brother of Perdiccas and future conqueror of Greece. On his return, Pelopidas was treacherously seized by the tyrant of Pheræ, and thrown into prison; nor was he liberated until Epaminondas, after the defeat of many inferior leaders, was sent into Thessaly, where he soon forced the tyrant Alexander to unconditional submission. Pelopidas, after his liberation, was sent as an ambassador to Persia, where his eloquence so charmed Artaxerxes, that he broke off his alliance with Sparta, and concluded a league with the Thebans. The greater number of the Grecian states refused to accede to this union, partly from their ancient hostility to Persia, partly from jealousy of Thebes. Epaminondas was therefore sent a third time into the Peloponnesus with a powerful army, to revive the spirit of the former confederacy against Sparta (B.C. 366). He wasted much precious time in trying to obtain a naval power, and he was long prevented from undertaking any enterprise of importance by the jealousy and dissensions of his allies, especially the Arcadians. Whilst he was thus employed, his colleague Pelopidas fell in a battle against Alexander, the tyrant of Pheræ (B.C. 364); and the Thebans, through sorrow for his death, made no public rejoicings for their victory. His loss was poorly compensated by the destruction of the tyrant, who was soon after murdered by his own family. In the following year, Epaminondas entered upon his last campaign, by marching against the Peloponnesian states that had separated from the Theban alliance. Knowing the unprotected condition of Sparta, he made a forced march, and appeared before the city while the army was at a considerable distance. His attack was fierce; but it was repelled by the valour of Archidamus, the son of Agesilaus, who, with a handful of men, compelled the Thebans to retreat. Foiled in this attempt, he resolved to surprise the wealthy city of Mantinæa; and would have succeeded, had not a squadron of Athenian cavalry accidentally reached the place a little before the appearance of the Thebans, and by their determined valour baffled the utmost efforts of the assailants. These repeated disappointments induced Epaminondas to hazard a pitched battle. It was fought in the neighbourhood of Mantinæa, and was the most arduous and sanguinary contest in which the Greeks had yet engaged. Epaminondas fell in the arms of victory; and the Thebans, neglecting to pursue their advantages, rendered this sanguinary struggle indecisive, and productive of no other consequence that a general languor and debility in all the Grecian states. The glory of Thebes perished with the two great men who had raised her to fame: a general peace was established by the mediation of Artaxerxes (B.C. 362), on the single condition, that each republic should retain its respective possessions.

Sparta was anxious to recover Messenia; but this being opposed by the Persian king, Agesilaus, to punish Artaxerxes, led an army into Egypt, where he supported one rebel after another, and acquired considerable wealth in this dishonourable war. On his return home, he died in an obscure port on the Cyrenaic coast, at the advanced age of eighty-four years (B.C. 361). At the commencement of his reign, Sparta had attained the summit of her greatness; at its close, she had sunk into hopeless weakness. And, notwithstanding all the praise bestowed upon this monarch by the eloquent Xenophon, it is undeniable that most of Sparta's misfortunes were owing to the ambition, the obstinacy, and the perfidy of Agesilaus.

Section VI.—*The Second Sacred War. Destruction of Grecian Freedom.*

FROM B.C. 361 TO B.C. 336.

Scarcely had the third Peloponnesian war terminated, when the Athenians, by their tyranny and rapacity towards the maritime states, were deprived of all the advantages they had derived from the patriotism of Conon. Chares, a blustering, vulgar demagogue, raised to power by pandering to the passions of a licentious populace, exhorted his countrymen to supply their exhausted treasury by plundering the wealth of their allies and colonies. This counsel was too faithfully obeyed. The weaker states complained; but the islands of Chios, Coos, and Rhodes, together with the city of Byzantium, prepared openly to revolt, and entered into a league for their mutual protection (B.C. 358). Chares was sent to chastise the insurgents: he laid siege to the city of Chios, but was driven from its walls with disgrace and loss; Chabrias, the best leader that the Athenians possessed, falling in the engagement. The insurgents, encouraged by this success, began to assume the offensive, and to ravage the islands that remained faithful to Athens. A new armament was prepared to check their progress, and it was entrusted to the joint command of Chares, Timotheus, and Iphicrates; but Chares, having been hindered by his colleagues from hazarding a battle off Byzantium under very unfavourable circumstances, procured their recall, and had them brought to trial upon a charge of treachery and cowardice. Venal orators conducted the prosecution; and a degraded people sentenced the two illustrious commanders to pay an exorbitant fine. They both retired into voluntary exile, and never again entered the service of their ungrateful country. Chares, left uncontrolled, wholly neglected the commission with which he had been entrusted, and hired himself and his troops to the satrap Artabazus, then in rebellion against Artaxerxes Ochus, king of Persia. This completed the ruin of the Athenians. Ochus threatened them with the whole weight of his resentment, unless they instantly recalled their armament from the East; and with this mandate the degraded republicans were forced to comply (B.C. 356). The confederate states regained complete freedom and independence, which they preserved for twenty years, when they, with the rest of Greece, fell under the dominion of the Macedonians.

Sparta, Thebes, and Athens, having successively lost their supremacy, the Amphictyonic council, which, for more than a century, had been a mere pageant, began to exercise an important influence in the affairs of Greece. They issued a decree subjecting the Phocians to a heavy fine for cultivating some lands that had been consecrated to Apollo, and imposing a similar penalty on the Spartans for their treacherous occupation of the Cadmeia (B.C. 357). The Phocians, animated by their leader Philomelus, and secretly encouraged by the Spartans, not only refused obedience, but had recourse to arms. In defiance of the prejudices of the age, Philomelus stormed the city of Delphi, plundered the sacred treasury, and employed its wealth in raising an army of mercenary adventurers. The Thebans and Locrians were foremost in avenging this insult to the national religion; but the war was rather a series of petty skirmishes than regular battles. It was chiefly remarkable for the sanguinary spirit displayed on both sides; the Thebans murdering their captives as sacrilegious wretches; the Phocians retaliating these cruelties on all the captives that fell into their hands. At length Philomelus, being forced to a general engagement under disadvantageous circumstances, was surrounded, and on the point of being made prisoner, when he threw himself headlong from a rock, to escape falling into the hands of his enemies (B.C. 353). Onomarchus, the lieutenant and brother of the Phocian general, safely conducted the remnant of the army to the fastnesses of Delphi. He proved an able and prudent leader. With the treasures of the Delphic temple he purchased the aid of Lycophron, the chief of the Thessalian princes; and, thus supported, he committed fearful ravages in the territories of Bœotia and Locris. The Thebans, in great distress, applied for aid to Philip, king of Macedon, who had long sought a pretext for interfering in the affairs of Greece (B.C. 352): he marched immediately to their relief, completely routed the Phocians in the plains of Thessaly, and suspended from a gibbet the body of Onomarchus, which was found among the slain. He dared not, however, pursue his advantages further; for he knew that an attempt to pass the straits of Thermopylæ would expose him to the hostility of all the Grecian states, which he was not yet prepared to encounter.

Phayllus, the brother of the two preceding leaders of the Phocians, renewed the war, and again became formidable. Philip, under the pretence of checking his progress, attempted to seize Thermopylæ; but had the mortification to find the straits pre-occupied by the Athenians. He returned home, apparently wearied of Grecian politics; but he had purchased the services of venal orators, whose intrigues soon afforded him a plausible pretext for renewed interference. The war lingered for two or three years; the treasures of the Delphic temple began to fail, and the Phocians longed for peace. But the vengeance of the Thebans was insatiable: they besought Philip to crush the impious profaners of the temple; and that prince, having lulled the suspicions of the Athenians, in spite of the urgent warnings of the patriotic Demosthenes, passed the straits without opposition, and laid the unhappy Phocians prostrate at the feet of their inveterate enemies (B.C. 347). Their cities were dismantled, their country laid desolate, and their vote in the Amphictyonic council transferred to the king of Macedon.

A new sacred war was excited by the artifices of Æschines, the Athenian deputy to the Amphictyonic council, a venal orator, who had long sold himself to Philip. He accused the

Locrians of Amphissa of cultivating the Cirrhean plain, which had been consecrated with such solemn ceremonies in the first sacred war. The Locrians, after the example of the Phocians, refused obedience to the sentence of the Amphictyons; and the charge of conducting the war against them was entrusted to Philip (B.C. 339). He hastened to Delphi, marched against Amphissa, took it by storm; and soon after revealed his designs against the liberties of Greece, by seizing and fortifying Elateia, the capital of Phocis. The Athenians and Thebans instantly took up arms; but they entrusted their forces to incompetent generals; and when they encountered the Macedonians at Chæroneia, they were irretrievably defeated. The independence of the Grecian communities was thus destroyed; and in a general convention of the Amphictyonic states at Corinth (B.C. 337), Philip was chosen captain-general of confederate Greece, and appointed to lead their united forces against the Persian empire.

CHAPTER XI.

THE HISTORY OF MACEDON.

SECTION I.—*Geographical Outline.*

THE range of Mount Hæmus separates Thrace and Macedon from northern Europe, and the Cambunian mountains on the south divide the latter country from Thessaly. The space intervening between these mountain-chains was, during a long succession of ages, distinguished by different appellations, according as the barbarous nations that tenanted these regions rose into temporary eminence. The most ancient name of Macedonia was Æmathia; but the time and cause of the appellation being changed are unknown. It is difficult to describe the boundaries of a country whose limits were constantly varying; but in its most flourishing state, Macedon was bounded on the north by the river Strymon, and the Scardian branch of Mount Hæmus; on the east by the Ægean Sea; on the south by the Cambunian mountains; and on the west by the Adriatic. It was said to contain one hundred and fifty different nations; and this number will not appear exaggerated, when it is remembered that each of its cities and towns was regarded as an independent state.

The western division of the country, on the coast of the Adriatic, was for the most part possessed by the uncivilised Taulantii. In their territory stood Epidamnus, founded by a Corcyrean colony, whose name the Romans changed to Dyracchium (*Durazzo*), on account of its ill-omened signification; and Apollonia, a city colonised by the Corinthians. South of the Taulantii, but still on the Adriatic coast, was the territory of the Alymiotæ, whose chief cities were Elyma and Bullis. East of these lay a little inland district called the kingdom of Orestes, because the son of Agamemnon is said to have settled there after the murder of his mother.

The south-eastern part of the country, called Æmathia, or Macedonia Proper, contained Ægæa, or Edessa, the cradle of the Macedonian monarchy, and Pella, the favourite capital of its most powerful kings. The districts of Æmathia that bordered the sea were called Pieria, and were consecrated to the Muses: they contained the important cities Pydna, Phylace, and Dium. North-east was the region of Amphaxitis, bordering the Thermaic Gulf: its chief cities were Therma, subsequently called Thessalonica (*Salonichi*), and Stagira, the birthplace of Aristotle.

The Chalcidian peninsula, between the Thermaic and Strymonian Gulfs, has its coast deeply indented by noble bays and inlets of the Ægean Sea. It contained many important trading cities and colonies, the chief of which were Pallene, in the headland of the same name; Potidæa, a Corinthian colony; Torone, on the Toronaic Gulf; and Olynthus, famous for the many sieges it sustained. In the region of Edonia, near the river Strymon, was Amphipolis, a favourite colony of the Athenians, Scotussa, and Crenides, whose name was changed to Philippi by the father of Alexander the Great.

The most remarkable mountains of Macedon were the Scardian and other branches from the chain of Hæmus; Pangæus, celebrated for its rich mines of gold and silver; Athos, which juts into the Ægean Sea, forming a remarkable and dangerous promontory; and Olympus, which partly belonged to Thessaly. Most of these, but especially the Scardian chain and Mount Athos, were richly wooded, and the timber they produced was highly valued by ship-builders. The principal rivers falling into the Adriatic were the Panyasus, the Apsus, the Laüs, and the Celydnus; on the Ægean side were the Haliacmon, the Erigon, the Axius, and the Strymon, which was the northern boundary of Macedon, until Philip extended his dominions to the Nessus.

The soil of Macedonia was very fruitful; on the sea-coast especially it produced great abundance of corn, wine, and oil; and most of its mountains were rich in mineral treasures. Macedonia was celebrated for an excellent breed of horses, to which great attention was paid; no fewer than thirty thousand brood mares being kept in the royal stud at Pella.

Section II.—*History of the Macedonian Monarchy.*

FROM B.C. 813 TO B.C. 323.

An Argive colony, conducted by Caranus, is said to have invaded Æmathia by the command of an oracle, and to have been conducted by a flock of goats to the city of Edessa, which was easily stormed (*B.C. 813). The kingdom thus founded was gradually enlarged at the expense of the neighbouring barbarous nations; and was fast rising into importance when, in the reign of King Amyntas, it became tributary to the Persians (B.C. 513), immediately after the return of Darius from his Scythian campaign. After the overthrow of the Persians at Platææ, Macedon recovered its independence; which, however, was never recognised by the Persian kings. Perdiccas II. (B.C. 454), on coming to the throne, found his dominions exposed to the attacks of the Illyrians and Thracians, while his brother was encouraged to contest the crown by the Athenians. He was induced by these circumstances to take the Spartan side in the first Peloponnesian war, and much of the success of Brasidas was owing to his active co-operation.

Civilisation and the arts of social life were introduced into Macedonia by Archelaus, the son and successor of Perdiccas (B.C. 413). His plans for the reform of the government were greatly impeded by the jealous hostility of the nobles, who were a kind of petty princes, barely conceding to their kings the right of precedence. He was a generous patron of learning and learned men; he invited Socrates to his court; and munificently protected Euripides when he was forced to depart from Athens.

Archelaus was murdered by Craterus, one of his favourites (B.C. 400); and his death was followed by a series of civil wars and sanguinary revolutions, which possess no interest or importance. They were terminated by the accession of Philip (B.C. 360), who, on the death of his brother Perdiccas III., escaped from Thebes, whither he had been sent as a hostage, and was chosen king in preference to his nephew, whose infancy disqualified him from reigning in a crisis of difficulty and danger.

Philip found his new kingdom assailed by four formidable armies, and distracted by the claims of two rival competitors for the throne, one of whom had the powerful support of the Athenians. Educated in the arts of war and state-policy by the great Epaminondas, Philip displayed valour and wisdom adequate to the crisis: he purchased, by large bribes, the forbearance rather than the friendship of the Illyrians, Pæonians, and Thracians; he then marched with his whole force against Argæus and his Athenian auxiliaries, whom he defeated in a general engagement. Argæus was slain, and his supporters remained prisoners of war. Philip, anxious to court the favour of the Athenians, dismissed his captives without ransom, and resigned his pretensions to Amphipolis.

Having restored tranquillity to his kingdom, he began to prepare for its security by improving the tactics and military discipline of his subjects. Epaminondas, at Leuctra and Mantineia, had shewn the superiority of a heavy column over the long lines in which the Greeks usually arranged their forces; and, improving on this lesson, he instituted the celebrated Macedonian phalanx. He soon found the advantage of these improvements: having been forced to war by the Pæonians, he subdued their country, and made it a Macedonian province; and then, without resting, he marched against the Illyrians, whom he overthrew so decisively, that they begged for peace on any conditions he pleased to impose.

While Athens was involved in the fatal war against the colonies, Philip, though professing the warmest friendship for the republic, captured Amphipolis, Pydna, and Potidæa; and stripped Cotys, king of Thrace, the most faithful ally the Athenians possessed, of a great portion of his dominions. Thence he turned his arms against the tyrants of Thessaly and Epirus; and received from the Thessalians, in gratitude for his services, the cession of all the revenues arising from their fairs and markets, as well as all the conveniences of their harbours and shipping. When the campaign was concluded (B.C. 357), he married Olympias, daughter of the king of Epirus, a princess equally remarkable for her crimes and her misfortunes.

While Greece was distracted by the second sacred war, Philip was steadily pursuing his policy of extending his northern frontiers, and securing the maritime cities of Thrace. He was vigorously opposed by Kersobleptes and an Athenian army; in spite, however, of these enemies, he captured the important city of Methone; but he deemed the conquest dearly purchased by the loss of an eye during the siege. His attention was next directed to the sacred war, which he was invited to undertake by the Thebans. Having subdued the Phocians, he made an attempt to seize Thermopylæ (B.C. 352), but was baffled by the energetic promptitude of the Athenians. They were roused to this display of valour by the eloquent harangues of the orator Demosthenes, whose whole life was spent in opposing Philip's designs against Grecian liberty. He was soon after doomed to meet a second disappointment; his troops being driven from the island of Eubœa by the virtuous Phocion, the last and most incorruptible of the long list of generals and statesmen that adorned the Athenian republic.

These disappointments only stimulated his activity. Having purchased, by large bribes, the services of several traitors in Olynthus, he marched against that opulent city (B.C. 349), while the venal orators at Athens, whom he had taken into his pay, dissuaded the careless and sensual Athenians from hastening to the relief of their allies. The noble exhortations, solemn warnings, and bitter reproaches of Demosthenes, failed to inspire his countrymen with energy: they wasted the time of action in discussions, embassies, and fruitless expeditions; and when they began to prepare for some more serious interference, they were astounded by the intelligence that Olynthus was no more. It had been betrayed to Philip, who levelled its walls and buildings to the ground, and dragged the inhabitants into slavery. This triumph was followed by the conquest of the whole Chalcidian peninsula, with its valuable commercial marts and sea-ports. His artifices and bribes disarmed the vengeance of the Athenians, and lulled them into a fatal security, while Philip finally put an end to the sacred war by the utter destruction of the Phocians. They even permitted him to extend his conquests in Thebes, and to acquire a commanding influence in the Peloponnesus, by leading an armament thither, which completed the humiliation of the Spartans.

For several years Philip was engaged in the conquest of the commercial cities in the Thracian Chersonese and on the shores of the Propontis, while the Athenians made some vigorous but desultory efforts to check his progress. At length the third sacred war against the Locrians of Amphissa gave him an opportunity of again appearing as the champion of the national religion of Greece. He entered Phocis, and thence marched to Amphissa, which he totally destroyed (B.C. 338). Before the southern Greeks could recover from their astonishment, he threw off the mask which had hitherto concealed his plans, and announced to the states his design of becoming their master, by seizing and fortifying Elateia. The Thebans and Athenians united in defence of Grecian liberty, but unfortunately they entrusted their forces to feeble and treacherous commanders. They encountered the Macedonians, headed by Philip and his valiant son Alexander, in the plains of Chæroneia, and were irretrievably ruined. They were forced to accept of peace dictated by the conqueror, who treated the Thebans with dreadful severity, but shewed great forbearance and kindness to the Athenians. In the following year a general convention of the Grecian states was held at Corinth, where it was resolved that all should unite in a war against the Persians, and that Philip should be appointed captain-general of the confederate forces. While preparations were making for this great enterprise, Philip was stabbed to the heart by Pausanias, a Macedonian nobleman (B.C. 336), whose motives for committing such an atrocious crime cannot be satisfactorily ascertained.

Alexander, deservedly surnamed the Great, succeeded his father, but on his accession had to contend against a host of enemies. The Thracians, the Illyrians, and the other barbarous tribes of the north, took up arms, hoping that they might easily triumph over his youth and inexperience. But they were miserably disappointed. Alexander, in an incredibly short space of time, forced their fastnesses, and inflicted on them so severe a chastisement, that they never again dared to attempt a revolt. But, in the meantime, a report had been spread in Greece, that Alexander had fallen in Illyria. The different states began to make vigorous preparations for shaking off the yoke of Macedon; and the Thebans took the lead in the revolt, by murdering the governors that Philip had appointed, and besieging the garrison in the Cadmeia (B.C. 335). Fourteen days had scarcely elapsed, when Alexander, eager for vengeance, appeared before the walls of Thebes. After a brief struggle, the city was taken by storm, and levelled with the ground. The conqueror spared the lives of those who were descended from Pindar, of the priestly families, and of all who had shewn attachment to the Macedonian interest; but the rest of the inhabitants were doomed to death or slavery. This dreadful calamity spread terror throughout Greece: the states hastened to renew their submission; and Alexander, whose whole soul was bent on the conquest of Asia, accepted their excuses, and renewed the confederacy, of which his father had been chosen chief. He then entrusted the government of Greece and Macedon to Antipater, and prepared to invade the great empire of Persia with an army not exceeding five thousand horse and thirty thousand foot (B.C. 334). He led his forces to Sestus in Thrace, whence they were transported across the Hellespont without opposition, the Persians having totally neglected the defence of their western frontier.

The Persian satraps rejected the prudent advice of Memnon, who recommended them to lay waste the country, and force the Macedonians to return home by the pressure of famine; but they collected an immense army, with which they took post on the Granicus, a river that flows from Mount Ida into the Propontis. Alexander did not hesitate a moment in engaging the enemy, notwithstanding the vast superiority of the hostile forces. He forded the river at the head of his cavalry, and, after being exposed to great personal danger, obtained a decisive victory, with the loss of only eighty-five horsemen and thirty of the light infantry. This glorious achievement was followed by the subjugation of all the provinces west of the river Halys, which had formed the ancient kingdom of Lydia; and before the first campaign closed, Alexander was the undisputed master of Asia Minor.

The second campaign opened with the reduction of Phrygia, after which the Macedonian hero entered Cilicia, and, marching through the pass called the Syrian Gates, reached the bay of Issus, where he expected to meet Darius and the Persian army. But that monarch, persuaded by his flatterers that Alexander was afraid to meet him and trembled at his approach, had entered the defiles in quest of the Greeks, and was thus entangled in the narrow valleys of the Syrian straits, where it was impossible to derive advantage from his vast superiority of numbers. Alexander instantly prepared to profit by this imprudence. He attacked the barbarian columns with his resistless phalanx, and broke them to pieces. The valour of the Greek mercenaries in the pay of Persia for a time rendered the victory doubtful; but the Macedonians, victorious in every other part of the field, attacked this body in flank, and put it to a total rout. Darius fled in the very beginning of the engagement, leaving his wife, his mother, his daughters, and his infant son, to the mercy of the conqueror. The Persians, entangled and crowded in the defiles of the mountains, suffered so severely in their flight, that they made no effort to defend their camp, which, with all its vast treasures, became the prey of the Macedonians. The conduct of Alexander after this unparalleled victory proved that he deserved success. He treated the captive Persian princesses with the greatest respect and kindness, and dismissed without ransom the Greeks whom he had made prisoners while fighting against their country.

Before invading Upper Asia, Alexander prudently resolved to subdue the maritime provinces. He encountered no resistance until he demanded to be admitted into the city of Tyre, when the inhabitants boldly set him at defiance. It would be inconsistent with our narrow limits to describe the siege of this important place (B. C. 332). Suffice it to say, that, after a tedious siege and desperate resistance, Tyre was taken by storm, and its inhabitants either butchered or enslaved. This success was followed by the submission of all Palestine, except

Gaza, which made as obstinate a defence as Tyre, and was as severely punished. From Gaza the Macedonians entered Egypt, which submitted to them almost without a blow.

Having received during the winter considerable reinforcements from Greece, Macedon, and Thrace, Alexander opened his fourth campaign by crossing the Euphrates at Thapsacus; thence he advanced to the Tigris, and, having forded that river, entered the plains of Assyria. He found Darius with an immense army, composed not merely of Persians, but of the wild tribes from the deserts east of the Caspian, encamped near the village of Gaugamela; but as this place is little known, the battle that decided the fate of an empire is more usually named from Arbela, the nearest town of importance to the plains on which it was fought (B.C. 331). Having halted for a few days to refresh his men, Alexander advanced early in the morning against the vast host of Darius. The battle was won by the Macedonian phalanxes breaking the barbarian lines; for there is no instance, either in ancient or modern times, of an Asiatic army having rallied when once thrown into confusion.

Forty thousand Persians fell in the battle or the pursuit; the loss of the Greeks did not exceed five hundred men. The triumph was, however, sullied by the wanton destruction of Persepolis, which Alexander is said to have burned at the instigation of an Athenian courtezan, when heated with wine during the rejoicings after the victory.

The first intention of Darius after his defeat was to establish himself in Media; but hearing that Alexander was approaching Ecbatana, he fled to Hyrcania with a small escort. Here he was deposed by the satrap Bessus, and thrown into chains. On receiving this intelligence, Alexander advanced against Bessus with the utmost speed; but he came too late to save the unhappy Darius, who was savagely stabbed by the rebels, and left to expire at the road-side. His fate was soon avenged by his former enemy. Alexander continued the pursuit so vigorously, that Bessus was soon taken, and put to death with the most horrible tortures. Spitamenes, and several other satraps, still maintained a desperate struggle for independence, assisted by the barbarous tribes of the desert. Four years were spent in subduing these chiefs and their allies; in the course of which time Alexander conquered Bactria, Sogdiana, and the countries now included in southern Tartary, Khorassán, and Kabúl (B.C. 327). But, still desirous of further triumphs, he resolved to invade India.

Whilst Alexander was thus engaged, the Lacedæmonians, instigated by their warlike monarch Agis, declared war against Macedon; but were speedily subdued by Antipater. They sent ambassadors into Asia to supplicate the clemency of the Macedonian monarch, and were generously pardoned by Alexander (B.C. 330). Another proof of the young hero's respect for the ancient Grecian states, was his permitting the Athenians to banish Æschines, the ancient friend of Macedon, after he had been conquered by Demosthenes in the most remarkable oratorical contest recorded in the annals of eloquence. Æschines accused Ctesiphon for having proposed that a golden crown should be given to Demosthenes as a testimony to the rectitude of his political career. Æschines assailed the whole course of policy recommended by Demosthenes, declaring that it had caused the ruin of Grecian independence. Demosthenes defended his political career so triumphantly, that Æschines was sent into banishment for having instituted a malicious prosecution.

Alexander, having made all necessary preparations for the invasion of India (B.C. 327), advanced towards that country by the route of Kandahar, which is that generally used by caravans to and from Persia at the present day. One division of his army, having pushed forward to the banks of the Indus, prepared every thing requisite for fording the river, while the king was engaged in subduing such cities and fortresses as might be of service in forming magazines, should he advance, or securing a retreat, if he found it necessary to return. No opposition was made to the passage of the Indus. Alexander received on its eastern bank the submission of Taxiles, a powerful Indian prince, who supplied him with seven thousand Indian horse as auxiliaries. Continuing his march through the country now called the Punj-áb, or land of the five rivers, he reached the banks of the Hydaspes (*Jhilúm*), and found the opposite side occupied by an Indian prince, called Porus by the historians, though that name, like Brennus among the Gauls, and Darius among the Persians, more properly designates an office than an individual.

The Indian army was more numerous than the Macedonian, and it had besides the support of three hundred war-chariots and two hundred elephants. Alexander could not pass the river in the presence of such a host without danger; but by a series of stratagems he lulled the enemy into false security, and reached the right bank with little interruption. A battle ensued, in which the Indians were totally defeated, and Porus himself made prisoner. The conqueror continued his march eastwards, crossing the Acesines (*Chunáb*) and the Hydraotes (*Raví*); but when he reached the Hyphasis (*Sutleze*), his troops unanimously refused to continue their march; and Alexander was reluctantly forced to make the Punj-áb the limit of his conquests. He determined, however, to return into central Asia by a different route from that by which he had advanced, and caused vessels to be built on the Hydaspes to transport his troops down that stream to its junction with the Indus, and thence to the ocean. His navigation employed several months, being frequently retarded by the hostilities of the natives, especially the warlike tribe of the Malli. After having wistfully surveyed the waters of the Indian Ocean, Alexander determined to proceed towards Persepolis through the barren solitudes of Gedrosia (B.C. 325), while his fleet under Nearchus was employed in the survey of the Persian Gulf, from the mouth of the Indus to that of the Euphrates. He endured many hardships; but at length arrived, with less loss than might reasonably have been anticipated, in the fertile provinces of Persia. His active mind was next directed to securing the vast empire he had acquired, and joining Europe to Asia by the bonds of commercial intercourse. No better proof of the wisdom of his plans can be given than the fact that most of the cities he founded as trading marts are still the places of most commercial importance in their respective countries. But while he was thus honourably and usefully employed, his career was cut short by a fever, the consequence of excessive drinking,—a vice in which all the Macedonians were prone to indulge after the fatigues of war (B.C. 324, May 28th). His sudden death prevented him from making any arrangements respecting the succession or a regency; but in his last agony he gave his ring to Perdiccas, a Macedonian nobleman who had obtained the chief place in his favour after the death of Hephæstion.

Section III.—*Dissolution of the Macedonian Empire.*

FROM B.C. 324 TO B.C. 301.

Perdiccas was the only one of Alexander's followers that refused a portion of his treasures when the young hero shared them among his friends, just before his invasion of Asia. Possessing no small share of the enthusiasm of his late illustrious master, tempered by policy and prudence, Perdiccas seemed the best fitted of all the generals to consolidate the mighty empire which Alexander had acquired. But the Macedonian nobles possessed a more than ordinary share of the pride and turbulence that distinguishes a feudal aristocracy; they had formed several conspiracies against the life of the late monarch, by whose exploits and generosity they had so largely profited; and consequently they were not disposed to submit to one who had so recently been their equal. Scarcely had the regency been formed, when the Macedonian infantry, at the instigation of Meleager, chose for their sovereign Arrhidæus, the imbecile brother of Alexander. The civil war consequent on this measure was averted at the very instant it was about to burst forth, by the resignation of Arrhidæus; and as his incapacity soon became notorious, all parties concurred in the propriety of a new arrangement. It was accordingly agreed that Perdiccas should be regent, but that Arrhidæus should retain the shadow of royalty; provision was made for the child with which Roxana, Alexander's widow, was pregnant; and the principal provinces were divided among the Macedonian generals, with the powers previously exercised by the Persian satraps.

During these dissensions the body of Alexander lay unburied and neglected, and it was not until two years after his death that his remains were consigned to the tomb. But his followers still shewed their respect for his memory by retaining the feeble Arrhidæus on the throne, and preventing the marriage of Perdiccas with Cleopatra, the daughter of Philip; a union which manifestly was projected to open a way to the throne.

But while this project of marriage occupied the attention of the regent, a league had secretly been formed for his destruction; and the storm burst forth from a quarter whence it was least expected. Alexander, in his march against Darius, had been contented with receiving the nominal submission of the northern provinces of Asia Minor, inhabited by the barbarous tribes of the Cappadocians and Paphlagonians. Impatient of subjection, these savage nations asserted their independence after the death of Alexander, and chose Ariarathes for their leader. Perdiccas sent against them Eumenes, who had hitherto fulfilled the peaceful duties of a secretary; and sent orders to Antigonus and Leonatus, the governors of Western Asia, to join the expedition with all their forces. These commands were disobeyed; and Perdiccas was forced to march with the royal army against the insurgents. He easily defeated these undisciplined troops, but sullied his victory by unnecessary cruelty. On his return he summoned the satraps of Western Asia to appear before his tribunal, and answer for their disobedience. Antigonus, seeing his danger, entered into a league with Ptolemy the satrap of Egypt, Antipater the governor of Macedon, and several other noblemen, to crush the regency. Perdiccas, on the other hand, leaving Eumenes to guard Lower Asia, marched with the choicest divisions of the royal army against Ptolemy, whose craft and ability he dreaded even more than his power.

Antipater and Craterus were early in the field; they crossed the Hellespont with the army that had been left for the defence of Macedon, and on their landing were joined by Neoptolemus, the governor of Phrygia. Their new confederate informed the Macedonian leaders that the army of Eumenes was weak, disorderly, and incapable of making the slightest resistance. Seduced by this false information, they divided their forces; Antipater hastening through Phrygia in pursuit of Perdiccas, while Craterus and Neoptolemus marched against Eumenes. They encountered him in the Trojan plain, and were completely defeated. Neoptolemus was slain in the first onset, and Craterus lay mortally wounded, undistinguished among the heaps of dead. Eumenes, having learned the state of Craterus, hastened to relieve him; he found him in the agonies of death, and bitterly lamented the misfortunes that had changed old friends into bitter enemies. Immediately after this great victory, Eumenes sent intelligence of his success to Perdiccas; but two days before the messenger reached the royal camp the regent was no more. His army, wearied by the long siege of Pelusium, became dissatisfied; their mutinous dispositions were secretly encouraged by the emissaries of Ptolemy. Python, who had been formerly employed by the regent in the ruthless massacre of some Greek mercenaries for disobedience of orders, organised a conspiracy, and Perdiccas was murdered in his tent (B.C. 321). Had the news of the victory obtained by Eumenes reached the camp earlier, the regent's life might have been saved; but now the news served only to aggravate the malice of the insurgent satraps.

In the meantime a brief struggle for independence had taken place in Greece, which is commonly called the Lamian war, from the town in whose neighbourhood the principal contests occurred. Instigated by the orators Hyperides and Demosthenes, the Athenians boldly proclaimed themselves the restorers of Grecian freedom, and called on the other states to second them in the great struggle for liberty. The Ætolians, and the hardy mountaineers of Doris and Phocis, eagerly responded to the summons; but of the other states, Thebes no longer existed, Sparta was too proud to act under her ancient rival, the Achæans and Arcadians too prudent to risk their present tranquillity for the doubtful chances of war (B.C. 323). Alarmed by the intelligence of this confederacy, Antipater marched to secure the straits of Thermopylæ; but he was met by the Athenians under Leosthenes, and his forces put to the rout. The remnant of the Macedonian army sought refuge in Lamia, a strong fortress on the Malian Gulf, which the victorious army closely besieged. Unfortunately for the Athenians, Leosthenes was slain in a sally, and the command of the confederates entrusted to Antiphilus, a general of great valour, but deficient in skill and discretion. Intoxicated by a second victory over the Macedonians, he kept careless guard, of which Antipater took advantage to break through the hostile lines, and form a junction with a fresh army from Macedon. Thus reinforced, he attacked the confederates, and completely annihilated their army. The Athenians had no resource but submission: they were compelled to abolish the democracy, to receive garrisons into their fortresses, and to give up their patriotic orators to the conqueror's vengeance. The cruel Antipater put Hyperides to death, after having subjected him to insult and torture. Demosthenes escaped a similar fate by committing suicide. Undismayed by these calamities, the Ætolians resolved to continue the war; and Antipater, eager to march into Asia against Perdiccas, was forced to grant them peace on favourable conditions.

As soon as Ptolemy had been informed of the murder of Perdiccas, he came to the royal army with a large supply of wine and provisions. His kindness and courteous manners so won upon these turbulent soldiers, that they unanimously offered him the regency; but he had the prudence to decline so dangerous an office. On his refusal, the feeble Arrhidæus and the traitor Python were appointed to the regency, just as the news arrived of the recent victory of Eumenes. This intelligence filled the royal army with indignation. Craterus had been always a favourite with the soldiers; Eumenes was despised on account of his former unwarlike occupation. They hastily passed a vote proclaiming Eumenes and his adherents public enemies, and denouncing all who afforded them support or protection. The advance of an army to give effect to these decrees was delayed by a new revolution. Eurydice, the wife of Arrhidæus, a woman of great ambition and considerable talent for intrigue, wrested the regency from her feeble husband and Python, but was stripped of power on the arrival of Antipater, who reproached the Macedonians for submitting to the government of a woman; and, being ably supported by

Antigonus and Seleucus, obtained for himself the office of regent.

No sooner had Antipater been invested with supreme power than he sent Arrhidæus and Eurydice prisoners to Pella, and entrusted the conduct of the war against Eumenes to the crafty and ambitious Antigonus. Cassander, the son of Antipater, joined the expedition with a thousand horse, and, being himself a selfish and cunning statesman, he soon penetrated the secret plans of Antigonus, and vainly warned the regent of his dangerous designs. A quarrel soon took place between the worthy colleagues; and Cassander returned to Europe, where he was about to commence a career as bold and bloody as that of Antigonus in Asia. Eumenes was unable to cope with the forces sent against him; having been defeated in the open field, he took shelter in Nora, a Cappadocian city, and maintained a vigorous defence, rejecting the many tempting offers by which Antigonus endeavoured to win him to the support of his designs (B.C. 318). The death of Antipater produced a new revolution in the empire; and Eumenes in the meantime escaped from Nora, accompanied by his principal friends, on fleet horses that had been trained for this especial service.

Antipater, at his death, bequeathed the regency to Polysperchon, excluding his son Cassander from power on account of his criminal intrigues with the wicked and ambitious Eurydice. Though a brave general, Polysperchon had not the qualifications of a statesman: he provoked the powerful resentment of Antigonus by entering into a close alliance with Eumenes; and he permitted Cassander to strengthen himself in southern Greece, where he seized the strong fortress of Munychia. His next measures were of still more questionable policy: he recalled Olympias, the mother of Alexander, whom Antipater had banished on account of her turbulent disposition; and he proclaimed his intention of restoring democracy in the Grecian states. The latter edict was received with the utmost enthusiasm at Athens; an urgent embassy was sent to the regent, requesting him to send an army to protect the city from Cassander and his partisans. Polysperchon sent his son Alexander with a considerable force into Attica; and no sooner were news of his approach received, than the restoration of democracy was voted by a tumultuous assembly, and a decree passed for proceeding against all aristocrats, as capital enemies of the state (B.C. 317). Several illustrious individuals, and among others the virtuous Phocion, fell victims to this burst of popular violence, which the regent made no effort to check or control.

Cassander, however, remained master of the ports of Athens, and was thus enabled to fit out a considerable fleet, which he sent to the Thracian Bosphorus, under the command of his friend Nicanor, to second the enterprises of Antigonus. Nicanor was at first defeated by the royal navy; but being reinforced, he renewed the engagement, and captured all the enemies' ships except the admiral's galley. The news of this victory rendered the power of Antigonus paramount in Lower Asia, and gave Cassander possession of Athens. The Athenians, however, suffered no injury from the change; the government of their city having been entrusted to Demetrius Phalereus, who ruled them with justice and moderation during ten years.

Polysperchon, unable to drive Cassander from Attica, entered the Peloponnesus to punish the Arcadians, and engaged in a fruitless seige of Megalopolis. In the meantime Olympias, to whom he had confided the government of Macedon, seized Arrhidæus and Euridyce, whom she had murdered in prison. Cassander hasted, at the head of all his forces, to avenge the death of his mistress: Olympias, unable to meet him in the field, fled to Pydna; but the city was forced to surrender after a brief defence, and Olympias was immediately put to death. Among the captives were Roxana the widow, Alexander Ægus the posthumous son, and Thessalonica the youngest daughter, of Alexander the Great. Cassander sought and obtained the hand of the latter princess, and thus consoled himself for the loss of his beloved Euridyce. By this marriage he acquired such influence, that Polysperchon did not venture to return home, but continued in the Peloponnesus, where he retained for some time a shadow of authority over the few Macedonians who still clung to the family of Alexander.

In Asia, Eumenes maintained the royal cause against Antigonus, though deserted by all the satraps, and harassed by the mutinous dispositions of his troops, especially the Argyraspides, a body of guards that Alexander had raised to attend his own person, and presented with the silver shields from which they derived their name. After a long struggle, both armies joined in a decisive engagement; the Argyraspides broke the hostile infantry, but learning that their baggage had in the meantime been captured by the light troops of the enemy, they mutinied in the very moment of victory, and delivered their leader, bound with his own sash, into the hands of his merciless enemy (B.C. 315). The faithful Eumenes was put to death by the traiterous Antigonus; but he punished the Argyraspides for their treachery: justly dreading their turbulence, he sent them in small detachments against the barbarians; and thus sacrificed in detail the veterans that had overthrown the Persian empire.

Antigonus, immediately after his victory, began openly to aim at the sovereignty of the entire Macedonian empire. The weight of his power was first directed against the satraps whose rebellious conduct had enabled him to triumph over Eumenes. Peucestes of Persia was banished, Python of Media put to death, and Seleucus of Babylon could only escape a similar fate by a precipitate flight into Egypt. The Macedonian governors in the west, instigated by Seleucus, formed a league for mutual defence, and sent an embassy to Antigonus, who answered their proposals with menace and insult. But at the same time he prepared to wage a more effectual war than one of words: while his armies overran Syria and Asia Minor, he roused the southern Greeks, the Ætolians, and Epirotes, to attack Cassander in Macedon. He bribed the mountaineers and northern barbarians to attack Lysimachus in Thrace, while his son Demetrius, afterwards named Poliorcetes, or the conqueror of cities, marched against the Egyptian Ptolemy.

The first important operations of the war took place in southern Syria. Ptolemy overthrew Demetrius near Gaza, and, in consequence of his victory, became master of Palestine and Phœnicia. But the Egyptians were defeated in their turn at the commencement of the next campaign; their recent acquisitions were lost as rapidly as they had been gained; and Demetrius would have invaded their country with great prospect of success, had he not been involved in an unwise contest with the Arabs.

We have already mentioned that the excavated city of Petra was the great depôt of the caravan-trade between the southern countries of Asia and northern Africa. Athenæus, a general in the army of Antigonus, was sent to seize its rich stores: he surprised the inhabitants by a rapid march and unexpected attack, and was returning laden with plunder to join the main army; but the Nabathæan Arabs, enraged by their loss, hastily collected their forces, and, urging their dromedaries through the desert, overtook Athenæus near Gaza, where they not only recovered the spoil, but almost annihilated his army. Demetrius eagerly hasted to avenge this loss, but he was baffled by the fastnesses of Arabia Petræa; and when he returned into Syria, he received intelligence that directed all his attention to the state of Upper Asia.

After Ptolemy's victory at Gaza, Seleucus, with a small but gallant band of attendants, boldly threw himself into his ancient satrapy of Babylon, and was received with so much enthusiasm that he obtained possession of all his former power without striking a blow. The Persian and Median satraps appointed by Antigonus hastened to destroy the dangerous enemy that had thus suddenly arisen; but they were totally routed, after a brief but ineffectual struggle (B.C. 312). This battle, from which a new dynasty may be dated, forms an important epoch in Grecian history, called the era of the Seleucidæ.

Alarmed by these occurrences, Antigonus hastened to conclude a peace with his other opponents; and a treaty was ratified which was pregnant with the elements of future war. Cassander agreed to restore the freedom of the Grecian cities, without the slightest intention of performing his promise. Ptolemy consented that Antigonus should retain his present possessions, while he was preparing a fleet to seize the Asiatic islands, previous to invading Syria; Lysimachus was resolved to annex the northern provinces of Asia Minor to his satrapy of Thrace; and all agreed to acknowledge the son of Alexander for their sovereign, though a resolution had been already formed for his destruction. Alarmed by the murmurs of the Macedonians, Cassander caused Roxana, Alexander Ægus, and Hercules, the last survivor of the great conqueror, to be assassinated; and soon after consigned the princess Cleopatra to the same fate, dreading that she might bestow her hand on some of the rival satraps.

It was not long before Antigonus discovered that he had been deceived in the recent treaty by Cassander and Ptolemy. He sent his son Demetrius into Greece, under the pretence of restoring the liberty of the states; and Athens, still enamoured of the memory of its freedom, opened its gates to the young prince (B. C. 308). Thence he sailed to Cyprus, and gained a decisive victory over the Egyptian fleet that came to protect the island. He was baffled, however, in an attempt to invade Egypt; and when he went from thence to besiege Rhodes, he was recalled to Greece by the prayers of the Athenians, who were exposed to imminent danger from the power of Cassander.

The success of Demetrius induced his father to nominate him captain-general of Greece,—an injudicious measure, which led to the formation of a new confederacy against Antigonus. Cassander renewed his attacks on southern Greece; Ptolemy entered Syria; Lysimachus, with an army of veterans, invaded Thrace; while Seleucus marched westwards with the numerous forces of Upper Asia, including four hundred and eighty elephants. The junction of Lysimachus and Seleucus in Phrygia necessarily brought on a decisive engagement, which Antigonus, reinforced by his gallant son Demetrius, shewed no anxiety to avoid (B. C. 301). The battle that decided the fate of an empire was fought at Ipsus in Phrygia: it ended in the defeat and death of Antigonus, and the destruction of the power that he had raised. The consequences of this victory were, a new partition of the provinces, and the erection of the satrapies into independent kingdoms. Seleucus became monarch of Upper Asia; Ptolemy added Syria and Palestine to Egypt; Lysimachus obtained the northern provinces of Asia Minor as an appendage to his kingdom of Thrace; and the services of

Cassander were rewarded not only with the sovereignty of Macedon and Greece, but also of the rich province of Cilicia. Thus, in the course of a single generation, the mighty empire of Alexander had risen to unparalleled greatness, and fallen into hopeless ruin; while not a single descendant of the illustrious founder was spared to transmit his name to posterity.

CHAPTER XII.

HISTORY OF THE STATES THAT AROSE FROM THE DISMEMBERMENT OF THE

MACEDONIAN EMPIRE.

SECTION I.—*The History of Macedon and Greece from the Battle of Ipsus to the Roman Conquest.*

FROM B.C. 301 TO B.C. 146.

AFTER the fatal battle of Ipsus, Demetrius fled to Greece, hoping to obtain a refuge from the Athenians, whom he had essentially served in the days of his prosperity; but the harbours and gates of the city were closed against him. Having obtained, however, the restoration of the ships and money he had deposited there, he established himself in the Peloponnesus, and commenced a desultory naval war against Lysimachus. Seleucus sought an alliance with his ancient enemy, and married Stratonice, the daughter of Demetrius, and this union was equally advantageous to both parties. Cassander did not long survive the establishment of his power: on his death (B.C. 296), he left Macedonia to his three sons, of whom Philip speedily followed his father to the grave. The survivors quarrelled about the division of their inheritance. Antipater murdered his mother Thessalonica, on account of the favour she shewed to his brother Alexander. The vengeance of his brother being, however, supported by the general feeling of the Macedonians, he fled to the court of his father-in-law Lysimachus, where he died prematurely. Dreading the resentment of the Thracian monarch, Alexander sought the aid of Pyrrhus, king of Epirus, and Demetrius Poliorcetes, who both entered Macedon, in the hope of gaining some advantage. The ambition of Demetrius soon provoked the jealousy of the son of Cassander, and he attempted to remove so formidable a competitor by stratagem; but he was counterplotted and slain. The vacant throne was seized by Demetrius, who possessed, in addition to Macedon, Thessaly, a great portion of southern Greece, with the provinces of Attica and Megaris, to which, after a fierce resistance, he added Bœotia. But his restless ambition led him to form plans for the recovery of his father's power in Asia. Seleucus and Ptolemy, in great alarm, roused Lysimachus, king of Thrace, and Pyrrhus, king of Epirus, to attack him at the same time. The Macedonians, terrified by such a confederacy, mutinied; and Demetrius fled, disguised as a common soldier, into the Peloponnesus, which was governed by his son Antigonus (B.C. 287). Pyrrhus obtained possession of the vacant kingdom; but after a brief reign of seven months, he was forced to yield to the superior power or popularity of Lysimachus, and retire to his native Epirus. Demetrius had in the meantime sailed to Asia, with the hope of seizing the provinces belonging to Lysimachus (B.C. 286); but he was driven into Cilicia, and forced to surrender to his father-in-law Seleucus, by whom he was detained in prison until the day of his death (B.C. 284). But his son Antigonus maintained himself in the Peloponnesus, waiting with patience a favourable opportunity of restoring the fortunes of his family.

Lysimachus was unfortunate in his domestic relations: at the instigation of his queen, the wicked Arsinoë, he put to death his gallant son Agathocles, upon which Cassandra, the widow of the young prince, with her brother Ptolemy Ceraunus, fled to the court of Seleucus, and stimulated that prince to war. Lysimachus was defeated and slain (B.C. 282); but in the following year Seleucus was murdered by Ptolemy Ceraunus, who availed himself of the treasures of his victim, and the yet remaining troops of Lysimachus, to usurp the throne of Macedon. In the same year that Seleucus fell (B.C. 281), Pyrrhus invaded Italy as an ally of the Tarentines; the Achæan league was revived in southern Greece; and several Asiatic provinces, especially Cappadocia, Armenia, and Pontus, in the north, and Parthia and Bactria in the east, became independent kingdoms.

Ceraunus did not long retain the crown he had procured by treachery and assassination. An innumerable multitude of Gauls, who had, about two centuries before, settled in Pannonia, driven by want, or perhaps instigated by their restless disposition, poured into Thrace and Macedon, desolating the entire country with the reckless fury of ferocious savages. Ceraunus led an army against them, but was defeated and slain (B.C. 279). In the following year, his successor Sosthenes met the same fate; and the Gauls, under the guidance of their brenn, or chief, advanced into southern Greece. The Athenians, aided by the Ætolians, made a brave defence at the straits of Thermopylæ; but the latter being called home to defend their own country, invaded by a Gallic division, the Athenians were unable any longer to defend the pass, and the main body of the Gauls, entering Phocis, marched to plunder Delphi. Here, however, the success of the invaders ended: the detachment sent against Ætolia was cut to pieces by a nation scarcely less ferocious than the Gauls themselves; and the main body, after suffering severely from cold and storms in the defiles of Mount Parnassus, was almost annihilated by the enthusiastic defenders of the national temple. The miserable remnant of the invaders fell back upon a fresh body of their countrymen, with whom they passed over into Asia; and after inflicting many calamities on the states of Anatolia, obtained possession of the province which received from them the name of Galatia.

Antigonus Gonnatas, the son of Poliorcetes, deriving his name from Gonni in Thessaly, where he had been educated, obtained the throne of Macedon, and transmitted it to his posterity; but he did not, like his predecessors, possess the sovereignty of southern Greece, whose independence had been secured by the Achæan league. This association had been originally revived by the towns of Patræ, Dyme, Tritæa, and Pharæ; but it did not become formidable until it was joined by Sicyon (B.C. 251), after the noble Aratus had freed that city from tyrants.

The return of Pyrrhus from Italy was followed by a new revolution in Macedon; the mercenaries revolted to the Epirote monarch, and Antigonus was driven from the throne. He retired into southern Greece, whither he was soon followed by his rival, who had been solicited to place Cleonymus on the throne of Lacedæmon. Pyrrhus professed that his chief object in entering the Peloponnesus was to deliver the cities from the yoke of Antigonus; but his actions were inconsistent with his declarations, for he ravaged the lands of Laconia, and made an attempt to surprise Sparta. Being defeated in this enterprise, he turned his arms against Argos, and was admitted into the city by some of his secret partisans. But the Argives opened another gate to Antigonus, who entered with a chosen body of troops. A fierce struggle ensued, which was terminated by the death of Pyrrhus. An Argive woman, whose son he was about to slay, struck him with a tile from the roof of the house; he fell from his horse, and was trampled to death in the press (B.C. 271). After a short contest with Alexander, the son of Pyrrhus, Antigonus regained the throne of Macedon, and retained it to his death.

The Achæan league was joined by Corinth, Trœzene, and Epidaurus, when Aratus, by a bold attempt, had driven the Macedonian garrison from the Corinthian citadel. It was finally joined by Athens (B.C. 229), and continually grew in strength, though opposed by the Macedonians and Ætolians. On the death of Antigonus Gonnatas (B.C. 243), his son Demetrius II. became king of Macedon. The ten years of his reign were spent in war with the Ætolians, who had formed a confederacy similar to that of the Achæans. After his death (B.C. 233), Antigonus Doson, cousin to the late monarch, succeeded to the throne, nominally as guardian of the infant prince Philip II., just as a revolution in the Peloponnesus was about to effect a great and important change in the political aspect of Greece.

The ancient laws of Lycurgus were only nominally observed in Sparta: the plunder of foreign countries had introduced wealth and luxury; a law sanctioning the alienation of landed estates had effaced the ancient equality of property; and the gradual decrease of the ruling caste of Spartan families had rendered the oligarchy as weak as it was odious. A bold plan of reform, including a fresh division of landed property, an abolition of debts, and the weakening of the power of the ephori, was brought forward by king Agis III. (B.C. 244): it was at first very successful, but the unsteadiness of Agis, and the opposition of the other king, Leonidas, brought about a counter-revolution (B.C. 241). Agis was strangled by order of the ephori, and his mother and grandmother shared the same fate.

Leonidas compelled the widow of Agis to marry his youthful son Cleomenes, not foreseeing that she was likely to inspire the prince with the principles of her former husband. Soon after his accession to the throne, Cleomenes, relying on the reputation he had acquired by defeating the efforts of Aratus to force Sparta into the Achæan league, renewed the reforms of Agis (B.C. 227); and, as he was unscrupulous in the use of the means requisite to effect his object, he speedily overthrew the ephori, and opened the right of citizenship to all the Lacedæmonians. He then turned his arms against the Achæans (B.C. 224), compelled Argos and Corinth to secede from the league, defeated the confederates at Dyme, and reduced Aratus to such difficulties that he was forced to solicit assistance from the king of Macedon. Antigonus II. readily embraced so favourable an opportunity of restoring the influence of his family in southern Greece. He entered the Peloponnesus, and, after some minor operations, he obtained a complete victory over Cleomenes at Sellasia, on the borders of Laconia, which placed Sparta at his mercy (B.C. 222). Cleomenes fled to Egypt, and the ancient constitution of Lacedæmon was restored. Antigonus did not long survive his victory; he died generally lamented by the Greeks (B.C. 221), and was succeeded by Philip II., son of Demetrius.

The Ætolians were greatly dissatisfied with the peace that followed the battle of Sellasia. No sooner had they received intelligence of the death of Antigonus, than, despising the youth and inexperience of Philip, they commenced a series of piratical attacks on the Messenians and Macedonians, which speedily rekindled the flames of war. Aratus was sent to expel the Ætolians from Messenia, and entered into a convention with their leaders for the purpose; after which he imprudently dismissed the greater part of his army. The Ætolians took advantage of his weakness to attack him unexpectedly, and they then, having ravaged the greater part of the Peloponnesus, returned home laden with plunder.

Philip, being invited to place himself at the head of the

Achæan league, went to Corinth, where a general assembly of the states was held. A declaration of war against the Ætolians was voted by all the southern Greeks, except the Spartans and Eleans, who were both adverse to the league; and active preparations for hostilities were made on both sides. While these affairs engaged attention throughout Greece, little regard was paid to the commercial war between the Byzantines and Rhodians, in consequence of the heavy tolls exacted by the former from all vessels entering the Euxine Sea (B.C. 222). It terminated in favour of the latter, and the Byzantines were forced to abolish the onerous duties.

The war between Philip and the Ætolians was conducted with great obstinacy and cruelty on both sides; Philip's progress was aided by his fleet, which soon rose into importance; but it was also greatly checked by the intrigues of Apelles and other wretches who envied Aratus, and weakened the influence of his prudent counsels. The increasing power of the Romans and Carthaginians, who were already contending for the empire of the world in the second Punic war, at length inclined all the Greeks to peace, for they felt that it would be soon necessary to defend the independence of Greece either against Rome or Carthage, whichever should prove victorious. A treaty was accordingly concluded between the general assembly of the Ætolian states at Naupactus and the representatives of the Achæan confederacy (B.C. 217): Philip attended in person, and greatly contributed to the success of the negotiations.

The Macedonian monarch possessed the ambition but not the military talents of Pyrrhus. Like the great Epirote, he hoped to become the conqueror of Italy, and entered into a strict alliance with Hannibal, who had already invaded the peninsula. About the same time, to get rid of the remonstrances of Aratus, who frequently warned the king of the dangers that would result from his indulgence in ambitious projects, he caused the old general to be poisoned; a crime that filled all Greece with horror and indignation.

The Romans resolved to find Philip so much employment in Greece, that he should not have leisure to attack Italy. They prevailed on the Ætolians to violate the recent treaty, promising them, as a reward, the possession of Acarnania and the Ionian islands. To this confederacy the republics of Sparta and Elis, and the kings of Pergamus and Elis, acceded (B.C. 211). Philip, on the other hand, was supported by the Acarnanians, the Bœotians, and the Achæans. The Romans, and their ally Attalus, king of Pergamus, became masters of the sea; but the former were too much engaged by the presence of Hannibal in Italy to continue their aid to the Ætolians; and Attalus was recalled home to defend his own kingdom from an invasion of the Bithynians. Nearly at the same time, Philopœmen, the worthy successor of Aratus, as head of the Achæan league, defeated and slew with his own hand Machanidas, the usurper of Lacedæmon. The Ætolians, thus deprived of all their allies, made overtures of peace, which were readily accepted (B.C. 208). The Romans made some efforts to interrupt the treaty; but the Ætolians had suffered too severely to continue the war any longer. Scarcely had peace been restored, when Philip entered into an alliance with Prusias, king of Bithynia, against Attalus, king of Pergamus; and with the Syrian monarch against the infant ruler of Egypt. As if these enemies were not sufficient, he declared war against the Rhodians; but was soon punished by the overthrow and ruin of the Macedonian fleet at Chios (B.C. 202). The Athenians were next added to the number of his enemies; and this once-powerful people, no longer able to protect their fallen fortunes, supplicated the Romans for aid. A fleet and army was sent to secure this illustrious city, and it reached Athens just in time to save it from a sudden attack of the Macedonians. The Roman army in Epirus advanced into Macedon, and gained some advantages; but in the second campaign, when the conduct of the war was confided to the consul Flamininus, Philip's fortunes declined so rapidly, that his allies, especially the Achæans, lost all courage, and accepted terms of peace. Though deserted, the Macedonian monarch did not resign all hope; he assembled an army in Thessaly nearly equal to that of his enemies, but inferior in discipline and equipment, with which he took post on a range of low hills, called from their singular shape Cynoscephalæ, or the dogs' heads. In the early part of the decisive battle, the Macedonians at first had the advantage, their right wing having borne down the opposing divisions; but the consul, observing that the left of the Macedonians had not been formed into order of battle, charged them with his cavalry and elephants, and scattered them in a few moments; he then assailed the victorious Macedonian wing in flank and rear. The phalanx, admirable for attack, was an inconvenient body to manœuvre; the phalangites attempted to face about, broke their lines, and were in a moment a disorderly mass, unable to fight or fly. The rout was complete: eight thousand Macedonians fell; five thousand remained prisoners; while the loss of the Romans did not exceed seven hundred men. Without an army and without resources, Philip was forced to beg a peace (B.C. 197); he purchased it by the sacrifice of his navy and the resignation of his supremacy over the Grecian states. The Romans, thus successful, went through the farce of proclaiming the liberties of Greece at the Isthmian games, amid the wildest exultation of the spectators. But Flamininus shewed his insincerity by secretly labouring to weaken the Achæan league; which, however, was strengthened, after the murder of the tyrant Nabis (B.C. 192), by the accession of Sparta.

Antiochus, king of Syria, instigated by Hannibal, who had sought refuge in his court when exiled from his native country, declared war against the Romans (B.C. 194); but instead of attacking their power in Africa or Italy, he passed over into Greece, and was gladly welcomed by the turbulent Ætolians. The Achæans, of course, joined the Romans as soon as their ancient enemies had declared for Antiochus; and Philip, notwithstanding his recent defeat, lent his interest to the same cause. The campaigns of Antiochus were mere repetitions of error and presumption; at length he returned to Asia (B.C. 191), leaving his allies exposed to the vengeance of their enemies. The Ætolians were the most severely treated; the only terms of peace which the Romans would consent to grant reduced them to poverty and deprived them of independence (B.C. 189); but Antiochus having been defeated utterly by the Scipios in Asia, they had no alternative, and were forced to bend their stubborn necks to the heavy yoke imposed upon them. About the same time Sparta was captured by the Achæans, under the command of Philopœmen, and the constitution of Lycurgus finally abolished.

The Romans affected great indignation at the sufferings of the Spartans, and compelled the Achæans to modify the terms they had imposed on the conquered. But this was a trifling calamity compared with that which the league sustained by the loss of Philopœmen, the last great general that maintained the glory of the Hellenic race (B. C. 183). He was made a prisoner by the enemy in a petty war between the Messenians and Achæans, and compelled to swallow poison.

Philip had in the meantime borne very impatiently the overbearing conduct of the Romans; but the exertions of his son Demetrius, whom he had given as a hostage after his defeat at Cynoscephalæ, with the leading men at Rome, prevented a rupture. On this account Demetrius was enthusiastically received by the Macedonians on his return home,—a circumstance of which his elder brother Perseus took advantage to accuse the young prince of treason. Philip delivered this promising young man to the executioner; but soon after his death, discovering his innocence, the wretched monarch died of a broken heart (B.C. 179). Perseus ascended the throne with the certainty that he was secretly hated by the Romans and his own subjects. Pretences for war were easily found: a Roman army crossed the sea, and passed through Epirus and Athamania into Thessaly. Perseus neglected many opportunities of attacking his enemies at a disadvantage; and when he asked for peace, after having triumphed in slight skirmishes, he found that the Romans were more haughty after defeat than after victory. The alliance of Gentius, king of Illyria, might probably have turned the scale of war in favour of the Macedonian monarch; but he defrauded his ally of the subsidy he had promised to enable him to levy an army; and the Romans, landing in Illyria, subdued the whole kingdom within thirty days. Soon afterwards the consul Lucius Æmilius Paulus appeared in Macedon; and his name gave confidence to the friends of Rome, while it filled the partisans of Perseus with confusion (B.C. 169). After some indecisive skirmishes, the

Macedonian monarch was forced to hazard a decisive engagement at Pydna, in which he was irretrievably ruined. Twenty thousand Macedonians were slain; Perseus himself was taken prisoner, and was led in chains to Rome to adorn the triumph of his haughty conqueror.

By the victory at Pydna the fate of Macedon and Greece was sealed: the Romans permitted both, indeed, for a time to enjoy a qualified independence; but they exercised over them a galling supremacy, which rendered their freedom an empty name. Above a thousand of the most eminent Achæans were summoned at one time to Rome, and detained there seventeen years in prison, without being admitted to an audience. Some of these, on their return, stimulated their countrymen to insult the Roman ambassadors at Corinth, who had come to arrange some disputes between the Achæans and the Spartans (B.C. 148). This of course led to a war: the Achæans were every where defeated, and at length Corinth was taken by Mummius, the Roman consul (B.C. 146), who razed that splendid city to the ground. Thenceforward Greece, under the name of Achaia, became a Roman province, and Macedon had been reduced to the same condition some years previously. The shadow of freedom, however, was left to some of the cities, but especially to Athens, which became the university of the Roman empire.

SECTION II.—*History of the Kingdom of Syria under the Seleucidæ.*

FROM B.C. 312 TO B.C. 64.

THE victory of Seleucus over the satraps of Persia and Media, already mentioned (p. 244), gave that monarch possession of the principal part of Upper Asia. In less than four years he became master of the countries between the Oxus, the Indus, and the Euphrates (B.C. 306); and, reviving the projects of Alexander, he invaded India. More fortunate than his illustrious master, he penetrated as far as the Ganges, where he entered into a treaty with Sandracottus, the king of the rich country between the Sutlege and the Ganges. The great number of elephants which Seleucus obtained by this alliance enabled him to turn the scale at the battle of Ipsus; but a more important advantage was, the commercial intercourse established between his subjects and those of Sandracottus. After the death of Antigonus at Ipsus, Seleucus, having obtained the greater part of the late satrap's provinces, made Syria the seat of his government,—an unfortunate choice, since it exposed his kingdom to the jealousy of Egypt, involved it in the troubled politics of the western world, and led the rulers to neglect the rich countries on the Tigris and the Euphrates. During the eighteen years of peace that followed the death of Antigonus, Seleucus founded or embellished several important cities, especially Antioch in Syria, which he made the capital of his dominions, and two Seleucias; one on the Tigris, the other on the Orontes. Anxiety to add Macedon to his dominions induced Seleucus to invade Europe; but in the midst of his career he was murdered by Ptolemy Ceraunus (B.C. 281). He was succeeded by his son Antiochus, surnamed Sóter (*the saviour*), who had for some time governed the provinces of Upper Asia.

Antiochus pursued his father's plans of conquest in Asia Minor; but he ceded his claims over Macedon to Antigonus Gonnatas, and gave his step-daughter in marriage to that monarch. The northern states in Asia Minor that had asserted their independence rapidly attained maturity: Antiochus was defeated by Nicomedes, king of Bithynia, who had obtained the support of the Gallic hordes after their defeat in Greece (B.C. 275), and he was similarly unsuccessful in a war with the king of Pergamus (B.C. 263), whose complete defeat of the Syrians gave security to all the new states. Nor was Soter more fortunate in a war he undertook against Egypt: Magas, the brother of the Egyptian Ptolemy, having married into the Syrian royal family, hoped that by this alliance he would be enabled to establish a new kingdom in Cyrene. Antiochus united with the usurper, and both marched against Ptolemy. The Syrians were defeated in every engagement; their coasts were laid waste by the Egyptian fleet; and Magas was speedily hurled from his throne. On his return, Antiochus marched against the Gauls, who had advanced towards Ephesus (B.C. 262), and in the neighbourhood of that city he was defeated and slain.

Antiochus II. avenged his father's death on the Gauls, and received, from the excessive adulation of his subjects, the surname Theos (*god*). In his reign the provinces of Upper Asia began to slip from the grasp of the Seleucidæ, owing to the progress of the Parthian tribes, the exactions of the provincial governors, and the unwise efforts of the monarch to force the Grecian customs and religion on his subjects. In order to encounter his eastern enemies with effect, Theos deemed it necessary to tranquillise the west, and he accordingly made peace with the king of Egypt. In pursuance of the conditions of this treaty, Antiochus married Berenice, the daughter of Ptolemy, divorcing his former wife Laodicè, and excluding her children from the succession. On the death of Ptolemy, the divorced queen was restored to her station; but she could not forget the insult she had received, nor conquer her dread of being sacrificed to some future arrangement. Influenced by these motives, she poisoned her husband (B.C. 247), and procured the murder of Berenice and her infant son.

Seleucus, surnamed Callinicus (*illustrious conqueror*), succeeded to the throne by his mother's crime, and was immediately engaged in war with Ptolemy Evergetes, who was eager to avenge his sister's murder. Crossing the Syrian deserts with a numerous army, Ptolemy overran rather than conquered Palestine, Babylonia, Persia, and the wealthy provinces of Upper Asia. He returned, bringing with him enormous spoils, among which were the Egyptian idols which Cambyses had taken from Memphis and Thebes. On his way back he encountered Seleucus, whom he defeated with great slaughter, and forced to take refuge in Antioch. He then returned to Egypt, having gained immense treasure, but no additional territory, in his expedition. Eumenes, king of Pergamus, took advantage of the Egyptian war to enlarge his dominions at the expense of the Syrian monarch; and Hierax, the brother of Seleucus, aided by a body of Gauls, attempted to usurp the throne. The rebellion was at first successful; but the ravages of the Gauls provoked such general indignation, that Seleucus found all his subjects rising in one body to support him; and, thus strengthened, he assailed the army of the rebels and invaders in Babylonia. The battle was fierce; but it ended in the total defeat of the Gauls, who were almost annihilated in the pursuit. Hierax fled to the Egyptian court, but was thrown into prison by Ptolemy, where he languished thirteen years, and only escaped to perish by the hands of robbers in the Syrian desert. Callinicus then turned his arms against the Parthians (B.C. 238), but was defeated by their king Arsaces; and the Parthians date the origin of their monarchy from this battle. In a second campaign, Seleucus fell into the hands of his enemies (B.C. 236), and was detained a prisoner by the Parthians to the day of his death (B.C. 227).

Seleucus III., surnamed Ceraunus (*the thunderbolt*), succeeded his father; but, after a brief reign, was removed by poison (B.C. 224). The hopes of his murderers, however, were frustrated by the vigour of his cousin Achæus, who secured the inheritance for Antiochus, the younger brother of the deceased monarch, who had been satrap of Babylon.

In the early part of his reign, Antiochus III., surnamed the Great, was brought into great danger by the intrigues of his prime minister Hermeias, a native of Caria. Deceived by the artifices of this crafty vizier, Antiochus quarrelled with Achæus, to whom he was mainly indebted for his crown, and set Molon and Alexander, the brothers of Hermeias, over the important provinces of Media and Persia. The new satraps raised the standard of revolt, and defeated the royal generals sent against them. At length Antiochus took the field in person, contrary to the wishes and remonstrances of his minister. When the armies were about to engage, the rebel forces, by an almost intuitive movement, threw down their arms, and submitted themselves to their youthful sovereign. Molon and Alexander escaped a public execution by suicide, and Hermeias expiated his complicated treasons on the scaffold (B.C. 220). Whilst Antiochus was thus engaged in the remote east, Achæus, whom he had forced into rebellion, had strengthened himself in

Asia Minor; and the Egyptian monarch Ptolemy Philopater was becoming formidable on the southern frontiers of Syria. Antiochus obtained possession of Cœle-Syria by the treachery of Theodotus, its governor; but he was soon after defeated by Ptolemy, at the battle of Raphia near Gaza (B.C. 217), and forced to purchase peace by the sacrifice of the newly-acquired province. This defeat was in some degree compensated, the following year, by the capture of Achæus, whose ravages to support his troops having provoked the resentment of the kings of Lesser Asia, he was besieged in the citadel of Sardis by the joint forces of Antiochus and Attalus, king of Pergamus, treacherously betrayed, and ungratefully put to death.

Freed from the dangers of this war, Antiochus turned his attention to the affairs of Upper Asia, and gained several victories over the Parthians and Bactrians (B.C. 214). He was, however, forced to recognise the independence of both nations. To secure his dominions, he gave his daughter in marriage to Demetrius, the son of the Bactrian monarch, and joined that prince in an important expedition against northern India (B.C. 206). In return, he made some efforts to revive the commercial system of Alexander the Great, and paid particular attention to the trade of the Persian Gulf. On the death of Ptolemy Philopater (B.C. 203), and the accession of his infant son, Antiochus entered into an alliance with Philip, king of Macedon, to wrest Egypt from the family of the Ptolemies. He conquered Cœle-Syria and Palestine; but was prevented from pursuing his success by the interference of Attalus, the Rhodians, and the Romans. Checked in this direction, he revived the claims of his family on the northern states of Europe and Asia. While his generals besieged Smyrna and Lampsacus, he conquered the Thracian Chersonese, and prepared to invade Greece (B.C. 196). The Romans again interfered; but the Syrian monarch, instigated by Hannibal, who had sought refuge at his court, treated their remonstrances with disdain. War immediately followed. Antiochus lost the fairest opportunities of success by neglecting the advice of Hannibal: driven from Europe into Asia, he was forced to act solely on the defensive, until his total defeat at Magnesia, near Mount Sipylus, laid him prostrate at the feet of his enemies. The Romans deprived him of all his dominions in Asia Minor, the greater part of which were annexed to the kingdom of Pergamus. The unfortunate monarch did not long survive his defeat: he was murdered by his servants (B.C. 187); but the cause and manner of the crime are uncertain.

Seleucus IV., surnamed Philopater (*a lover of his father*), succeeded to a throne fast falling into decay. His reign lasted eleven years, but was not distinguished by any remarkable event. Anxious to have the aid of his brother Antiochus, who had been given as a hostage to the Romans, Seleucus sent his son Demetrius to Rome in exchange. Before Antiochus could reach home, Heliodorus poisoned Seleucus, and usurped the crown (B.C. 176). This is represented by many Jewish writers as a providential punishment of the king, who had employed that very minister to plunder the sacred treasury of Jerusalem.

Antiochus IV. soon expelled the usurper, and assumed the surname of Epiphanes (*illustrious*), which his subsequent conduct induced his contemporaries to change into that of Epimanes (*madman*). He sought to combine the freedom of Roman manners with the ostentatious luxury of the Asiatics, and thereby provoked universal hatred. His reign commenced with a war against Egypt, in consequence of the claim made by the Ptolemies to Cœle-Syria and Palestine. Antiochus was very successful: in two campaigns he penetrated to the walls of Alexandria, and gained possession of the person of Ptolemy Philometer, the rightful heir of the Egyptian throne, who had been driven from Alexandria by his brother Physion. With this prince the Syrian monarch concluded a most advantageous peace; but scarcely had he returned home, when Philometer entered into an accommodation with his brother, and both combined to resist the power of Syria. Justly enraged at this treachery, Antiochus returned to Egypt; but his further progress was stopped by the interference of the Romans, at whose imperious command he found himself compelled to resign all his conquests (B.C. 169).

The ambition of Antiochus was next directed against his own subjects: he resolved to establish uniformity of worship throughout his dominions, and to Hellenise all his subjects. His intolerance and rapacity engendered a determined spirit of resistance (B.C. 168). The Jews, headed by the gallant Maccabees, commenced a fierce struggle, which, after much suffering, ended in the restoration of their former independence; and the Persians, equally attached to their ancient faith, raised the standard of revolt. Antiochus hasted to suppress the insurrection in Upper Asia; but being severely defeated (B.C. 165), he died of vexation on his road to Babylon.

Eupator, the young son of the deceased monarch, was placed on the throne by the Syrians; but Demetrius, the son of Seleucus Philopater, having escaped from Rome, no sooner appeared in Asia than he was joined by such numerous partisans, that he easily dethroned his rival (B.C. 162). With the usual barbarity of Asiatic sovereigns, he put the young prince to death, and found means to purchase the pardon of his crimes from the Roman senate. After an inglorious reign, he was slain in battle by Alexander Balas (B.C. 150), an impostor who personated the unfortunate Eupator, and was supported in his fraud by the Maccabees and the Romans. Balas was in his turn defeated by Demetrius Nicator, the son of the late monarch (B.C. 145), and forced to seek refuge in Arabia, where he was murdered by his treacherous host.

Nicator, having lost the affections of his subjects, was driven from Antioch by Tryphon, who placed the crown on the head of young Antiochus, the son of Balas; but in a short time murdered that prince, and proclaimed himself king. Demetrius was withheld from marching against the usurper by the hope of acquiring a better kingdom in Upper Asia, whither he was invited by the descendants of the Greek and Macedonian colonists, to defend them from the power of the Parthians (B.C. 140). He was at first successful, but was finally captured by his enemies, who detained him a prisoner for ten years. In the meantime his brother Antiochus Sidetes, having overthrown Tryphon, seized the crown of Syria. He appears to have been a good and wise sovereign; but unfortunately he was induced, by the provincials of Upper Asia, to wage war against the Parthians, and was treacherously murdered by his own allies

(B.C. 130). Demetrius, about the same time, escaped from prison, and was restored to the throne. But after a brief reign he was defeated and slain by Zebinas (B.C. 126), a pretended son of the impostor Balas.

Seleucus, the son of Demetrius, was waging a successful war against Zebinas, when he was treacherously murdered by his own mother Cleopatra, who wished to secure the crown for her favourite child Antiochus Gryphus. She also prevailed on her relative, the king of Egypt, to declare war against the usurper; and Zebinas was soon defeated and slain. Gryphus no sooner found himself secure on the throne than he put his mother to death for the murder of Seleucus (B.C. 122); and it must be added, that this measure was necessary to secure his own life. After some years, Cyzicenus, the half-brother of Gryphus, attempted to usurp the throne; and during the civil war that ensued, many cities and provinces separated from the Syrian kingdom. Gryphus was assassinated (B.C. 97). His five sons and the son of Cyzicenus engaged in a dreary series of civil wars; until the Syrians, weary of enduring the calamities and bloodshed of their protracted dissensions, expelled the entire family, and gave the crown to Tigranes, king of Armenia (B.C. 83). Tigranes, after a long and not inglorious reign, was involved in a war with the Romans, which ended in his complete overthrow; and he was forced to resign Syria to the conquerers (B.C. 64). Thus the kingdom of the Seleucidæ was made a Roman province, and the family soon after became extinct in the person of Seleucus Cybrosactes (B.C. 57). He was raised to the throne of Egypt by his wife, the princess Berenice, and afterwards murdered by her orders.

SECTION III.—*History of Egypt under the Ptolemies.*

FROM B.C. 301 TO B.C. 30.

PTOLEMY the son of Lagus was the wisest statesman among the successors of Alexander. No sooner had the battle of Ipsus put him in possession of the kingdom of Egypt, than he began to provide for the happiness of his new subjects by a regeneration of their entire social system. Unlike the Seleucidæ, he made no attempt to Hellenise the Egyptians; on the contrary, he revived, as much as altered circumstances would permit, their ancient religious and political constitution: the priestly caste was restored to a portion of its ancient privileges; the division of the country into nomes was renewed; Memphis, though not the usual residence of the monarchs, was constituted the capital of the kingdom, and its temple of Phtha declared the national sanctuary, where alone the kings could receive the crown. But not less wise was the generous patronage accorded to literature and science: the Museum was founded in Alexandria as a kind of university for students, and a place of assembly for the learned; the first great national library was established in another part of the society; and the philosophers and men of letters were invited to seek shelter from the storms which shook every other part of the world in the tranquil land of Egypt. Impressed by the example of his illustrious master, Ptolemy paid great attention to trade and navigation. Colonists from every quarter of the globe were invited to settle at Alexandria, and the Jews flocked thither in great numbers to escape the persecution of their Syrian masters. So many of that singular people became subjects of the Ptolemies, that the Septuagint version of the Old Testament from Hebrew into Greek was made for their use, and a Jewish temple erected in Egypt similar to that at Jerusalem. The double harbour of Alexandria, on the sea and on the Maræotic lake, were constructed at the same time; and the celebrated Pharus, or light-house, erected at the entrance of the haven.

The external security of Egypt was strengthened by the conquest of the Syrian frontiers, the ancient kingdom of Cyrene, a considerable part of Ethiopia, and the island of Cyprus. Hence, during the administration of Ptolemy I., Egypt was free from the fear of foreign invasion; and its inhabitants, for the first time during several centuries, were free to develop the great internal resources of the country. Few sovereigns were more deservedly lamented than the son of Lagus (B.C. 284): his death spread universal sorrow among his subjects, who at once lamented him as a father and worshipped him as a god.

The reign of Ptolemy II., surnamed Philadelphus (*a lover of his brethren*), was disturbed only by the rebellion of Magas, which was supported by Antiochus II., as has been mentioned in the preceding section. Under the peaceful administration of Philadelphus, Egyptian commerce made the most rapid strides; ports for the Indian and Arabian trade were constructed on the Red Sea, at Arsinoë (*Suez*), Myos Hormes (*Cosseir*), and Berenice. From the two latter stations caravan-roads were made to the Upper Nile, and the lower river was united to the Red Sea by a canal, which was further continued to the lesser harbour of Alexandria, on the Maræotic lake. The Æthiopian trade was revived with great spirit; and remote countries of central and southern Africa were opened to the enterprise of the Alexandrian merchants. Unfortunately, the luxury of the court increased in the same proportion as the wealth of the country. Philadelphus fell into all the effeminate dissipation of the Asiatic sovereigns, and adopted their pernicious habits of intermarriages between near relations. He set the example by repudiating his first wife, and marrying his own sister Arsinoë, who exercised the greatest influence over her husband. She brought him no children, but she adopted the offspring of her predecessor.

Philadelphus was succeeded by his son Ptolemy III., surnamed Evergetes (*the benefactor*) (B.C. 246). Unlike his father, he was a warlike, enterprising prince, and his conquests extended into the remote regions of the east and south. His war with Seleucus II., in which the Egyptian army penetrated as far as Bactria, has been described in the preceding section; but the result of the Asiatic campaigns was plunder, not any permanent acquisition of territory: very different was the result of the southern wars, by which a great part of Abyssinia and the Arabian peninsula were added to the Egyptian dominions, and new roads for trade opened through these remote countries.

With the death of Evergetes (B.C. 221), ended the glory of the Ptolemies. His son Ptolemy, surnamed Philopator (*a lover of his father*), was a weak, debauched prince, who was, during his whole life, under the tutelage of unworthy favourites.

At the instigation of his first minister, Sosibius, he put to death his brother Magas, and Cleomenes the exiled king of Sparta. Antiochus the Great, who then ruled in Syria, took advantage of Philopator's incapacity to wage war against Egypt; but was defeated at Raphia, as already mentioned in the preceding section. After his victory, Ptolemy visited Jerusalem, and made an attempt to enter the sanctuary of the Temple; but being prevented by the priests, he was so indignant, that, on his return to Egypt, he prepared to exterminate all the Jews that had settled in the kingdom. Tradition says that his cruel project was miraculously frustrated, and the Jews were again restored to favour. Soon afterwards the king murdered his wife and sister, and transferred his affections to Agathoclea, whose brother, the infamous Agathocles, succeeded to the power of Sosibius. At length his continued dissipation broke down his constitution, and he died of premature infirmity, though in the very prime of life (B.C. 204). He left behind him only one son, a child about five years old.

The guardians of Ptolemy V., surnamed Epiphanes (*illustrious*), proving unworthy of their trust, the regency was transferred to the Roman senate, a circumstance that saved Egypt from being involved in the Macedonian or Syrian war. Epiphanes was a weak, debauched prince, and, before he attained his thirtieth year, he died, the victim of dissipation or poison (B.C. 181). He left behind him two sons, Ptolemy, surnamed Philometor (*a lover of his mother*), and Physcon, both of immature age.

The claims of the Egyptians on Cœle-Syria led to a war between the regents and the king of Syria, in the course of which Philometor fell into the hands of Antiochus Epiphanes, as has been related in the preceding section. After the retreat of the Syrians, Philometor being a second time expelled by Physcon, appealed to the Romans, who divided the Egyptian dominions between the two brothers. He supported the pretender Balas against Demetrius, and mainly contributed to the placing of that impostor on the Syrian throne; but, being ungratefully treated, he led an army against Balas, and defeated him (B.C. 145). But the victory was fatal to Philometor; he died of the wounds that he had received in the engagement.

Physcon, by marrying Cleopatra, who, according to the infamous practice of the Ptolemies, was Philometor's wife and sister, succeeded to the Egyptian throne. On the very day of his marriage he murdered his infant nephew; and his conduct towards every class of his subjects was in accordance with this atrocious crime. At length he was compelled by the Alexandrians to abandon his kingdom, and the crown was given to his sister Cleopatra, whom he had previously divorced in order to marry her daughter, who had the same name. He was subsequently restored by the aid of a mercenary army, and retained the sceptre to the day of his death (B.C. 116). He left behind him two sons by his niece Cleopatra, Ptolemy, surnamed Lathyrus, from the resemblance of a wart on his face to a small pea; and Ptolemy, surnamed Alexander.

Cleopatra endeavoured to secure the crown for her younger son, but was compelled by the Alexandrians to allow Lathyrus to ascend the throne. She, however, compelled him to exchange Egypt for Cyprus with Alexander. The new king, unable to bear the tyranny of his mother, caused her to be murdered, upon which his subjects revolted, and restored Lathyrus. The remainder of this prince's reign was passed in tranquillity. He died B.C. 81, leaving behind him one legitimate daughter, Berenice, and two natural sons, Ptolemy of Cyprus, and Ptolemy Auletes (*the flute-player*). A long series of obscure civil wars, and uninteresting intrigues with the Roman senate, followed. They ended in placing Ptolemy Auletes on the throne, which, however, he retained only three years.

Auletes left four legitimate children; but his daughter, the too-celebrated Cleopatra, set aside the claims of her brothers and sister by the influence which her personal charms gave her with Julius Cæsar, and afterwards with Mark Antony. The battle of Actium was fatal to her and her protector. In the year following that decisive engagement she was taken prisoner by Augustus Cæsar, and poisoned herself to avoid being led in triumph (B.C. 30). Egypt thenceforth became a

Roman province, but it preserved its commercial importance; and Alexandria long continued to be the most wealthy and busy city of trade in the world.

SECTION IV.—*History of the Minor Kingdoms in Western Asia.*

FROM B.C. 301 TO THE BIRTH OF CHRIST.

THE principal kingdoms formed from the fragments of the Macedonian monarchy in Western Asia were—1. Pergamus; 2. Bithynia; 3. Paphlagonia; 4. Pontus; 5. Cappadocia; 6. Greater Armenia; 7. Lesser Armenia; 8. Judæa; to which may be added, 9. the republic of Rhodes. The little kingdom of Pergamus, in Mysia, was founded by Philelærus, the lieutenant of Lysimachus, during the wars of that monarch with Seleucus. It did not attain any eminence before the accession of Attalus I. (B. C. 24), whose alliance with the Romans during the Ætolian and Macedonian wars was rewarded by the protection of the republic. He was a generous patron of literature and science, as were his immediate successors, Eumenes and Attalus II. The latter was the most faithful ally the Romans had in the east, and his services were rewarded by a gift of the rich provinces that had been taken from Antiochus. His nephew, Attalus III., bequeathed his dominions to the Romans, who made this inheritance their first Asiatic province (B. C. 130). Brief as was the duration of this little kingdom, the patronage of its enlightened sovereigns conferred the most important benefits on letters. To them we owe the invention of parchment (*charta Pergamena*), and the establishment of a library that rivalled the library of Alexandria; to which city, indeed, it was transferred by Antony, as a present to Cleopatra.

Bithynia was created into a kingdom about the same time as Pergamus. Its most remarkable sovereign was Prusias, a devoted ally of the Romans, who offered to resign Hannibal to their vengeance, and had the meanness to style himself a freedman of that republic (B.C. 82). He was murdered by his own son Nicomedes; and the parricide was, in his turn, assassinated by Socrates, a son that trod in his father's footsteps. Socrates was placed on the throne by the aid of Mithridates, king of Pontus; but, on the defeat of that monarch, he was deposed by Sylla, and the crown given to Nicomedes III. This monarch died after a brief reign (B.C. 75), and bequeathed his dominions to the Romans.

Paphlagonia was, for the most part, subject to the kings of Pontus, and shared the fortunes of that country. Even under the Persian empire the kings of Pontus enjoyed a qualified independence, and were said to be descended from the royal family of the Achæmenidæ, as well as the Persian kings. Pontus became independent after the battle of Ipsus; but the first of its monarchs remarkable in history was the last that swayed its sceptre, Mithridates VII., deservedly surnamed the Great. He came to the throne while yet a boy (B.C. 121): by devoting himself to manly sports, and inuring his body to support extreme hardships, he acquired such great personal strength, that he defeated all the plots formed for his assassination by his treacherous guardians. As he grew up, he became formidable to the neighbouring princes, from whom he wrested several important provinces. He then directed his attention to the countries around the Black Sea, conquered the kingdom of Colchis, and delivered the Greek cities in the Tauric Chersonese from their Scythian oppressors. His rising greatness excited the jealousy of the Romans, who had good reason to suspect that he was a deadly enemy of their power. To strengthen himself for the coming contest, Mithridates gave his daughter in marriage to Tigranes, king of Armenia, and invited that monarch to attack the allies of the republic. At length war was openly declared (B.C. 89), and Mithridates, in the two first campaigns, became master of Lesser Asia. He made a cruel use of his victory, by ordering all the Italian merchants, resident in Asiatic cities, to be murdered, and secured the execution of his sanguinary edict, by giving up their properties as rewards to the assassins. From Asia he passed into Greece, and having captured several of the islands, made himself master of Athens. At length Sylla was sent against him: he defeated the Greek partisans of Mithridates in three successive battles, all fought within the confines of Bœotia; while Fimbria, another Roman general, was equally successful in Asia. Mithridates was thus forced to beg terms of peace, which Sylla readily granted (B.C. 85), because he was jealous of Fimbria, who belonged to a rival faction, and was, besides, anxious to return to Italy, in order to rescue his party from the destruction with which it was threatened by Marius.

The large forces raised by Mithridates, under the pretence of subduing the Colchians and other nations on the eastern shores of the Black Sea, gave umbrage to Muræna, the Roman pro-consul of Asia, as the ancient kingdom of Pergamus was rather ostentatiously named by the senate (B.C. 83). Without any formal declaration of war, he invaded Pontus, but was severely defeated by Mithridates, and compelled to renew the peace by command of Sylla. Taking advantage of the civil wars that raged in the Roman territories between the partisans of Marius and Sylla, the king of Pontus made several large additions to his kingdom, and finally seized on Bithynia, which Nicomedes had recently bequeathed to the Romans (B.C. 75). He even attacked the Roman province; but was driven out by Julius Cæsar, then a young student in the island of Rhodes, who, without any orders from the government, assembled a few troops, and defeated the king's lieutenants.

When the Roman senate heard of the state of affairs in Asia, they appointed Lucullus to undertake the management of the war; but the soldiers placed under his command were so mutinous, that Mithridates was at first victorious both by land and sea. Encouraged by this success, the king laid siege to Cyzicus; but, scarcely had he completed his lines, when he found himself blockaded in turn by Lucullus, and, after enduring the most dreadful hardships, was forced to purchase a retreat by the sacrifice of the greater part of his army. His fleet was, soon after, almost wholly annihilated in a naval engagement, and several of his best towns taken. Finally, his army mutinied, and he was forced to abandon Pontus, and seek refuge with his son-in-law, Tigranes, in Armenia.

Tigranes readily joined Mithridates in renewing the war;

but was defeated by Lucullus (B.C. 70). His courage, however, was soon re-animated by a great victory which the king of Pontus gained over Triarius, a lieutenant of Lucullus, who, contrary to his better judgment, had been forced to hazard an engagement by the impetuosity of his soldiers. The main army mutinied against Lucullus when they heard of this defeat, and his enemies at home made it the pretext for procuring his recal. Glabrio, his successor, remained inactive during his year of office; and at length the celebrated Pompey was appointed to conduct the Mithridatic war, and extraordinary powers were conferred on him by the Manilian law,— a law that announced too plainly the speedy downfal of the Roman republic. Pompey, after some minor successes, blockaded the king in his camp, and reduced him to great distress; but Mithridates, by an unexpected sally, broke, with his army, through the hostile lines, and took the road to Armenia. He was hotly pursued, overtaken, and his army routed with great slaughter. The unfortunate monarch, at the head of eight hundred horse, cut his way through the Roman army; but, being closely pressed, he abandoned these faithful followers, and, with only three attendants, continued his flight to Armenia. Tigranes gave no welcome reception to the fugitive, and Mithridates was forced to seek shelter in the wilds of Scythia. Pompey followed the enemy of Rome into the deserts; but, after two years spent in warring against the barbarous nations round the Black Sea, he was unable to hear any tidings of Mithridates, and returned fully convinced of his death.

Scarcely had the Romans rested from the fatigues of this expedition, when they were astounded by the intelligence of Mithridates having returned into Pontus at the head of a considerable army, and recovered several important fortresses. But the unfortunate monarch found in his kingdom and family worse enemies than his open foes. His daughters were betrayed to the Romans by a faithless escort; his army mutinied; and, finally, his own son revolted, and was acknowledged king by the soldiers.

Borne down by this complication of misfortunes, the aged monarch attempted to commit suicide, but weakness prevented him from giving himself a mortal wound: in the meantime the Roman army broke into his retreat. He was found languid, bleeding, and deserted, by a Gallic soldier, who, compassionating his misery, put an end to his pain and life together (B.C. 64). Thus ended the kingdom of Pontus: after some years it was permitted to have nominal sovereigns; but even this shadow of independence was removed by the emperor Nero, and the country became a Roman province.

Cappadocia was one of the Asiatic kingdoms founded after the battle of Ipsus: none of its monarchs were remarkable in history, and the country itself was proverbial for the infamy of its inhabitants.

The two Armenias did not become kingdoms until after the defeat of Antiochus the Great by the Romans (B.C. 190), when the lieutenants of the king of Syria proclaimed their independence. The only Armenian monarch requiring notice was Tigranes, the son-in-law of Mithridates. He was involved in the fate of the king of Pontus, and his dominions were subjected to the Romans, under whose sway both the Armenias continued until near the commencement of the Christian era, when they were seized by the Parthians. For several centuries the possession of Armenia was contested by the Romans and Parthians; and, when the latter power was overthrown, the same country continued to be a constant source of war between the eastern empire and the restored kingdom of Persia.

When the Jews were restored to their country by the edict of Cyrus (B.C. 536), they found their country partly occupied by the Samaritans, who zealously exerted themselves to prevent the restoration of Jerusalem and the holy Temple. These obstacles were overcome by the great zeal of the priests and the people; but the Samaritans built a rival temple on Mount Gerizim,—a circumstance which led to the most inveterate hatred between the two races. Judæa was nominally subject to the Persian satraps of Syria; but the chief authority was usurped by the high priests, who retained their power under

Alexander, the Ptolemies, and Seleucidæ. Palestine was conquered by Ptolemy I. (B.C. 312), who removed a vast number of the Jews into Egypt. It was recovered by Antigonus; but after his overthrow it was again annexed to Egypt, and continued a province of that kingdom for nearly a century. In the second war of Antiochus the Great against Egypt (B.C. 203), the Jews transferred their allegiance to the Syrian monarch, and supported him enthusiastically in his arduous struggle with the Romans. Their fidelity was badly rewarded by the next monarch, Antiochus Epiphanes, who attempted to Hellenise the nation by main force, and to abolish the worship of Jehovah. His tyranny provoked the rebellion of the gallant Maccabees (B.C. 164); three brothers of this family ruled in succession, Judas, Jonathan, and Simon, and succeeded in establishing the independence of their country. On the death of Simon (B.C. 135), his son, John Hyrcanus, ascended the throne, and not only secured Judæa, but reduced the Samaritans and Idumæans to subjection. Scarcely, however, were the Jews delivered from a foreign yoke, when they were involved in the horrors of civil dissensions, by the disputes between the rival sects of the Pharisees and Sadducees. Thenceforward Jewish history is a mere repetition of domestic feuds and the violences of faction, until the last of the degenerate Maccabees was dethroned by Herod, an Idumæan, who was placed on the throne by the Romans (B.C. 37), to whom he became tributary. The Romans permitted a qualified independence to the Jewish nation until the death of Herod Agrippa (A.D. 44), when Judæa was annexed to the province of Syria.

After the death of Alexander, Rhodes first became remarkable by its gallant resistance when besieged by Demetrius Poliorcetes. Thirty thousand men were employed in the labours of this siege. When the first wall crumbled under the blows of the helepolis (*taker of cities*), a formidable engine of destruction invented by Demetrius during the siege, the brave garrison erected a second with the materials of their temples, their theatres, and their houses; and when that was demolished, they erected a third. Fifty deputies from the states of Greece came to the besiegers' camp as mediators: Demetrius granted peace on condition of receiving one hundred hostages and a small auxiliary force (B.C. 305). During the siege he had shewed his respect for the works of art that ornamented this splendid city, by preventing his engines from playing upon the buildings in which the most celebrated paintings of Protogenes were preserved. It was in memory of this siege that the wonderful Colossus was erected.

In the war between Antiochus and the Romans, the Rhodians joined with the latter: though at first defeated in a naval engagement, they exerted themselves so strenuously, that they soon became masters of the eastern sea, and obtained a decisive victory over the Syrian fleet, even though it was commanded by the illustrious Hannibal. But jealousies soon arose between the two republics; and in the second Macedonian war the Rhodians preserved a strict but suspicious neutrality. The Roman senate sent ambassadors to the islanders, who acted as supreme magistrates rather than as envoys; and thenceforward the Rhodian independence existed only in name. Mithridates attacked the island when he invaded Greece; but he was repulsed by the inhabitants, whose fidelity was rewarded by the constant protection of Sylla.

During the great civil war of Rome between Pompey and Cæsar, the Rhodian fleets fought sometimes on one side and sometimes on the other; but maintained, under all circumstances, a very high character. Pompey was refused admittance into the island after his defeat at Pharsalia; and the murderers of Cæsar were similarly excluded during the great civil war that followed his assassination. Cassius, in consequence, besieged the city of Rhodes, into which he obtained admittance by the treachery of some of the inhabitants: he resigned the unfortunate citizens to the discretion of his licentious soldiery, and extorted from the inhabitants all that he could obtain by violence or threats. In the reign of the emperor Claudius Cæsar, the Rhodians were deprived of their liberties for having crucified two Roman citizens; but their privileges were subsequently restored. At length the island was made a Roman province by Vespasian (A.D. 70).

SECTION V.—*History of Bactria and Parthia.*

FROM B.C. 256 TO A.D. 226.

THE Bactrian kingdom differed from those whose history was described in the preceding section, in being a Grecian state, although established at the extreme eastern verge of the ancient Persian empire. It was formed into a state by Diodatus, the Grecian governor (B.C. 254), who threw off his allegiance to the Syrian king, Antiochus II. The Bactrian monarchs made extensive conquests in India, and at one time (B.C. 181) their dominions extended to the banks of the Ganges and the frontiers of China. The nomad hordes of the desert that reside to the east of the Caspian Sea, and who, both in ancient and modern times, have frequently changed the political aspect of the western world, poured down on the descendants of the Macedonian colonists, and forced them to retreat towards the south. The Greeks, driven from Bactria, appear to have ascended the Oxus (B.C. 126), and to have maintained their independence in the fastnesses of the lofty mountains called the Indian Caucasus (*Hindú Kúsh*) to a very late period, while their ancient territory was annexed to the Parthian empire. It is not yet determined whether any traces can be found of this Greek colony at the present day; but it is to be hoped that some of the enterprising travellers now exploring northern India will direct their attention to the subject.

The Parthian kingdom was founded about the same time as the Bactrian, by some of the nomad hordes that subsequently overthrew the latter. Its general limits were the Euphrates, the Indus, and the Oxus; but its dominions were sometimes extended beyond these streams. Though thus holding the ancient empire of Persia, the Parthian monarchs never regarded themselves as descendants of Cyrus; they preferred the Greek religion, manners, and customs, to those of the Persians, and they conferred great privileges on the Grecian colonies that were established in their dominions. To the modern Persians this dynasty, which ruled their country for more than four centuries, is scarcely known even by name; a clear proof that the Parthians and their reigning family, the Arsacidæ, must have been foreigners. In one important respect they imitated the exclusive policy of the Tartar rulers of China, excluding strangers from their dominions, and sacrificing commerce to their watchful jealousy. Their establishment in the Persian empire consequently effected a great revolution in the lines of traffic between the eastern and western world. The East India trade, stopped in its passage through Babylonia, was thrown farther to the south, and began to shape its course through northern Arabia and the Red Sea. To this change the great wealth and splendour obtained by the great commercial cities Palmyra and Alexandria must be chiefly attributed.

Arsaces I. commenced the war of independence (B.C. 256) by putting to death the Syrian governor of Upper Asia, who had offered a grievous insult to his brother. The heads of the Parthian tribes that supported him formed a government similar to the feudal aristocracy of Europe in the middle ages, giving to the monarch little more than nominal authority, and making the crown elective, under the restriction, however, that the monarch should be chosen from the family of the Arsacidæ. War with the Syrian kings, of course, followed; but the light cavalry of the Parthian troops, which have always formed the main strength of the armies of central Asia, by their rapid evolutions disconcerted the steady discipline of the Syrians and Macedonians. It was a remarkable peculiarity of the Parthian evolutions, that their armies were never so formidable as in flight: when the enemies advanced in pursuit, as if to assured victory, these active horsemen turned on their steeds, and assailed them with a flight of arrows which invariably threw them into confusion. The wars between the Parthians and Syrians terminated (B.C. 131) in the total annihilation of the Syrian army led by Antiochus Sidetes.

During half a century after their deliverance from the rivalry of the Syrians, the attention of the Parthian monarchs was chiefly engrossed by the eastern nomad tribes, whom the fall of the Bactrian kingdom had set at liberty to attack the rich provinces of southern Asia. These hordes were either subdued or incorporated with the Parthian army; and scarcely had this danger been averted, when the Romans, being brought into contact with the Parthians by their occupation of the kingdom of Mithridates, prepared to contend with them for the empire of Asia.

The war commenced by Crassus, the Roman triumvir, invading Parthia (B.C. 53); his incapacity led to the utter annihilation of his army and the loss of his own life. In the Roman civil wars the Parthians supported the cause of Pompey, and afterwards that of Brutus and Cassius. Subsequently, alarmed at the great power to which Augustus Cæsar attained, they sought terms of peace, and purchased it by surrendering the arms and standards which had been taken from the army of Crassus. The wars between the Parthians and the succeeding Roman emperors were almost incessant; but none of them produced any decisive result. After Christianity began to spread, its progress was tolerated, if not directly encouraged, by the Parthian monarchs, who liberally afforded shelter to Christians flying from the persecutions of the pagans, and, we must add, from those of their brethren who belonged to a different sect. But, unfortunately, the Arsacidæ never gained the affections of their Persian subjects: after the lapse of more than four centuries, the Parthians continued to be an army of occupation, separated by habits, prejudices, and feelings, from the great bulk of the nation. At length Ardeshír Babezan, called by the Greeks Artaxerxes, a native Persian, of the illustrious house of Sassan, descended, or claiming to be descended, from the ancient line of Cyrus and Jemshíd, raised the national standard of Persia, and drove the Parthians into the northern mountains and deserts (B.C. 226). Irân, the ancient national name of Persia, was revived; the religion of Zerdusht restored in its pristine splendour; the progress of Christianity eastwards was checked, and it was thrown back on the western world, bearing unfortunately too many marks of its having been brought into close contact with Oriental mysticism and superstition. The destruction of the Parthian kingdom in Asiatic annals holds the same place as the overthrow of the Roman empire in European: it forms the epoch that separates ancient from modern history. We shall resume Persian history under the princes of the house of Sassan in the second volume of this work.

CHAPTER XIII.

HISTORY OF ANCIENT ITALY.

SECTION I.—*Geographical Outline.*

ITALY, in its earliest signification, was the name given to the small tongue of land between the Sylletic and Nepetic Gulfs, that is, the southern portion of Bruttium; but it was gradually extended to include more northern provinces, until, in the reign of the Emperor Augustus, it was applied to the great peninsula included between the Alps, the Adriatic, the Tyrrhenian and Mediterranean Seas. It was also called Hesperia, from its western situation; Saturnia, from the fable of Saturn's flight thither; Ausonia and Œnotria, from some of the most ancient tribes of inhabitants.

The most convenient division of the peninsula is into three portions: Cisalpine Gaul in the north, Italy Proper in the centre, and Magna Græcia in the south.

Subalpine Italy received the name of Gaul from the Gallic hordes that settled in the northern and western districts; it was called for distinction Cisalpine, or Citerior, because it lay on the side of the Alps next to Rome, and Togata, because, in a late age, its inhabitants began to use the toga, or national dress of the Romans. From the Alps, this province at first extended to the city of Ancona, in the province of Picenum; but, in the later ages of the Roman republic, the river Rubicon (*Rugone*), between Ravenna and Ariminum, was considered the limit of its frontiers.

The principal Subalpine tribes were the Vediantii, inhabiting the small tract lying on the east bank of the Varus (*Var*), and extending from the territory of Nicæa (*Nice*), to the Maritime Alps, or that branch of the mountain-chain which joins the Western Mediterranean; the Vagænni, north of the Maritime Alps, near the source of the river Padus (*Po*); and the Taurini, at the other side of the Padus, on which stood their capital, Taurasia, subsequently called Augusta Taurinorum (*Turin*).

North of the Taurini, and among the mountains, was the kingdom of Cottius, who gave his name to the Cottian Alps. From thence to the Greek Alps, which extended to Mons Jovis (*Great St. Bernard*), there were several warlike Gallic tribes, but none of any particular note in history.

Liguria lay south of the river Padus, extending to the Mediterranean Sea, between the rivers Macra and Varus. Its chief cities on the sea-coast were Nicæa (*Nice* or *Nizza*), erected by the Massilians to protect their frontier against the Ligurian mountaineers; Portus Herculis Monœci (*Monaco*), Albium Intemelium (*Vintimiglia*), Albium Ingannum (*Albengia*), Sabata (*Savona*), Genua or Janua (*Genoa*), Portus Delphini (*Porto Fino*), and Portus Lunæ (*Golpho delle Spezie*). Of these Genua was the most important, being the great emporium of Ligurian commerce. The principal towns in the interior were Pollentia (*Pollenza*), Asta (*Asti*), and Industria (*Tortona*). This last city was called Bodencomacgum by the earlier Ligurians, because it stood on the Po, which they named Bodencus, a word in their language signifying "bottomless." Next to Liguria lay the district named Gallia Cispadana, or Gaul south of the Po; it was chiefly inhabited by the Boii, the Lingones, and the Senones. The principal towns of the Boii were Placentia, Parma, Mutina (*Modena*), and Bononia (*Bologna*). The Lingones possessed Ravenna, Faventia (*Faenza*), Solona (*Citta di Sole*), and Cæsena; and to the Senones belonged Ariminum (*Rimini*), Pisaurum (*Pesaro*), Sena Gallica (*Sinigaglia*), and Ancona.

Gallia Transpadana, or north of the Padus, had the great Alpine chain on the north and west, between which and the Po it extended to the river Formio (*Il Risano*), which separated it from Istria. It was inhabited by the Orobii, the Insubres, the Lævi, the Cenomanni, the Euganei, and the Veneti. The principal cities in the territory of the Orobii were Conrum, (*Conro*), Bergamum (*Bergamo*), and Forum Licinii (*Berlasina*); the Insubres possessed Mediolanum (*Milan*), Laus Pompeii (*Lodi*), and Forum Intuntorum (*Crema*): to the Cenomanni belonged Brixia (*Brescia*), Cremona, Mantua, and Verona: the Euganei owned Sabium, Voberna, Edrum, and Vannia, cities long since demolished: and the Veneti were masters of Patavium (*Padua*), Vicentia (*Vicenza*), Ateste (*Este*), Forum Allieni (*Ferrara*), Tarvisum (*Treviso*), Aquileia (*Aquilea*), Forum Julii (*Friuli*), and Tergeste (*Trieste*). In later ages, a horde, called the Carni, wrested from the Veneti the cities and country between the rivers Formio and Telaventum (*Piave*).

Central or Proper Italy extended along the Adriatic coast from the city of Ancona to the river Frento (*Fortore*), and on the Mediterranean side was limited by the rivers Macra and Silarus (*Sele*). It comprehended Etruria, Umbria, Sabinium, Latium, Picenum, with the countries of the Vestini, Marrucini, Peligni, Marsi, Frentani, Samnites, Hirpini, Campani, and Picentini.

Etruria was inhabited by two distinct races, that seem to have very slowly amalgamated, the Tyrrheni and the Hetrusci. It was bounded on the east by the river Tiber, on the west by the Macra, on the north by the chain of the Apennines, and on the south by that portion of the Mediterranean commonly called the Tuscan Sea. It was divided into a dodecarchy, or government of twelve tribes and cities. These ruling cities in the most flourishing period of Etrurian history were, Volsinii (*Bolsena*), Clusium (*Chiusi*), Perusia (*Perugia*), Cortona, Aretium (*Arezzo*), Falerii (*Civita Castellana*), Volaterræ (*Volterra*), Vetulonium (*Grosseto*), Rusellæ (*Cerveteri*), and the cities of Veii, Tarquinii, and Cære, which at present lie in ruins. There were many other places of importance in Etruria: on the sea-coast were Luna (*L'Erice*), Pisæ (*Pisa*), Portus Herculis Liburni (*Livorno* or *Leghorn*), Papulonia now in ruins, Talamon (*Telamone*), Centumcellæ (*Civita Vecchia*), and Alsium (*Palo*). There were besides, in the interior, Nepete (*Nepe*), Sutrium (*Sutri*), Fanum Voltumnæ (*Viterbo*), Hortanum (*Orti*), Herbanum (*Orvieto*), Senæ Juliæ (*Saona*), Florentia (*Fiorenza*, or *Florence*), Pistoria (*Pistoia*), and Luca (*Lucca*).

Umbria was bounded on the south by the river Nar (*Nera*), on the north by the Adriatic sea, on the east by the Æsis (*Fiumicino*), and on the west partly by the Tiber, and partly by the Bedesis (*Il Roneo*), which falls into the Adriatic near Ravenna. But the maritime part of Umbria having been early conquered by the Senonian Gauls, the cities it contains have been already mentioned in the account of Gallia Cispadana. The Umbrian cities on the Adriatic side of the Apennines were Sarsina, Urbinum (*Urbino*), Metaurense (*Castel Durante*), Sentinum (*Sentino*), and Camers (*Camerino*). On the other side of these mountains were Iguvium (*Ugubio*), Mevania (*Bagagna*), Spoletium (*Spoleti*), Tifernum (*Citta di Castella*), Nuceria (*Nocera*), Asisium (*Asisi*), Hispellum (*Ispello*), Fulginium (*Foligno*), Interamnium (*Terni*), Narnia (*Narni*), and Ocriculum (*Otriculi*).

The territory of the Sabines lay between the Nar, which divided it from Umbria, and the Anio (*Teverone*), by which it was separated from Latium. It contained the cities of Cures, whose inhabitants, migrating to Rome, are said to have given its citizens the name of Quirites; Reate (*Riete*), Nursia (*Norcia*), Eretum (*Monte Rotondo*), and Amiternum (*Lamentaria*).

Latium was at first restricted within very narrow limits, being bounded by the Tiber, the Anio (*Teverone*), and the Circæan promontory (*Monte Circilli*); but, after the subjugation of the Æqui, Hernici, Volsci, and Ausones, it was extended to the Liris (*Garigliano*); and hence arises the distinction between Old and New Latium. The chief cities of Old Latium were Rome, Tibur (*Tivoli*), Præneste (*Palestrina*), Tusculum (*Frascati*), Aricia, Lanuvium (*Citta Lavina*), Alba Longa (*Albano*), Laurentum (*Paterno*), and Ostia. There were, besides, four Latin towns, of which the ruins can now scarcely be traced, Gabii, Antemnæ, Collatia, and Ardea. The chief cities of the Æqui were Carsula (*Arsuli*), Valeria (*Vico Varo*), Sublaqueum (*Subiaco*), and Algidum, now in ruins. To the Hernici belonged Anagnia (*Anagni*), Alatrium (*Alatri*), Verulæ (*Veroli*), and Ferentinum (*Ferentino*). In the country of the Volsci were Antium, Circæi, and Suessa Pometia, all three long since ruined; Anxur (*Terracina*), Velitræ (*Veletri*), Privernum (*Piperno*), Aquinum (*Aquino*), Casinum (*Monte Casino*), Arpinum (*Arpino*), Fregellæ (*Ponte Corvo*), and Interamna (*L'Isola*). The Ausones possessed Careta (*Gaeta*), Fundi (*Fondi*), and Formiæ (*Mola*).

Picenum extended from the Adriatic to the Apennines, between the Æsis (*Esino*) and the Aternus (*Pescara*). The chief cities of the Picentes were Ancona, Asculum (*Ascoli*), Interamnium (*Teramo*), and Atria (*Atri*). Several other nations besides the Picentes were included within the boundaries of Picenum. Of these, the Vestini possessed Angulus (*Civita di Sancto Angelo*) and Avella; the Marrucini owned but one city, Teate (*Chiete*); the Peligni possessed Corfinium, now in ruins, and Sulmo (*Sulmona*); the Marsi, in the interior of the country, close to the Apennines, had only one important town, Marrubium (*Morrea*). On the southern sea-coast were the Frentani, whose chief cities were Ortona, Anaxonum (*Lanzano*), and Histonium (*Guasto d'Amone*): the Samnites possessed the country between the territory of the Frentani and the Apennines; their chief cities were Bovianum (*Boiano*), Æsernia (*Isernia*), Sepinum (*Sepina*), Allifæ (*Alifi*), and Telesia (*Telesi*). Finally, the Herpini held the south-western side of the Apennines, and possessed Beneventum (*Benevento*), Equotuticum (*Ariano*), and Compsa (*Conza*).

Campania, the most pleasant and fruitful division of Italy, extended between the territories of the Samnites and Herpini and the Mediterranean from the river Liris to the promontory of Minerva. On its coast were Liternum (*Torre di Patria*), Baia (*Baie*), Misenum (*Monte Miseno*), Parthenope or Neapolis (*Naples*), and Sorrentium (*Sorrento*), together with the cities of Herculaneum and Pompeii, overwhelmed by an eruption of Mount Vesuvius. In the interior of the country were Capua, Suessa Aurunca (*Sessa*), Venafrum (*Venafro*), Casilinum (*Nova Capua*), Teanum Sidicinum (*Tiano*), Calatia (*Cajazzo*), Cales (*Calvi*), Atella (*Aversa*), Acerræ (*Acerra*), Nola and Nuceria (*Nocera*). Between the promontory of Minerva and the river Silarus (*Sele*) was a small district inhabited by a Picentine colony, whose chief city was Salernum (*Salerno*).

Magna Græcia, so called from the number of Greek colonies that settled in it, comprised Apulia, Lucania, and the territory of the Bruttii.

Apulia (*La Puglia*) extended from the river Frento (*Fortore*) to the Japygian promontory (*Capo di Leuca*), at the south-eastern extremity of Italy. It was divided into three portions: Daunia, lying between the Frento and the Aufidus (*Ofanto*);

Peucetia, stretching from the Aufidus to the isthmus between Brundusium and Tarentum; and Japygia, or Calabria, comprising the south-eastern peninsula of Italy, or the heel of the boot to which Italy has been fancifully compared.

In the first two divisions were Teanum Apulum (*Civitate Tragonara*), Lipuntum (*Liponto*), Luceria (*Lucera*), Arpi (*Foggia*), Asculum Apulum (*Asicli*), Venusia (*Venosa*), Acherontia (*Acirenza*), Canusium (*Canosa*), Cannæ (*Canna*), Salapia (*Salpe*), Barium (*Bari*), and Egnatia (*Terra d'Anazzo*). The chief cities of Calabria were Brundusium (*Brindisi*), Hydruntum (*Otranto*), Callipolis (*Gallipoli*), Neritum (*Nardo*), and Aletium (*Lezze*).

Lucania lay between the Silarus and the Laüs (*Laino*). It was divided from Peucetia by the Bradanus (*Brandano*), and from Calabria by the upper part of the Tarentine Gulf. On the Mediterranean, or Tyrrhenian Sea, stood Pæstum or Posidonia (*Pesto*), Velia (*Pisciotta*), and Buxentum (*Policastro*). On the Tarentine Gulf were Metapontum (*Terre di Mare*) and Heraclea, called also Sybaris and Thurii (*Policore*). The inland cities were Potentia (*Potenza*) and Grumentum (*Clarimonte*).

Greek colonies occupied the south-western peninsula of Italy. Their chief cities on the western coast were Cerilli (*Cirella*), Clampetia (*Amantea*), Tomsa (*Torre Loppa*), Lametia (*Sant' Euphemia*), Scyllæum (*Sciglia*), and Rhegium (*Reggia*). On the eastern coast stood Locri Epizephyrii (*Jeraces*), Caulonia (*Castel Veteri*), Scylaceum (*Squillaci*), Croto (*Crotone*), Petilia (*Belicastro*), and Ruscianum (*Rossano*). The chief cities of the interior were Consentia (*Cosenza*) and Hipponium, called by the Romans Vibo Valentia (*Monte Leone*).

The chief Italian mountains are the Alps, which extend round the north of the peninsula in an irregular chain about eight hundred miles in length; and the Apennines, which go through Italy from the Maritime Alps to the straits of Sicily. The Massic, Gaurian, and Garganian mountains are detached ridges, celebrated for their fertility; and Vesuvius, near Naples, has been long remarkable for its volcano.

From the Alps flow the Padus (*Po*), the Druria (*Dora*), the Sessites (*Sessia*), the Ticinus (*Tessino*), the Addua (*Adda*), the

Ollius (*Oglio*), the Mincius (*Mincio*), the Tanarus (*Tanaro*), the Trebia, and the Rhenus Bonomensis (*Reno di Bologna*): all these are tributaries of the Padus. The Athesis (*Adige*) has also its source in the Alps, but it falls into the Adriatic. The Arnus (*Arno*) and the Tiber flow from the Apennines into the Mediterranean: the tributaries of the latter river are the Clanis (*Chiana*), the Nar (*Nera*), and the Anio (*Teverone*). Besides these, there are the Liris (*Garigliano*), separating Latium from Campania; the Vulturnus (*Voltorno*), in Campania; the Silarus (*Silaro*), severing the territories of the Picentini and Lucani; the Sybaris (*Cochile*) and the Crathis (*Crati*), in Lucania; the Aufidus (*Ofanto*), in Apulia; and the Aternus (*Pescara*) and Metaurus (*Metauro*), in Picenum.

Italy has ever been celebrated for its fertility and beauty: its inhabitants were once the triumphant conquerors and lords of the known world; but ages of misgovernment have blighted this lovely peninsula, and it is now among the most degraded and miserable countries in Europe.

Section II.—*Historical Notices of the early Inhabitants of Italy.*

(CHRONOLOGY UNCERTAIN.)

The earliest inhabitants of Italy appear to have been branches of the great Pelasgic nation. Of these, the Œnotrians occupied the south of the peninsula, the Sicilians possessed the plain of the Tiber, and the Tyrrhenians were settled in Etruria. In process of time, the Œnotrians were subjugated by Hellenic colonies, the Sicilians subdued by some mountain-tribes who took the name of Latins, and the Tyrrhenians conquered by the Hetrusci, a people that probably descended from the Rhætian Alps.

Between Œnotria and Tyrrhenia was the territory of the Opicans or Oscans, called also Ausonians. Their language was intelligible to the Latins; for the Latin tongue is compounded of Greek and Oscan. To this race the Æqui and Volsci appear to have belonged.

The Latins, according to tradition, were driven down the Anio by the Sabines, and they in their turn expelled a great portion of the Siculians from their habitations, who proceeded southwards, and passed over the strait of Messina into the island which took from them the name of Sicily. In the old legends these Latin conquerors are called Sacrani; they were also named Priscans and Cascans. From the latter name, and the similarity of language, they must have been a branch of the Oscan nation. The agreement between the Greek and Latin languages in words that relate to agriculture and the arts of social life, while they differ wholly in the names of objects belonging to war or the chase, is a strong proof that the agricultural labourers or serfs were of Pelasgian origin, and the warriors a superior caste of Oscan descent. Little is known of the religion of the ancient Latins, or the deities they worshipped. Janus, or Dianus, was the god of the sun, Saturn the vivifying power of nature, and his wife Ops the productive energy of the earth; but the distinctive character of these deities was lost when, in a late age, the native legends of Latium were blended and confounded with the mythology of Greece.

The Sabines and their cognate tribes are included under the common name of Sabellians; they were the most widely extended and the greatest people in Italy when the Romans advanced beyond the frontiers of Latium. Their original home was in the neighbourhood of Amiternium, among the highest of the Apennines that are now included in Abruzzo Ultra. From these they descended at a very remote age, driving the Cascans before them in one direction, and the Umbrians in another. Their colonies were sent out according to a singular religious institution called the "Ver Sacrum," or sacred spring. Every twenty years the children and cattle born within the twelvemonth were consecrated and set apart for founding a colony; and, as soon as they reached mature age, were sent forth for the purpose. One of these occupied Picenum, then inhabited by the Pelasgians; another passed into the land of the Opicans, or Oscans, and became the founders of the great Samnite race. To the Sabellian race belonged also the Frentanians on the coast of the Adriatic, the tribes that conquered Campania, the powerful nation of the Lucanians, and the four confederate tribes of Marsians, Manucinians, Pelignians, and Vestinians. The Hernicans were a sub-colony of the Marsians.

The Lucanians, pushing their conquests into Œnotria, were soon involved in war with the Greek colonies, most of which they subdued. They were joined by the Samnites from Campania (B.C. 437), who gained possession of Vultumum. They soon advanced to the Laüs (B.C. 423), and confirmed their power by the total defeat of the Thurians (B.C. 387). At length they were brought into hostile contact with the Romans, and soon stripped of all their power.

The Sabellian tribes, more especially those in the north, were distinguished for their love of divination, the rigid severity of their morals, and their cheerful contentedness. In other respects their characters differed. The Sabines and most of the northern tribes lived in open villages; the Samnites fortified the hills on which they dwelt; and the Lucanians became attached to residence in cities. The want of union between the Sabellian tribes prevented that race from becoming predominant in Italy. The Samnites owed their downfal to the want of a central metropolis, and the unity it confers. It was only in time of war that they elected a commander-in-chief, called *embrator;* a term which the Latins borrowed, and changed into *imperator*, using it instead of their old words *dictator* and *prætor*.

The Etrurians, or Etruscans, who conquered the Tyrrhenian Pelasgi, were called in their own tongue "Rasena:" they established a kind of feudal supremacy over the subjugated nation, and deprived the Tyrrhenians of all political privileges. All public affairs were decided in the general council of the Lucumones, a sacerdotal caste whose privileges descended by inheritance. From the want of a free and respectable commonwealth, the Etruscans, though possessed of great wealth and power, having been at one time masters of the commerce and navigation of the western Mediterranean, proved unequal to cope with the Romans, whose infantry was composed of free citizens. The regal office was not hereditary, but elective, and the power of the kings was very limited. Before the conquest the Tyrrhenians were remarkable for their piracies, and the Etruscans followed the same course. Their corsairs were the terror of the western Mediterranean, until their navy was almost annihilated, in a sea-fight off Cumæ, by Hiero, king of Syracuse. About two centuries afterwards, they partially recovered their power, and extended their piracies even into the Ægean Sea; but they were finally subdued by the Rhodians.

The Etruscans had made great advances in the arts and sciences. The ruins of their public works rival those of ancient Egypt in magnitude, and surpass them in utility; especially the dykes for fencing the delta of the Po, and the tunnels for draining the lakes that formed in the craters of extinct volcanoes. Their pottery and metal works, if not of Greek origin, were certainly improved by Grecian artisans, and may therefore be attributed to the Pelasgic Tyrrhenians. No Italian nation was so religious, or rather superstitious, as the Etrurians: from them the Romans borrowed most of their ritual and ceremonies, the rules of augury and divination, and the solemnities in the declaration of peace or war. At a very early age Greek literature supplanted the native literature of Etruria, and the ancient lore of the Tuscans fell into what seems to have been unmerited oblivion.

The Umbrians were a nation consisting of several distinct races, the most remarkable being the Camertes and the Sarsinates. Their language appears to have been a mixture of Etrurian and Oscan. It is the misfortune of the Umbrians that their greatness had disappeared before the age of certain history; their glory seems to have passed away when the rich countries bordering on the sea-coast were occupied by the Gauls.

The south-east of Italy, or Japygia, was occupied by the Messapians, the Peucetians, and the Daunians. The Messapians are said to have been an old Pelasgian colony from Crete; they were a very powerful people until the city of Tarentum had acquired sufficient strength to contend for the supremacy of southern Italy, when, after a tedious struggle, they were compelled to enter into an alliance of inferiority with the Tarentines.

The Peucetians appear to have been a Liburnian colony from Illyria; the Daunians, a Pelasgic colony from Ætolia. The latter were subdued by the Apulians, an Oscan horde, and their name was lost in that of their conquerors. The language of the inhabitants of that part of Italy called Japygia was Greek.

The Ligurians and Venetians appear to have been branches of the great Liburnian nation, which at one time possessed both sides of the northern Adriatic. The former were a brave, warlike people; for more than forty years they resisted the Roman arms; and it is perhaps on this account that they are stigmatised as liars and deceivers by classical writers. On the other hand, the Venetians submitted without a struggle; but it is probable that the evils they had suffered from the invasion made them anxious to obtain the protection of some powerful state.

SECTION III.—*The Greek Colonies in Italy.*

FROM B.C. 1030 TO B.C. 277.

THE earliest Greek settlement in Italy, of which we have any certain historical information, came from Chalcis in the island of Eubœa, and settled at Cumæ (B.C. 1030). This city soon attained a high degree of prosperity, established a powerful navy, and founded flourishing colonies, of which Neapolis and Zancle (afterwards called Messana) was the chief. Its form of government was aristocratic; but this constitution was subverted (B.C. 544) by the tyrant Aristodemus. Freedom was restored after his assassination; but the Cumans, weakened by internal dissensions, suffered severely in a war with the Eretrians and Daunians (B.C. 500), and were finally subdued by the Campanians. Cumæ was annexed to the Roman dominions (B.C. 345); but in consequence of its harbour at Puteoli, it retained a considerable share of its importance even after the loss of its independence.

Tarentum was founded by the Parthenii from Sparta, under Phalantus (B.C. 707), as has been already mentioned. The colonists had to maintain long wars against the Italian tribes in their neighbourhood, especially the Messapians and Lucanians; but they prevailed over these uncivilised barbarians, and made their city one of the most flourishing maritime states in western Europe. Luxury, however, finally brought effeminacy and weakness. To escape from the grasping ambition of the Romans, the Tarentines invited Pyrrhus, king of Epirus, into Italy; but after the departure of that monarch, the city became dependent on Rome (B.C. 277).

Croton was founded by the Achæans (B.C. 710). Even in the first century of its existence the city attained such power as to be able to raise an army of one hundred and twenty thousand men. The constitution was in a great degree democratic, and continued so until the philosopher Pythagoras came to reside in Croton (B.C. 540). He established a secret association among his disciples, the chief object of which was to secure a monopoly of political power to the members of the Pythagorean society. In a few years three hundred men, all Pythagoreans, held the sovereignty of Croton; and the influence of the new sect was established not only in the Greek cities of Italy and Sicily, but over a great part of ancient Greece and the islands of the Ægean. The Crotonians soon after engaged in war with the Sybarites, and destroyed their city. Success proved ruinous; the inferior ranks of men in Crotona, intoxicated with prosperity, and instigated by the artful and ambitious Cylon, whose turbulent manners had excluded him from the order of Pythagoras, into which he had repeatedly attempted to enter, became clamorous for an equal partition of the conquered territory of Sybaris; which being denied, as inconsistent with the nature of the oligarchy established by the Pythagoreans, they secretly conspired against their magistrates, attacked them by surprise in the senate-house, put many to death, and drove the rest from their country. Pythagoras himself died soon afterwards at Metapontum, in Lucania, having lived just long enough to witness the ruin of the structure he had laboured so anxiously to raise. Croton never perfectly recovered from the fatal effects of this civil war; it was repeatedly captured by the kings of Syracuse; and after the departure of Pyrrhus from Italy, it became dependent on Rome.

Sybaris was founded by an Achæan colony (B.C. 720). The extreme fertility of the soil, and the generous admission of all strangers to the right of citizenship, caused the population to increase so rapidly, that, in a war against the Crotonians, the Sybarites are said to have brought three hundred thousand men into the field. Its vast wealth, derived chiefly from an extensive trade in wine and oil with northern Africa and Gaul, rendered it the most extensive, populous, and luxurious city in Europe, from about B.C. 600 to B.C. 550; so that the debauchery and effeminacy of the Sybarites became proverbial. Disputes arose between the aristocratic and democratic factions, which led to a civil war. At length Telys, the leader of the multitude, obtained possession of the supreme power, and expelled five hundred of the principal nobles, who fled for refuge to Crotona. The Sybarites sent to demand these refugees, and, meeting with a refusal, put to death the Crotonian ambassadors. Such an outrage naturally led to a war between the two cities (B.C. 510). With far inferior forces the Crotonians defeated the Sybarites in the field, took their city by storm, and rased it to the ground.

The Sybarites, driven from their habitations, besought the Lacedæmonians and Athenians to restore them, requesting them, at the same time, to send a colony to share in the new city they had resolved to build. The ambassadors were rejected at Sparta; but the Athenians, who delighted in such applications, cheerfully granted their aid (B.C. 446). A squadron of ten ships, having a considerable number of troops on board, was sent to Italy, under the command of Lampo and Xenocrates; and, at the same time, proclamation was made throughout Greece, that all persons willing to emigrate to the new colony should receive the protection of the Athenian fleet. Great numbers availed themselves of the proposition, and the Sybarites, aided by the new settlers, soon recovered their former possessions, and founded Thurium, near the site of their ancient city. Peace did not long inhabit these new dwellings; the inhabitants coming from so many various quarters, could not forget their old animosities, and began to dispute which section among them could claim to rank as founders of the city. An appeal was made to the Delphic oracle (B.C. 433): the priests of that temple declared the city to be a colony of Apollo. But this did not put an end to discord; the Sybarites, believing that they had the best right to their own country, began to exclude the foreign colonists, who were by far the majority, from all honours and employments: this provoked a civil war, which ended in a second expulsion of the Sybarite families. The Thurians then invited fresh colonists from Greece, and formed themselves into a commonwealth, choosing Charondas, of Catana, for their legislator. They soon sunk under the enervating effects of luxury, and, being unable to defend themselves against the Lucanians, placed themselves under the protection of the Romans. This afforded the Tarentines an excuse for attacking the city, of which they made themselves masters, and thus brought upon themselves the vengeance of Rome. At the close of the Tarentine war Thurium became a Roman dependency. It suffered very severely in the second Punic war, and, having been almost depopulated, was occupied by a Roman colony (B.C. 190).

The city of Locri Epizephyrii was inhabited by the people of the same name. The original colonists were sent out by the Locri Ozolæ (B.C. 683); but these were joined by a great variety of settlers, chiefly from western Greece. Zaleucus, one of their own citizens, became the legislator of the Locrians, and his wise institutions remained unchanged for nearly two centuries. The constitution appears to have been a judicious mixture of aristocracy and democracy. The Locrians continued to be honourably distinguished by their peaceful condition, quiet conduct, and good manners, until Dionysius II., tyrant of Syracuse, having been expelled by his subjects, sought refuge in Locri, which was the native country of his mother (B.C. 357). His insolence, his licentiousness, and the excesses of his followers, brought the state to the verge of ruin; and, when he returned to Syracuse (B.C. 347), the Locrians revenged their wrongs on his unfortunate family. When Pyrrhus invaded Italy, he placed a garrison in Locri (B.C. 277); but the Locrians rose in revolt, and put the intruders to the sword. The king of Epirus, in revenge, stormed and plundered the city. After his return home, it submitted to the Romans, and was one of the places that suffered most severely in the second Punic war.

Rhegium was colonised jointly by the Chalcidians and Messenians (B.C. 668); but the chief power was possessed by the Messenian aristocracy. This oligarchy was subverted by Anaxilaus (B.C. 494), and an absolute despotism established. After some time the Rhegians recovered their freedom, and attempted to secure tranquillity by adopting from the Thurians the constitution of Charondas. Thenceforward Rhegium enjoyed tranquillity and happiness, until it was captured and destroyed by Dionysius I., of Syracuse (B. C. 392). It was partially restored by Dionysius II.; but, during the wars of Pyrrhus in Italy, it was still so weak as to require the protection of a Roman garrison. A legion, raised in Campania, was sent to Rhegium, under the command of Decius Jubellus. These soldiers having been used to a life of hardship, began soon to envy the luxurious ease and wealth of the citizens they had come to protect, and they formed a perfidious plan for their destruction (B.C. 281). They forged letters from the Rhegians to Pyrrhus, offering to put that monarch in possession of the city, and, under this pretence, they put the principal part of the citizens to death, and drove the rest into exile. The Roman senate was not slow in punishing this atrocious outrage; they sent an army against the guilty Campanians, who had been reinforced by several bands of profligate plunderers, and, after a severe struggle, obtained possession of the city. The survivors of the wicked legionaries were beaten with rods, and beheaded in bands of fifty at a time; and the few Rhegians that survived were reinstated in possession of their estates, liberties, and laws. But the city was too weak to maintain its independence, and it became thenceforth subject to Rome.

CHAPTER XIV.

HISTORY OF SICILY.

SECTION I.—*Geographical Outline.*

THE fertile island of Sicily was known by various names to the ancients. It was called Triquetra, or Trinacria, from its triangular shape; Sicania and Sicilia from the Sicani and Siculi, Italian hordes who peopled a great part of the country. Its three extreme promontories were named Pelorum (*Faro*), Pachynum (*Passaro*), and Lilybæum (*Boco*): the first of these faces Italy, the second Greece, and the third Africa. From the narrowness of the strait opposite Pelorum, it has been supposed that Sicily was broken off from Italy by some convulsion of nature; and the Greek city Rhegium, which stood on the Italian side of the strait, derives its name from this common opinion.* The strait is remarkable for the rapidity of its currents, and for the rock Scylla, and whirlpool Charybdis, the passage between which was accounted very dangerous. These places are frequently described by the Latin poets. Ovid thus alludes to the opinion of Italy having been joined to Sicily near the city of Zancle, or Messana:

> " So Zancle to the Italian earth was ty'd,
> And men once walk'd, where ships at anchor ride;
> Till Neptune overlook'd the narrow way,
> And in disdain pour'd in the conqu'ring sea."

Virgil describes the strait and its dangers more fully in the advice which he represents Helenus as offering to Æneas respecting his voyage to Italy:

> " When parted hence, the wind that ready waits
> For Sicily, shall bear you to the straits:
> Where proud Pelorus opes a wider way,
> Tack to the larboard and stand off to sea:
> Veer starboard sea and land. Th' Italian shore
> And fair Sicilia's coast were one, before

* From ῥήγνυμι, *to break.*

An earthquake caus'd the flaw, the roaring tides
The passage broke, and land from land divides.
Distinguish'd by the straits, on either hand
Now rising cities in long order stand,
And fruitful fields (so much can time invade
The mouldering work that beauteous Nature made).
Far on the right her dogs foul Scylla hides:
Charybdis roaring on the left presides;
And in her greedy whirlpool sucks the tides:
Then spouts them from below; with fury driven,
The waves mount up and wash the face of heaven.
But Scylla from her den with open jaws
The sinking vessel in her eddy draws;
Then clashes on the rocks: a human face
And virgin-bosom hides her tail's disgrace.
Her parts obscene below the waves descend,
With dogs enclos'd, and in a dolphin end."

The most remarkable cities on the eastern coast of Sicily were Zanclé, or Messana (*Messina*), deriving its first name from the old Sicilian word Zanclos, signifying a reaping-hook, to which its curved shore bears some fanciful resemblance; and its second from the Messenian exiles, who conquered the city: Taurominium (*Taormina*), on the river Taurominius (*Cantara*), near which was the coast called Copria, or "the dunghill," from the number of wrecks cast upon it by the whirlpool of Charybdis: Catana, a Chalcidian colony on the river Amenes (*Judicello*): Morgantium, a city of the Italian Siculi, near the mouth of the Sigmæthus (*La Jaretta*): Leontini, a flourishing Chalcidian colony: Hybla, celebrated for its honey, founded by the Sicanians, and subsequently colonised by the Megarians: and Syracuse, the ancient capital of the island.

Syracuse contained within its walls, which were eighteen miles in circumference, four very considerable cities united into one, like London, Westminster, Southwark, and Lambeth. Acradina, the largest of the four, contained the principal public buildings, such as the Prytaneum, the palace of justice, and the temple of Jupiter Olympius. Tyche,* which stood between Acradina and the hill Epipolæ, contained the gymnasium for the exercise of youth, and several temples, especially one

* From τυχη, *fortune*.

dedicated to Fortune, from which this division of the city derived its name. The third quarter, called Ortygia, was an island, connected with the other parts by a bridge: it contained two beautiful temples, one sacred to Diana, and the other to Minerva, the tutelary deities of Syracuse. Neapolis, or the new city, was the latest erected: it contained the temples of Ceres and Proserpine, and the statue of Apollo Temenites, celebrated by Cicero as the most valuable monument of Syracuse.

Near Syracuse was a steep hill named Epipolæ, defended in the later ages by a fort called Labdalon. On this hill was the famous prison called Latomiæ, on account of its being partly excavated from the living rock.* It was a cave one hundred and twenty-five paces long and twenty feet broad, constructed by order of Dionysius the tyrant, who imprisoned there those whom he suspected of being opposed to his usurpation. A winding tube, constructed on the model of the human ear, ascended from the cavern to a private apartment, where the tyrant used to sit and listen to the conversation of his unhappy captives.

The celebrated fountain of Arethusa, now dried up, arose in the island of Ortygia. The poets fabled that the Alpheus, a river of Elis, in the Peloponnesus, rolled its waters either through or under the waters of the sea, without mixing with them, as far as the fountain of Arethusa; which gave occasion to the following lines of Virgil:

> "Thy sacred succour, Arethusa, bring,
> To crown my labour; 'tis the last I sing:
> So may thy silver streams beneath the tide,
> Unmix'd with briny seas, securely glide!"

On the African side of Sicily stood Camarina, between the rivers Oanus (*Frascolari*) and Hipparis (*Camarana*): it was anciently a very wealthy city; but its inhabitants having drained a marsh by which the city was protected, the enemies found easy access, and destroyed it; hence *Ne moveas Camarinam*, "remove not Camarina," has passed into a proverb. Following the line of coast westwards, we meet Gela (*Terra Nova*), now in

* From λααϛ, *a stone*, and τεμνω, *to cut*.

ruins, and Agragas or Agrigentum (*Girgenti*), between the rivers Agragas (*San Biaggio*) and Hypsa (*Drago*). It was anciently the rival of Syracuse; and we may judge of its former strength and splendour from the following description given of it by the historian Polybius: "It exceeds most of the Sicilian cities in strength, beauty, and situation, and magnificent edifices. Though erected at the distance of eighteen hundred furlongs from the sea, it can conveniently import all kinds of provision and munitions of war. From its natural strength, increased judiciously by fortifications, it is one of the most impregnable places in the island. Its walls are built upon a rock, rendered inaccessible by art. The river from which the city takes its name protects it on the south, and it is covered by the Hypsa on the west; on the east it is defended by a fortress, built on the brink of a precipice, which serves instead of a ditch." The citadel, called Omphale, which stood at the mouth of the Agragas, was more ancient than the city itself.

The other cities on the African side were Minoa Heraclea (*Castel Bianco*), deriving its first name from a Cretan, and its second from a Lacedæmonian colony, on the banks of the Halycus (*Platani*); and Selinus (*Terra delle Pulci*), on the river Selinus (*Madiuni*), founded by a colony from Megara.

On the coast opposite Italy were the cities Lilybæum (*Marsala*), celebrated in ancient times for its excellent harbour; Drepanum (*Trapani*), deriving its name from a fancied resemblance of its coast to a scythe;* Eryx (*Trepano del Monte*), on a mountain of the same name; Segesta, or Egesta, now in ruins, supposed to have been founded by a Trojan colony, who named the streams that watered their territory the Scamander and the Simois, in memory of the rivers of their native land; the former of these is now *Il fiume di San Bartolomeo*, the latter a rivulet without a name; Panormus (*Palermo*), the present capital of Sicily, originally founded by the Phœnicians, between the Orothus (*Amiraglio*) and the Leutherus (*Baiaria*). In the neighbourhood of Panormus was a mountain-fortress called Ereta (*Monte Pelegrino*): Himæra, Alæsa, and Agathyrna, are now in ruins.

* From δρεπανον, *a scythe.*

In the interior of the country were Adranum (*Aderno*), near the foot of Mount Ætna; Enna (*Castro Janni*), sacred to Ceres; and Engyum (*Mandania*), near the springs of the Alæsus (*Casonia*).

The most remarkable natural object in Sicily is the celebrated volcano of the lofty Mount Ætna, covered with eternal snows, though ever burning. It has been rather powerfully described by Silius Italicus:

> "Its lofty summits, wondrous to be told,
> Display bright flames amid the ice and cold;
> Above, its rocks with flames incessant glow,
> Though bound in icy fetters far below:
> The peak is claim'd by winter as its throne,
> While glowing ashes o'er its snows are shewn."

The fire which continually burns in the bowels of the mountain made the poets place here the forges of Vulcan and his Cyclopean attendants, and the prison of the giants who rebelled against Jupiter. This fiction is beautifully related by Virgil, in his description of the mountain:

> "The port capacious, and secure from wind,
> Is to the foot of thund'ring Ætna join'd.
> By turns a pitchy cloud she rolls on high;
> By turns hot embers from her entrails fly,
> And flakes of mountain-flames that lick the sky.
> Oft from her bowels massy rocks are thrown,
> And shiver'd by the force come piece-meal down.
> Oft liquid lakes of burning sulphur flow,
> Fed from the fiery springs that burn below.
> Enceladus, they say, transfix'd by Jove,
> With blasted limbs came trembling from above;
> And when he fell, the avenging father drew
> This flaming hill, and on his body threw:
> As often as he turns his weary sides,
> He shakes the solid isle, and smoke the heavens hides."

The Æolian or Vulcanian islands lie off the north coast of Sicily, in the Tuscan Sea. The most remarkable are Lipara (*Lipari*) and Strongylæ (*Stromboli*). North of Cape Lilybæum were the islands called Ægates, or Ægades: they are three in number; Phorbantia (*Levanzo*), Ægusa (*Favignano*), and Hiera (*Maretino*).

Section II.—*Historical Notices of the ancient Inhabitants of Sicily.*

CHRONOLOGY UNCERTAIN.

The Cyclopians and Læstrigons are said to have been the first inhabitants of Sicily. It is impossible to trace their origin; we only know that their settlements were in the vicinity of Mount Ætna. Their inhumanity towards strangers, and the flames of Ætna, were the source of many popular fables and poetic fictions. It was said that the Cyclops were giants; that they had but one eye, placed in the centre of their forehead; that they fed on human flesh; and that they were employed by Vulcan to forge the thunderbolts of Jove.

Next in antiquity were the Sicanians, probably an Italian horde driven southwards by the pressure of the Pelasgi, though many ancient writers assert that they came from Spain. They finally settled in the western part of the island, and were said to have joined the Trojan exiles in building Eryx and Egesta.

After the Sicani had been for some ages exclusive masters of the island, the Siculi, an ancient people of Ausonia, crossed the strait; and having defeated the Sicanians in a sanguinary engagement, confined them in a narrow territory, and changed the name of the island from Sicania to Sicily. Some centuries after this revolution, Greek colonies began to settle on the Sicilian coast: the principal states that founded settlements in the island were Chalcis in Eubœa, Megara, Corinth, the Dorians from Rhodes and Crete, and the Messenians, driven from their native country by the Spartans. To these may be added two Italian colonies, the Morgetes and the Mamertines.

The Siculi were first united under one head by a king named Æolus, whose age is uncertain. Their most renowned sovereign was Deucetius, who engaged in a long war with the Syracusans; but having been frequently defeated, he was forced to surrender himself to their mercy. With unusual clemency, the Syracusans granted him liberty and life, and assigned a pension for his support on condition of his living in the territories of their parent city, Corinth. Having removed this formidable rival, the Syracusans reduced the whole country of the Siculi, stormed their chief city, Triquetra, and levelled it to the ground. When the Athenians invaded Sicily under the command of Nicias, they were joined by the Siculi, who gave them very effective assistance. They likewise aided the Carthaginians in their first attempts to gain possession of the island. Having been subsequently induced to join the Syracusans, they were disgracefully betrayed to the Carthaginians by the tyrant Dionysius, and were forced to bear a cruel yoke, until their independence was restored by Timoleon.

Section III.—*The History of Syracuse.*

FROM B.C. 735 TO B.C. 212.

Syracuse was founded by a Corinthian colony (B.C. 735), under the guidance of Archytas, a nobleman of rank, compelled to quit his native country by some political dispute. Its form of government for two centuries and a half was republican; and though, during this period, the state does not appear to have risen to any considerable height of power, yet the Syracusans founded the colonies of Acræ, Casmenæ, and Camarina. An aristocratic faction having cruelly oppressed the citizens, the populace at length combined to throw off the yoke, and drove the tyrannical nobles into exile (B.C. 485). They fled to Gela, then ruled by Gelon, an able and ambitious usurper, who had recently become sovereign of his country. Gelon levied an army, and, accompanied by the exiles, marched to Syracuse, of which he easily made himself master. Under his administration the city rose rapidly in wealth and importance, while Gelon himself acquired so much fame, by repeated victories over the Carthaginians, that the Athenians and Spartans, then menaced by the Persian invasion, earnestly sought his assistance. Gelon demanded to be appointed captain-general of the confederate Greeks; a stipulation to which the Athenians and Spartans returned a stern refusal; and, before any further steps could be taken, he learned that Xerxes had engaged the Carthaginians to attack the Greek colonies in Sicily and Italy, while he invaded the parent state. After spending three years in making preparations, the Spartans sent against Sicily an immense armament, under the command of Hamilcar, said to consist of three hundred thousand men, two thousand ships of war, and three thousand vessels of burden. Having effected a landing, Hamilcar laid siege to Himera, then ruled by Theron, the father-in-law of Gelon. The king of Syracuse, though unable to muster more than fifty thousand men at this sudden emergency, marched with all expedition to raise the siege. On his road he had the good fortune to intercept a messenger from the Selonuntines to the Carthaginian general, promising to send him a stipulated body of cavalry on an appointed day. Gelon led an equal number of his horse to the Carthaginian camp at the specified time, and, having gained unsuspected admission, so disconcerted the enemy by a sudden attack, that the whole host was thrown into confusion, and the Syracusans won an easy victory. Hamilcar was slain, and his mighty army all but annihilated. Carthage humbly sought peace, which was generously granted by the conqueror. During the brief remainder of his reign, Gelon strenuously exerted himself for the benefit of his subjects; and though no one can justify the means by which he acquired supremacy, there are few who will not pardon his original error on account of the use he made of his power. His subjects, after his death, honoured him as a demigod.

Hiero I. succeeded his brother Gelon (B.C. 477): his administration was more brilliant than useful; he protected the arts and sciences; but he also encouraged a taste for luxury and magnificence, contrary to the policy of his more enlightened predecessor. He subdued the cities of Catana and Naxus, expelled the ancient inhabitants, and supplied their place with fresh colonies from Syracuse and the Peloponnesus. A more honourable and useful achievement was his decisive victory over the Etrurian pirates off Cumæ: these had long been the terror of the western Mediterranean; but, after their overthrow by Hiero, they ceased to infest the seas for several centuries. After this exploit he engaged in war with the tyrant of Agrigentum, who was forced to abdicate the government, and his subjects placed themselves under the protection of Hiero.

Thrasybulus, likewise a brother of Gelon, became sovereign of Syracuse on the death of Hiero (B.C. 459); but his tyranny and cruelty soon provoked a revolution; he was dethroned, and the republican constitution restored. But the Syracusans gained little by the change. A system of secret voting, called *petalism*,* was introduced, precisely similar to the Athenian ostracism, and most of the leading statesmen were banished by a giddy populace. It was at this period that the Athenians made their unfortunate attempt to conquer Sicily, whose results have been already described in the chapter on Grecian history. After the complete destruction of the Athenian armaments (B.C. 413), the Egestans, who had invited the invaders, sought and obtained the aid of Carthage: this led to a series of sanguinary wars, which have been noticed in the chapter on the history of Carthage.

Taking advantage of the political disturbances in Syracuse, Dionysius I. usurped the government (B.C. 405), and, though deservedly branded as a tyrant, it must be confessed that his vigorous administration was crowned with success abroad and prosperity at home. The greater part of his reign was passed in wars against Carthage and the cities of Magna Græcia, and also against the ancient race of the Siculi, whose choice of party generally decided the success of these wars.

Dionysius I. was cut off by poison (B.C. 368), and was succeeded by his youthful son Dionysius II., under the guardianship of the virtuous Dio. But neither Dio nor his friend the philosopher Plato, could improve the corrupted character of the young prince. He drove Dio into banishment (B.C. 360), and then gave a loose reign to his passions, indulging in the most extravagant luxury and debauchery. Dio returned (B.C. 357), and, after a long struggle, restored the republican form of government. He was, however, assassinated (B.C. 353). Syracuse became the prey of sanguinary factions, of which Dionysius, after ten years of exile, took advantage to recover his throne. His tyranny, and the treachery of Icetas the Leontine, who, when invited to aid the Syracusans, betrayed their interests to the Carthaginians, compelled the citizens to seek succour from Corinth. Timoleon, the most splendid example of a true

* From πεταλον, *a leaf.*

republican that ancient history affords, was sent to their assistance, but with very inadequate forces (B.C. 345). His abilities were, however, of more value than an army; he dethroned Dionysius, expelled Icetas, and, by a brilliant victory, humbled the pride of the Carthaginians. Timoleon's death (B.C. 337) was followed by a long period of stormy weakness, which ended in the usurpation of Agathocles (B.C. 317). The wars of that usurper in Sicily and Africa will be found in the chapter on Carthaginian history.

After the death of Agathocles (B.C. 289), the Syracusans, harassed by intestine commotions, and closely pressed by the Mamertines and Carthaginians, suffered the most dreadful calamities; and were at length forced to supplicate the aid of Pyrrhus, king of Epirus. That monarch, after having conquered almost the entire island, so disgusted his supporters by his arrogance, that he was compelled to retire (B.C. 275). The Syracusans at length, wearied of anarchy, conferred the throne on Hiero II., descended from the ancient royal family of Gelon. Under this prince the city enjoyed peace and prosperity during the wars between Rome and Carthage, in which he had the wisdom to take the Roman side. He died of old age (B.C. 215), after a long and glorious reign. After his death, the Carthaginian party acquired supremacy in Syracuse, and made a profligate use of their power. The new rulers soon provoked the resentment of the Romans, who sent an army into Sicily, and, after a long siege, protracted by the ingenious mechanical inventions of the celebrated mathematician Archimedes, took it by storm (B.C. 212), and laid it level with the ground.

Most of the other Greek cities in Sicily were involved in the fortunes of Syracuse. Agrigentum having been used as a military and naval station by the Carthaginians in the first Punic war, was seized by the Romans so early as B.C. 262.

CHAPTER XV.

HISTORY OF THE ROMAN REPUBLIC.

SECTION I.—*Traditions respecting the Origin of the Romans.*

THE legends of Rome, preserved by her best historians, relate that Æneas, after the destruction of Troy, led a colony of his countrymen into Italy, and founded the city of Lavinium. It would be easy to shew that this tale is destitute of truth or importance, but it is worth while to trace its origin. That the Romans were partly of Pelasgic origin appears evident from the name of their city, which in Greek signifies "a fortress."* In almost every country where the Pelasgi settled we find a city named Ænus, which, therefore, was probably a generic rather than an individual name. If any of the Pelasgi who settled on the hills at the south side of the Tiber came from an Ænus, they most probably retained their ancient name Æneadæ; and the signification of that patronymic being forgotten in process of time, it was confounded with another similar name, preserved by an independent tradition, the Æneadæ, or followers of Æneas, who survived the destruction of their country.

The legends proceed to state that, three years after the landing of the Trojans in Italy, they were supernaturally guided to the spot where Lavinium was erected. Their rising power gave offence to the Rutulians and Etruscans: Turnus and Mezentius led an army to expel the intruders. A battle was fought on the banks of the river Numicius; Turnus was slain by Æneas, who in his turn fell a victim to Mezentius; or, as was more generally believed, disappeared in the stream, and became a god, under the name of Jupiter Indiges. Mezentius was ultimately slain by Iulus, or Ascanius, the son of Æneas, whose descendants became lords of Latium.

After the lapse of thirty years, Lavinium was deserted for the more secure city of Alba, erected on the Alban Mount

* Ῥωμη, *strength.*

(*Monte Cavo*); and here the thirty confederate cities of Latium offered common sacrifices to the gods of the Pelasgic nation.

The traditions then go on to state that, at an uncertain date after the erection of the city, Procas, king of Alba, leaving two sons at his death, bequeathed his kingdom to Numitor, the elder, and his treasures, including the ancient wealth that had been saved from the sack of Troy, to Amulius. His riches enabled the younger prince to bribe a band of supporters, dethrone his brother, procure the murder of Numitor's youthful son, and have his daughter Ilia, or Rhea Sylvia, appointed a vestal virgin. While going to draw water from a spring, for the service of the temple, she was violated by the god Mars, and became the parent of twin boys. Amulius caused Sylvia to be put to death, and the children thrown into the Anio. The helpless infants were borne down the stream to the Tiber; and as that river subsided from a recent overflow, they were deposited at the foot of the Palatine hill, beneath a fig-tree called the *ficus ruminalis*. They were suckled by a she-wolf, and fed by a woodpecker, until they were discovered by Acca Laurentia, wife of Faustulus, the royal shepherd. Amongst her twelve sons and the neighbouring shepherds, the twins became distinguished for courage, and were chosen heads of rival factions. The followers of Romulus were named Quinctilii; those of Remus, Fabii. When they grew up, Remus, being involved in a dispute with the herdsmen of the deposed Numitor, and being taken prisoner, was carried to Alba as a robber. The youthful prince, when brought into the presence of his grandfather, so charmed him by the intrepidity of his replies, that Numitor hesitated to pronounce sentence of death. In the mean time Romulus, having learned from the aged shepherd the secret of his birth, assembled his comrades to rescue Remus; and, being joined by some of his grandfather's old adherents, deposed Amulius, and restored Numitor to the throne.

Love for the spot where their lives had been thus miraculously preserved, induced the young men to solicit their grandfather for permission to erect a city on the banks of the Tiber. Scarcely had leave been granted, when a violent contest arose between the brothers; Romulus insisted that the city should be called Rome, and should be built on Mount Palatine; Remus demanded that it should be named Remuria, and erected on Mount Aventine. It was resolved that the question should be decided by the most favourable augury. Remus had the first omen, six vultures; but Romulus the more perfect, twelve vultures. A second dispute arose; but the party of Romulus prevailed, and the foundation of the new city was laid on Mount Palatine, with all the ceremonies of Tuscan superstition. Scarcely had the walls begun to appear above the surface, when Remus leaped over them in an insulting manner, and was slain either by Romulus or one of his followers.

According to Varro, whose authority has been followed by most chronologists, Rome was founded on the 21st of April, being the day sacred to Pales, the goddess of shepherds, in the third year of the sixth Olympiad, 431 years after the destruction of Troy, and 753 before the commencement of the Christian era. It was built in a square form, and contained originally about a thousand miserable huts. Such was the humble beginning of a city destined to be the capital of the world.

SECTION II.—*From the Foundation of the City to the Abolition of Royalty.*

FROM B.C. 753 TO B.C. 509.

IN order to procure inhabitants for his new city, Romulus opened an asylum for all whom guilt or misfortune compelled to quit their native country. When he had thus procured a competent number of citizens, he convened an assembly of the people to choose a constitution and rulers. As he had anticipated, he was elected king; but at the same time his power was limited by municipal institutions tending to secure a considerable degree of freedom. He divided the colony into three tribes, and these into thirty curiæ: next he constituted classes or orders of the state, separating the wealthier or more nobly born, whom he styled patricians, from the inferior rank of plebeians. The dignity of the patricians was hereditary; and eligibility to the principal offices of state was long confined to their order. To prevent envy or sedition arising from such a distinction, he engaged both classes to each other by the obligation of clientship. Every plebeian was allowed to choose "a patron" from the body of the patricians, to whom he became a client; and the sanctity of this mutual tie was preserved by the most awful denunciations, civil and religious, against its violation. A senate of 100 was chosen to aid the king by their counsels. Romulus nominated the first, who had the privilege of governing the city in his absence: each of the three tribes and thirty curiæ chose three, which completed the number. The senators, either from their age, or from the similitude of their care, were named Patres (*fathers*).

The next object that required the attention of Romulus was the formation of treaties of intermarriage with the neighbouring states; but these, despising the mean origin of the Romans, rejected his proposals with scorn. But though they thus refused alliance, they flocked to witness the Consualia, splendid games which Romulus proclaimed in honour of Consus or Neptune. While the strangers gazed unsuspectingly on the spot, their maidens were seized by an armed band of young Romans, who compelled them to become their wives by force. Several of the injured cities had recourse to arms, but were suceessively defeated. At last Titus Tatius, king of the Sabines, led a more powerful army against them; and Romulus, unable to withstand him in the field, retreated into the city, leaving a garrison to protect an important outpost on the Capitoline hill. Tarpeia, the daughter of the governor, dazzled by the splendid bracelets of the Sabines, agreed to betray the fortress "for what the besiegers wore on their arms." The Sabines, either mistaking her meaning, or anxious to punish her treachery, threw their shields on her as they entered, and crushed her to death. The Romans found themselves obliged, by the loss of this important outpost, to hazard a general engagement; but while victory was still doubtful, the Sabine women rushing between the armies induced them, by earnest supplications, to make terms of peace. It was agreed that the Sabines should erect a new city on the Quirinal and Capitoline hills; that there should be a "comitium," or place of common assembly for both nations, in the space between the Palatine and Capitoline hills, and that Romulus and Tatius should reign conjointly. The murder of Tatius, not long after, at Lavinium, left Romulus sole monarch of both nations.

The romantic circumstances just narrated bear every mark of having been derived from some national ballad or legendary lay, and consequently are not to be received as historic truth. Even less confidence is due to the narrative of the Tuscan wars, with which the Latin historians have filled the blank of thirty-seven years in the life of Romulus. But a second heroic lay recited, that, after a long reign, he disappeared from earth, and became a god, under the name of Quirinus. Opposed to this was an ancient tradition, that he was torn to pieces by an aristocratic faction in the senate-house (B.C. 717).

On the death of Romulus, the senate appeared anxious to retain the supreme power, and each senator in rotation was to enjoy regal authority for one day, under the title of *interrex.* This form of government continued a year, when the people compelled the senate to elect a king. Their choice fell upon Numa, a Sabine, from the little town of Cures, to whom Tatius had given his daughter in marriage. The history of Numa is as legendary as that of Romulus: it was generally believed that he had been a disciple of Pythagoras, and this opinion maintained its ground in spite of many chronological difficulties. The traditions declare that when Numa was informed of his election, he refused to enter on his office, until assured that the gods, by their auguries, had confirmed the choice of the senate. His first care was to regulate the laws of property; he divided among the citizens the lands that Romulus had conquered, and founded the worship of Terminus, the god of boundaries, thus protecting the limits of estates by a religious sanction. His most important labour, however, was the regulation of the national worship: pretending to be secretly guided by the goddess Egeria, he framed the entire ritual law of the Romans, including regulations for the priesthood and for the prayers and worship of the people. His tranquil reign is said to have lasted forty years; the temple of Janus, which he had erected, and ordained to be open in time of war, and shut in peace, remained closed during the entire period, and his pious example diffused the blessings of tranquillity throughout the whole Italian peninsula. He died of old age (B.C. 679); and the legend adds, that the nymph Egeria, through grief for his loss, melted into a fountain.

After an interregnum, as in the former case, Tullus Hostilius, the son of a Roman captain who had been eminently distinguished by his valour in the wars of Romulus, was chosen king. The history of his reign, though still retaining much of legendary fiction, especially in the account of the Alban war, contains some circumstances that may be regarded as facts. In the very beginning of his reign, mutual acts of violence led to a war between the Romans and the Albans. The armies of both cities were drawn up against each other at the Fossa Cluilia, where it was agreed to avert a battle by a combat between three brothers on each side, the Horatii and Curiatii, whose mothers were sisters, and had each brought three children into the world at a birth. The three Curiatii and two of the Horatii fell upon the field. The surviving Horatius sullied his victory by slaying his sister, who was bewailing the death of her cousin, to whom she had been betrothed; and was about to be executed by Tullus, but he appealed to the people, and the Romans unanimously insisted on the pardon of their champion.

In consequence of the previous agreement, Alba became subject to Rome. Tullus next engaged in war with the Fidenates, and summoned his new vassals to his aid. Mettius Fuffetius, the Alban dictator, broke his faith with the Romans, but had not courage to complete his defection. His meditated treachery was punished with death. Soon afterwards the Romans surprised Alba and levelled it to the ground, sparing only the temples of the gods; no injury, however, was done to the citizens; they were removed to Rome, and habitations assigned them on the Cœlian hill. The destruction of Alba, and the settlement of its citizens on the Cœlian, may be regarded as historical facts; the other circumstances are clearly disguised by poetic fiction.

After the conquest of Alba, Tullus waged successful wars

against the Latins and Sabines; but he was cut off in the midst of his victorious career (B.C. 640), by some superstitious experiments recommended to him as a remedy for sickness, which the legends declare brought down upon him the vengeful thunderbolts of the gods.

Ancus Martius, said to have been the grandson of Numa, was the next king. Like his ancestor, he turned his attention to the regulation of religious ceremonies, especially those used in declaring war or proclaiming peace; he also caused the principal parts of the Roman ritual to be transcribed on tables, that all might know how to conduct themselves in public or private worship. His peaceful labours were interrupted by a war with the Latins, whom he subdued, and carried several thousand of them to Rome, where they were assigned settlements on Mount Aventine. His conquests were extended into Etruria, and along both banks of the Tiber to the sea. He founded the town and port of Ostia at the mouth of the river; but it is probable that this first naval establishment of the Romans was intended rather for piracy than trade. Nor did he pay less attention to the city than to its dominions; a new line of fortifications, the first bridge over the Tiber, and the first public prison, now the oldest remaining monument in Rome, are generally ascribed to Ancus. Of still greater importance was his legal constitution of the plebeian order in the state, and the assignment of lands to this body from the conquered territories. His death (B.C. 618) is said by some authors to have been accelerated by violence.

We now approach one of the most important, but also one of the most obscure, periods in the early history of Rome; the reigns of Tarquinius Priscus and his son-in-law Servius Tullius. Lucius Tarquinius Priscus is said to have been the son of Damaratus, one of the Bacchiads who fled from Corinth to avoid the vengeance of Cypselus. Niebuhr has pointed out the many chronological difficulties involved in this statement, but these do not furnish sufficient reason for rejecting the legend altogether: by the simple change of "son" into "descendant," by no means an improbable substitution, the truth of the story is brought within the verge of possibility.

His original name is said to have been Lucumo; this we know to have been an Etrurian title of dignity; and if we understand by it that he held a magisterial office in his native country, it will explain the respect with which he was received at Rome, and the trust reposed in him by Ancus. He is said to have removed from Tarquinii, his native city, partly because his foreign descent exposed him to envy, and partly at the instigation of his wife Tanaquil, who was celebrated for her skill in augury. With this history there seems to be intermingled the traditions respecting Cœles Vibenna, a leader of independent companies, who hired his soldiers as mercenaries in the Tuscan wars, and finally came and settled at Rome with his followers, in an uncertain age.

Tarquinius Priscus was appointed guardian of the young sons of Ancus; but by his influence with the people, he had the claims of these princes set aside, and was himself chosen king. He introduced many Etrurian customs and ceremonies into Rome, especially those connected with the dignities of kings and magistrates. The accounts of his wars with the Etruscans, Latins, and Sabines, are very contradictory; but it seems not improbable that, towards the close of his reign, these three nations acknowledged his supremacy. His victory over the Sabines was owing to his superiority in cavalry. It had been originally his intention to add three new centuries to the equestrian order; but this plan was opposed by the celebrated augur, Attus Nævius, whose authority, in an age of superstition, rivalled that of the kings. A mode was found for reconciling the opponents; new centuries were established, but no addition was made to the names assigned by Romulus; so that henceforward there were the first and second Ramnes, Tities, and Luceres. But Tarquin's name is rendered still more memorable by the stupendous public works he commenced for the security and improvement of the city, especially the great sewers, the embankments of the Tiber, the foundation of the city-walls, the porticoes in the forum, and the race-course of the circus. To console the people under their toils, he instituted the great or Roman games, which were celebrated annually in September. Tarquinius is said to have reigned thirty-eight years, when he was assassinated by the agents of the sons of Ancus Martius (B.C. 578), who dreaded that he would bequeath the kingdom to his son-in-law Servius Tullius, the darling of the Roman people.

Servius Tullius for some time concealed the fact of Tarquin's death; but when he had secured the votes of the people, he made it public; and having convened an assembly to elect a sovereign, was unanimously chosen king. In the old legends, the birth of Servius Tullius is described as equally marvellous and humble. His mother was said to have been a captive named Ocresia; his father, a deity. While yet an infant, sleeping in the cradle, lambent flames, playing round his forehead, predicted his future greatness; and Tanaquil, encouraged by the omen, had him brought up in the palace as a prince, and gave him her daughter in marriage. Opposed to this is the testimony of the emperor Claudius Cæsar, derived from lost Tuscan authorities. In a speech, recommending some Lugdunensian Gauls for admission into the senate, he says,—"Servius Tullius, according to the Latin authorities, was the son of the captive Ocresia; but if we pay any regard to the Tuscans, he was the most faithful follower of Cœles Vibenna, and a sharer in his varied adventures. When harassed by the vicissitudes of fortune, he quitted Etruria with the remains of the army that Cœles had commanded. He occupied the Cœlian Mount, which he thus named in honour of his old commander. In Tuscany he was called Mastama; but he exchanged this for the Roman name, Servius Tullius. Having been chosen king, he exercised his authority to the highest advantage of the state." Though Servius waged several successful wars, his military famé was far inferior to his political glory; for his institutions not only laid the foundation, but completed the frame-work of the future republic. He formed a federal union between the Latin cities, placing Rome at the head of the league; and cemented the union by instituting common sacrifices for the united states on Mount Aventine. Of still greater importance was his institution of the census, or record of the property possessed by the citizens, and his distribution of the right of suffrage (*comitia centuriata*) to centuries, arranged according to the property of the six classes into which the census divided the people. All his laws were designed to secure free and equal government, and an impartial administration of justice. His wise and beneficent laws were received by the patricians with sullenness and anger; they were indignant at the restraints imposed upon their tyranny and exactions; accordingly they entered into a conspiracy with Lucius Tarquinius, the son of the late monarch, who had married the daughter of Servius. The plot exploded in the senate-house: the aged king was murdered, and his body flung into the streets (B.C. 534). Tullia, his wicked daughter, in her haste to congratulate Tarquin on his success, drove her chariot over her father's corpse, and proceeded onwards, though her vest was stained with his blood.

Tarquin, surnamed the Proud, was raised to the throne by the patricians, without the assent of the people being asked. In the history given of his reign, it is scarcely possible to separate what is merely legendary from what is worthy of credit; but it seems pretty certain that he gratified his supporters by diminishing the privileges of the plebeian order, and that he soon after made the patricians themselves feel the weight of his tyranny. He confirmed the supremacy of Rome over the Latins, united the Hernicans to the confederation by treaty, and gained several advantages over the Volsci. While the tyrant was besieging Ardea, his son Sextus violated the honour of Lucretia, a noble Roman lady. She summoned her relatives, and, having informed them of the outrage, committed suicide. Lucius Junius Brutus, who up to this time is said to have concealed patriotic resolutions under the mask of pretended insanity, though he held an important magistracy, convoked an assembly of the people, and exhibited the bleeding body of Lucretia to the multitude (B.C. 509). A decree was immediately passed for expelling the Tarquins and abolishing royalty. The army sent in its adhesion; and Tarquin, finding himself universally shunned, fled into Etruria.

Section III.—*From the Establishment of the Roman Republic to the Burning of the City by the Gauls.*

FROM B.C. 509 TO B.C. 386.

The abolition of royalty was a purely patrician revolution, from which the great body of the people gained no immediate advantage. Two annual magistrates, at first called prætors, but afterwards consuls, chosen from the patrician ranks, inherited the entire royal power, but did not, like the kings, possess any priestly dignity. The first magistrates elected under the new system were Brutus, and Collatinus the husband of Lucretia. Scarcely had they entered on their office, when ambassadors arrived from Etruria to plead the cause of Tarquin. Though these deputies met with no public success, they were enabled to organise a conspiracy among the younger patricians, who had shared in the tyrant's debaucheries; and among the accomplices of the plot were the sons of Brutus and the nephews of Tarquin. The plans of the conspirators were accidentally overheard by a slave, concealed in the apartment where they assembled, and information of the treason given to the consuls. Public duty triumphed over parental affection: Brutus not only pronounced sentence of death upon his sons, but witnessed their execution without shedding a tear. The property of the Tarquinii was confiscated; the whole family condemned to perpetual banishment; and the consul, Collatinus, whose relationship to the late family excited suspicion, was included in the sentence. Publius Valerius was elected to the vacant magistracy. Soon after, in an engagement between the Etruscans and Romans, Ancus the eldest son of Tarquin, and Brutus, fell by mutual wounds; but the victory was decided in favour of the young republic.

Valerius delayed some time before proceeding to the election of a new colleague. This circumstance, and a splendid house he was erecting on one of the Roman hills, inspired a suspicion that he was aiming at royalty. To prove his innocence, he demolished the building, proposed laws for restraining the consular power, and resigned the ensigns of his dignity to Spurius Lucretius. For this patriotic conduct Valerius was honoured with the surname Poplicola (*a friend of the people*). In the following year Valerius and Horatius were chosen consuls, the latter of whom had the honour of dedicating the national temple of Jupiter Capitolinus. In this sanctuary were preserved the Sibylline oracles, and the records of the pontiffs and augurs.

To the first year after the banishment of the Tarquins belong the celebrated *lex de provocatione* (law of appeal), and the first treaty between Rome and Carthage. The patricians had always the right of appeal from the sentence of the supreme magistrate to the general council of their own body: a similar right of trial by their peers was secured to the plebeians by the law of Valerius Poplicola, to which the senate seems to have yielded a very ungracious assent.* The treaty with Carthage shews how extensive the possessions of Rome had been under the monarchy: Ardea, Antium, Aricia, Circeii, and Terracina, are enumerated as subject cities, and Rome stipulates for them as well as herself.

From these historical facts we now turn to a legendary narrative, in which truth is so blended with fiction, that it is impossible to determine more than one or two circumstances on which any reliance can be placed. After their former defeat, the Tarquinii had recourse to the aid of Lar Porsenna, king of Clusium, the most powerful of the Tuscan princes, who at once led an overwhelming force to the Janiculum, a fortified hill on the north bank of the Tiber, joined to the city by a wooden bridge. The Romans were defeated, and fled over the bridge; the enemy would have gained admission into the city along with the fugitives, had not Horatius Cocles, with two companions, defended the entrance of the bridge until it was broken down behind him, when he leaped into the Tiber, and swam safely to his friends. As a mark of gratitude, every citizen, during the famine caused by the subsequent siege, brought him a portion of provision; a statue was erected to

* The Valerian law was imperfect in its sanction; there was no other penalty to enforce it than the declaration that he who violated it acted wrongly.

him at the expense of the republic, and as much land was bestowed upon him as he could plough round in a day. Porsenna continuing to blockade the city, a youth, named Caius Mucius, undertook, with the approbation of the senate, the task of assassinating the invading king. He entered the camp in disguise, but slew only a secretary instead of Porsenna. When brought before that monarch, to shew his contempt for tortures, he thrust his right hand into a fire that burned upon the altar, and held it there until it was consumed. The king, admiring such heroism, gave him his life and liberty: Mucius, in gratitude, informed him that three hundred Roman youths had similarly sworn his destruction; and Porsenna, alarmed for his life, immediately offered terms of peace to the Romans. In memory of his daring exploit Mucius was thenceforth named Scævola (*left-handed*), and was rewarded as munificently as Cocles. Hostages were given by the Romans for the due performance of the treaty; and the legend relates that one of them, a noble lady named Clœlia, won the admiration of Porsenna by escaping from her guards, and swimming on horseback over the Tiber, amid a shower of darts hurled at her by her baffled pursuers. The aid which the Romans subsequently afforded Porsenna when he was defeated before Aricia, induced him to render back the territory which had been yielded to him as part of the price of the peace.

Thus far the legend: but there is certain evidence that, in this war, the Romans surrendered their city and became tributary to the Tuscans, but that they embraced the opportunity afforded them by the defeat of Porsenna in Latium, to regain their independence.

A war with the Sabines, who wished to take advantage of the weakened condition of the republic, followed. It was chiefly remarkable for the migration of Attus Clausus, a noble Sabine, with all the members and clients of his house, to Rome. There he changed his name to Appius Claudius, and founded one of the most distinguished families of the republic. Though they lost their able leader, Poplicola, the Romans were victorious in three successive campaigns; and the Sabines were forced to purchase peace with corn, money, and a part of their lands.

Tarquin's son-in-law, Mamilius, induced the Latins to arm themselves in behalf of the exiled king, taking advantage of the violent disputes that raged between the patricians and plebeians respecting the law of debt. Ever since the expulsion of the king, the Roman nobles, after the abolition of royalty, had, by a series of iniquitous measures, usurped the most fertile portion of the conquered lands, which they leased out to the plebeians. Having thus the monopoly of the only property existing at the period, they became the sole capitalists of the republic, and lent out money at an exorbitant rate of usury. By the Roman law, those who were unable to discharge their debts became slaves to their creditors (*nexi*), and were subject to whatever punishment barbarous masters pleased to inflict. Goaded to madness by their wrongs, the plebeians refused to enlist in defence of their country until their grievances were redressed. The reasonable demands of the people were strenuously supported in the senate by Marcus Valerius, the brother of Poplicola; but they were obstinately opposed by Appius Claudius, whose haughty and selfish counsels had a predominant effect on a short-sighted aristocracy. After long delay, it was resolved to elect a single supreme magistrate, with the title of dictator, and invest him with absolute authority (B.C. 497). The people assented to the law; and Titus Lartius, one of the consuls, was appointed to the new office. After having ravaged the territories of the enemy, he dismissed all his prisoners without ransom; and this generosity so gratified the Latins, that they agreed upon a suspension of arms.

When the truce was expired, war again commenced, and the senate again appointed a dictator. Aulus Posthumius, the second dictator, encountered the Latins at the lake of Regellus, and inflicted on them a decisive defeat. Tarquin, thus frustrated in his last hope, retired to Cumæ in Campania, where he soon after died in exile.

While Tarquinius excited alarm, and the wars with Latium and Etruria continued, the senate ruled with some shew of justice and moderation. But when danger was passed, the patricians began to treat the plebeians as slaves. To the palace of every noble was attached a prison for debtors; and, in seasons of distress, after the sittings of the courts, herds of sentenced slaves were led away in chains to the private gaols of the patricians. At length the plebeian armies, after having been frequently deceived by false promises, deserted their officers in the very midst of war, and marched in a body to a hill called Mons Sacer, on the river Anio, within three miles of Rome, where they were joined by vast multitudes of their discontented brethren (B. C. 493). The patricians and their clients took up arms; their numbers were not contemptible; but, unaccustomed to military service, they dared not encounter a peasantry inured to warfare. The pressure of foreign enemies rendered an accommodation necessary; ten senators were sent to negotiate a peace with the plebeians, and a treaty was concluded, by which all the contracts of insolvent debtors were cancelled, those who had been reduced to slavery were set at liberty, the Valerian laws were restored to their former efficacy, and five annual magistrates were chosen to watch over the rights of the people, whose persons were declared to be inviolable. In the same year a league was made with the Latins, not, as before, on the basis of Roman superiority, but on terms of perfect equality. A similar federation was subsequently made with the Hernicans; and both these treaties prove, indisputably, that the disturbances produced by aristocratic tyranny, subsequent to the abolition of royalty, had seriously diminished the Roman power.

These losses began to be retrieved by successful wars against the Æquians and Volscians. The common histories of this period are full of extraordinary difficulties and contradictions; the account extracted from them must, therefore, be received with the suspicion that necessarily attaches to all traditionary legends. We are informed, that the success of the Volscian war was mainly owing to a young nobleman, Caius Marcus, who acquired the surname of Coriolanus, from his conduct at the capture of Coriola. Soon after, Rome suffered grievously by a famine; but a Sicilian prince hearing of the dearth, sent a large supply of corn to relieve the distresses of the citizens. Coriolanus proposed in the senate that this corn should not be distributed to the poor until the plebeians had resigned all the privileges they had acquired by their recent secession. For this detestable attempt he was impeached by the tribunes (B. C. 490), and brought to trial before that form of assembly (*comitia tributa*) in which the plebeians had the superiority. He was condemned to exile, and in his rage joined the Volsci. Guided by his superior talents, the Volscians defeated the Romans in every engagement, and at length laid siege to the city. Rome must have fallen, had not Veturia the mother, and Volumnia the wife of Coriolanus, prevailed upon the enraged exile to grant his countrymen terms of peace. On his return to the Volscian territories he was put to death in a tumult raised by Attius Tullius, a celebrated chief of the Volsci, who envied the fame of Coriolanus, and persuaded his countrymen that the illustrious exile had betrayed them. An opposing tradition is recorded by several historians, namely, that Coriolanus lived to a very advanced age, and often used to exclaim, "How miserable is the state of an old man in banishment!" It is impossible to ascertain which deserves the greater credit; but it is sufficiently manifest that the history of Coriolanus is not to be received without a considerable share of scepticism.

The Volsci, after the death of Coriolanus, lost rapidly all the advantages they had acquired, and were besides involved in a war with the Æqui, their former allies. But the Romans could not avail themselves of these favourable circumstances, being harassed by disputes respecting the agrarian law proposed by Spurius Cassius. The general purport of the law was, that lands conquered from the enemy should be divided into small estates, and assigned to the plebeians, instead of being leased out in large portions to the patricians. This appears to have been merely a revival of the ancient constitution of Servius, and was obviously based in equity; for no persons had a better claim to the public lands than those by whose valour and labours they had been acquired. The senate and patricians obstinately opposed a project that threatened to destroy the source of their profits; and Spurius Cassius, in his anxiety to accomplish his great objects, is said to have aimed at royalty. He was brought to trial on this charge before the collective body of the patricians, which has been by later writers confounded with the general assembly of the people (B.C. 484). He was convicted, and thrown from the Tarpeian rock. Another account of the death of Cassius has been given by some historians, not unworthy of credit. They inform us that he was put to death by his own father, as a traitor to his order.

There are few circumstances in Roman history more remarkable than that during seven consecutive years (from B.C. 483 to B.C. 479) one of the seats in the consulship was held by some member of the Fabian family. This arose from the powerful support which that family gave to the older patrician houses in their effort to monopolise the chief dignities. Civil dissensions were thus aggravated; the populace demanded an agrarian law; the minor patrician houses clamoured for a share in the honours of the state; and the senate could only evade the difficulty by keeping the nation constantly involved in war. At length the soldiers refused to conquer; and Cæso Fabius had the mortification to see a certain victory wrested from his hands by the determination of his followers not to pursue their advantages. This unexpected disgrace had such an effect on the Fabii, that they resolved to conciliate the favour of the commonalty, and declared themselves the patrons of popular measures. They thus lost the favour of the senate; and though the affection of the soldiers enabled them to acquire military glory, they were unable to carry any of the measures that they advocated. Weary of disappointment, they resolved to establish a colony of the members of their family, their clients, and dependents, on the frontiers, to guard the Roman territories from the Virentes. The number of persons capable of bearing arms mustered by this single house amounted to three hundred and six. They took post on the Cremera, where they were all cut off by the Etrurians (B.C. 476). It is said that only one young man of the Fabii escaped from this ruin of his family, and became the progenitor of a new race; but this is manifestly an exaggeration.

The Etruscans, following up their success, advanced within sight of Rome, formed a camp on the Janiculum, ravaged both sides of the river, and crowded the city with fugitives. The consuls, Virginius and Servilius, at length attacked the enemy in different quarters, and, after a desperate battle, forced them to retreat. From this time fortune began to favour the Romans, probably on account of the Etrurians being engaged in war with Hiero, king of Syracuse; and peace was at length concluded for forty years (B.C. 470). Niebuhr conjectures, with apparent plausibility, that it was at this time the Romans recovered the territory of which they had been deprived by Porsenna.

In the year after the conclusion of the peace, Cneius Genucius, tribune of the people, impeached the consuls, Furius and Manlius, before the general assembly of the commonalty, for refusing to give effect to the agrarian law. The consuls made a feeble defence; and the patricians, failing to bribe or intimidate the bold tribune, had him assassinated. Taking advantage of the consternation produced by this daring crime, the consuls ordered a general levy, intending to divert the people from their purpose by engaging them in foreign war. This plan would have succeeded, had not the refusal of one man, Volero Publius, to serve in the ranks, after having previously held the commission of centurion, led to a fierce commotion, which frustrated the consular plans. Volero, being chosen tribune by his countrymen, instead of seeking personal revenge, by impeaching the consuls, struck a fatal blow at the supremacy of the patrician faction, by transferring the election of the tribunes from the centuries to the tribes, and establishing the right of the general assembly of the commonalty to deliberate on all matters affecting the common weal, which should be brought before them by the tribunes; a law which was in effect the same as the establishment of the liberty of the press in our own days. While these laws were under discussion, the consul, Appius Claudius, was pre-eminently distinguished by his opposition to the popular claims; and when they were extorted from the senate, he unwisely vented his dissatisfaction on the army that he led against the Volsci. His soldiers, in revenge, fled before the enemy. Appius punished them by decimation, putting every tenth man to death. When his year of office expired, he was impeached capitally for such atrocious vengeance; but he escaped the penalty of his tyranny by committing suicide.

For several years the Roman history presents little more than a repetition of the struggles between the patricians and plebeians; desultory wars with the Æqui and Volsci; and a succession of physical calamities, uniting the horrors of plague, pestilence, and famine. Appius Herdonius, a Sabine adventurer, took advantage of these circumstances, and one night surprised and seized the capitol with an army of about four thousand men, composed of outlaws and slaves (B. C. 459). Instigated by the tribunes, the people refused to take up arms unless security was given that their grievances should be redressed; particularly insisting on the legal restriction of the consular power by a written code, according to the proposal of Terentillus (*lex Terentilla*) a few months before. The consul Valerius promised compliance; and the people stormed the capitol, slew Herdonius, and punished his associates: but Valerius having fallen in the assault, the senate refused to fulfil the conditions he had stipulated.

During the Æquian war (B. C. 457), a consular army was intercepted by the enemy in the defiles of Mount Ægidus, and so closely blockaded, that there seemed no choice between death or disgraceful submission. Some horsemen, breaking through the hostile lines, brought the news to Rome; and the senate, in alarm, resolved to create a dictator. Their choice fell upon Titus Quinctius Cincinnatus, a patrician violently opposed to the popular claims, but celebrated for personal integrity. His son Cæso had recently fled from Rome to escape a trial for high crimes and misdemeanours; and Cincinnatus had been reduced to great pecuniary distress by being compelled to pay the surety he had given for his son's appearance. The dictator delivered the consul Minucius and the army from their danger; but before resigning office he used the absolute power with which he was invested, to recal his son Cæso from banishment, and drive his accuser into exile. There is, indeed, some reason to believe, that the dictatorship of Cincinnatus, which has been so much lauded, was a mere artifice to baffle the demand of the people for a written code of laws. It, however, failed of success: the tribunes succeeded in getting their numbers increased from five to ten: Sicinius Dentatus, a veteran plebeian of approved valour, stimulated his order to fresh exertions in behalf of their freedom; and at length the senate yielded a reluctant assent to the formation of a code.

Ambassadors having been sent to the principal Grecian states and colonies for the purpose of collecting the best codes of celebrated legislators; on their return, ten persons, hence called decemviri, were chosen, with consular power, to arrange and digest a body of laws. A new constitution was established, known in history as the laws of the Twelve Tables, which continued down to the time of the emperors to be the basis of all civil and penal jurisprudence. It established the legal equality of all the citizens; but it preserved some of the most odious privileges of the aristocracy, especially the exclusive eligibility to the consulship, and it prohibited the intermarriage of patricians and plebeians (B.C. 450). The patricians, hoping to procure some modification in laws which they regarded as ruinous to their interests, and the plebeians, gratified by the advantages they had obtained, united to continue the decemviral authority for another year. The decemvirs, now secure of power, threw off the mask, grievously oppressed the people, and treacherously betrayed old Sicinius Dentatus, whose approved valour they dreaded, to the enemy. At length Appius, one of their number, attempted to make Virginia, the daughter of a brave officer, the victim of his lust, by illegally assigning her as a slave to one of his creatures. Her father Virginius slew the girl in the public court to save her from dishonour, and, aided by her lover Icilius, raised such a storm against the decemvirs, that they were forced to resign their office, and the ancient forms of government were restored. The tribunician power was not only re-established, but formidably increased by a law of the consul Valerius (B.C. 446), which invested the votes of the commons with the force of laws.*

* Lex Valeria; ut quod tributim plebes jussisset, populum teneret.

Civil commotions were renewed in consequence of the exertions made by the tribune Canuleius to abolish the law against intermarriages, and to open the consulship to plebeians. The repeal of the marriage-law was conceded, after a difficult struggle (B. C. 445); and the second popular demand was evaded by transferring the consular power to the annual commanders of the legions,* who were to be six in number, and one half chosen from the people (B. C. 443). But even this concession was for some time evaded by the senate, under the pretence of informalities in the election of those officers. Soon afterwards (B. C. 442), new magistrates, called censors, were chosen, not only to regulate the taking of the census, but also to superintend public morals; a power that soon enabled these magistrates to take rank among the very highest dignitaries of the state. These changes, however, did not conciliate the people, and a severe famine (B. C. 438) aggravated their discontent. In the midst of this distress, Spurius Mælius, a plebeian knight, purchased from his private fortune a large quantity of corn in Tuscany, which he distributed gratuitously to the people. His object probably was to become the first plebeian consul, which laudable object the patricians perverted into the crime of aiming at the sovereignty. They therefore appointed Cincinnatus dictator, who at once sent Spurius Ahala, his master of the horse, to summon Mælius before his tribunal. The knight was standing unarmed in the forum when thus called upon to take his trial; he shewed some reluctance to obey the dictator's command, and was cut down by Ahala. The old dictator applauded this murder of a defenceless man, as an act of pure patriotism; but the people took a different view of the transaction, and Ahala only escaped condemnation by voluntary exile.

While these commotions raged in the city, the Romans were engaged in desultory wars against the Sabines, the Æquians, and the Volscians, which generally terminated to the advantage of the republic, though they led to no decisive result. A more important affair was the war against Veii,

* Tribuni militum consulari potestate.

provoked by Lar Tolum'nius, king of the Veien'tes, who put to death the Roman ambassadors to the people of Fídenæ. Satisfaction being refused for this outrage (B.C. 404), the Romans came to the resolution of destroying Veii, which, being the richest city of Etrúria, had long been a dangerous rival of their republic. To effect this object, it was necessary to have a permanent standing army; and a property-tax was levied to supply payment for the troops. After the blockade and siege had continued nearly ten years, Fúrius Camil'lus, who had distinguished himself by defeating the Etrurian armies that attempted to aid the Veien'tes, was chosen dictator. By his directions a mine was constructed from the Roman camp into the Veientine citadel, through which an entrance was obtained, and Veii taken (B.C. 395). Its riches were shared by the soldiers, its inhabitants enslaved or held to ransom, and the images of its gods transferred to Rome.

Notwithstanding his great services, Camil'lus was condemned to exile on the charge of having embezzled part of the plunder of Veii; but scarcely had he departed, when the Romans were involved in the most calamitous war that had yet occurred in their history. The barbarous Gauls, having crossed the Alps in numerous hordes, laid waste the fertile fields of Etrúria, and besieged the important city of Clúsium. The Etrurians sought aid from the Romans, who sent some of the young nobility to remonstrate with the Bren'nus, or chieftain of the Gauls. This barbarous chieftain treated the deputies with such scorn, that, forgetting their sacred character, they entered the besieged city, and joined in a sally of the garrison. The Bren'nus, enraged at such a violation of the law of nations, demanded satisfaction from the senate; and when this was refused, broke up his camp, and marched direct against Rome. A body of troops, hastily levied to repel the invasion, took post on the river Al'lia, about eleven miles from Rome (B.C. 389). In the very commencement of the engagement, the Romans, seized with sudden panic, broke and fled; they were pursued with dreadful slaughter to their very gates; and had not the victors paused to gather the spoil an end would have been put to the Roman name and nation.

To defend the city of Rome was impossible; it was therefore resolved to place the best troops as a garrison in the citadel, supplying them with whatever provisions remained in the city, whilst the mass of the population should seek refuge in the neighbouring towns. The priests and principal objects of religious reverence were removed to the old Pelasgic city Cære Agylla. About eighty of the chief pontiffs and patricians, probably devoting themselves, according to the superstition of the age, for the safety of the republic, remained quietly sitting on their curule chairs in the forum. When the Gauls entered the city, they were amazed to find it deserted: pursuing their march, they entered the forum, and slew those whom they found there. They then laid siege to the capitol; but soon became weary of so tedious a task, especially after their attempt to take the citadel by storm had been frustrated by the cackling of the sacred geese kept in the temple of Juno, and the valour of Marcus Manlius. They finally agreed to quit the city, on receiving a ransom of one thousand pounds' weight of gold. According to the ordinary legend, Camillus, recalled from banishment by a hasty decree of the people assembled at Veii, appeared with an army while the gold was being weighed, defeated the Gauls, and liberated his country. Polybius, a Greek historian, gives a much more probable account. He says, that the Gauls returned home to protect their own country from an invasion of the Veneti, and intimates that they bore off their plunder without interruption.

SECTION IV.—*From the Rebuilding of the City to the first Punic War.*

FROM B.C. 363 TO B.C. 264.

So helpless was Rome after the departure of the Gauls, that it was exposed to repeated insults from the neighbouring townships, which had hitherto been subject to its sway. The citizens looked forward with dismay to the task of rebuilding their walls and houses: they clamoured for an immediate removal to Veii, and were with difficulty prevented from accom-

moval to Veii, and were with difficulty prevented from accomplishing their purpose by the firmness of Camil'lus. While the subject was under discussion, a lucky omen, probably preconcerted, decided the irresolute. Just as a senator was rising to speak, a centurion, coming with his company to relieve guard, gave the usual word of command, 'Ensign, plant your colours; THIS IS THE BEST PLACE TO STAY IN!'[1] The senators rushed out of the temple, exclaiming, 'A happy omen; the gods have spoken: we obey.' The multitude caught the enthusiasm, and exclaimed with one voice, 'ROME FOR EVER!'

Under the prudent guidance of Camil'lus, the military strength of Rome was renewed, and the states which had triumphed in the recent humiliation of the city were forced again to recognise its superiority. Man'lius, the brave defender of the capitol, finding himself excluded from office by the jealousy of his brother patricians, declared himself the patron of the plebeians. This revived the old dissensions with all their former virulence. Camil'lus was appointed dictator; and by his orders Man'lius was brought to trial, convicted of treason, and thrown from the Tarpeian rock (B.C. 382). A plague, which burst forth soon after, was popularly attributed to the anger of the gods at the destruction of the hero who had saved their temples from pollution. By their triumph over Man'lius, and their steadiness in opposing popular claims, the patricians acquired such strength that the populace became overawed, and the commons ceased to display the spirit and courage they had previously shown in their contests with the nobles. 'Rome was on the point of degenerating into a miserable oligarchy; her name is the utmost we should have known of her, had not her irretrievable decline been arrested at the moment by the appearance of two men, who changed the fate of their country and of the world.'[1]

The renovators of the constitution were Caíus Licin'ius Stólo, and Lúcius Sex'tius Lateránus. They were aided in their patriotic labours by Mar'cus Fábius Ambus'tus, a patrician, the father-in-law of Licin'ius, who is said to have espoused the

* Hīc manebimus optimè. † Niebuhr.

popular cause to gratify the ambition of a favourite daughter. There were three rogations, or bills, brought forward by Licinius: the first opened the consulship to the plebeians; the second prohibited any person from renting more than five hundred acres of public land, and forbade any individual to feed on a common pasturage more than one hundred head of large, and five hundred of small cattle. It also fixed the rent of the public lands at the tenth of the corn produce (*fruges*), and a fifth of the produce of vines, aloes, and other fruit-trees. The third proposed, that, in all cases of outstanding debts, all the interest which had been paid should be deducted from the capital, and the balance paid by equal annual instalments in three years. The patricians protracted their resistance to these laws during five years, using every means of force and fraud in their power to frustrate the designs of Licinius. At length the people took arms, and occupied Mount Aventine. Camillus, being chosen dictator, saw that nothing but concession could avert the horrors of a civil war; and the senate allowed the three bills to become law (B.C. 366), stipulating only that the consuls should no longer act as civil judges, and that new magistrates should be chosen, with the title of prætors, to exercise judicial functions. The plebeians having once made good their claim to the consulship, acquired successively, as a matter of course, participation in the other high offices of state: the dictatorship was opened to them B.C. 353; the censorship, B.C. 348; the prætorship, B.C. 334; and even the priestly office, B.C. 300.

During these civic struggles the Romans maintained their reputation abroad by several victories over their enemies, especially the Gauls and the Etrurians. But they were soon engaged in a more important struggle with the Samnites; and this contest, which lasted, with little intermission, more than half a century, opened a way for the subjugation of Italy, and laid the foundation of Rome's future greatness. The Samnites having invaded Campania, the people of Capua, to ward off impending danger, declared themselves subjects of Rome (B.C. 343). Ambassadors being sent to warn the Samnites against invading the new province, the Samnites treated their remonstrances with contempt, and war was immediately declared. It was carried on slowly at first, but generally to the advantage of the Romans, until the Samnites sought terms of truce. During this interval the Latins attacked the Samnites, who requested assistance from their recent enemies, and orders were issued by the senate that the Latins should desist from hostilities. These commands being disobeyed, war was declared against the Latins, and the conduct of it entrusted to the consuls Manlius and Decius. To prevent the confusion that might arise between armies speaking the same language, Manlius commanded that no Roman soldier should quit his ranks under pain of death (B.C. 330). The consul's own son, challenged to single combat by a commander of the enemy, disobeyed these orders, and was instantly sent to execution by the stern father. In the engagement that ensued, the Romans were on the point of being routed, until Decius, the plebeian consul, devoting himself, according to the superstitions of the age, for the good of his country, rushed into the thickest of the fight, and fell covered with wounds. The soldiers, now sure that the gods had been conciliated, renewed the fight with enthusiastic confidence, and the Latins were completely defeated. The Romans followed up their success with so much spirit during the three ensuing campaigns, that all Latium and Campania were subdued, and annexed as provinces to the territory of the republic.

These great advantages gained by their rivals alarmed the Samnites; and many of the states in southern Italy, especially the Lucanians and Tarentines, became jealous of the rising greatness of Rome. Papirius Cursor was appointed dictator to crush this dangerous confederacy: he gained several victories over the Samnites; and these successes being improved by the generals that followed him, reduced the enemies so low, that they were once more forced to solicit a cessation of arms (B.C. 321). But these peaceful appearances lasted only a few months: Pontius, an able Samnite general, stimulated his countrymen to renew the war, and bade defiance to the Roman power. The consuls, Veturius and Posthumius, were sent with a large army to invade Samnium (B.C. 320); but the crafty Pontius contrived to draw these generals, with their leaders, into a rocky defile, called the Caudine Forks, where they could neither fight nor fly; and while they were in this situation, his Samnites blockaded all the passages. The Romans being forced to capitulate, Pontius sent to ask his father in what manner the persons should be treated: the old man recommended that they should either be dismissed with all honour and freedom, or slaughtered without mercy. Pontius unwisely adopted a middle course; he spared the lives of the Romans, but compelled them all, officers and soldiers, to pass under the yoke, and forced the consuls to give hostages for evacuating Samnium.

This disgraceful treaty was disavowed by the senate, and the officers who had signed it were sent bound to Pontius, that he might wreak his vengeance upon them; but the Samnite general spurned such poor satisfaction, and vainly demanded either that the whole Roman army should be again placed in his power, or that the articles of capitulation should be strictly observed. The Romans turned a deaf ear to these proposals; Papirius Cursor once more shewed them the way to victory; his successors in command followed his example; and the Samnites, completely humbled, sought and obtained conditions of peace (B.C. 303). But amity could not long subsist between nations aspiring each to the supremacy of Italy: the war was renewed (B.C. 297); and Fabius Maximus, with his colleague the younger Decius, rivalled the exploits of Papirius Cursor. The Samnites were aided by the Umbrians, the Etrurians, and the Gauls; but the desperate valour of the Romans enabled them to triumph over this formidable confederacy. Once they were on the point of being defeated by the Gauls (B.C. 294); but the younger Decius, imitating the example of his father, devoted himself an offering to the gods, and, at the sacrifice of his life, purchased a decisive victory for his countrymen. At length the Samnites, having lost their brave general Pontius, were completely subdued by Curius Dentatus (B.C. 290), and forced to submit to the terms dictated by the conquerors. In the same year the Sabines were conquered; and Curius had the unusual honour of having two triumphs decreed to him in one consulate.

The Tarentines, and the other states in southern Italy, dreading that the Romans would take vengeance on them for their having aided the Samnites, incited the Gauls to attack the republic. These barbarians were at first successful; but they were finally crushed by Dentatus and Fabricius. Preparations were made for a war against Tarentum, and its luxurious citizens placed themselves under the protection of Pyrrhus, king of Epirus. That royal knight-errant, believing that it was in his power to found as extensive an empire in the western world as Alexander the Great had recently established in Asia, readily obeyed the summons; and having sent his friend Cineas with a strong detachment to secure the citadel of Tarentum, soon followed with a powerful army, having some elephants among his forces, the first that had been used in the wars of western Europe (B. C. 279). It was solely to these animals that Pyrrhus was indebted for his first victory over the consul Lævinus; and so little were the vanquished terrified by defeat, that they vainly offered him a renewal of battle before the termination of the campaign. He was still more unsuccessful in his attempts at negotiation; his bribes were rejected by the Roman consul and ambassador Fabricius; and the offers of peace which he sent to the senate by the orator Cineas were peremptorily rejected.

A second time Pyrrhus defeated the Romans; but was so little satisfied with his success as to exclaim, "Another such victory, and I am undone!" The war then lingered, and Pyrrhus passed over into Sicily, with his usual inconstancy, to deliver the Greek states in that island from the Carthaginians. During his absence his allies suffered very severely, and sent pressing messages soliciting his return; an excuse of which Pyrrhus readily availed himself to cover the shame of his failure in Sicily (B.C. 274). Curius Dentatus and Cornelius Lentulus were chosen consuls to oppose him, and two considerable armies were placed at their disposal. Pyrrhus marched against the former, hoping to surprise him in his camp near

Beneventum; but his lights failing him, he was obliged to halt, until the dawn revealed his approach to the Romans. Instead of being the assailant, the Epirote monarch was himself attacked by Dentatus; his elephants were driven back on his own lines by fire-balls and torches; and, after vainly endeavouring to stop the slaughter of his bravest troops, he was forced to fly with a small escort to Tarentum. Thence he returned to Greece, leaving a garrison under the command of Milo in the citadel, which, however, finally surrendered to the Romans. The Samnites, Bruttians, and Lucanians, who had joined Pyrrhus, were easily subdued after his departure; and Rome established her supremacy over all the countries in Italy, from the northern frontiers of Etruria to the Sicilian straits, and from the Tuscan Sea to the Adriatic.

SECTION V.—*From the Commencement of the Punic Wars to the Beginning of the Civil Dissensions under the Gracchi.*

FROM B.C. 264 TO B.C. 134.

THE Mamertine mercenaries, who had seized Messena and slaughtered the citizens, justly dreading the vengeance of the Syracusans, divided into two parties; one seeking the protection of the Carthaginians, the other that of the Romans. Thus the first pretence of quarrel between the two mightiest republics of ancient times was, which should have the honour, or rather dishonour, of shielding from merited punishment a piratical banditti, stained by every species of crime. The Romans were long delayed by their reluctance to acknowledge such discreditable allies; but finding that the Carthaginians had gained possession of the Messenian citadel, they made speedy preparations to prevent their rivals from becoming masters of Sicily. An army, entrusted to the command of the consul Appius Claudius, was conveyed across the straits (the vigilance of the Carthaginian fleet being eluded by stratagem), and gained possession of Messena. Successive victories over the Syracusans and Carthaginians soon procured the Romans allies among the Sicilian states, and inspired them with the hope of becoming masters of the island. Hiero, king of Syracuse, deserted his former allies, and, by his early alliance with Rome, secured the tranquillity of his kingdom in the coming contest. The Carthaginians, on the other hand, who had looked upon Sicily as an almost certain conquest, were filled with rage when they learned the danger that threatened their possessions in that island. They hired a vast number of mercenaries in Gaul, Liguria, and Spain; they made Agrigentum their chief naval and military depôt, storing it plentifully with the munitions of war. Notwithstanding the great natural and artificial strength of Agrigentum, the Romans, eager to seize the Carthaginian magazines, laid siege to the city, and defeated an immense army that had been sent to its relief (B. C. 262). Dispirited by this misfortune, the garrison abandoned the city, which, with all its stores, fell into the hands of the Romans. But this success only roused the senate and people of Rome to fresh exertions; they saw that their conquests could not be secure while the Carthaginians held the supremacy of the sea, and they therefore directed all their energies to the preparation of a fleet.

Though not wholly unacquainted with ships, the Romans had hitherto paid little or no attention to naval affairs; and their model for building ships of war was a Carthaginian vessel that had been driven ashore in a storm. After some indecisive skirmishes, the consul Duilius, relying on his invention of the "corvus," a machine which served both as a grappling-iron and drawbridge, hazarded an engagement with the Carthaginian fleet (B. C. 260). No sooner had the hostile ships closed, than the Romans lowered the new machines on the enemies' decks, and, fighting hand to hand, carried no fewer than fifty galleys by boarding. The Carthaginian admiral finding naval tactics of no avail, drew off the rest of his fleet. To commemorate this their first victory by sea, the Romans erected a rostral* column in the forum, which still continues in excellent preservation, the chief injury it has sustained being the loss of part of the inscription. In a second naval engagement,

* That is, ornamented with representations of the rostra, or beaks of ships.

near the island of Lipara (B. C. 256), the Carthaginians lost eighteen vessels, of which eight were sunk, and ten taken.

The struggle between the rival republics had lasted about eight years, when the Romans, following the example of the Syracusan Agathocles, resolved to invade Africa, knowing that the native tribes of that continent were weary of the tyranny and rapacity of Carthage. An armament of three hundred and thirty ships was prepared for this great enterprise, and entrusted to the command of the consuls Regulus and Manlius (B. C. 255). A third sea-fight was a necessary preliminary to this invasion; the Carthaginians were once more defeated, sixty-four of their galleys were taken, and thirty destroyed. The victorious fleet pursued its voyage; Regulus effected a landing without loss, and took the city of Clypea by storm. Soon after, he defeated the Carthaginian army in a general engagement, and seized the city of Tunis. In great terror the Carthaginians sought for peace; but the terms demanded by Regulus were so harsh, that they resolved, at all hazards, to continue the war, and were confirmed in their determination by the arrival of a body of mercenary troops from Greece, under the command of Xanthippus, a Spartan general of high reputation. To this foreigner the Carthaginians entrusted the command of their army: he eagerly sought an opportunity of bringing the enemy to an engagement; the Romans did not decline his challenge; but they found that one man was sufficient to change the fortune of the war. Xanthippus won a complete victory; the greater part of the Romans were taken prisoners or cut to pieces, two thousand alone escaping to the city of Clypea; Regulus himself was among the captives. The Spartan general after this brilliant exploit returned home. A Roman fleet was sent to bring off the garrison of Clypea, and gained on the voyage a great victory over the Carthaginians; but on the return of the ships, three hundred and twenty of them, with all on board, were destroyed by a tempest. A second naval armament suffered a similar fate; and the Romans, disheartened by these repeated misfortunes, abandoned for a time the sea to their enemies. But they were in some degree consoled by a second triumph obtained near Panormus, in Sicily, over Asdrubal (B. C. 249), which gave them a decided superiority in the island.

The Carthaginians, daunted by this misfortune, took Regulus from his dungeon to go as their ambassador to Rome, trusting that, weary of a long captivity, he would urge the senate to grant favourable terms of peace. Regulus, however, persuaded his countrymen to continue the war, assuring them that the resources of Carthage were exhausted. It is generally stated, that the patriotic general, after his return to Africa, was tortured to death by the disappointed Carthaginians. On the other hand, there is reason to believe that he died a natural death; and that the tale of his savage murder was invented to excuse the cruelty with which his family treated their Carthaginian captives.

The renewed war began unfavourably for the Romans, their entire fleet having been wrecked on the south coast of Sicily (B. C. 248), and Hamilcar Barca, the new commander of the Carthaginians, proving a worthy successor of Xanthippus. But they were not dispirited by these losses; a new fleet, of better construction than any they had yet possessed, was built, and placed under the command of the consul Lutatius Catulus; at the same time strong reinforcements were sent to the army in Sicily. The hostile navies met near the Ægates: the consul had lightened his vessels by landing all unnecessary burdens on one of these islands; but Hanno, the Carthaginian admiral, in his hurry to engage, left his vessels encumbered with baggage. The battle was brief but decisive; fifty of Hanno's vessels were sunk, and seventy taken; and the Carthaginians were for ever deprived of the empire of the sea (B. C. 241).

But the consequences of this defeat threatened still more fatal results to Carthage: Hamilcar Barca, with the last army on which the republic could depend, was closely blockaded in a corner of Sicily, and the Roman cruisers cut him off from all communication with Africa: were he forced to surrender, Carthage would be left at the mercy of the barbarous tribes in its neighbourhood. Under these circumstances the Carthaginians sought peace; but could obtain no better terms than those which Regulus demanded when in sight of their gates

(B. C. 240). These conditions were, that the Carthaginians should evacuate all the islands of the Mediterranean; restore the Roman prisoners without ransom; and pay three thousand talents of silver (about 600,000*l.*) to defray the expenses of the war.

After the termination of the first Punic war, Rome enjoyed a brief period of domestic and external tranquillity; and the temple of Janus was shut for the second time since the foundation of the city. Tedious wars were waged against the Ligurians and the Gallic tribes that had settled in northern Italy, when the people became weary of peace: but a more important contest was provoked by the piracies of the Illyrians, whose queen, Teuta, procured the murder of the ambassadors sent to remonstrate against the outrages of her subjects. A navy was soon established in the Adriatic, and an army sent into Illyricum, whose rapid successes compelled Teuta to purchase peace by resigning the greater part of her territories (B.C. 227). This speedy conquest diffused the fame of the Romans throughout eastern Europe; for most of the Greek states had suffered severely from the piracies of the Illyrians. The war was subsequently renewed (B.C. 218), and the Illyrians again overthrown with greater disgrace and loss.

The Carthaginians were anxious to compensate their losses in Sicily by the subjugation of Spain; and their extensive conquests in that peninsula gave great umbrage to their suspicious rivals. A pretext for interference was soon found. Hannibal, the son of Hamilcar Barca, who had been brought, while yet a child, to the altar by his father, and sworn never to relax in his enmity to Rome, laid siege to Saguntum, a Greek colony on the Iberus, and treated with contempt the remonstrances of the Roman ambassadors (B. C. 218). His conduct having been approved by the Carthaginian senate, both parties made instant preparations for renewing hostilities, and soon commenced the second Punic war.

Before the Roman armies were ready to take the field, Hannibal had completed the conquest of Spain, and crossed the Pyrenees on his road to Italy. The consul, Scipio, hastened to prevent him from passing the Rhone; but being frustrated by the superior diligence of the Carthaginian general, he sent the greater part of his forces into Spain, and sailed with the remainder for Italy, in order to intercept his enemies as they descended from the Alps. Even these formidable mountains caused but little delay to the enterprising Hannibal. He led his army across them in fifteen days (B. C. 217); and advancing through the country of the Taurini, took their capital city (*Turin*) by storm. Scipio hasted to meet the invaders on the banks of the river Ticinus; but he was defeated with great loss, and further weakened by the desertion of his Gallic mercenaries, who eagerly flocked to the standard of Hannibal, regarding him as another Brennus.

In the meantime Scipio had been re-inforced by Sempronius, the other consul; but he found that these succours were more than counterbalanced by the impetuosity of his colleague. Sempronius, eager to engage, imprudently forded the river Trebia, though its waters were swollen by rain and melted snow. The Romans, suddenly attacked as they came out of the river, were not able to cope with their enemies, who were fresh and vigorous; nevertheless they made a brave resistance, and the central division, unbroken, made its way from the field to the city of Placentia. The victory, however, was of the greatest service to Hannibal, as it secured him the alliance of the Gauls in northern Italy.

Flaminius, the consul of the next year, displayed even more impetuosity and imprudence than Sempronius. Marching incautiously in search of Hannibal, he fell into an ambuscade, near the Thrasymenian lake, and was slain, with the greater part of his army (B. C. 216). The Romans were so alarmed by the intelligence of this great calamity, that they created Fabius Maximus dictator, though, in the absence of the surviving consul, they were obliged to dispense with the legal formalities. Fabius adopted a new system of tactics; he declined fighting; but moving his camp along the summits of the hills, he closely watched the motions of the invaders, harassed their march, and intercepted their convoys. From his stedfast adherence to this policy, Fabius received the surname of Cunctator (*the delayer*). During this period, the Roman armies in Spain, under the command of the Scipios, gained many important advantages, and thus prevented the Carthaginians from sending succours to Hannibal.

At the close of the year, Fabius resigned his authority to the consuls Paullus Æmilius and Terentius Varro (B.C. 215). The latter hurried his more prudent colleague into a general action at the village of Cannæ, near the river Aufidus, where the Romans suffered a more severe defeat than any they had received since their fatal overthrow by the Gauls on the Allia. This victory gave Hannibal possession of southern Italy: it is even supposed, that he would have got possession of Rome itself, had he marched thither immediately after the battle.

But the Romans, notwithstanding their great losses, did not despair: Scipio, a young man destined at no distant period to raise his country to the summit of greatness, encouraged the nobles of his own age to stand firm at this crisis; and Fabius Cunctator being appointed to the command of the army, resumed the cautious system, whose advantages had been already so fully proved. Hannibal, in the meantime, led his forces to Capua, where his veterans were enervated by the luxury and debauchery of that licentious city. At the same time he concluded an alliance with Philip, king of Macedon; but the Romans, by their intrigues in Greece, found sufficient employment for that monarch at home, to prevent his interference in the affairs of Italy. They even sent an army against him, under the command of the prætor Lævinus; and thus, though exposed to such danger in Italy, they maintained a vigorous contest in Greece, Spain, and Sicily.

It was in Sicily that success first began to dawn upon the Roman cause (B.C. 211): the ancient city of Syracuse was taken by the prætor Metellus; and the celebrated mathematician, Archimedes, by whose engines the defence had been protracted, was slain in the storm. Two years afterwards, Agrigentum, the last stronghold of the Carthaginians, was betrayed to Lævinus; and the Romans remained masters of the entire island, which henceforth became a regular province.

In the meantime the war lingered in Italy; the Roman generals were rarely able to cope with Hannibal, though Marcellus is said to have gained a general battle over the Carthaginians.

On the other hand, Hannibal, receiving no reinforcements from Carthage, feared to peril his limited resources in any decisive enterprise. At length he summoned his brother Asdrubal, who had long maintained the Carthaginian cause against the Scipios in Spain, to join him in Italy; and Asdrubal, without encountering any great difficulty, soon crossed the Pyrenees and Alps. The consuls, Livius and Nero, having discovered the direction of the Carthaginian's march, hastened to intercept him. Asdrubal, misled by his guides, was forced to hazard an engagement at a disadvantage on the banks of the Metaurus, and was cut to pieces with his whole army (B. C. 206). The first information Hannibal received of this great misfortune, was the sight of his brother's gory head, which the consuls caused to be thrown into his camp. Soon after, the Romans alarmed the Carthaginians by the prospect of a war in Africa, having entered into a treaty of alliance with Massinissa, the legitimate king of Numidia, and also with the usurper Syphax.

At length Scipio, the conqueror of Spain, was chosen consul, and, contrary to the strenuous exertions of Fabius, he prevailed upon the senate to permit him to transfer the war into Africa; and this was the more readily conceded, as the conclusion of peace with Philip (B. C. 203) had placed a fresh army at their disposal. Scipio, on landing in Africa (B. C. 202), found that Syphax had been won over to the Carthaginian side by his wife Sophonisba, the daughter of Asdrubal. The Roman general knowing, however, the inconstancy of the Numidian, commenced negotiations, which were protracted with equal duplicity. While Syphax was thus amused, Scipio suddenly surprised and burned his camp; then attacking the Numidians in the midst of the confusion, he put forty thousand of them to the sword. After this achievement Scipio laid siege to Utica: the Carthaginians raised a large army to relieve a place of so much importance; but they were routed with great slaughter, and pursued to their very walls. This victory exposed Carthage itself to the perils of a siege; Tunis, almost within sight of the city, opened its gates to the Romans; and the Carthaginian senate, driven almost to despair, recalled Hannibal from Italy to the defence of his own country.

Hannibal, on his return home, would have made peace on reasonable terms, had not the Carthaginian populace, elated by the presence of the hero of a hundred fights, obstinately resisted any concession. With a heavy heart the brave old general made preparations for a decisive engagement in the field of Zama. Hannibal's abilities were not less conspicuous in this fatal fight than in the battles he had won in Italy; but the greater part of his forces were raw troops, unfit to cope with Scipio's disciplined legions. After a dreadful struggle, the Romans prevailed, and they followed up their advantages with so much eagerness, that twenty thousand of the Carthaginians fell in the battle or the pursuit. Hannibal, after having performed every thing that a skilful general or brave soldier could do to restore the fortune of the day, fled with a small body of horse to Adrumetum, whence he was soon summoned to Carthage to assist the tottering republic with his counsels (B. C. 201). There he informed the senate that "Carthage had no resource but in peace;" and these words, from the mouth of the warlike Hannibal, were decisive. Ambassadors were sent to seek conditions from the conqueror; and the humbled Carthaginians accepted the terms of peace dictated by Scipio, who from henceforth was honoured with the title of Africanus. The chief articles of the treaty were, that Carthage should deliver up to the Romans all their deserters, fugitive slaves, and prisoners of war; surrender all her ships of the line, except ten triremes, and all her elephants; restore Numidia to Massinissa; enter into no war without the permission of the Roman people; pay as a ransom ten thousand talents of silver (about two millions sterling); and give one hundred hostages for the performance of the treaty. To these harsh terms the Carthaginians subscribed: Scipio returned home, and was honoured with the most magnificent triumph that had yet been exhibited in Rome.

Rome was now become a great military republic, supreme in western Europe, and commanding a preponderating influence in the east, where the kingdoms formed from the fragments of Alexander's empire had sunk into weakness from the exhaustion of mutual wars. The Athenians, exposed to the attacks of Philip, king of Macedon, sought the protection of the Romans, which was readily granted, as the senate had long been anxious to find a pretext for meddling in the affairs of Greece (B. C. 206). War was declared against Philip, notwithstanding the opposition of the tribunes of the people; and it was resolved to follow up Scipio's policy, by making the enemy's country the theatre of hostilities. An army was sent into Macedonia, and its conduct was soon entrusted to Quintius Flamininus, whose diplomatic skill was even more conspicuous than his military talents. After some minor engagements, in none of which did Philip evince much ability as a general or statesman, a decisive battle was fought at Cynoscephalæ (B. C. 206), in which the Macedonians were irretrievably overthrown, and forced to submit to such terms of peace as the conquerors pleased to dictate. This success was followed by the solemn mockery of proclaiming liberty to Greece at the Isthmian games, which filled the foolish spectators with so much delight, that they virtually became slaves to the Romans through gratitude for freedom.

Antiochus, king of Syria, hoping to establish the empire of the Selucidæ in the east, soon caused a renewal of the wars in Greece. Hannibal was accused to the Romans by his treacherous countrymen of having secretly intrigued with this monarch; and having reason to fear that he would be surrendered to his enemies, he fled to Antiochus in Asia. The great general, however, found that the vain-glorious Syrian was unable to comprehend his prudent plans for conducting the war, and had the mortification to find himself suspected of being secretly in league with the Romans. In the meantime the Ætolians, displeased by the policy which the Romans were pursuing, invited Antiochus into Europe; and that monarch, passing over into Greece, made himself master of the island of Eubœa (B. C. 191). War was instantly declared; the consul, Acilius Glabrio, appeared in Greece with a powerful army; he gained a signal victory over the Syrians at the straits of Thermopylæ, and reduced the Ætolians to such great extremities, that they were forced to beg a peace; but the senate demanded such harsh conditions, that they resolved to endure the hazards of war a little longer (B.C. 190).

In the following year the senate entrusted the conduct of the war to Lucius Scipio, under whom his brother Africanus served as a lieutenant. Having soon tranquillised Greece, the two brothers passed into Asia: after many minor successes, they forced Antiochus to a general battle near the city of Magnesia, in which that monarch was completely overthrown (B.C. 189). He was forced to purchase peace by resigning all his possessions in Europe, and those in Asia north of Mount Taurus; paying a fine of fifteen thousand Eubœan talents (about three millions sterling); and promising to give up Hannibal. That illustrious exile fled for refuge to Prusias, king of Bithynia; but finding that he was still pursued by the vindictive hatred of the Romans, he put an end to his life by taking poison, which, in anticipation of such an extremity, he always carried with him concealed in a ring.

On their return home the Scipios were accused of having taken bribes from Antiochus and embezzling the public money (B.C. 186). Africanus refused to plead, preferring to go into voluntary exile at Liternum, where he died. Lucius was condemned; and on his refusal to pay the fine imposed, all his property was confiscated. About the same time Rome exhibited the first example of religious persecution: a sect called the Bacchanalians, having been accused of the most monstrous crimes, several laws were enacted for its extirpation; but it is scarcely possible to discover how far the charges against this unfortunate society were supported by evidence.

The mastery assumed by the Romans in Greece gave great and just offence to the principal states; but their yoke was felt by none so grievously as Perses, king of Macedon, who opened for himself a way to the throne by procuring the judicial murder of his brother Demetrius. Mutual complaints and recriminations soon led to open war (B.C. 170). Perses having collected his forces, entered Thessaly, captured several important towns, defeated a Roman army on the river Peneus, and was joined by the greater part of the Epirote nation. His successes continued until the Romans entrusted the conduct of the war to Æmilius Paullus, son of the general that had fallen in the battle of Cannæ, though he was past the age at which they usually sent out commanders. While the new general advanced against Macedon, the prætor Anicius invaded Illyricum, whose monarch had entered into alliance with Perses, and subdued the entire kingdom in the short space of thirty days. Perses being hard pressed, resolved to hazard a battle near the walls of Pydna (B. C. 167). After both armies had remained for some days in sight of each other, an accident brought on an engagement contrary to the wishes of the leaders; it ended in the complete victory of the Romans. Perses fled to Samothrace, but was soon forced to surrender, and was reserved to grace the triumph of the conqueror. Macedon, Epirus, and Illyricum, were reduced to the condition of provinces, and it became evident that the independence of the remaining Grecian states would not long be respected.

The destruction of the Macedonian monarchy was soon followed by that of the miserable remains of the once proud republic of Carthage. To this war the Romans were stimulated by the rigid Cato, surnamed the Censor, who was animated by his envy of Scipio Nasica, on account of his great influence in the senate, and by a haughty spirit of revenge for some slights which he imagined he had received from the Carthaginians when sent as ambassador to their state. The pretext for the war was some quarrels between the Carthaginians and the Numidians, in which, however, the former only acted upon the defensive. At first, the Carthaginians attempted to disarm their enemies by submission; they banished all who had incurred the displeasure of the Romans, and surrendered their arms and military stores to the consuls; but when informed that they must abandon their city and consent to its demolition, they took courage from despair, and set their insulting foes at defiance (B. C. 168). They made the most vigorous exertions to supply the place of the weapons they had surrendered; men of every rank and station toiled night and day in the forges; the women cut off their long hair, hitherto the great sources of their pride, to furnish strings for the bows of the archers, and engines of the slingers; and the banished Asdrubal was recalled to the defence of his country.

From this unexpected display of courage and patriotism the Romans found Carthage not quite so easy a conquest as they had anticipated: during the first two years of the war they suffered repeated disappointments; but at length they entrusted the command of their armies to Scipio Æmilianus, the adopted son of the great Africanus (B.C. 147). On his arrival in Africa, Scipio's first care was to restore the discipline of the soldiers, who had been allowed by their former commanders to indulge in dangerous licentiousness. His strictness and moderation won him the friendship of the African nations, and enabled him in his second campaign (B.C. 146) to press vigorously the siege of Carthage. After a severe struggle, the Romans forced an entrance into the city on the side of Cothon, or the port, and made themselves masters of the great wall. Thence Scipio, with a large body of soldiers, cut his way to the principal square of the city, where he bivouacked all the following night. On the next morning the fight was renewed, and the whole city, except the citadel and the temple of Æsculapius, taken: six days were spent in preparation for the siege of these strongholds; but, on the seventh, the garrison in the citadel surrendered at discretion; and the deserters in the temple of Æsculapius, setting fire to that building, perished in the flames.

Scanty as are our limits, two incidents connected with the destruction of this ancient commercial metropolis, so long the rival of Rome for supremacy in the western world, must not be omitted. When Scipio beheld Carthage in flames, his soul was softened by reflections on the instability of fortune, and he could not avoid anticipating a time when Rome herself should experience the same calamities as those which had befallen her unfortunate competitor. He vented his feelings, by quoting from Homer the well-known lines in which Hector predicts the fall of Troy: —

"Yet come it will, the day decreed by fates;
(How my heart trembles, while my tongue relates!)
The day when thou, imperial Troy, must bend,
And see thy warriors fall, thy glories end."

The second incident is still more tragic: Asdrubal, the first mover of the war, had fled with the deserters, accompanied by his wife and children, to the temple of Æsculapius, but went over to the Romans a little before the destruction of that edifice. While the fire was kindling, the wife of Asdrubal, having decked herself in the best manner she could, appeared with her two children on the top of the temple, whence, calling out to Scipio, she begged him to punish her husband according to his deserts, that traitor to his God, his country, and his family. Then directing her speech to Asdrubal — "Thou wicked, perfidious wretch," she exclaimed, "thou most cowardly of men! This fire will quickly consume me and my children: but thou, once ruler of mighty Carthage, what a triumph shalt thou adorn! And what punishment wilt thou not suffer from him at whose feet thou art sitting." This said, she cut the throats of her children, threw their bodies into the burning building, and sprung after them into the very centre of the flames.

During the third Punic war, the disturbances excited in Macedonia by an impostor, Andriscus, who pretended to be the son of Philip, kindled a new war, which proved fatal to the independence of Greece. The Achæans, stimulated by some factious leaders, took up arms, but were subdued the very same year that Carthage was destroyed. Mummius, the consul who conducted this war, sacked and burned Corinth; and after having plundered the city of its statues, paintings, and most valuable effects, levelled its walls and houses to the ground. Thebes and Chalcis soon after shared the same sad fate. If we may believe Velleius Paterculus, Mummius was so little acquainted with the value of the beautiful works of art which fell into his possession, that he covenanted with the masters of the ships, whom he hired to convey from Corinth to Italy a great number of exquisite pieces of painting and statuary, that "if they lost any of them, they should furnish others in their stead."

Spain next began to attract the attention of the Romans. No nation that the republic had subdued defended its liberties with greater obstinacy. The war for the subjugation of the Spaniards commenced six years after the expulsion of the Carthaginians from the western peninsula, and was exceedingly obstinate (B. C. 200). This struggle was protracted partly from the natural state of the country, which was thickly populated and studded with natural fortresses, partly from the courage of the inhabitants, and partly from the peculiar policy of the Romans, who were accustomed to employ their allies to subdue other nations. The chief enemies against whom the invaders had to contend were the Celtiberians and Lusitanians; and so often were the Romans defeated, that nothing was more dreaded by the soldiers at home than an expedition against such formidable foes. At length the Lusitanians found a leader worthy of their bravery (B. C. 146) in Viriatus, who, from a shepherd, became a hunter and a robber; and in consequence of his distinguished valour was chosen general-in-chief by his countrymen. This bold leader long maintained his ground against the Roman armies, and was equally formidable whether victorious or vanquished. Indeed, he was never more to be dreaded than immediately after defeat, because he knew how to make the most of the advantages arising from his knowledge of the country, and of the dispositions of his countrymen. Unable to compete with Viriatus, the consul Cæpio treacherously procured his assassination (B. C. 140); and the Lusitanians, deprived of their leader, were easily subdued.

The Numantine war in hither Spain had been allowed to languish while the Lusitanians remained in power; it was now renewed with fresh vigour on both sides, and the pro-consul Pompey laid siege to Numantia. He was soon compelled to raise the siege, and even to enter into a treaty with the Numantines; but dreading the resentment of the senate, he disavowed the negotiation, and, by his great interest, escaped the punishment of his perfidy. A similar disgrace befel Pompey's successor Mancinus; and the Romans, alarmed by the great victories of the Numantines, raised Scipio Æmilianus a second time to the consulship, and assigned him Spain as his province.

Scipio spent his entire consular year in restoring the discipline of soldiers dispirited by defeat, and neglected by their former generals; he then, with the inferior title of pro-consul, directed all his attention to concluding the war. Having obtained reinforcements from Africa, he laid close siege to Numantia, blockading every avenue to the town. After a protracted defence of more than six months, the Numantines destroyed their wives and children, set fire to their city, threw themselves on their swords or into the flames, and left the victors nothing to triumph over but empty walls (B. C. 133). Spain from henceforth became a Roman province, governed by two annual prætors.

A rich province in Asia was obtained nearly at the same time on much more easy terms. Attalus king of Pergamus dying, bequeathed his dominions to the Roman republic; and the senate took possession of the valuable inheritance, without heeding the remonstrances of the legitimate heir. But this acquisition of the wealthiest and finest districts in Asia Minor eventually cost the Romans very dear, both by the corruption of morals consequent on the great influx of Asiatic wealth, and the dreadful wars in which this legacy involved them with Mithridates, king of Pontus.

SECTION VI.—*From the Beginning of the Civil Dissensions under the Gracchi, to the Downfal of the Republic and Death of Pompey.*

FROM B. C. 134 TO B. C. 48.

DURING the Punic, Macedonian, and Spanish wars, the power of the senate, on which the administration of the government necessarily devolved, increased very rapidly, and the form of the constitution consequently was changed more and more into that of a hateful aristocracy, against which the tribunes of the people struggled rather as factious demagogues than as honest defenders of popular rights. The aristocracy acquired vast wealth in the government of the provinces, and they employed their acquisitions in extending their political influence. The most obvious means of effecting this purpose was jobbing in the public lands, undertaking the management of extensive tracts, and sub-letting them to a crowd of needy dependents.

Tiberius Gracchus, the son of a consul, whose mother Cornelia was a daughter of the celebrated Scipio Africanus, witnessed with indignation the progress of corruption, and, to check it, resolved to enforce the Licinian prohibition against any individual renting more than five hundred acres of the public land. His office of tribune enabled him at once to commence operations; but before committing himself to the hazards of a public struggle, he sought the advice of the most virtuous and respectable men in Rome, all of whom sanctioned his project. Not daring to oppose directly the attempt to enforce a well-known law, the corrupt nobles engaged one of the tribune's colleagues to thwart his measures. Grieved, but not disheartened, Tiberius procured the deposition of this unworthy magistrate, and carried a law, constituting a triumvirate, or commission of three persons, to inquire into the administration of the public lands, and the violations of the Licinian law (B. C. 132). This was followed by a proposal, that the treasures which Attalus king of Pergamus had bequeathed to the Romans should be distributed among the poorer classes of the people. During the agitation of this and some similar laws, his year of tribuneship expired, and the patricians resolved to prevent his re-election by absolute violence. So great was the uproar on the first day of the comitia, that the returning officer was obliged to adjourn the proceedings. Early in the following morning, when the assembly met, Tiberius received information that some of the nobles, accompanied by bands of armed retainers, had resolved to attack the crowd and take his life. Alarmed by this intelligence, he directed his friends to arm themselves as well as they could with staves; and when the people began to inquire the cause of this strange proceeding, he put his hand to his head, intimating that his life was in danger. Some of his enemies immediately ran to the senate, and reported that Tiberius Gracchus openly demanded a crown from the people. Scipio Nasica, a large holder of public lands, seized this pretext to urge the consul to destroy the reformer. On the refusal of that magistrate to embrue his hands in innocent blood, Nasica, accompanied by a large body of the patricians, with their clients and dependents, assaulted the unarmed multitude; Tiberius was slain in the tumult, and many of his friends were either murdered or driven into banishment without any legal process. So great was the odium Nasica incurred by his share in the murder of his kinsman, that the senate, to screen him from popular resentment, sent him to Asia, under a pretext of public business, but in reality as a species of honourable exile: he died in a few months, the victim of mortification and remorse.

While the city was thus disturbed by civil tumults, Sicily was harassed by the horrors of a servile war; and the new province of Pergamus was usurped by Aristonicus, a natural brother of the late king Attalus. Both wars were terminated by disgraceful means, which the Romans would have scorned to have used at an earlier period of their history: Eunus, the leader of the slaves, was betrayed by some wretches the consul had bribed; and Pergamus was not subdued until the springs which supplied water to the principal towns were poisoned.

Caius Gracchus had been a mere youth when his brother Tiberius was so basely murdered; but, undaunted by that brother's fate, he resolved to pursue the same course, and was confirmed in his determination by his mother Cornelia, a woman of undaunted spirit, animated by the purest principles of patriotism. He commenced his career by offering himself a candidate for the office of quæstor, to which he was elected without opposition. His integrity and ability in this station won him "golden opinions from all sorts of men." On his return to Rome he was chosen tribune of the people; and he immediately began to take measures for enforcing the agrarian law (B. C. 122). In his second tribuneship, he procured the enactment of a law, transferring the power of judging corrupt magistrates from the senators to the equestrian order; a change rendered absolutely necessary by the impunity that had long been granted to the grossest delinquency and extortion. At length the senate set up Drusus, another tribune, as a rival in popularity to Gracchus. This wretched minion of an unprincipled faction made several grants of public money and remissions of taxes to the people, with the direct sanction of the senate; and soon became a favourite with the ignorant multitude. A severer blow was the exclusion of Gracchus from the tribuneship when he stood candidate the third time, the officers having been bribed to make a false return; and this was followed by the election of Opimius, the most violent of the aristocratic faction, to the consulship.

A contest could not long be avoided: the nobles, confiding in the numbers of their armed retainers, were anxious to provoke a battle; but Gracchus, though personally menaced by the consul, was desirous that peace should be preserved. An accident precipitated the struggle. While the consul was performing the customary morning sacrifice, Antylius, one of his lictors, carrying away the entrails, said, with contemptuous voice and gesture, to the friends of Gracchus and Fulvius—"Make way there, ye worthless citizens, for honest men!" The provoked bystanders instantly assaulted the insolent lictor, and slew him with the pins of their table-books.

This imprudence afforded Opimius the opportunity he had so eagerly desired; the senate hastily assembled, and passed a vote investing him with dictatorial power.* Gracchus, with his most zealous followers, took possession of Mount Aventine: here he was soon attacked by the sanguinary Opimius; three thousand of his followers were slain, and their bodies thrown into the Tiber; and Caius himself chose to fall by the hands of a faithful slave, rather than glut his cruel enemies by his tortures (B. C. 120). With the Gracchi perished the freedom of the Roman republic; henceforth the supreme power of the state was wielded by a corrupt, avaricious, and insolent aristocracy, from whose avarice and oppression even the worst tyranny of the worst of the emperors would have been a desirable relief.

The profligacy and corruption of the senate, now that the

* The vote by which absolute power, in cases of emergency, was given to the consuls, consisted in the following formula:—"*Ut darent operam consules ne respublica quid detrimenti caperet.*"

check of popular control was removed, soon became manifest by their conduct in the Jugurthine war. Micipsa king of Numidia, the son of Massinissa, divided his monarchy on his death-bed between his two sons Hiempsal and Adherbal, and his nephew Jugurtha, though the latter was of illegitimate birth. Jugurtha resolved to obtain possession of the entire inheritance, procured the murder of Hiempsal, and compelled Adherbal to seek refuge at Rome. The senate at first seemed disposed to punish the usurper; but soon won over by his bribes, they actually voted him a reward for his crimes, decreeing that the kingdom of Numidia should be divided equally between him and Adherbal. Impunity only stimulated Jugurtha to fresh iniquities; he declared war against his cousin, gained possession of his person by a capitulation, and, in violation of the terms, put him to death. Even this atrocity failed to rouse the senate; and Jugurtha would have escaped unpunished, had not Memmius, one of the tribunes, exposed the profligate venality of the aristocracy in a general assembly of the people, and persuaded them to send Cassius the prætor into Africa, to bring Jugurtha thence to Rome, on the public faith, in order that those who had taken bribes might be convicted by the king's evidence.

Júgurtha being brought before the assembly, was interrogated by Mem′mius; but Bæ′bius, another tribune, who had been bribed for the purpose, forbade the king to make any reply. The Numidian, however, soon added to his former crimes, by procuring the murder of his cousin Massíva in Rome, suspecting that he was likely to be raised to the throne of Numidia by a party in the senate. Such an insult could not be borne; Júgurtha was instantly ordered to quit Italy (B.C. 109), and an army raised against him was intrusted to the command of the consul Al′binus. Instead of prosecuting the war, Al′binus left his brother Aúlus, a vain, avaricious man, in command of the army, and returned to Italy. Aúlus invaded Numidia, hoping that Júgurtha would purchase his forbearance by a large sum; but he was surrounded, betrayed, and forced to capitulate on the most disgraceful terms. The Roman people was roused to exertion by this infamy; a com-

Digitized by Google

mission was issued for inquiring into the criminality of those who had received bribes; several of the leading nobles, among whom was Opimius, the murderer of Caius Gracchus, were convicted on the clearest evidence, and sentenced to different degrees of punishment. Finally, the conduct of the war was entrusted to Quintus Metellus, a strenuous partisan of the aristocracy, but an able general, and an incorruptible statesman. When Metellus had almost completed the conquest of Numidia, he was supplanted by his lieutenant Caius Marius, a man of the lowest birth, but whom valour, talent, and a zealous devotion to the popular cause, had elevated to fame and fortune. Raised to the consulship, and entrusted with the conduct of the war against Jugurtha, by the favour of the people, Marius shewed little respect for the vote of the senate that had continued Metellus in command. He raised fresh levies, and passed over into Africa just when Jugurtha had been forced to seek refuge with Bocchus king of Mauritania (B. C. 106). The principal cities and fortresses of Numidia were speedily subdued, and the united army of Jugurtha and Bocchus routed with great slaughter. The Moorish king, terrified by his losses, was at length prevailed upon to betray Jugurtha to Sylla, a young nobleman who held the important office of quæstor in the army of Marius; and this wicked usurper, after having been exhibited in the conqueror's triumph, was starved to death in prison.

In the meantime, the barbarous hordes of the Cimbri and Teutones were devastating Transalpine Gaul, and had defeated the Roman armies sent to check their ravages. At length their total defeat of Cæpio's army, and slaughter of eighty thousand men, spread such general consternation, that the senate and people combined to raise Marius to the consulate a second time, contrary to law. It was not, however, until his fourth consulship (B. C. 100), that Marius brought the Teutones to a decisive engagement at Aquæ Lutiæ. The annals of war scarcely record a more complete victory; more than one hundred thousand of the invaders having been slain or made prisoners. He was no less fortunate in a second engagement with the Cimbrians; but on this occasion his old quæstor, but now his rival, Lucius Sylla, had fair grounds for claiming a large share in the honours of the day. About the same time a second servile war in Sicily was terminated: so cruelly was the revolt of these unhappy men punished, that more than a million of the insurgents are said to have perished in the field, or been exposed to wild beasts in the arena.

A much more dangerous war, called the Marsic, the Social, and the Italic, was provoked by the injustice with which the Romans treated their Italian allies. The different states having in vain sought a redress of grievances from the senate and people, entered into a secret conspiracy, which soon extended from the Liris eastwards to the extremity of ancient Italy. The Marsi, long renowned for their bravery, were foremost in the revolt, and hence their name is frequently given to the war. After a tedious contest of three years, in which half a million of men are supposed to have perished, the Romans granted the freedom of their city to the states that laid down their arms (B. C. 87), and tranquillity was restored in Italy.

But the Roman power was exposed almost to equal danger in Asia by the rising greatness of Mithridates, the celebrated king of Pontus, who, in a short time, made himself master of all the towns and islands in Asia Minor, with the single exception of Rhodes. Marius and Sylla eagerly contended for the chief command in this important war; the latter prevailed, and procured the banishment of his rival, who very narrowly escaped with his life. Sylla departed with his army to Asia; but, during his absence, the consul Cinna recalled Marius, and Italy was involved in all the horrors of civil war (B. C. 86). At length, the aged exile, having every where defeated the partisans of the nobles, made his triumphant entry into Rome, and filled the entire city with slaughter. Having caused the murder of most of the leading senators and knights that had joined in procuring his banishment, he declared himself consul without going through the formality of an election, and died soon after, in the seventy-first year of his age.

In the meantime Sylla defeated the armies of Mithridates in Greece, took Athens by storm, slaughtering its citizens without mercy or compunction, and compelled the king of

Pontus to solicit peace. Sylla willingly consented; for he had neither ships nor money to carry on the war; and he longed impatiently to be in Italy, that he might revenge himself on his enemies, who were so cruelly persecuting his partisans.

On the news of the approach of Sylla with a victorious army (B. C. 83), the consuls Cinna and Carbo made every preparation for the impending war; but the former was murdered by his mutinous troops, and the latter, though aided by the younger Marius, did not possess abilities adequate to the crisis. After a severe struggle, Sylla prevailed, and became master of Rome. He surpassed even the cruelties of Marius, slaughtering without mercy not merely his political opponents, but all whom he suspected of discontent at his elevation. While the city was filled with mourning and consternation, he caused himself to be elected dictator for an unlimited time (B. C. 81); but, to the great astonishment of every body, he resigned his power at the end of three years, and retired into private life. He died soon after (B. C. 77) of a loathsome disease, brought on by intemperance and debauchery.

The consul Lepidus attempted to seize the power which Sylla had abdicated; he was declared a public enemy, defeated in the field, forsaken by his friends, and abandoned by his faithless wife: he sunk under this complication of misfortunes, and died of a broken heart. But though the senate escaped this danger, they were alarmed by the rapid progress of the Marian faction in Spain (B. C. 76), where Sertorius had collected a powerful army from the relics of that party. After some deliberation, the management of this war was entrusted to Pompey, afterwards surnamed the Great, though he had not yet attained the consular age, and was still a simple Roman knight. Sertorius proved more than a match for the young general, defeating him in several engagements: but treachery proved more efficacious than valour; the bold adventurer was murdered by Perperna (B. C. 73); and the insurgents, deprived of their able leader, were finally subdued by Pompey (B. C. 70). Before the Spanish war was terminated, Italy was thrown into confusion by the daring revolt of Spartacus (B. C. 72). This dangerous insurgent, with about eighty companions, forced his way out of a school for training gladiators at Capua, and resolved, instead of hazarding his life in the arena, for the brutal sport of the Roman populace, to make war on the republic. Two brilliant victories so established his fame, that the slaves, deserting their masters, flocked to his standard from all quarters, and he soon found himself at the dead of ten thousand men. Fresh successes now crowned his arms; prætors and consuls were sent against him, and defeated; his forces rapidly increased to one hundred and twenty thousand; and he even attempted to make himself master of Rome. At length the prætor Crassus succeeded in suppressing his formidable revolt; but his victory was chiefly owing to the want of union and discipline in the army of the insurgents (B. C. 70). Spartacus himself fell in the field, and great numbers of his followers were crucified by the barbarous conquerors.

Crassus and Pompey were chosen consuls the next year: both were ambitious of supreme power, and both began to pay their court to the people; Crassus by largesses of corn and money, Pompey by restoring the tribunitian power, and repealing many of the unpopular laws of Sylla. These measures gave Pompey so much influence, that he was chosen to manage the war against the Cilician pirates, in spite of the most vigorous opposition of the senators; and to this commission there were added, by the Manilian law, the government of Asia, and the entire management of the war against Mithridates (B. C. 65). Little did the tribune Manilius foresee that he was placing the whole power of the Roman empire in the hands of a man who would soon become the most strenuous supporter of the senate.

Pompey made a judicious use of the power with which he was entrusted; he subdued Mithridates, and established the sway of the Romans over the greater part of western Asia. But while he was thus engaged gathering laurels in the remote east, the republic narrowly escaped destruction from the conspiracy of Catiline (B. C. 62). The original contriver of this celebrated conspiracy, Sergius Catiline, was a young man of noble birth, sullied, however, by the most infamous debauchery and crimes. The recent examples of Marius and Sylla stimulated him to attempt making himself master of his country; and he found many associates among the profligate young nobles, whom their riotous extravagance had overwhelmed with a load of debt. The great impediment to the success of the plans of the conspirators was the vigilance of the consul Cicero, who had raised himself to the highest rank in the state by his consummate eloquence and great skill in political affairs. His murder was deemed a necessary preliminary to any open efforts; but Cicero received secret warnings of his danger from Curius, one of the conspirators, whose mistress had been bribed by the consul; and he was thus enabled to disconcert all the plans of Catiline. While the city was alarmed by rumours of danger, Catiline had the hardihood to present himself in the senate-house, where Cicero pronounced so dreadful an invective against him, that the hardened conspirator was unable to reply, and fled from the city to commence open war.

In the meantime his associates in the city attempted to form an alliance with the Allobroges, a people of Gaul that had sent ambassadors to petition the senate for some relief from the load of debt with which their nation was oppressed. These ambassadors betrayed the negotiations to Cicero, who took his measures so well, that he arrested the chiefs of the conspiracy with the proofs of their guilt on their persons. After a warm debate in the senate, it was resolved that the traitors should be put to death; Julius Cæsar, who was now fast rising into notice as the chief of the popular party, protesting almost alone against the dangerous precedent of violating the Porcian law, which forbade the capital punishment of a Roman citizen. When Catiline heard of the fate of his associates, he attempted to lead his forces into Gaul; but he was overtaken by a consular army, defeated, and slain. So pleased were the senate with the conduct of Cicero on this occasion, that they gave him the honourable title of FATHER OF HIS COUNTRY.

Pompey soon afterwards returned to Rome, and the old jealousies between him and Crassus were renewed; but Julius Cæsar, whose eminent abilities were now known and valued, succeeded in bringing the rivals together, and uniting them with himself in a partnership of power, generally called " the first triumvirate" (B.C. 59). They were supported in this project by the infamous Clodius, whose sole aim was to be revenged on Cicero for having given evidence against him on a criminal trial. To wreak his vengeance more effectually, he had himself transferred from the patrician order to the plebeian; and then becoming a candidate for the tribuneship, was elected without much opposition. By the exertions of Clodius, Cicero was driven into banishment; but he was honourably recalled after a year's exile, and restored to his dignity and estates. While Clodius, by his violence, kept the city in constant agitation, Pompey and Crassus were again elected consuls together; the former chose Spain, the latter Syria, for his province, hoping that its wealth would be the prey of his boundless avarice (B.C. 54). Cæsar was in the meantime winning fame by the conquest of Gaul, and establishing a military reputation which soon eclipsed that of all his contemporaries.

The union of the triumvirs was first disturbed by the death of Julia, Cæsar's daughter, who had been married to Pompey, and exercised great influence over both her father and her husband. But the compact was completely broken by the unfortunate termination of the rash expedition which Crassus undertook against the Parthians, in which he perished, with the greater part of his army (B.C. 52).

Cæsar's victorious career in Gaul lasted nearly eight years (from B.C. 57 to B.C. 49). During this space of time he subdued all the barbarous and warlike tribes between the Pyrenees and the German Ocean; he even crossed the Rhine, and gained several victories over the Germans; and, passing over into Britain, he subdued the southern part of the island. Pompey at first favoured all the projects of his colleague, procured him a prolongation of his command and supplies of troops; but he soon became envious of exploits that obscured the fame of his own achievements; his creatures began to detract from the brilliancy of Cæsar's victories, and many of that general's official letters were suppressed by the senate. It became soon obvious that the jealousies of the two surviving triumvirs could be arranged only in the field of battle, and their partisans began to prepare for combat long before the principals had any notion of breaking the peace. The poet Lucan has very ably sketched the character of both leaders at the commencement of the contest, in a passage whose innate beauty will be perceptible even through the defects of an imperfect translation, as the image of the sun retains a portion of its lustre though viewed through a distorted medium.

You, Pompey, fear lest modern deeds efface
Your ancient triumphs o'er the pirate race;
*You** a long series of heroic deeds
And fierce impatience of a greater leads:
Pompey no rival, Cæsar brooks no lord;
Yet who more justly drew the hostile sword
We dare not know. Cato and Heav'n divide;
It chose the victor's, he the vanquish'd side.
Ill were they match'd; the one now aged grown,
Unlearn'd the warrior in the peaceful gown:
He courts the fame that follow'd him so long,
And buys the plaudits of a hireling throng.
Pleas'd with the venal shouts, no triumphs now
Replace the laurels fading on his brow;
His sole reliance is his former fame;
He stands the shadow of a mighty name.
Like the proud oak, that, in a fruitful field,
Sustains the wasting helm and mouldering shield—
The faint memorials of forgotten days,
Chieftains unknown, and unremember'd frays—
Whose perish'd roots no more the trunk sustain;
Fix'd by its weight, still triumphs in the plain,
Still are its naked boughs to heaven display'd;
The naked trunk alone extends a shade.
Yet though it quivers in each passing breeze,
Ready to fall, though round it younger trees
In all the pride of youthful bloom are shewn,
It stands unrivall'd, honour'd, and alone.
Cæsar relies not on an empty name,
War his delight, defeat his only shame;
Tameless and fierce, as hope or anger burns,
Th' impatient warrior with new fierceness turns;
Conquest impels him to more glorious deeds,
Believing fate his friend: whate'er impedes
His proud career soon owns the victor's sway:
He views with triumph ruins mark his way.

* Cæsar.

Thus bursts from angry clouds the flashing levin
Rushing in thunders o'er the startled heaven;
The echoing globe reverberates the crash,
Its pale inhabitants are dumb—the flash,
Darting athwart, closes each eye in pain,—
Its own wild flames consume its own proud fane:
No fence restrains it, and no limits bound,
It spreads a waste of ruin all around;
Then to its clouds on wings of flame retires,
And bears to heaven its re-assembled fires.

The contest began by Cæsar's demanding permission to hold the consulship while absent. He had secured his interest and increased his adherents in Rome by the most lavish bribes, having spent nearly half a million on the purchase of Caius Curio alone. This powerful and popular tribune placed the senate in a very difficult position, by proposing that both Pompey and Cæsar should resign their offices, and retire into private life (B.C. 51). Some time was wasted in negotiations; but at length the senate (Jan. 7, B.C. 49) passed a decree by which Cæsar was commanded to disband his army before a specified day, under penalty of being declared a public enemy. Mark Antony and Quintus Cassius, tribunes of the people, put their negative on this vote; but their prerogative was disputed; and a debate ensued, in the course of which many severe speeches were made against them. Finally, the vote for suspending the constitution passed by a large majority in a very full house. It was decreed that "the consuls, prætors, proconsuls, and other magistrates near Rome, should take care that the republic received no detriment." Antony and Cassius fled from the city the same night, disguised as slaves. They were followed by Curio and Cælius.

When Cæsar received this intelligence, he resolved to march immediately into Italy, before Pompey could collect forces sufficient for the defence of the peninsula. The rapidity of his movements disconcerted his enemies; and the news of his having passed the Rubicon, spread such alarm at Rome, that the senate and Pompey's party abandoned the city, leaving the public treasure behind them. All Italy was subdued in sixty days. On the 17th of March, Pompey sailed from Brundusium for

Greece, abandoning his country to his rival. Sicily and Sardinia speedily followed the fate of the peninsula.

Elated by this great success, Cæsar returned to Rome, took the funds from the public treasury; and, after a brief respite of six or seven days, set out to attack Pompey's lieutenants in Spain. He met with unexpected resistance from the city of Marseilles; but, leaving a detachment to besiege the place, he continued his march to Ilerda, where he found his enemies posted under the command of Afranius and Petreius. An undecisive battle was fought at Ilerda; but Cæsar, taking advantage of the inexperience and incapacity of his opponents, soon reduced them to such straits, that they were forced to surrender at discretion. The reduction of the remainder of the Spanish peninsula was soon completed, and Cæsar returned into Gaul to finish the siege of Marseilles. Cæsar's presence soon forced the citizens to surrender. Their lives were spared; but they were forced to give up all their arms, magazines, and money. But while he was thus every where victorious in person, the armies commanded by his lieutenants met some severe reverses in Illyricum and Africa.

On his return to Rome, Cæsar was created dictator. Having made proper arrangements for the government of the city, he prepared to follow Pompey into Greece, where that general had collected an immense army from the principal states of the East. His inferiority by sea exposed Cæsar's soldiers to great dangers and hardships in their passage from Brundusium to Dyracchium; but they were finally transported into western Greece, and a tedious campaign began, in which both leaders shewed themselves equally reluctant to hazard a general engagement. From Epirus both armies moved into Thessaly; and on the 30th of July (B. C. 48), the battle, which decided the fate of the world, was fought on the plains of Pharsalia. Pompey's forces were completely routed; their camp stormed; and the bodies of fugitives that preserved a semblance of regularity in their retreat, forced to yield themselves prisoners. The unfortunate general himself made no effort to retrieve the fortune of the day: when his squadrons of cavalry, on which he placed his principal reliance, were routed, he retired to his tent, whence he fled in disguise when the enemy began to storm his entrenchments.

From the field of battle Pompey fled to the Ægean sea, probably designing to renew the war in Syria; but finding the Asiatic states inclined to withdraw their allegiance when they heard of his defeat, he steered for Egypt, accompanied by his wife Cornelia, trusting that he would receive protection from the young king of that country, with whose father he had been united by the strictest bonds of friendship. But the guardians of the young king resolved to murder the unfortunate fugitive, and entrusted the execution of the crime to Septimius, a Roman deserter, and Achillas, the captain of the Egyptian guards. Lucan has given a very vivid description of the catastrophe.

Now in the boat defenceless Pompey sate,
Surrounded and abandon'd to his fate;
Nor long they held him in their power aboard,
Ere every villain drew his ruthless sword:
The chief perceiv'd their purpose soon, and spread
His Roman gown, with patience, o'er his head:
And when the curs'd Achillas pierc'd his breast,
His rising indignation close repressed.
No sighs, no groans, his dignity profaned,
No tears his still unsullied glory stained:
Unmoved and firm he fixed him on his seat,
And died—as when he liv'd and conquer'd—great.

At the sad sight of the Egyptian treachery, Cornelia's attendants, disregarding her lamentations, weighed anchor and stood out to sea. Pompey's body was flung into the waves; but it was dragged out in the night by one Cordus, who had been Pompey's quæstor in Cyprus, and interred with the Roman rites of sepulture. Plutarch informs us that his ashes were subsequently removed to Italy, and deposited in a vault in his Alban villa, by Cornelia: but Lucan asserts that they remained in Egypt; and he thus spiritedly remonstrates against the neglect shewn to the remains of the hero:—

And thou, old Rome, by whose forgetful hand
Altars and temples rear'd to tyrants stand,
Canst thou neglect to call thy hero home,
And leave his ghost in banishment to roam?

What, though the victor's frown and thy base fear
Bade thee, at first, the pious task forbear?
Yet now, at least, oh! let him now return,
And rest with honour in a Roman urn.
Nor let mistaken superstition dread,
On such occasions, to disturb the dead.
Oh! would commanding Rome my hand employ,
The impious task would be perform'd with joy;
How would I fly to tear him from that tomb,
And bear his ashes in my bosom home!

SECTION VII.—*The Establishment of the Roman Empire.*

FROM B.C. 48 TO B.C. 30.

THE news of Pompey's death occasioned a fresh division among his fugitive friends. Many who were attached personally to him, and who held out in hopes of seeing him again at their head, determined to have recourse to the conqueror's clemency. Cornelia returned to Italy, well knowing that she had nothing to apprehend from Cæsar. Cato, with Pompey's two sons, remained in Africa, and marched overland to join Varus and Juba, king of Numidia. We shall see immediately how they renewed the war, and exposed the victor to fresh fatigues and dangers.

Cæsar, immediately after his victory, commenced a close pursuit of his competitor; and did not hear of his death until his arrival in Alexandria, when messengers from the Egyptian king brought him Pompey's head and ring. Cæsar turned with disgust from these relics. He ordered the head to be inhumed with due honour; and, to shew his disapprobation of Egyptian treachery, he caused a temple to be erected near Pompey's tomb, dedicated to Nemesis, the avenging power of cruel and inhuman deeds. His next task was to arrange the disputed succession of the crown; but, seduced by the charms of the princess Cleopatra, he shewed an undue preference for her interests, and thus induced the partisans of the young king Ptolemy to take up arms. As Cæsar had only brought a handful of men with him to Alexandria, he was exposed to great danger by this sudden burst of insurrection. A fierce battle was fought in the city. Cæsar succeeded in firing the Egyptian fleet; but unfortunately the flames extended to the celebrated public library, and the greater part of that magnificent collection of the most valuable works of ancient times perished in the flames. After the struggle had been protracted for some time, Cæsar at length received reinforcements from Syria, and soon triumphed over all his enemies. From Egypt he marched against Pharnaces, the unnatural son of the great Mithridates, and subdued him so easily, that he described the campaign in three words, "VENI, VIDI, VICI"—(*I came, I saw, I conquered*).

Having thus settled the affairs of the East, he departed for Rome, having been created dictator in his absence; and found on his return the affairs of the city in the greatest confusion, caused by the quarrels between Antony and Dolabella. Cæsar with difficulty reconciled their differences, and began to make preparations for his war in Africa against Cato and the sons of Pompey. On his arrival in Africa, he did not find victory quite so easy as he had anticipated; but at length he forced his enemies to a decisive engagement at Thapsus, and gave them a complete overthrow. From thence he advanced to Utica, which was garrisoned by the celebrated Cato, whose hostility to Cæsar was inflexible. It was not, however, supported by his followers; and Cato, seeing his friends resolved on yielding, committed suicide. The sons of Pompey made their escape into Spain, where they soon collected a formidable party.

Having concluded the African war in about five months, Cæsar returned to Rome (B.C. 45) to celebrate his triumph. The senate placed no bounds to their adulation, passing, in their excessive flattery, the limits even of ordinary decency. They decreed that in his triumph his chariot should be drawn by four white horses, like those of Jupiter and the Sun: they created him dictator for ten years, and inspector of morals for three: they commanded his statue to be placed in the capitol, opposite to that of Jupiter, with the globe of the earth beneath his feet, and with this inscription;—"To Cæsar, the demigod."

During his residence at Rome, the dictator distinguished himself by several acts of clemency, more truly honourable to his character than all the titles conferred upon him by a servile senate. Having provided for the safety of the city during his absence, he hasted into Spain to terminate the civil war by crushing the relics of his opponents, who still made head under the sons of Pompey. Early in the spring (B.C. 44), the two armies met in the plains of Munda: the battle was arduous and well contested; Cæsar had never been exposed to such danger; even his veterans began to give ground. By leading, however, his favourite tenth legion to the charge, he restored the fortune of the field, and his exertions were crowned with a decisive victory, which put an end to the war. The elder of Pompey's sons was taken and slain; Sextus the younger escaped to the mountains of Celtiberia.

Having thus completely extinguished the last embers of the civil war, Cæsar contemplated several vast designs for extending and improving the empire he had acquired. He resolved to revenge the defeat and death of Crassus on the Parthians; he undertook to rebuild and repair several towns in Italy, to drain the Pomptine marshes, to dig a new bed for the Tiber, to form a capacious harbour at Ostia, and to cut a canal through the isthmus of Corinth. But these gigantic projects did not compensate, in the minds of his countrymen, for the criminal design he was understood to have formed of making himself king of Rome. Mark Antony, it is supposed at Cæsar's secret instigation, offered the dictator a regal crown at the feast of the Lupercalia, which Cæsar, perceiving the displeasure of the people, deemed it prudent to refuse: Antony, however, had it entered in the public acts, "That by the command of the people, as consul, he had offered the name of king to Cæsar, perpetual dictator; and that Cæsar would not accept of it."

A large body of the senators, regarding Cæsar as a usurper, conspired for his destruction, among whom Brutus and Cassius were the most conspicuous. They resolved to put their plot into execution in the senate-house (March 15, B.C. 44); but they very narrowly escaped detection, from a variety of untoward accidents. As soon as Cæsar had taken his place, he was surrounded by the conspirators, one of whom, pretending to urge some request, held him down by his robe: this was the signal agreed upon; the other conspirators rushed upon him with their daggers, and he fell, pierced by twenty-three wounds, at the base of Pompey's statue. The murderers had no sooner finished their work, than Brutus, lifting up his dagger, congratulated the senate, and Cicero in particular, on the recovery of liberty; but the senators, seized with astonishment, rushed from the capitol and hid themselves in their own houses. Tranquillity prevailed until the day of Cæsar's funeral, when Mark Antony, by a studied harangue, so inflamed the passions of the populace, that they stormed the senate-house, tore up its benches to make a funeral pile for the body, and raised such a conflagration that several houses were entirely consumed. This was a clear warning to the conspirators, who immediately quitted Rome, and prepared to defend themselves by force of arms.

The superstition of the Roman people led them to invent or imagine many omens and prodigies, which they believed to have portended the death of Cæsar. They are thus enumerated by the poet Ovid:—

Not gods can alter fate's resistless will!
Yet they foretold by signs the approaching ill.
Dreadful were heard, among the clouds, alarms
Of echoing trumpets and of clashing arms:
The sun's pale image gave so faint a light,
That the sad earth was almost veiled in night.
The ether's face with fiery meteors glowed,
With storms of hail were mingled drops of blood;
A dusky hue the morning star o'erspread,
And the moon's orb was stained with spots of red;
In every place portentous shrieks were heard,
The fatal warnings of the infernal bird:
In every place the marble melts to tears;
While in the groves, rever'd through length of years,
Boding and awful sounds the ear invade,
And solemn music warbles through the shade.
No victim can atone the impious age,
No sacrifice the wrathful gods assuage;

Dire wars and civil fury threat the state,
And every omen points out Cæsar's fate.
Around each hallow'd shrine and sacred dome,
Night-howling dogs disturb the peaceful gloom;
Their silent seats the wand'ring shades forsake,
And fearful tremblings the rock'd city shake.
Yet could not by these prodigies be broke
The plotted charm, or staid the fatal stroke;
Their swords the assassins in the temple draw,
Their murd'ring hands nor gods nor temples awe;
This sacred place their bloody weapons stain,
And virtue falls, before the altar slain.

Mark Antony long deceived the conspirators by an appearance of moderation, and an affected anxiety to procure an act of amnesty; but when joined by Octavius Cæsar, the nephew and heir of the murdered dictator, he threw off the mask, and proposed extraordinary honours to the memory of Cæsar, with a religious supplication to him as a divinity. Brutus and Cassius at length discovering that Antony meditated nothing but war, and that their affairs were daily growing more desperate, left Italy, and sought refuge in the East. Octavius Cæsar, becoming jealous of Antony, joined the party of the senate; and Antony, retiring into Cisalpine Gaul, levied an army of veterans, and came to an engagement with the armies of the republic, in which both the consuls were slain. Antony, defeated in the field, fled to Lepidus in Spain; and Octavius Cæsar, whom the death of the consuls had placed at the head of the army, entered secretly into a correspondence with the enemies of the senate. Their mutual interests led to the formation of a league between Octavius, Lepidus, and Antony, called the second triumvirate (November 27, B.C. 43), and their confederacy was cemented by the blood of the noblest citizens of Rome, shed in a proscription more ruthless and sanguinary than those of Marius and Sylla. The most illustrious of the victims was the celebrated Cicero, whose severe invectives against Antony had procured him the relentless hatred of the triumvir. Octavius is said to have hesitated long before consenting to the sacrifice of the greatest orator that Rome ever produced, and the most patriotic of her recent statesmen; but at length he permitted the fatal consent to be extorted, and Cicero fell a victim to a band of assassins, headed by a tribune whom he had formerly defended and preserved in a capital cause.

The triumvirs having taken vengeance on their enemies in Italy, began to prepare for carrying on war against Brutus and Cassius. Macedonia became the theatre of the new civil war: the republicans at first seemed destined to conquer; they appeared to possess superior talents and greater forces both by land and sea. But in the double battle at Philippi, fortune rather than talent gave the victory to the triumvirs; and Cassius destroyed himself after the first contest, and Brutus after the second (B.C. 42). Antony made a cruel use of his victory, putting to death his political opponents without mercy. Octavius emulated the crimes of his colleague, and treated the most illustrious of his prisoners with barbarity and abusive language.

After his victory Antony visited Greece, where he was received with the most refined flattery. Thence he passed into Asia, where all the sovereigns of the East came to offer him homage; but he was most gratified by a visit from the celebrated Cleopatra, who rendered the voluptuous triumvir a captive to her charms. Resigning all his plans of war against the Parthians, he followed this celebrated beauty into Egypt, and in her company neglected all care of public affairs. Octavius Cæsar, on the other hand, proceeded to Italy, and took the most efficacious means for securing the permanence of his power. Lucius the brother, and Fulvia the wife of Antony, excited a new war against Octavius; but they were soon defeated, and the capture of their principal stronghold, Perusia (B.C. 41), rendered Cæsar's nephew master of Italy, and almost the recognised heir of his uncle's power.

Antony was still immersed in pleasure at Alexandria, when he received the account of his brother's defeat, and the ruin of his party in Italy; and that Octavius had made himself master of both Gauls, and had got all the legions into his hands that were quartered in those districts. He was roused by these tidings from his lethargy, and immediately proceeded towards Italy; but blaming Fulvia for all his disasters, he treated her with so much contempt, that she died of a broken heart. This circumstance paved the way to a reconciliation; Antony married Octavia, the half-sister of his rival, and a new division was made of the Roman empire. Sextus Pompey, who during the troubles had become powerful by sea, was included in the new arrangements, and obtained the possession of the Peloponnesus and several important islands.

But the mutual jealousies of the triumvirs rendered peace of short duration. Octavius drove Pompey from Sicily, and compelled him to seek refuge in the East, where he was put to death by one of Antony's lieutenants; and about the same time he deprived Lepidus of all his power, and took possession of his dominions. Antony, while his rival was thus acquiring strength, disgraced himself by an unsuccessful war against the Parthians; after which he returned to Alexandria, and lost all regard to his character or his interest in the company of Cleopatra. Octavia went to the East, hoping to withdraw her husband from the fascinating syren; but the infatuated triumvir refused to see her, and sent her orders to return home. He completed this insult by sending her a bill of divorce, and professing a previous marriage with Cleopatra. Preparations for war were instantly made on both sides; but Antony's debauchery, and slavery to the caprices of an abandoned woman, disgusted his best friends, and many of them deserting him brought such an account of his extravagance to Rome, that the indignant citizens passed a decree for deposing him from the consulship.

The great rivals were soon in readiness for action. Antony had the most numerous forces; but Octavius had the advantage of a more disciplined army, and, at least in appearance, a better cause. Their fleets and armies were soon assembled at the opposite sides of the gulf of Ambracia, where they remained for several months without coming to a decisive engagement. At length, Antony, instigated by Cleopatra, formed the fatal resolution of deciding the contest by a naval battle. The fleets met off the promontory of Actium (September 2, B.C. 31), while the hostile armies, drawn up on the shore, were simple spectators of the battle. For a long time success was doubtful; until Cleopatra, wearied with expectation, and overcome with fear, unexpectedly tacked about, and fled towards the Peloponnesus with the Egyptian squadron of sixty sail; and, what is more surprising, Antony himself, now regardless of his honour, fled after her, abandoning his men who so generously exposed their lives for his interest. The battle, notwithstanding, continued till five in the evening, when Antony's forces were partly constrained to submit by the great conduct of Agrippa, and partly persuaded by the liberal promises of Octavius. The army of Antony could not believe in the flight of their general, and held out for seven days in expectation of his returning to join them; but hearing no tidings of him, and being deserted by their allies, they hasted to make terms with the conqueror.

Antony and Cleopatra continued their flight to Egypt, where the queen displayed more courage and enterprising spirit than her lover. She caused some of her galleys to be carried over the isthmus (of Suez) into the Red Sea, proposing to save herself, with her treasures, in an unknown world; but the Arabians having burned her vessels, she was forced to abandon a design so full of difficulties, and she therefore commenced fortifying the avenues of her kingdom, and making preparations for war. She also solicited foreign assistance, addressing herself to all the princes in the alliance of Antony. While Cleopatra was thus employed, Antony exhibited the most lamentable weakness: at first he affected to imitate Timon the misanthrope, and shut himself up without either friends or domestics; but his natural temper did not allow him to remain long in this state, and quitting his cell, he gave himself up to feasting and every kind of extravagance.

In the meantime the forces of Octavius advanced on each side of Egypt. Cornelius Gallus took possession of Paretonium, which was the key of Egypt on the west side; and Antony, who speeded with his fleet and army to wrest it out of his hands, was forced to retire with great loss, especially of his ships. Pelusium, the eastern security of the kingdom, was surrendered to Octavius at the first summons: it was reported that Seleucus the governor betrayed the place by Cleopatra's orders; but she, to clear herself from such an imputation, delivered up his wife and children into Antony's hands. Cæsar advanced to besiege Alexandria: Antony made an effort to impede his march, but he was abandoned by his soldiers; and finding he could not die with glory in the field, he returned to Alexandria, overcome with rage and fury, running and crying out, "that Cleopatra had betrayed him, when he had ruined all his fortunes for her sake alone." The queen, hearing of his violent transports, retired in terror to a monument she had erected, secured the doors, and caused a report to be spread of her death. Upon this news Antony attempted to commit suicide, and inflicted on himself a mortal wound: hearing, however, in the midst of his agonies, that Cleopatra still lived, he caused himself to be transported to her monument, and expired in her presence.

Cleopatra seems to have formed some hope of obtaining the same influence over Octavius Cæsar that she had exercised over Antony; but finding the conqueror insensible to her charms, and having received secret information that he reserved her to adorn his triumph, she bribed a countryman to convey an asp to her in a basket of figs, and applied the venomous creature to her arm, and thus died. Egypt was then reduced into the form of a Roman province, and its immense riches were transported to Rome, which enabled Octavius to pay all he owed to his soldiers. On his return to Rome the senate saluted him by the honourable name of Augustus, and by a unanimous vote conceded to him the entire authority of the state.

The era of the Roman empire is usually dated from Jan. 1st, B.C. 28. The title of Augustus was at first only personal, and did not convey any idea of sovereignty: several of the imperial family took it who were never emperors, such as Germanicus. The female line, who had not the least shadow of sovereignty with the Romans, had it, as Antonia Major; and thus Livia first took the name of Augusta when she was adopted, by her husband's will, into the Julian family. After the time of Dioclesian it was changed into Semper Augustus; and this title was, in modern times, assumed by the emperors of Germany and Austria. It may appear surprising that the Romans made no vigorous effort to recover their republican constitution; but, in truth, Roman liberty was destroyed when the Gracchi were murdered: all the subsequent civil dissensions were contests for power between different sections of the oligarchy; and the people, weary of the oppression of the aristocracy, gladly sought shelter from the tyranny of the nobles in the despotic sway of a single master.

CHAPTER XVI.

GEOGRAPHICAL AND POLITICAL CONDITION OF THE ROMAN EMPIRE.

SECTION I.—*European Countries. Spain.*

IN general the boundaries of the Roman empire may be described as the great western ocean, the rivers Rhine and Danube in Europe, the chain of Mount Caucasus, the river Euphrates and the Syrian deserts in Asia, and the sandy deserts of Africa. It thus included the fairest portions of the known world surrounding the Mediterranean sea.

Its most western province was the Spanish peninsula, whose boundaries being fixed by nature continue unvaried. This great country, usually called Iberia by the Greeks, either from a colony of Iberians, or from the river Iberus (*Ebro*), was known to the Romans by the names Hispania or Hesperia. It was usually divided into three great portions, Lusitania, Bœtica or Hispania Ulterior, and Tarraconensis or Hispania Citerior.

The limits of Lusitania were never regularly defined; the Anas (*Guadiana*) was usually deemed its southern boundary, and the Durius (*Douro*) its northern. The chief tribes that inhabited this district were the Lusitani, the Celtici, the Vettones, and the Turdetani. The chief towns were Olisippo (*Lisbon*), founded by the Phœnicians; Conimbrica (*Coimbra*); Augusta Emerita, the capital of the Roman colony founded by a body of veterans to whom Augustus assigned lands in lieu of their arrears of pay; Salmantica (*Salamanca*); Pax Julia (*Beja*), the chief city of the Turdetani; and Salacia (*Alacor do Sal*). The chief promontories were the Promontorium Sacrum (*Cape St. Vincent*), the Promontorium Barbârium (*Cape Spiabel*), and the Promontorium Magnum (*Cape de Rocca Sintra*). The chief ranges of mountains were Herminius Major (*Sierra de Estretta*), and Herminius Minor (*Sierra de Maroao*).

The most celebrated rivers were the Anas, the Tagus, and the Durius. It was said that gold-dust, in considerable quantities, was obtained from the sands of the Tagus. The Lusitanians preferred plundering their neighbours to cultivating the fertile lands of their own country. They were a fierce, warlike race, and long resisted the Roman power.

Bœtica was so named from the river Bœtis (*Guadalquiver*), which falls into the sea near the ancient Tartessus, which we have already mentioned as probably the first great station of the Phœnicians, and the place from which the Hebrews gave the name of Tarshish to western Europe. The principal tribes in this division were, the Bastuli, supposed to have come originally from Africa, the Turduli, and the Bastetani. When the Romans took possession of this country, they nominated the four principal places assize towns (*conventus juridici*), to facilitate the administration of justice; these capitals were Gades (*Cadiz*), Corduba (*Cordova*), Hispalis (*Seville*), and Munda. The site of the ancient Tartessus is much disputed; but the weight of evidence is in favour of the little town of Nocadillo, distant about four miles from Gibraltar. Calpe (*Gibraltar*) and Mount Abyla, on the opposite or African side of the strait that unites the Mediterranean to the Atlantic, were usually called the Pillars of Hercules. The principal chain of mountains was the Orospeda (*Sierra Morena*).

Tarraconensis was divided into two unequal portions by the river Iberus (*Ebro*), and derived its name from the ancient city of Tarraco (*Tarragona*). The chief tribes were the Callœci, the Astures, the Cantabri, and the Vascones, in the north; the Celtiberi, Carpetani, and Ilergetes, in the interior; and along the coast of the Mediterranean, the Indigetes, the Cosetani, the Comsi, the Lacetani, and many others. The chief towns were Saguntum (*Murviedro*), Valentia (*Valencia*), Complutum (*Alcala*), Toletum (*Toledo*), Carthago Nova (*Carthagena*), Ilerda (*Lerida*), and Numantia (*Loria*).

The chief islands were the major and minor Baleares (*Majorca* and *Minorca*), whose inhabitants were celebrated for their skill as slingers and archers.

SECTION II.—*Transalpine Gaul.*

ANCIENT Gaul was bounded on the north and south by the sea, on the west by the Pyrenees, and on the east by the rivers Rhine and Var. It was divided into three great sections, Belgia, Aquitania, and Gallia Propria; in which the language, manners, and customs, differed considerably. The Gauls or Celts, who inhabited Gallia Propria, were subdivided into the Comati, or those who wore long hair; the Bracchati, whose national dress was a kind of loose trousers; and the Togati, who wore the Roman toga. Gallia Narbonensis, or Braccata, was bounded on the west by the Pyrenees, on the east by the Varus (Var), and on the north by the chain of Mount Cebenna (*Cevennes*). The chief tribes were the Allobroges, the Volcæ, and the Calyes. The principal towns were Narbo (*Narbonne*), which gave its name to the province; Tolosa (*Toulouse*); Nemausus (*Nismes*); Massiliæ (*Marseilles*), founded, as has been already described, by the fugitive Phocæans; and Vienna (*Vienne*).

Gallia Lugdunensis, or Celtica, was bounded on the south and west by the Liger (*Loire*), on the north by the Sequana (*Seine*), and on the east by the Arar (*Saone*), which, though only a tributary to the Rhodanus (*Rhone*), was regarded as one of the most important rivers in Gaul. The different tribes that inhabited this district were all of Celtic origin; the most remarkable were the Ædui, the Lingones, the Parisii, and the Cercomanni. The chief towns were Lugdunum (*Lyons*), Lutetia Parisiorum (*Paris*), and Alesia (*Alise*).

Gallia Aquitanica was unequally divided by the Garumna (*Garonne*); its boundaries were the Pyrenees on the south, and the Liger on the north and east. The chief tribes were the Aquitani, who appear to have been of Iberian origin, and several Celtic hordes, of which the most remarkable were the Pictones, the Beturiges, and the Averni. The principal towns were Clunberis and Burdegala (*Bourdeaux*), the principal seaport of the province.

Gallia Belgica had the Rhine on the north and east, the Arar on the west, and the Rhodanus on the south; so that it comprised the Rhenish provinces and Helvetia, which were afterwards separated from it, under the names of Germania Superior and Inferior. The northern tribes, such as the Neuri, Bellovaci, and Suessones, were of Belgic origin; the Treviri, Ubii, and others along the Rhine, were Germans; but the great hordes of the Helvetii and Sequani in the interior were Celts.

The principal towns in the interior were Vesantio (*Besançon*), Verodunum (*Verdun*), Colonia Agrippina (*Cologne*), Mogontiacum (*Mayence*), and Argentoratum (*Strasburg*).

The religion of the ancient Gauls, like that of the ancient Britons, was Druidical; they worshipped a supreme deity called Hesus, or Æsar, to whom they believed the oak to be sacred, especially if the parasitical plant called mistleto were found growing upon it. Their rites were very sanguinary: human victims were sacrificed in their groves and circles of stone; and it is said that their nobles occasionally volunteered to offer themselves upon the national altars. Temples were not erected in Gaul until after its conquest by the Romans; but long before that period the worship of a crowd of inferior deities had been introduced.

The several Gallic tribes were usually independent of each other; but on great occasions a general council of the nation was summoned, especially when preparations were made for any of the great migrations which proved so calamitous to Greece and Italy. Their superior valour rendered these tribes very formidable to all the southern nations: it was commonly said, that the Romans fought with others for conquest, but with the Gauls for actual existence. But from the time of the subjugation of their country by Julius Cæsar, their valour seemed to have disappeared together with their liberty; they never revolted, except when the extortions of their rulers became insupportable; and their efforts were neither vigorous nor well-directed.

Section III.—*Britain.*

Though Britain was not reduced to the form of a Roman province until long after the time of Julius Cæsar, yet, as that general brought it nominally under subjection, it will be better to describe its ancient state here than to interrupt the history of the empire in a subsequent chapter. The name of Britain was originally given to the cluster of islands in the Atlantic now called British, the largest of which bore the name of Albion. The southern part of Albion, or England, was originally colonised from Gaul; the tribes that inhabited the east and north are said to have been of German descent; and there is a constant tradition, that the Scots in the north-west came originally from Ireland.

That part of Britain now included in the kingdom of England and principality of Wales was anciently divided among seventeen tribes, to whom probably some of inferior note were subject.

The Damnonii inhabited what may perhaps be called the western peninsula formed by the counties of Devonshire and Cornwall. Their principal places of note were, the Promontorium Belterium, or Antivestæum (*Land's End*); Promontorium Ocrinum, or Damnonium (*the Lizard*); Voliba (*Falmouth*); Isca Damnoniorum (*Exeter*), Tamaré (*Tavistock*), and Uxella (*Lostwithiel*).

East of the Damnonii were the Durotriges, inhabiting the present county of Dorset. Their chief city was Durnium (*Dorchester*).

To the north and east of the Durotriges were the Belgæ, who possessed Somersetshire, Wiltshire, and Hampshire: they had the following places of note, Magnus Portus (*Portsmouth*); Trisantonis Portus, or Clausentum (*Southampton*), which derived its first name from the river Trisanto (*Hampton*); Venta Belgarum (*Winchester*); Aquæ Calidæ or Aquæ Solis (*Bath*); and Ischalis (*Ilchester*).

The Attrebattii, a Gallic tribe, like the former, bordered on the Belgæ, possessing the county of Berkshire. Their chief city was Calcua or Caleva (*Wallingford*).

Surrey, Sussex, and part of Hampshire, was possessed by the Regni, the site of whose capital, Noviomagus, is unknown.

By far the most civilised of the British tribes were the Cantii, who inhabited the present county of Kent. Their chief places were Durovernum (*Canterbury*); Durobrives (*Rochester*); Rutupæ (*Richborough*), with its harbour, the Portus Rutupensis (*Stonar*), whence was the most usual passage in ancient times to the opposite coast of Gaul, at the harbour of Gesiacum (*Boulogne*); Portus Dubris (*Dover*); Regulbium (*Reculver*); and Portus Lemanis (*Lyme*). Londinum (*London*) was sometimes reckoned among the cities of the Cantii.

North of the Thames, near its source, was the residence of the Dobuni, who possessed the present counties of Oxfordshire and Gloucestershire. Their chief city was Corinium, called also Durocornovium (*Cirencester*).

The Cattieuchlani or Cassii, a powerful and warlike tribe, possessed the counties of Buckingham, Bedford, and Herts. Their chief cities were Verulamium (*Verulam*), supposed to have been the metropolis of Casswelaules, taken by Cæsar; Lactodurum (*Bedford*); Magrovinium (*Ashwell*); and Durocobrivis (*Hertford*).

The Trinobantes possessed the counties of Middlesex and Essex; their chief city, Londinum (*London*), did not exist in the time of Julius Cæsar, but so early as the age of Tacitus it had become a place noted for trade, and the concourse of merchants. Their other remarkable towns were Durolitum (*Leiton*); Cononium (*Cannonden*); Camalodunum, the first Roman colony established in Britain (*Maldon*); and Colonia (*Colchester*).

The counties of Suffolk, Norfolk, Cambridge, and Huntingdon, were inhabited by the Sceni, called by Cæsar the Cænomagni. Their chief places were Villa Faustini (*St. Edmondbury*); Cambrelonium (*Brettenham*); Sitomagus (*Thetford*); Venta Scenorum (*Castle*); Sciani (*Saleborough*); Garienis Ostium (*Yarmouth*); Brannodium (*Brettenham*); Druobrivæ (*Domford*); and Camboritum (*Cambridge*).

Bordering on the Sceni were the Coutani, whose territories included Northamptonshire, Leicestershire, Rutlandshire, Lincolnshire, Nottinghamshire, and Derbyshire. They possessed the towns of Lindum (*Lincoln*); Tripontium (*Towcester*); Benaventa (*Northampton*); Rata (*Leicester*); Verometum (*Burrowhill*); Pontes (*Panton*); and Adelocum (*Idleton*).

Farther to the west were the Cornavii, possessing Warwickshire, Worcestershire, Staffordshire, Shropshire, and Cheshire. Their chief towns were Branovium (*Worcester*); Præsidium Avonæ (*Warwick*); Uriconium, their capital (*Wrockcester*), now a small village, but from its ruins rose the present town of Shrewsbury; Deva (*Chester*), a celebrated military station in the later ages of the empire; and Condaté (*Congleton*).

The principality of Wales, formerly comprehending the whole country beyond the Severn, was inhabited, in the Roman times, by the Silures, the Demetæ, and the Ordovices. The last-named tribe possessed North Wales, and long bade defiance to the Roman power in their mountain-fastnesses. The island of Mona (*Anglesey*), celebrated as the ancient seat of the Druids, belonged to the Ordovices.

A numerous and powerful people, called the Brigantes, or Brigæ, possessed Yorkshire, and the bishopric of Durham in the east, together with Lancashire, Cumberland, and Westmoreland, in the opposite direction. Their chief places were Danum (*Doncaster*), Eboracum (*York*), Mancunium (*Manchester*), and Aballaba (*Apelby*). The little town of Blatobulgium (*Bulness*) was generally regarded as the most remote limit of the Roman province of Britain. A little beyond it, some traces of the foundation of the great wall, built to restrain the incursions of the northern barbarians, may still be discovered at low water.

The county of Northumberland, and the south of Scotland, as far as the Firth of Forth, was inhabited by the Ottadini; west of these were the Selgovæ, or Damnii; and the inhabitants of the country beyond the Firths of Solway and the Forth were named Metæ and Caledonii, but, in a later age, the Picts and Scots. Juverna, or Hibernia (*Ireland*), was known only by name to the Romans.

Three walls were successively raised to check the incursions of the Picts and Scots by the emperors Adrian, Antoninus, and Severus. The last was the most important, according to Camden, who seems to have traced it with great care. It began at Blatobulgium (*Bulness*), on the Irish sea, kept along the side of Solway Firth, by Burgh-upon-sands, to Lugovallum (*Carlisle*), where it passed the Ituna (*Eden*). Thence it was carried on over the little rivers Cambeck, Living, and Poltrose, into the Northumbrian hills, along which it passed to the German ocean. This wall was about eight feet thick, and was protected by a ditch twelve yards broad.

When Britain was first visited by the Romans, the inhabitants had made considerable advances in civilisation. Their country was well peopled and stocked with cattle; their houses were as good as those of the Gauls, and they used iron and copper plates for money. They made little use of clothes, instead of which they painted and tattooed their skins. In war they made use of chariots, with sharp blades fixed to the axle-trees, which they drove at full speed against the hostile ranks. Their chief traffic was with the Gauls and the Phœnicians, who came to the Cassiterides (*Scilly islands*) for tin. Little is known respecting their religion, except that they were held in mental thraldom by a caste of priests named Druids, and that they were guilty of offering human sacrifices to their gods. Each tribe had its own king; but in cases of emergency, a common chief was elected, who possessed, however, little more than a nominal authority. The most singular monument of the Druids remaining is Stonehenge in Wiltshire, a circular edifice of enormous stones, which probably was the national temple. Britain was finally abandoned by the Romans in the early part of the fifth century.

Section IV.—*The Northern Provinces of the Empire.*

Italy, Greece, Sicily, Macedon, &c. having been already described in former chapters, we shall conclude the account of the Roman empire in Europe by a notice of the countries south of the Danube, which were formed into provinces during the reign of Augustus Cæsar.

Vindelicia was bounded on the north by the Danube, on

the east by the Ænus (*Inn*), on the west by Helvetia (*Switzerland*), and on the south by Rhætiâ: it derived its name from the river Vindo (the *Wert*). Its chief tribes were the Vindelicii and Brigantii. Two others are mentioned by Horace in his ode celebrating the conquest of this country by Tiberius and Drusus, addressed to Augustus:—

> Of late the Vindelicians knew
>   Thy skill in arms, and felt thy sword,
> When Drusus the *Genanni* slew,
>   And *Brenni* swift, a lawless horde.
> The towers which covered all around
>   The rugged Alps enormous height,
> By him were levell'd with the ground,
>   And more than once confess'd his might.

Their principal towns were Augusta Vindelicorum (*Augsburgh*) and Brigantia (*Bregenz*), neither of which were remarkable in ancient history. The principal rivers were the Vedo and the Lycus (*Lech*).

Rhætia nearly coincided with the country now called the territory of the Grisons; it had Vindelicia on the north, the Ænus (*Inn*) on the east, the chain of the Alps from Lacus Verbanus (*Lago Maggiore*) to Lacus Birgantinus (*Lake of Constance*) on the south, and Helvetia on the west. The principal tribe were the Rhæti, whom some have identified with the Rasena or ancient Etrurians. They were a brave, but cruel people; and when they invaded Italy in the reign of Augustus Cæsar, their ravages exceeded those that had been in earlier times perpetrated by the Gauls. Hence, Horace, in the ode from which we have already quoted, describes the Rhætians as the most formidable of the barbarian tribes subdued by the young Neros.

> The elder branch of Nero's blood,
>   Amid the battle's fiercest flame,
> With Rhætians huge the field bestrew'd,
>   O'ercome by thy auspicious name.

The chief towns were Curia (*Chur*), which became the capital of the province in the reign of the emperor Adrian, Veldidena (*Wilden*), and Tridentum (*Trent*).

Noricum, formerly a kingdom, but afterwards a Roman province, extended between the Danube and the Alpes Noriæ in the neighbourhood of Trent, from the Ænus (*Inn*) to Mons Cetius (*Kahlenberg*), and consequently included a great portion of modern Austria, the archbishopric of Saltzburgh, and all Styria and Carinthia. Its southern boundaries were the Julian Alps and the Savus (*Save*). Its chief cities were, in Noricum Ripense, or the part bordering on the Danube, Jovavum or Jovavia (*Saltzburgh*), Boiodurum (*Innstadt*), so named from the Boii, the most important of the Noric tribes; Lentia (*Lenz*) and Lauriacum (*Lorch*). In the interior, or Noricum Mediterraneum, we find Pons Æni (*Innspruck*), Viscelli (*Weltz*), Graviacii (*Gurch*), Aguntum (*Innichen*), Teurnia (*Villach*), and Solva, once the capital of the country, but long since buried in its ruins.

Pannonia was divided into Superior and Inferior. The former had the Danube on the east and north, the Arrabo (*Raab*) on the west, and the chain of Mons Cetius (*Kahlenberg*) on the south. It consequently comprehended Carniola, Croatia, Windesch, Mark, and part of Austria. Pannonia Inferior had the Arrabo on the north, the Danube on the east, and the Savus (*Save*) on the south. The chief cities were Segesta or Sescia (*Siseck*) on the Save; Amona (*Unterlaubach*), a Roman colony; Nauportum (*Oberlaubach*), upon the river Nauportus (*Laubach*); Vindoniana or Vindebona (*Vienna*), obscure in ancient times, but now the capital of the Austrian empire; Scarabantia (*Scarbing*); Mursa (*Esseg*); Sirmium (*Sirmich*), the ancient metropolis of Pannonia on the Save; and Taurunum (*Belgrade*), an important frontier-fortress both in ancient and modern times.

Mœsia was the name given to the country between the conflux of the Save and Danube and the Euxine sea. It was divided into two unequal portions, Superior and Inferior. Mœsia Superior was bounded on the north by the Danube, on the south by the Scordian mountains, on the west by Pannonia, and on the east by the river Cebrus (*Ischia*). Its chief cities were Singidunum (*Semlin*) and Naissus (*Nissa*). This province comprehended the countries now called Bosnia and Servia.

Mœsia Inferior, nearly coinciding with the modern Bulgaria, was bounded on the north by the Danube, on the west by the Cebrus, on the south by Mount Hæmus (*the Balkan*), and on the east by the Euxine sea. Its chief cities were Odessus (*Varna*) and Tomi (*Temeswar*). The part of Lower Mœsia bordering on the Euxine was frequently named Pontus; and hence, Tomi, the place of the poet Ovid's exile, is called a city of Pontus, though it did not belong to the kingdom of that name. Tomi is said to have derived its name from Medea's having cut her brother Absyrtus to pieces in that place,* in order that her father's pursuit of her might be delayed, whilst he gathered the scattered limbs of his child. To this Ovid alludes in a well-known distich :—

Tomi its name from horrid murder bore,
For there a brother's limbs a sister tore.

North of the Danube was the province of Dacia, annexed to the Roman empire in the reign of Trajan. Some geographers describe it loosely as including all the country between the Borysthenes (*Dnieper*) and the Danube; but its proper boundaries were Montes Carpatii (*the Krapack chain*) on the north, the Tibiscus (*Theiss*) on the west, the Hierasus (*Pruth*) on the east, and the Danube on the south. It consequently included Upper Hungary, Transylvania, Moldavia, and Wallachia. The inhabitants were called Getæ by the Greeks, and Daci by the Romans: they possessed no city of importance.

Thrace was long permitted to retain its own sovereigns, on the condition of acknowledging the supremacy of the Romans; but in the reign of the Emperor Claudian it was reduced to the form of a province. It was nearly enclosed by the chain of mount Hæmus and the sea. The principal cities of Thrace were the Greek colonies, which have already been noticed in a preceding chapter.

Illyricum is a name sometimes given to all the countries south of the Danube, but it is properly applied only to the strip of land on the north-east coast of the Adriatic, from the Rhætian Alps to the river Drinus (*Drino*), and easterly to the Savus

* From τεμνω, *to cut.*

(*Save*). Its inhabitants were remarkable for their skill in naval architecture; and infamous for their inveterate attachment to piracy. Their chief cities were Salona, Epidaurus (*Ragusa*), and Scodra (*Scutari*).

Section V.—*Asiatic and African Provinces.*

The Roman provinces in Anatolia were—1. Asia, as the Romans with proud anticipations named the first cession of country made to them east of the Ægean: 2. Bithynia, together with Paphlagonia and part of Pontus: and, 3. Cilicia, with Pisidia. These provinces were in general the most tranquil portion of the empire; and the most peaceful, if not the most happy, period in the history of Asia Minor was that during which it remained subject to Rome. The various divisions of Syria, Phœnicia, Palestine, and Commagene, for the purposes of government, cannot easily be enumerated. At first, several states were permitted to retain a qualified independence; but before the close of the first century of the Christian era, they were all absorbed in the empire. Armenia and Mesopotamia became provinces in the reign of Trajan, and part of Arabia paid nominal allegiance to that emperor; but these acquisitions were abandoned in the reign of his successor.

The African provinces were—1. Egypt, which became a province after the battle of Actium: 2. Cyrenaica, which soon followed the fate of Egypt; Crete was annexed to this government: 3. Numidia and Africa Proper, which were finally subdued by Julius Cæsar: and, 4. Mauretania, whose king was dethroned A.D. 41, and the country divided into two provinces, separated by the river Mulucha (*Mahala*), called Cæsariensis and Tingitania. The chief towns in Mauretania Cæsariensis were, Igilgilis (*Zezeli*), Saldæ (*Delluz*), Iomnium (*Algiers*), Rususcucum (*Koleah*), Cæsarea (*Teunez*), and Siga (*Sigale*). The most remarkable tribe was the Massæsyli, on the river Mulucha, near the sea-coast.

Mauretania Tingitana derived its name from its chief city Tingis (*Tangiers*), on the Fretum Gaditanum (*Straits of Gibraltar*). It contained also the towns and ports of Busadir (*Melilla*), and Abyla (*Ceuta*), in the Mediterranean. There were besides, on the Atlantic ocean, Zilis, or Julia Constantina (*Arzillo*); Banasa Valentia (*Mehedund*), and Sala (*Sallee*): but these were scarcely known to the Romans until a very late period of the empire. The Gætulians, first made known to the Romans during the Jugurthine war, never were subdued by their armies; but in later ages paid homage to the proconsul or præfect of Africa.

Though the Romans had thus succeeded in Asia to the great commercial marts of the Phœnicians, Greeks, and Egyptians, and had acquired in Africa the ancient stations of the Carthaginians, they made little or no effort to encourage traffic. They do not seem to have opened a single new route for trade; and under their government many of the ancient highways of commerce, particularly in Asia, fell into disuse. One principal cause of this was, the distance of Rome from the chief trading stations in the eastern seas, by which the attention of the ruling powers was withdrawn from the great abuses that prevailed in the provincial administration and colonial government. This appears evident from the vast improvement in the commerce between Europe and Asia, which took place immediately after the seat of government was transferred from Rome to Byzantium (*Constantinople*); and, however some politicians may be disposed to blame the division of the empire, a slight glance at the nations that pressed on the frontiers of the Roman dominions will shew that the interests and dangers of the eastern and western empires were so very different, that the course of policy which suited the one would be injurious to the other.

SECTION VI.—*The principal Nations on the Frontiers of the Empire.*

GERMANY was a name loosely given by the Romans to all the countries north of the Rhine and Danube. Sarmatia, in as uncertain a sense, was applied to the countries now called Poland and Lithuania; while the greater part of the vast dominions of Russia in Europe and Asia were included under the general name of Scythia, and were almost wholly unknown in ancient times. In the north-west of Europe the countries about the Sinus Codarius (*Baltic Sea*), though probably visited in very ancient times by the enterprising Phœnicians, remained unvisited, or at least unexplored, by the Romans, who were never remarkable for their zeal in maritime discovery. Indeed, they seem to have regarded Scandinavia, or Scandia (*Sweden*), Nerigon (*Norway*), and Eningia, or Furningia (*Finland*), as isles of the German Ocean. When Britain was circumnavigated, the Orcades (*Orkney islands*) were discovered; but, previous to that time, some indistinct account had been received of a distant island, named Thule, which some believe to have been one of the Zetland cluster, and others Iceland.

The Germans took their name from their own language, Gharmans signifying warlike men, or warriors; for, like most savage tribes, they principally prided themselves on their military virtues. They were called in the earliest ages Cimbri and Teutones by the Romans; but it is not easy to determine whether these may not have been very different races, accidentally united in a common migration. The Cimbri gave their name to the Chersones Cimbrica (*Jutland*); from that of the Teutones the modern names Teutschen and Dutch have manifestly been derived. A confederation of several tribes, formed in the third century, took the name of Allemanni, or All-mans, that is, complete men, from which the French at the present day call Germany Allemagne.

It would be impossible, within our limits, to enumerate all the tribes of ancient Germany; but a few of the principal may be noticed. On the east bank of the Albis (*Elbe*), between that river and the Vistula, were the Cimbri and Saxones, of whom the former were the more remarkable in ancient times, and the latter during the middle ages. West of the Albis were the Upper and Lower Chauci, divided from each other by the Visurgis (*Weser*); and the Ficsii, separated from the Chauci by the river Amasia (*Erus*), whose territory still preserves the name of Friezland. The Marcomanni anciently possessed all the country between the sources of the Rhenus (*Rhine*) and the Ister, or Danubius (*Danube*): they afterwards fixed themselves in Bohemia and Moravia, and also in part of Gaul, driving the Boii before them.

On this side of the Rhine, between that river and the Mosa (*Maese*), were the Ubii, who were invited by Agrippa to this country during the reign of Augustus. To commemorate this migration they named their capital Colonia Agrippina (*Cologne*), in honour of their patron. Higher up the Rhine, and beyond the Mosella (*Moselle*), were the Treviri, whose chief city was Augusta Trevirorum (*Triers*), and some minor tribes, possessing the city of Argentoratum, or Argentinæ (*Strasburgh*). The Hercynian forests and mountains, by which the Romans seem to have understood all the unexplored part of eastern Germany, appear to have been the original abode of the Quadi, the Suevi, and the Hermanduri, who became very formidable to the Romans in the age of the Antonines. The original seat of the Longobardi, celebrated in history under the name of Lombards, were at first settled on the upper part of the Elbe: they are said to have derived their national appellation from their "long barts," or spears; but others think that they were so called from the length of their beards, or from having been formed by a coalition of the Lingones and Bardi. Near the mouth of the Vistula were the Gepidæ; and it is supposed that the first seat of the warlike Burgundians was on the same river; but they, as well as the Semnones, had pushed forward to the Elbe in the first century of the Christian era. The Æstui, celebrated for their trade in amber, resided on the coasts of the Baltic sea.

Besides the Hercynian forest already mentioned, Germany contained Sylva Meliboca (*the Hartz*), Sylva Bacenia (*the Black Forest*), Sylva Sudeta (*the Thuringian Forest*), and Sylva Cæsia (*Forest of Teutoberg*). Most of the rivers have been already mentioned; but we must notice the northern embouchure of the Rhine, called Flavum Ostium (*Vlie*), in the territory of the Batavians; the Isela (*Isel*), separating the Bructeri from the Frisii; the Lupias (*Lippe*), in the territory of the Marsi; and the Viadrus (*Oder*), near whose source many authors place the original habitation of the Burgundians.

In considering the state of ancient Germany, it must be

borne in mind that the tribes frequently migrated from one quarter to another, especially after the second century of our era; and that the name of a principal tribe, such as that of the Suevi, was frequently given to a large confederation. This is particularly the case with the Franks (*free men*), who were not so much a tribe, as a union of several hordes determined to maintain their national independence.

The religion of the ancient Germans seems to have resembled that of the Gauls, except that it was rather more sanguinary, and that greater regard was paid to oracles and old prophetesses. Their chief deity was Odin, or Woden, their god of war, whose name is preserved in our Woden's day, or Wednesday. Their notion of future happiness was to sit for ever in Odin's presence, quaffing beer from the skulls of their enemies. This opinion is forcibly expressed in the death-song which Lodbrog sings for himself in the Edda:—

> With flashing swords our might we proved;
> But this my hearty laughter moved,
> That bliss eternal shall be mine
> Where the halls of Odin shine;
> To him, great sire, my deeds are known,
> For me he has prepared a throne,
> Where richest ale incessant flows
> In the hollow skulls of foes.
> The brave man never shrinks at death,
> Gladly I resign my breath;
> No regrets my soul appal
> As I haste to Odin's hall.

This is manifestly the creed of a savage race of warriors, and such all the Germans were; they took no pleasure but in military weapons; they never attended any festival or public assembly without arms; and so sacred was the sword among them, that their most solemn oath was taken by kissing its naked blade.

In Asia, the Roman empire was bounded by the wild tribes of the Caucasus, and the kingdoms of Armenia and Parthia. On the south it was limited by the unconquered Arabs, who defied every effort made to reduce them to obedience.

India became known to the Romans after the conquest of

Egypt; and some efforts were made to establish an extensive commerce with that empire by the route of the Red Sea, in the reigns of the later emperors. It was divided into India Proper, or India at this side of the Ganges, whose western coast (*Malabar*) appears to have been pretty well known; and India beyond the Ganges, which included the Burman empire and the peninsula of Malacca. The extreme south of the Indian peninsula, called Regio Pandionis (*the Carnatic*), was said to have been the seat of a powerful and enlightened dynasty, whose capital was Madura. Malacca was known as the Chersonesus Aurea (*golden peninsula*); the island of Ceylon was called Taprobane or Salice, and that of Sumatra, Labodii or Hordei.

The frontier races of the empire in Africa have been mentioned in the preceding section.

SECTION VII.—*Topography of the City of Rome.*

ROME was originally built in a square form, whence it was called Roma Quadrata, on the Palatine hill. When the city was founded, and when it was at any subsequent period enlarged, the first care was to mark out the Pomœrium, a consecrated space round the walls of the city on which it was unlawful to erect any edifice. This custom manifestly arose from the necessity of preventing besiegers from finding shelter near the fortifications; and in this, as in a thousand other instances, the early legislators gave utility the sanction of superstition. A set form was prescribed for marking the Pomœrium; a bullock and heifer were yoked to a bronze or copper ploughshare, and a furrow was drawn marking the course of the future wall. The plough was so guided that all the sods fell to the inside, and if any went in an opposite direction, care was taken that they should be turned into the proper way. As the plough was sacred, it would have been profanation if any thing impure passed over the ground which it had once touched; but as things clean and unclean must necessarily pass into a city, the plough came to a place where the builders designed to place a gate, it was taken up and carried to the spot where the wall was resumed. Hence the Latins named a gate *porta*, from the verb *portare*, to carry. The comitium, or place of public assembly, was next consecrated: the most remarkable part of this ceremony was the preparation of a vault, named *mundus*, in which were deposited the first-fruits of all things used to support life, and a portion of each colonist's native earth. To this structure many superstitious notions were attached: it was supposed to be the entrance to the invisible world; and it was opened three days in the year, with many solemn forms, to admit the spirits of the deceased.

It is probable that the first extension of the Pomœ'rium was occasioned by enclosing the Quirinal hill for the Sabines, when, under Tátius, they united themselves to the people of Rom'ulus. The next addition was the Cœlian hill, on which the followers of Cœ'les Viben'na, whoever that Etruscan adventurer may have been, erected their habitation. Tul'lus Hos'tilius enclosed the Viminal hill after the destruction of Al'ba, to which An'cus Mar'tius added the Aventine, which was regarded as the peculiar habitation of the plebeians. In the reign of the first Tar'quin, Rome was increased by the Esquiline and Capitoline; these completed the number of the seven hills for which the city was celebrated. At a much later period the Pincian and Vatican mounts were added; and these, with the Janic'ulum on the north bank of the Tiber, made the number ten.

An'cus Mar'tius was the first who fortified the city with outworks, especially by raising a castle and garrison on the Janic'ulum, which was connected with Rome by a wooden bridge (*pons sublicius*). But the elder Tar'quin was the first who beautified his capital with splendid buildings, not only ornamental, but useful. To him the great sewer by which the city was drained, whose vast proportions still claim admiration, is generally attributed.

Though Rome began to be more regularly built when it was restored after the departure of the Gauls, and many splendid

splendid edifices, both public and private, were erected, when wealth was so vastly increased as it must have been after the conquest of Carthage and Western Asia,—it could scarcely be called a splendid city before the reign of Augustus, who boasted that "he found it brick, and left it marble." When Corinth was subdued by Mummius, so little were the Romans acquainted with the fine arts, that many precious pieces of statuary were destroyed for the sake of their materials; but from that time taste was improved by a more constant intercourse with the Greeks, especially when Athens became the university of the empire. But the long civil wars between the aristocratic and democratic factions prevented the development of these improvements, until the battle of Actium gave Rome tranquillity and a master. In the days of its greatest prosperity the circumference of Rome, enclosed by walls, was about twenty miles; but there were also very extensive suburbs. The city had thirty gates, some authors say more, of which the most remarkable were the Tergeminal, the Carmental, the Triumphal, and the Naval; to which we may add the Capena, near the great aqueduct.

The most remarkable buildings were the amphitheatres, the capitol with its temples, the senate-house, and the forum.

The first amphitheatre was the Circus Maximus, erected by Tarquinius Priscus; but so enlarged by subsequent additions, that it was capable of containing two hundred thousand spectators. In the arena were exhibited the cruel fights of gladiators, in which the Romans took a pleasure equally infamous and extravagant, together vith races, exhibitions of strange animals, and combats of wild beasts. A still larger edifice was erected for the same purpose in the reign of Vespasian, whose massive ruins are called the Colosseum. Theatres, public baths, and buildings for the exhibition of naumachiæ, or naval combats, were erected by the emperors, who seemed anxious to compensate the people for the loss of their liberty by the magnificence of their public shows and entertainments.

The capitol was commenced on the Saturnian hill, which received the name Capitoline from a human head being found by the labourers digging the foundation, in the reign of Tarquinius Priscus. It was erected on the northern summit of the hill; the rocky eminence to the south was called the Tarpeian cliff, to commemorate the treason of Tarpeia; and public criminals were frequently executed by being precipitated from its peak. The temple of Jupiter Capitolinus was usually regarded as the national sanctuary of the Romans: it was begun by Tarquinius Priscus, and finished by Tarquinius Superbus, and it was almost yearly improved by the rich presents that successful generals and foreign princes, eager to conciliate the Romans, offered as votive gifts. Augustus alone presented gold and jewels exceeding five thousand pounds in value. During the civil wars between Marius and Sylla this temple was burnt to the ground; but it was rebuilt with greater splendour; and Cicero informs us, that the statue of Jupiter Capitolinus was erected on its pedestal at the very time that the conspiracy of Catiline was discovered. It was destroyed twice again during the reigns of Vespasian and Domitian, but was restored each time with additional splendour. The Sibylline books, and other oracles, supposed to contain important predictions respecting the fate of the city, were preserved in the sanctuary, under the charge of fifteen persons of the highest rank, called the Quindecemviri. Here, also, were preserved the chronological archives of the city. A nail was annually driven into the temple by the chief magistrate; and this curious custom is supposed to have been the first rude mode of marking the lapse of time.

There were several other temples on this hill, the most remarkable of which was that of Jupiter Feretrius, erected by Romulus, where the *spolia opima* were deposited. The *spolia opima* were the trophies presented by a Roman general who had slain the leader of the enemy with his own hand; they were only thrice offered, by Romulus, Cossus, and Marcellus. From the *feretrum*, or bier, on which these spoils were borne to the temple, the deity was called Feretrius.

The capitol was the citadel of Rome, except in the reign of Numa, when the Quirinal was chosen as the chief place of strength. This circumstance tends greatly to confirm Niebuhr's theory, that an ancient Sabine town, named Quirium, stood on that hill, which modern writers confounded with Cures:

perhaps the double-faced Janus, whose temple was closed during peace, was the symbol of the united cities, and the opening of the temple-gates was to enable the inhabitants of the one in time of war to assist the other.

In the valley between the Palatine and Capitoline hills was the forum, or place of public assembly and great market. It was surrounded with temples, halls for the administration of justice, called *basilicæ*, and public offices; it was also adorned with statues erected in honour of eminent warriors and statesmen, and with various trophies from conquered nations. Among these memorials of conquest were several *rostra*, or prows of ships taken at Antium, which were used to ornament the pulpits from which the magistrates and public orators harangued the general assemblies of the people: from this custom the phrase "to mount the rostrum" originated. In the middle of the forum was a drained marsh, called the Curtian Lake, to which a singular legend was attached. Traditions recorded that an immense chasm had suddenly opened in this place, which the augurs declared could not be closed until the most precious things in Rome were thrown into it. Curtius, a Roman knight, armed and mounted, leaped into the yawning pit, declaring that nothing was more valuable than courage and patriotism; after which it is added that the fissure closed. A much more probable account is, that the place derived its name from a Sabine general named Curtius, smothered there while the place was as yet a swamp.

In the forum was the celebrated temple of Janus, built entirely of bronze, supposed to have been erected during the reign of Numa. Its gates were only closed three times in eight centuries, so incessant were the wars in which the Romans were engaged. Not far from this was the temple of Concord, in which the senate frequently assembled: storks were encouraged to build in the roof of the edifice, on account of the social instincts attributed to those birds. In the same quarter of the city was the temple of Vesta, where a perpetual fire was maintained by the Vestal virgins: in it were said to be preserved the Palladium, or sacred image of Pallas Minerva, on which the fate of Troy depended; and other relics consecrated by superstition.

The senate-house was above the pulpits belonging to the public orators; it was said to have been originally erected by Tullus Hostilius: but the senate had several other places of meeting, frequently assembling in the temples. Near it was the comitium, or court in which the patrician *curiæ* were convened: it was not roofed until the end of the second Punic war, soon after which the *comitia curiata* fell gradually into disuse. This space, before it was covered, was called a temple; because *templum* properly signifies not merely an edifice, but an enclosure consecrated by the augurs. The principal theatres and public baths were erected in this vicinity.

The elections of magistrates, reviews of troops, and the census or registration of the citizens, were held in the Campus Martius, which was also the favourite exercise-ground of the young nobles. It was originally a large common, which had formed part of the estate of the younger Tarquin, and, being confiscated after the banishment of that monarch, was dedicated to the god of war, because the Romans believed Mars to be the father of their founder. It long remained unimproved; but in the reign of Augustus it began to be surrounded by several splendid edifices; ornamental trees and shrubs were planted in different parts, and porticoes erected, under which the citizens might continue their exercises in rainy weather. Most of these improvements were due to Marcus Agrippa, the best general and wisest statesman in the court of Augustus. He erected, near the Campus Martius, the celebrated Pantheon, or temple of all the gods; the most perfect and splendid monument of ancient Rome that has survived the ravages of time.* At present it is used as a Christian church, and is universally admired for its circular form, and the beautiful dome that forms its roof. Near the Pantheon were the gardens and public baths, which Agrippa, at his death, bequeathed to the Roman people.

* The Colosseum in the Regent's Park is built on the model of the Pantheon.

Perhaps no public edifices at Rome were more remarkable than the aqueducts for supplying the city with water. Pure streams were sought at a great distance, and conveyed in these artificial channels, supported by arches, many of which were more than a hundred feet high, over steep mountains, deep valleys, and, what was still more difficult, dangerous morasses, which less enterprising architects would have deemed insuperable. The first aqueduct was erected during the censorship of Appius Cæcus, about four hundred years after the foundation of the city; but under the emperors not fewer than twenty of these stupendous and useful structures were raised, which brought such an abundant supply of water to the metropolis, that rivers seemed to flow through the streets and sewers. Even at the present day, when only three of the aqueducts remain, after the lapse of centuries, the neglect of rulers, and the ravages of barbarians, no city in Europe has a better supply of wholesome water than Rome.

It would be tedious to enumerate all the public buildings that decorated " the Eternal City;" we may therefore conclude by observing, that Rome, when in the zenith of its glory, contained four hundred and twenty temples, five regular theatres, two amphitheatres, and seven circuses of vast extent: there were sixteen public baths, built of marble, and furnished with every convenience that could be desired. From the aqueducts a prodigious number of fountains were supplied, many of which were remarkable for their architectural beauty. The palaces, public halls, columns, porticoes, and obelisks, were without number; and to these must be added the triumphal arches erected by the later emperors.

The public roads in the various parts of the empire, but more especially in Italy, though less ostentatious than the aqueducts, were not inferior to them in utility and costliness. Of these the most remarkable was the Appian road, from Rome to Brundusium, through the Pomptine marshes, which were kept well drained during the flourishing ages of the empire, but by subsequent neglect became a pestilential swamp. This road extended three hundred and fifty miles, and was paved through its entire length with enormous square blocks of hard stone.

Nineteen centuries have elapsed since it was formed, and yet many parts of it still appear nearly as perfect as when it was first made.

Rome was inferior to Athens in architectural beauty, but it far surpassed it in works of public utility. Every succeeding emperor deemed it necessary to add something to the edifices that had been raised for the comfort and convenience of the citizens: even after the seat of government had been transferred to Constantinople, we find the son of Constantine evincing his gratitude for the reception he met with in the ancient capital, by sending thither two magnificent obelisks from Alexandria in Egypt.

CHAPTER XVII.

HISTORY OF THE ROMAN EMPIRE.

SECTION I.—*The Reigns of the family of the Cæsars.*

FROM B.C. 30 TO A.D. 96.

THOUGH the battle of Actium made Octavius Cæsar sole sovereign of the empire, the forms of the republic were faithfully preserved; the senate sat as a council of state, and, though little weight was attached to its deliberations, the freedom of speech and comment preserved the government from sinking into absolute despotism. With supreme power, Octavius, or Augustus, as he was about this time named by the senate, assumed an entirely new character; the cruelty with which he may be justly reproached in the early part of his career disappeared; he became a mild and merciful ruler, truly anxious to ensure the happiness of the people entrusted to his charge. Under such a benignant administration, the Romans ceased to regret their ancient freedom, if, indeed, such a term can be applied to the oppressive government established by the aristocracy during the preceding century; and before the close of the first emperor's reign, the last traces of the republican spirit had disappeared. It is said that Augustus at first wished to resign his power, after the example of Sylla; but was dissuaded by his friends Agrippa and Mecænas, who represented to him, with great truth, that the Roman state could no longer be governed by its old constitution, and that he would retire only to make room for another master. He went through the form, however, of an abdication in the senate; but, on the urgent request of that body, he resumed his sway: instead, however, of taking the supreme authority for life, he would only accept it for a term of ten years. This example was followed by the succeeding emperors, and gave rise to the *sacra decennalia*, festivals celebrated at each renewal of the imperial authority.

Amid all the adulations of the senate and people, Augustus

felt that it was to the army he was indebted for empire, and therefore exerted himself diligently to attach the soldiers to his interest. He dispersed his veterans over Italy in thirty-two colonies, dispossessing, in many places, the ancient inhabitants to make room for these settlers. He maintained seventeen legions in Europe, eight on the Rhine, four on the Danube, three in Spain, and two in Dalmatia. Eight more were kept in Asia and Africa: so that the standing army of the empire exceeded one hundred and seventy thousand men. Twelve cohorts, amounting to about ten thousand men, were quartered in Rome and its vicinity; nine of these, called the prætorian bands, were intended to protect the emperor's person, the others were destined for the guard of the city. These household troops became afterwards the authors of many changes and revolutions, until they were all dismissed by Constantine the Great (A. D. 312). Two powerful fleets were established in the Italian seas; one at Ravenna, to guard the Adriatic, the other at Misenum, to protect the western Mediterranean. It is calculated that the revenues of the empire at this time exceeded forty millions sterling; but this sum was not more than sufficient to defray the expenses of the civil, naval, and military establishments, and of the public works undertaken to adorn the metropolis.

Some disturbances in Spain and Gaul induced the emperor to cross the Alps and Pyrenees: he subdued the Cantabrians, who inhabited the province now called Biscay, (a country whose mountains and defiles have always proved formidable obstacles to an invading army,) and the Asturians. To restrain these tribes in future, he erected several new fortified cities, of which the most remarkable were Cæsarea Augusta (*Saragossa*) and Augusta Emerita (*Merida*), so called because it was colonised by the veteran soldiers (*emeriti*). While resting at Tarraco (*Tarragona*) from the fatigues of his campaign, Augustus received ambassadors from the most remote nations, the Scythians, the Sarmatians, the Indians, and even the Seres, who inhabited northern China.

On his recovery from a fit of illness, which spread universal alarm throughout the empire, the senate conferred the tribuneship for life upon Augustus, which rendered his person sacrosanct. This dignity was henceforth annexed to the empire, and consequently all attempts against the life of the sovereign became high treason (*læsa majestas*). At the same time he declined the title of dictator, which had been rendered odious by the cruelties of Sylla. Having made a tour in the east of the empire, he was overwhelmed with adulations by the degenerate Greeks (B.C. 20); but the honour most gratifying to him and the Roman people was the restoration of the standards that had been taken from Crassus. On his return to Italy, he drove back the Rhætians, who had invaded the peninsula, and entrusted their subjugation to Tiberius and Drusus Nero, his stepsons, youths of great promise and valour. They succeeded in conquering Vindelicia, Rhætia, and Noricum; but their efforts to subdue Germany were baffled by the undaunted valour of the native tribes, and the great difficulties of the country, whose forests and marshes rendered discipline unavailing.

When the second decennial period of the imperial authority terminated, Augustus, harassed by domestic calamities, as well as the cares of empire, seemed really anxious to resign, and enjoy the quiet of domestic life; but the character of Tiberius, now generally regarded as his successor, gave so much alarm to the senate and people, that they cordially joined in supplicating the emperor to continue his reign. The greatest calamity he had to endure was the disgraceful conduct of his daughter Julia, whose scandalous debaucheries filled Rome with horror: she and the partners of her crimes were banished to various parts of the empire, and some of her paramours were put to death.

When peace was established in every part of the Roman dominions, Augustus closed the temple of Janus, and issued a decree for a general census, or enrolment, of all his subjects. It was at this period that Jesus Christ was born; and thus, literally, was his advent the signal of "on earth peace, and good will towards men."

The great prosperity of the reign of Augustus was first interrupted by the rebellion of the Germans, which the extortions of Quintilius Varus provoked. Arminius, a young prince of the Catti, united his countrymen in a secret confederacy; and then, pretending friendship to Varus, conducted him into the depths of a forest, where his troops could neither fight nor retreat. In this situation Arminius attacked the Romans, from whose camp he stole by night, and so harassed them that most of the officers slew themselves in despair (A.D. 10). The legionaries, thus left without leaders, were cut to pieces; and thus the Romans received the greatest overthrow that they had suffered since the defeat of Crassus. When the news of this calamity was brought to Rome, every body expected that the Germans would immediately cross the Rhine, and advance against the city. Augustus, though overwhelmed with sorrow, made every exertion to allay the general consternation: he sent his son-in-law and heir, Tiberius, to guard the Rhine; but he prohibited him from following the wild tribes to their fastnesses. For several months the emperor abandoned himself to transports of grief, during which he frequently exclaimed, "Varus, restore me my legions!" and he observed the fatal day as a mournful solemnity until his death. This event probably tended to hasten his dissolution: he was seized with a dangerous attack of illness at Naples, and as he was returning home to the capital, the disease compelled him to stop at Nola in Campania, where he expired (A.D. 14). It was currently reported that the empress Livia accelerated his death by administering poisoned figs, in order to secure the succession for Tiberius.

Tiberius Claudius Nero, or, as he was called after his adoption, Augustus Tiberius Cæsar, commenced his reign by procuring the murder of young Agrippa, grandson of the late emperor, whom he dreaded as a formidable rival. As soon as his accession was known at Rome, the consuls, senators, and knights, ran headlong into slavery, pretending to hail Tiberius with extravagant joy, whilst they professed equally extravagant sorrow for the loss of Augustus. Tiberius met them with duplicity equal to their own: he affected to decline the sovereign power; but after long debates, allowed himself to be won over by the general supplications of the senators. Having bound himself by oath never to depart from the regulations of his predecessor, he exerted himself to win the affections, or, rather, disarm the suspicions, of the virtuous Germanicus, whom Augustus had compelled him to declare his heir. But the jealousies of the emperor were greatly aggravated by a mutiny of the troops in Germany, who offered to raise Germanicus to the throne; and though he firmly refused and severely rebuked their disloyalty, yet Tiberius from thenceforth was resolved upon his destruction. The glory which the young prince acquired in several successful campaigns against the Germans, at length induced the emperor to recall him to Rome, under the pretence of rewarding him with a triumph. But Tiberius soon became anxious to remove from Rome a person whose mildness and virtue were so powerfully contrasted with his own tyranny and debauchery: he appointed him governor of the eastern provinces; but at the same time he sent Piso, with his infamous wife Plancina, into Syria, secretly instructing them to thwart Germanicus in all his undertakings. The wicked pair obeyed these atrocious commands; and the brave prince, after undergoing many mortifications, at last sunk under them. Attacked by a severe disease, aggravated by suspicions of Piso's treachery, whom he believed to have compassed his death by magic or by poison, he sent for his wife Agrippina, and having besought her to humble her haughty spirit for the sake of their children, expired, to the general grief of the empire (A.D. 19). His ashes were brought to Rome by Agrippina; and though she arrived in the very middle of the Saturnalia, the mirth usual at that festival was laid aside, and the whole city went into mourning.

In the early part of his reign Tiberius had affected to imitate the clemency of Augustus; but he soon began to indulge his natural cruelty, and many of the most eminent nobles were put to death under pretence of high treason. The emperor's depravity was exceeded by that of his minister, the infamous Sejanus, whose name has passed into a proverb. This ambitious favourite secretly aspired at the empire, and applied himself to win the favour of the prætorian guards: he is also accused of having procured the death of Drusus, the emperor's son, and of having tried to destroy Agrippina and her children.

But his most successful project was the removal of Tiberius from Rome, persuading him that he would have more freedom to indulge his depraved passions in Campania than in the capital. The emperor chose for his retreat the little island of Capreæ, where he wallowed in the most disgusting and unnatural vices; while Sejanus, with an entire army of spies and informers, put to death the most eminent Romans, after making them undergo the useless mockery of a trial. Tiberius, however, soon began to suspect his minister, and secret warnings were given him of the dangerous projects that Sejanus had formed. It was apparently necessary, however, to proceed with caution, and the emperor felt his way by withdrawing some of the honours he had conferred. Finding that the people gave no signs of discontent, Tiberius sent the commander of the prætorian guards privately to Rome with a letter to the senate, instructing him to inform Sejanus that it contained an earnest recommendation to have him invested with the tribunitian power. The minister, deceived by this hope, hastily convened the senate, and on presenting himself to that body, was surrounded by a horde of flatterers, congratulating him on his new dignity. But when the fatal epistle was read, in which he was accused of treason, and orders given for his arrest, he was immediately abandoned, and those who had been most servile in their flatteries became loudest in their invectives and execrations. A hurried decree passed condemning him to death, and was put in execution the very same day: a general slaughter of his friends and relations followed; his innocent children, though of very tender years, were put to death with circumstances of great barbarity; and the numerous statues that had been erected to his honour were broken to pieces by the fickle multitude. This memorable example of the instability of human grandeur is powerfully described by Juvenal, in his satire on the Vanity of Human Wishes. The passage is thus translated by Dryden:—

> Some ask for envy'd power, which public hate
> Pursues and hurries headlong to their fate;
> Down go the titles, and the statue crown'd
> Is by base hands in the next river drown'd.

The guiltless horses and the chariot-wheel
The same effects of vulgar fury feel:
The smith prepares his hammer for the stroke,
While the lung'd bellows hissing fire provoke;
Sejanus, almost first of Roman names,
The great Sejanus, crackles in the flames!
Form'd in the forge, the pliant brass is laid
On anvils; and of head and limbs are made
Pans, cans, and gridirons, a whole kitchen trade.
    Adorn your doors with laurel; and a bull,
Milk-white and large, lead to the capitol;
Sejanus, with a rope, is dragg'd along,
The sport and laughter of the giddy throng!
"Good Lord," they cry, "what Ethiop lips he bears!
See what a hang-dog face the scoundrel wears!
By Jove, I never could endure his sight;—
But, say, how came his monstrous crimes to light?
What is the charge, and who the evidence?
The saviour of the nation and the prince?"
"Nothing of this; but our old Cæsar sent
A tedious letter to his parliament."—
"Nay, sirs, if Cæsar wrote, I ask no more;
He 's guilty, and the question 's out of door."
How goes the mob?—for that's a mighty thing,—
When the king 's trump, the mob are for the king:
They follow fortune, and the common cry
Is still against the rogue condemn'd to die.
    But the same very mob, that rascal crowd,
Had cry'd Sejanus, with a shout as loud,
Had his designs, by fortune's favour blest,
Succeeded, and the prince's age opprest.

The cruelty of Tiberius was increased tenfold after the removal of his favourite: the least circumstance rendered him suspicious; and when once a noble was suspected, his fate was sealed. In all his extravagances he was supported by the servile senate; and this body, once so independent, never ventured even to remonstrate against his sanguinary decrees. At length, continued debauchery undermined the emperor's constitution; but, with the usual weakness of licentious sovereigns, he endeavoured to disguise the state of his health, not merely from his court, but his physicians. At length, finding death approach very rapidly, he bequeathed the empire to Caius

Caligula, the only surviving son of his nephew and victim, Germanicus. It is said that he chose this prince, though well aware of his natural depravity, that his own reign might be regretted, when contrasted with the still more sanguinary rule of his successor. Soon after having signed his will, Tiberius was seized with a fainting fit, and the courtiers believing him dead, hasted to offer their homage to Caligula; but the emperor rallied, and there was reason to fear his vengeance. Macro, the commander of the guards, averted the danger by smothering the weak old man with a weight of coverings, under pretence of keeping him warm (A.D. 37). In this reign, though the forms of the constitution were retained, its spirit and substance were completely altered; the government became a complete despotism; and the only use of the senate was to register the edicts of the sovereign. While Tiberius was emperor, Jesus Christ was crucified in Judæa, under the proprætorship of Pontius Pilate (A.D. 33). It is said, but on very doubtful authority, that Tiberius having received an account of his miracles, wished to have him enrolled amongst the gods, but that his designs were frustrated by the opposition of the senate.

Caius, surnamed Caligula, from the military boots (*caligæ*) which he was accustomed to wear, was received, on his accession, with the utmost enthusiasm by both the senate and the people, on account of the great merits of his father Germanicus. He began his reign by liberating all the state prisoners, and dismissing the whole horde of spies and informers whom Tiberius had encouraged. By these and other similar acts of generosity, he became so popular, that when he was attacked by sickness, the whole empire was filled with sorrow, and innumerable sacrifices were offered in every temple for his recovery. This sickness probably disordered his brain, for in his altered conduct after his restoration to health there appears fully as much insanity as wickedness. Young Tiberius, whom he had adopted, was his first victim; he then ordered all the prisoners in Rome to be thrown to wild beasts, without a trial. But Caligula was not satisfied with simple murder; it was his fiendish pleasure to witness the sufferings of his victims, and protract their tortures, in order that they might, as he said, feel themselves dying. Finding no one dare to oppose his sanguinary caprices, he began to regard himself as something more than a mere mortal, and to claim divine honours; and, finally, he erected a temple to himself, and instituted a college of priests to superintend his own worship. A less guilty but more absurd proceeding, was the reverence he claimed for his favourite horse Incitatus, whom he frequently invited to dine at the imperial table, where the animal fed on gilt oats, and drank the most costly wines from jewelled goblets. It is even said, that nothing but his death prevented him from raising this favoured steed to the consulship. While the whole city was scandalised by his outrageous licentiousness, men were suddenly astounded to hear that the emperor had resolved to lead an army against the Germans in person, and the most extensive preparations were made for his expedition. As might have been expected, the campaign was a mere idle parade; but Caligula, notwithstanding, claimed the most extravagant honours; and finding the senate slower in adulation than he expected, seriously contemplated the massacre of the entire body. At length the Romans became weary of a monster equally wicked and ridiculous; a conspiracy was formed for his destruction; and he was slain in one of the passages of the circus by Chærea, the captain of the prætorian guards (A.D. 40). His body lay a long time exposed, but was finally interred like that of a slave: his wife and infant child were murdered by the conspirators, who dreaded future vengeance.

Claudius, the brother of Germanicus and uncle of the late emperor, a prince of weak intellect, was raised to the throne by the conspirators, whose choice was sanctioned by the senate. The unfortunate idiot thus placed at the head of the empire, was, during his entire reign, the puppet of wicked and worthless favourites, among whom the most infamous were the empresses Messalina and Agrippina, the eunuch Posides, and the freedmen Pallas and Narcissus. His reign commenced with the punishment of those who had conspired against Caligula: they were slain, not for the crime they had committed, but because they were suspected of a design to restore the ancient constitution. Notwithstanding his weakness, Claudius undertook an expedition into Britain, where the native tribes were wasting their strength in mutual wars, and he commenced a series of campaigns which eventually led to the complete subjugation of the southern part of the island. The senate granted him a magnificent triumphal procession on his return; and Messalina, whose infidelities were now notorious, accompanied the emperor in a stately chariot during the solemnity. The cruelty of the empress was as great as her infamy: at her instigation Claudius put to death some of the most eminent nobles, and the confiscation of their fortunes supplied her with money to lavish on her paramours. At length she proceeded to such an extravagant length, that she openly married Silius, one of her adulterers; and Narcissus, whom she had displeased, gave the emperor private information of her guilt, and she was slain in the gardens that had been the chief theatre of her crimes.

Soon after the death of Messalina, Claudius married his niece Agrippina, the widow of Domitius Ahenobarbus, by whom she had one son, originally called after his father, but better known in history by the name of Nero. The new empress did not, like her predecessor, render the state subservient to her amours, but she grasped at power to indulge her insatiable avarice, boundless ambition, and unparalleled cruelty. She ruled the emperor and the empire, appeared with him in the senate, sat on the same throne during all public ceremonies, gave audience to foreign princes and ambassadors, and even took a share in the administration of justice. She at length prevailed upon Claudius to adopt her child Domitius (Nero), and constitute him heir of the sovereignty, in preference to his own son Britannicus. But Claudius shewing some signs of an intention to change the succession again, Agrippina procured him to be poisoned by his favourite eunuch and the state physician (A. D. 54). Having previously gained over Burrhus, the captain of the prætorian guards, to her interest, the empress concealed her husband's death until she had secured the army in favour of her son, rightly judging that the senate would confirm the choice of the soldiers.

Nero Claudius Cæsar had been nurtured in the midst of crimes, and educated for the stage rather than the state; he was still a youth of seventeen, and he looked on the empire as only an extensive field for the indulgence of his passions. He soon became weary of his mother's imperious rule; and Agrippina, finding herself neglected, threatened to restore the crown to Britannicus. This was the signal for the destruction of that young prince; poison was administered to him by one of the emperor's emissaries, and a few hours after his death his body was borne to the pile; for so little care had the emperor of concealing his share in the murder, that the preparations for the prince's funeral were made before the poison was administered. An infamous woman, Poppæa Sabina, who had abandoned her husband to live in adultery with the emperor, stimulated Nero to still greater crimes. Persuaded that during the lifetime of Agrippina she could not hope to remove Octavia, Nero's wife, and become herself a partner in the empire, she urged her paramour, by every means in her power, to the murder of his mother. Nero himself was anxious to remove one whom he so greatly feared; but he dreaded the resentment of the Romans, who, in spite of her crimes, reverenced the last representative of the family of Germanicus. After various attempts to destroy her secretly had failed, a body of armed men were sent to her house, and she was murdered in her bed. A laboured apology for this matricide was soon after published, which, it is painful to learn, was composed by the philosopher Seneca.

The death of Burrhus, whether by poison or disease is uncertain, led to a great deterioration of Nero's character; for the influence of that able statesman had restrained the emperor from many extravagancies in which he was anxious to indulge. Tigellinus, a wretch infamous for all the crimes that are engendered by cruelty and lust, became the new minister; and Nero no longer kept within the bounds of ordinary decency. Seneca was banished from the court; the empress Octavia was divorced, and afterwards murdered; finally, Poppæa was publicly married to the emperor. A tour through Italy gave Nero an opportunity of appearing as a singer on the stage at Naples, and he was excessively gratified by the applause with which the Neapolitans and some Alexandrians fed his vanity. Soon after his return to Rome, a dreadful conflagration, which lasted nine days, destroyed the greater part of the city; and it was generally believed that the fire had been kindled by the emperor's orders. Upon the ruins of the demolished city Nero erected his celebrated golden palace, which seems to have been more remarkable for its vast extent, and the richness of the materials used in its construction, than for the taste or beauty of the architectural design. To silence the report of his having caused the late calamity, Nero transferred the guilt of the fire to the new sect of the Christians, whose numbers were rapidly increasing in every part of the empire. A cruel persecution commenced; first, all who openly acknowledged their connexion with the sect were arrested and tortured; then, from their extorted confessions, thousands of others were seized and condemned, not for the burning of the city, but on the still more ludicrous charge of hatred and enmity to mankind. Their death and torture were aggravated with cruel derision and sport; for they were either covered with the skins of wild beasts, and torn to pieces by devouring dogs, or fastened to crosses, or wrapped up in combustible garments, that, when the daylight failed, they might serve, like torches, to illuminate the darkness of the night. For this tragical spectacle Nero lent his own gardens, and exhibited at the same time the public diversions of the circus; sometimes driving a chariot in person, and sometimes standing among the people as a spectator, in the habit of a charioteer.

The extravagant expenses of the golden palace, the restoration of the city, the emperor's luxuries, and the entertainments given to the people, exhausted the exchequer, and led to a system of plunder and extortion which nearly caused the dissolution of the empire. Not only Italy, but all the provinces, the several confederate nations, and all the cities that had the title of free, were pillaged and laid waste. The temples of the gods and the houses of individuals were equally stripped of their treasures; but still enough could not be obtained to support the emperor's boundless prodigality. At length a conspiracy was formed for his destruction by Cneius Piso, in which the greater part of the Roman nobility engaged. It was accidentally discovered; and Nero eagerly seized such a pretence for giving loose to his sanguinary dispositions. Among the victims were the philosopher Seneca, the poet Lucan, Piso, and most of the leading nobles. In the midst of the massacres Nero appeared on the stage as a candidate for the prize of music, which of course he obtained. About the same time he killed the empress Poppæa by kicking her while pregnant.

It may appear strange that such repeated atrocities should not have driven the Roman people to revolt; but the lower classes felt nothing of the imperial despotism, and did not sympathise with the calamities of the nobles, because the ancient oppressions of the aristocracy were still remembered. They were, besides, gratified by a monthly distribution of corn, by occasional supplies of wine and meat (*congiaria et eviscerationes*), and by the magnificent shows of the circus (*munera*). In fact, the periods of tyranny were the golden days of the poor; and Nero was far more popular with the rabble than any statesman or general of the republic had ever been.

Not satisfied with his Italian fame, Nero resolved to display his musical skill at the Olympic games, and for this purpose passed over into Greece. The applauses he received in this tour from the spectators so gratified him, that he declared "the Greeks alone perfectly understand music." He transmitted a particular account of his victories to the senate, and ordered thanksgivings and sacrifices to be offered for them in every temple throughout the empire. That no monuments of other victors might remain, he commanded all their statues to be pulled down, dragged through the streets, and either dashed to pieces or thrown into the common sewers. While he was thus engaged, the dreadful rebellion, which destroyed the Jewish nation, commenced in Palestine: Cestius Gallus, the governor of Syria, having been defeated in an attempt to besiege Jerusalem, the conduct of the war was entrusted to the celebrated Vespasian. Though Nero had been greatly delighted by the excessive adulations of the Achæans, he did not abstain from plundering their country; and Achaia suffered more from his peaceful visit than from the open war of Mummius or Sylla.

Soon after the emperor's return to Rome, formidable insurrections burst forth in the western provinces, occasioned by the excessive taxation to which they were subjected. Julius Vindex, descended from the ancient kings of Aquitain, was the first to raise the standard of revolt in Celtic Gaul, of which he was governor. Galba soon after was proclaimed emperor in Spain by his soldiers, and was supported by Otho, the governor of Lusitania. Nero was not much disturbed by the rebellion of Vindex; but the hostility of Galba filled him with consternation. He was, however, consoled for a time by the intelligence of the defeat of the Gauls, who were so completely overthrown by Virginius, the imperial lieutenant, that Vindex slew himself in despair. Galba would now have been ruined, had not Nymphidius, whom Nero had appointed the colleague of Tigellinus, seduced the prætorian guards to renounce their allegiance. The emperor was immediately abandoned by all his ministers and servants; he fled from Rome, and sought refuge in the house of Phaon, one of his freedmen. Here he soon learned that he had been declared an enemy to the state, and sentenced to be executed according to ancient custom (*more majorum*). Inquiring the nature of this punishment, he was informed that he was to be placed in a pillory, and beaten to death with rods (A.D. 68). At the prospect of such a cruel fate he was filled with horror, and declared that he would commit suicide; but his courage failed when he was about to use the dagger. At length, hearing the galloping of the horse sent to arrest him, he requested the aid of his freedman Epaphroditus, and received a mortal wound. He was not quite dead when the centurion, sent by the senate, arrived, and endeavoured to stop the blood. Nero, looking at him sternly, said, "It is too late. Is this your fidelity?" and soon after expired. His body was interred privately, but honourably; and many of the lower ranks, whose favour he had won by his extravagant liberalities, lamented his loss, honoured his memory, and brought flowers to decorate his tomb.

During this reign the provinces were harassed by frequent revolts: in addition to those we have already noticed, it may be necessary to mention the revolt of the Iceni in Britain, under the command of their heroic queen Boadicea. She took up arms to revenge the gross insults and injuries she had received; falling unexpectedly on the Roman colonies and garrisons, she destroyed a great number both of them and their allies; and could she have secured the co-operation of all the native tribes, might have liberated her country. This dangerous insurrection was quelled by Suetonius Paulinus, who added the island of Anglesey to the Roman dominions; thus taking from the Druids, the secret instigators of resistance to all foreign power, the great centre both of their religion and their influence.

The family of the Cæsars, properly speaking, ended with Caligula; but as both Nero and Claudius were maternally descended from Augustus, they are usually reckoned among the members of the Julian, or first imperial house. Its extinction, notwithstanding the vices of its later members, was a serious calamity to the empire; it led to a series of sanguinary wars, arising from disputed successions, during which the supreme authority of the state was wrested equally from the emperors and senate by a licentious soldiery.

Section II.—*From the Extinction of the Julian to that of the first Flavian Family.*

FROM A. D. 68 TO A. D. 96.

Servius Sulpitius Galba, universally acknowledged seventh emperor after the death of Nero, was descended from an illustrious family that had been eminently distinguished for warlike achievements during the later ages of the republic. He was now in the seventy-third year of his age, and, on account of his infirmities, travelled very slowly towards Rome. Nymphidius took advantage of this delay to make a struggle for empire by bribing the prætorian guards; but his conduct during the reign of Nero had rendered him so deservedly unpopular, that he was murdered by the very soldiers who had taken his money. This rash conspiracy induced Galba to sully the commencement of his reign by unseasonable severities, which gave the more offence to his subjects, as they had not been anticipated. It was soon discovered that the new emperor, however virtuous himself, was the tool of unworthy favourites, who, under the sanction of his name, plundered the people, and deprived the soldiers of their usual donative. A revolt of the legions in Upper Germany induced Galba to nominate a successor; he chose Cneius Piso, descended from the old triumvirs Crassus and Pompey, who was greatly esteemed for his talents, virtues, and engaging manners. But this appointment gave great offence to Otho, who had been foremost to espouse the cause of Galba: taking advantage of the discontent of the prætorian guards, he went to their camp, and easily induced these turbulent warriors to proclaim him emperor. Galba prepared to make a vigorous struggle for his crown, but his soldiers refused to obey the orders of their commander; and when he was borne in a litter to enforce obedience, those who carried him, terrified by the tumult, threw down the chair, and the aged emperor, thus lying helpless, was slain by one of the veterans (A. D. 69). His body was treated with great indignity by the factious troops; Piso, his appointed successor, was murdered; and the prætorian guards threatened destruction to all who did not acquiesce in their decision.

Otho, thus raised to the empire, was, during his brief reign, a passive instrument in the hands of the licentious soldiers. Scarcely had he been fixed upon the throne, when he found that he would have to struggle for empire with a formidable rival, Vitellius, the commander of the legions in lower Germany. Valens and Cæcina joined the usurper with numerous forces, and intelligence soon arrived of their advance towards Italy through Gaul. Their arrival in Italy filled Rome with consternation, which the licentious indolence in which Otho indulged by no means tended to abate. But on the near approach of danger, the emperor laid aside his pleasures and debaucheries, making the most vigorous preparations for resistance. Most of the provinces declared in his favour; and could he have protracted the war, he would probably have preserved his crown. But the prætorian guards, wearied of the unusual hardships of a campaign, and eager to return to the pleasures of the capital, demanded to be led instantly against the enemy. Otho withdrew to a place of safety, but ordered his generals to give battle without delay. The decisive engagement was fought at Bedriacum, near the banks of the Po: early in the day, the prætorian guards, attacked in flank by a Batavian column, fled in disorder, and threw the rest of the army into confusion. This unexpected disaster gave Vitellius an easy victory; and following up his success, he took possession of the imperial camp. Otho having learned the news of the battle, convened the rest of his soldiers, thanked them for their fidelity, and intimated his resolution not to permit his life to be the cause of further bloodshed. That night he committed suicide, having only reigned three months. He was honourably interred by his soldiers, who shewed sincere sorrow for his loss.

Vitellius was a slave to gluttony and debauchery; he received very coldly the congratulations of the senate on his victory and accession, and he was reluctant to expose himself to the dangers of the turbulences that the soldiers, both of his and Otho's army, excited in Italy. At length he made his public entrance into Rome, and endeavoured to win the favour of the populace by large donatives and expensive entertainments in the circus. Intrusting all the power of the state to unworthy favourites, he devoted himself wholly to the pleasures of the table, on which he squandered nearly seven millions of money in less than four months. Nothing, however, gave greater scandal to the higher ranks of the senators, than his solemnising, with great pomp, the obsequies of Nero, and compelling the Augustal priests, an order, consecrated by Tiberius for superintending the religious rites of the Julian family, to attend at that ceremony. While he was thus insulting his subjects, and wasting the wealth of the empire, fortune, or rather Providence, was raising him up a competitor in a distant province. Vespasian was carrying on the war against the Jews with great success when he heard of the death of Nero, and the election of Galba: he sent his son Titus to present his allegiance to the new emperor; but ere he could reach

Italy, Galba was no more, and Otho and Vitellius were contending for the empire. Titus returned to his father, whom he found ready to swear allegiance to Vitellius, though the army wished him to declare himself emperor. Vespasian's reluctance, whether real or affected, was overcome by the exhortations of Mucianus, governor of Syria, and the tributary monarchs of the east, whose friendship he had won by his justice and moderation. No sooner did he commence his march towards Europe, than the legions quartered in Illyricum and Pannonia declared in his favour; nor was there any province on which Vitellius could rely for support except Africa. Primus and Varus, at the head of the Illyrian armies, crossed the Alps, and made themselves masters of Verona, and at the same time the fleet at Ravenna declared in favour of Vespasian. Cæcina, who had the principal share in raising Vitellius to the throne, followed the same course; but his soldiers disapproved his conduct, and put him in irons. Primus, advancing southwards, encountered the forces of Vitellius near Cremona, and totally routed them, after a battle which lasted the entire day and a great part of the following night. The city of Cremona, after a desperate resistance, was taken by storm, and the greater part of the inhabitants put to the sword. Valens, who went to raise an army in the western provinces to support the emperor, was taken prisoner, upon which Gaul, Spain, and Britain, declared in favour of Vespasian.

Vitellius at first refused to believe the evil tidings that reached him from every quarter; but at length, on the near approach of danger, he hasted to secure the passes of the Apennines. Primus, however, by a hazardous march through the snow, forced his way over the mountains, and sent the head of Valens to be displayed to the imperial army, as a proof of his success in other quarters. Immediately Vitellius was abandoned by his troops: he fled hastily to Rome, and receiving no encouragement from the senate or people, abdicated his authority. Some of the prætorian guards, however, dreading the strict discipline of Vespasian, compelled the wretched monarch to resume the purple. The city was distracted by a horrid civil tumult, in which many of the principal nobles perished, and the capitol was burned to the ground. Primus, hearing of these disorders, advanced with all speed to Rome, forced an entrance into the city, and took the camp of the prætorian guards by storm. Vitellius hid himself in the palace, but was discovered in his retreat by the licentious populace, ready to rise under any pretext through hopes of plunder, dragged ignominiously through the streets to the place of common execution, and put to death with a thousand wounds (A.D. 69). His brother, Lucius Vitellius, who was advancing to his aid with an army from the south of Italy, surrendered at discretion, and was put to death. The factions that had been formed during this disgraceful reign of eight months, took advantage of the confusion to wreak mutual vengeance. Primus, and Vespasian's second son Domitian, abandoned themselves to debauchery and plunder: Rome appeared on the very brink of ruin from the madness of its own citizens.

At length tranquillity was restored by the arrival of Vespasian, whose accession diffused universal joy. His first care was to restore the discipline of the army, which he found in a shocking state of demoralisation: he next revived the authority of the senate, supplying its diminished ranks with eminent men from the provinces and colonies; finally, he reformed the courts of law, which had long ceased to be courts of justice. The virtues of Vespasian, supported by a firm temper, led to a great improvement in the social condition of Rome. His only fault was an extravagant love of money, which, however, was probably exaggerated by those who compared his parsimonious expenditure with the lavish extravagance of former emperors.

The early part of his reign was signalised by the final termination of the Jewish war, and the destruction of Jerusalem and its holy temple. It would be impossible to give even a faint outline of this memorable war here; suffice it to say, that the Jews, deceived by false prophets, who promised them a temporal deliverer, persevered in their rebellion long after every reasonable chance of success had disappeared; that they were divided into hostile factions, who fought against each other in the streets of Jerusalem, while the walls of the city quivered under the battering engines of the common enemy; and that they refused proffered mercy when the Roman ensigns were waving above their battlements. Dreadful was the punishment of this fated nation: their city and temple were reduced to heaps of shapeless ruins; their best and bravest fell by the swords of the Romans or each other; most of the wretched survivors were sold into slavery; and the Jews, since that period dispersed over the face of the earth, have become a mockery, a by-word, and a reproach among nations. Titus and his father triumphed together on account of this success, and rich ornaments of the temple were displayed in the procession. A triumphal arch was also erected for Titus, on which his noble deeds were sculptured; it continues nearly perfect to the present day, a lasting monument of his victories over the Jewish nation. The Batavian war, which threatened great dangers to the Roman dominions in Gaul and Germany, was concluded about the same time by the prudence and valour of Cerealis; and Comagene, which had been permitted to retain its own sovereigns, was reduced to a province.

Britain had yet been very imperfectly subdued, and the completion of its conquest was entrusted to Cneius Julius Agricola, a native of Gaul, justly celebrated for his great merits as a general and a statesman. His first enterprise was to recover the island of Anglesey from the Ordovices. His success was owing to his promptitude as much as to his valour: he appeared in the midst of the hostile country before the enemy knew of his having passed the frontiers; and the Britons, disconcerted by a sudden attack, agreed to purchase safety by submission. The advantages thus won by military prowess he resolved to confirm and secure by enlightened policy. He induced the Britons to lay aside their own barbarous customs, and adopt the Roman manners; but unfortunately, in giving them a knowledge of the arts of civilisation, he also inspired them with a taste for luxury. He next proceeded to attack the Caledonians; a fleet was ordered to examine the coast; and by this expedition Britain was first discovered to be an island.

The Caledonians drew together under the command of Galgacus, and hazarded a pitched battle with the army of Agricola, in which they were utterly routed, and pursued with great slaughter; but the fastnesses of the Scottish highlands were obstacles too formidable to be overcome; and the northern part of Britain was never subdued by the Romans.

Several conspiracies were formed against Vespasian, whose rigid rule was found a severe check on the licentiousness of the nobles; but they were all detected and punished. At length, his close attention to the affairs of state brought on a mortal disease. He retired to his country-seat for change of air; but the sickness was aggravated by the alteration, and he died in the seventieth year of his age (A. D. 78). He was the second of the Roman emperors that died a natural death, though some suspicion is attached to the fate of Augustus, and he was the first who was succeeded by his son. His obsequies were performed with extraordinary pomp by Titus; but the solemnity was disturbed by a ludicrous circumstance, too characteristic of the age to be omitted. The Romans were so preposterously fond of mimics and farces, that they were even exhibited at funerals, where actors personated the deceased, imitated his actions, mimicked his voice, and satirised his peculiarities. At Vespasian's obsequies, a pantomime named Favor personated that emperor, and took an opportunity of attacking his parsimony. Imitating the voice of the deceased emperor, he loudly demanded the price of the ceremony; a large sum was named in reply. "Give me the money," he continued, holding out his hand, "and throw my body into the Tiber."

Vespasian was succeeded by his son Titus, whose first action after his accession was a sacrifice of his dearest affections to the popular will. He dismissed the beautiful Berenice, daughter to Agrippa, the last king of Judæa, because he saw that his connexion with a foreigner was displeasing to the senate and people. Nor was this the only instance of his complaisance; he allowed the spectators to choose their own entertainments in the circus; and he never refused audience to a petitioner. His clemency was equally remarkable; he abolished the law of treason; and severely punished spies and informers.

In the first year of his reign, Campania was alarmed and devastated by the most dreadful eruption of Vesuvius on record; it laid waste the country for many miles around, overwhelming several cities with their inhabitants, among which Herculaneum and Pompeii were the most remarkable. This was followed by a dreadful conflagration at Rome, which lasted three days, and destroyed a vast number of edifices, both public and private. The exertions of Titus to remedy both these calamities procured him, from his grateful subjects, the honourable title of "benefactor of the human race." A plague afforded him fresh opportunities of displaying his native goodness of heart; but these exertions proved too much for his constitution; he was seized with a fever, which terminated fatally in a few days (A.D. 81). His death diffused universal sorrow throughout the empire; every family lamented as if it had been deprived of its natural protector; and his name has become a proverbial designation for wise and virtuous princes.

Flavius Domitian succeeded his brother without any opposition, though his character for debauchery and cruelty was sufficiently notorious. He was naturally timorous, and fear, of course, aggravated his sanguinary disposition; yet he professed a passionate attachment to military sports, and possessed so much skill in archery, that he could shoot arrows through the expanded fingers of a domestic placed at a considerable distance without ever inflicting a wound. In the beginning of his reign he studied to gain the favour of the people by a line of conduct worthy of an upright sovereign—disguising his vices, and affecting the opposite virtues. He presented large sums to his ministers and officers of state, that they might be raised above the temptation of receiving bribes; he refused the inheritances bequeathed to him, distributing the legacies among the nearest relations of the deceased; and he pretended to have such a horror of shedding blood, that he issued an edict forbidding the sacrifice of oxen or any other living animals. He confirmed all the grants made by the preceding emperors, increased the pay of the soldiers, and finished, at an immense charge, all the public buildings which had been begun by Titus.

In the second year of his reign he attacked the Catti, the most warlike of the German tribes; and, as the invasion was unexpected, made several of the peasants prisoners. Hearing, however, that the enemies were preparing an army, he retreated with great speed; yet the servile senate voted him a triumph for this pretended success. But flattery could not hide from the emperor his vast inferiority to Agricola, whose conquests in Britain were the theme of universal praise: he recalled this victorious general, who deemed it prudent to decline a triumph, and retire into the seclusion of private life. From this time forward the emperor indulged in the most sanguinary excesses, putting to death, without the form of trial, the most eminent senators and knights. The herd of informers, discouraged and punished during the preceding reign, once more came into favour; and such was their activity, that the most innocent conversation was frequently made the ground of a capital charge. The infamous vices of the palace were so far from being hidden, that they were ostentatiously exhibited to the public; and when Domitian had thus degraded himself in the eyes of his subjects to the condition of a beast, he required to be worshipped as a god, and all the streets leading to the capitol were daily crowded with victims to be offered in sacrifice before his altars and statues.

The Daci and Getæ, under their gallant king Decebalus, invaded the Roman frontiers, and defeated the generals sent to oppose them in two great battles. Domitian, encouraged by the news of a subsequent victory, resolved to take the field in person; but instead of marching against the Daci, he attacked the Quadi and Marcomanni, and was shamefully beaten. Discouraged by this overthrow, he concluded a dishonourable peace with the Dacians, engaging to pay Decebalus a yearly tribute: but he wrote to the senate, boasting of extraordinary victories; and that degraded body, though well aware of the truth, immediately decreed him the honours of a triumph.

Wearied by the tyranny of Domitian, Lucius Antonius, the governor of Upper Germany, raised the standard of revolt in his province, but was easily defeated and slain. This abortive insurrection stimulated the cruelty of the emperor; vast numbers were tortured and executed, under pretence of having been accomplices of Antonius. An edict was published, banishing all philosophers from Rome, and prohibiting instruction in the liberal sciences; for Domitian felt that all learning was a satire on his own ignorance, and all virtue a reproof of his infamy. But though thus tyrannical, Domitian had little fear of rebellion; he had secured the support of the troops by increasing their pay, and his splendid entertainments rendered him a favourite with the degraded populace. The adherents to the national religion were also gratified by a second general persecution of the Christians, who were odious to the emperor because they refused to worship his statues (A.D. 95). Among the most illustrious martyrs in the cause of truth on this occasion was Flavius Clemens, cousin-german of the emperor, whose example proves that the new religion was now beginning to spread among the higher ranks of society.

It was the custom of Domitian to inscribe on a roll the names of the persons he designed to slaughter. One day a young child with whom he used to divert himself took this paper from under the pillow on which the emperor was sleeping, and, unaware of its important contents, gave it to the empress Domitia. She saw with surprise and consternation her own name on the fatal list, as well as those of the imperial chamberlain and the captain of the prætorian guards, to whom she immediately communicated their danger. They at once conspired for his destruction, and he was murdered in his bed (A.D. 96). The Roman populace heard his fate with indifference; but the soldiers, whose pay he had increased, and with whom he had often shared his plunder, lamented him more than they had Vespasian or Titus; it is even said that they would have avenged his fate by a general massacre, had they not been restrained by their officers.

During this reign flourished a philosopher, Apollonius Tyaneus, whose austere life and extensive knowledge procured him so much fame, that he pretended to have the power of working miracles, and aspired to become the founder of a new religion. Like Pythagoras, he travelled into the remote east, and incorporated in his system many of the tenets that are now held by the Buddhists. During his life, this impostor enjoyed the highest reputation; but, in spite of all the efforts of his disciples, his system, after his death, sank rapidly into merited oblivion.

SECTION III.—*From the Extinction of the first Flavian Family to the last of the Antonines.*

FROM A.D. 96 TO A.D. 193.

DOMITIAN was the last of the emperors commonly called the twelve Cæsars: he was succeeded by Marcus Cocceius Nerva, who was chosen to the sovereignty by a unanimous vote of the senate. He was a native of Namia in Umbria, but his family came originally from Crete; and we may therefore regard him as the first foreigner placed at the head of the empire. Though past the age of seventy, he applied himself to the reformation of abuses with all the zeal of youth, punishing informers, redressing grievances, and establishing a milder and more equitable system of taxation. His greatest fault was excessive lenity, which encouraged the profligate courtiers to persevere in their accustomed peculations. The turbulent prætorian guards raised an insurrection, under pretence of avenging the death of Domitian, and not only compelled the emperor to abandon such victims to their fury as they demanded, but actually forced him to return them public thanks for their proper and patriotic conduct. This outrageous indignity, however, produced a highly beneficial result. Nerva, finding himself despised on account of his old age and infirmities, resolved to adopt Marcus Ulpius Trajan, the greatest and most deserving person of his age, as his colleague and successor, though he had many relations of his own, who might, without incurring the imputation of presumption, aspire to that dignity. The news of this appointment was received with great joy by the senate and people, and the soldiers immediately returned to their duty. Soon after, Nerva, while chiding severely an infamous informer, so heated himself, that he was seized with a fever, which proved mortal, in the sixteenth month of his reign

(A.D. 98). He was ranked amongst the gods by his subjects; and Trajan, out of gratitude, caused several temples to be erected to his memory both at Rome and in the provinces.

Trajan was by birth a Spaniard, descended from a family that had some claim to royal honours. He was equally great as a ruler, a general, and a man; free from every vice, except an occasional indulgence in wine. After completely abolishing the trials for high treason (*judicia majestatis*), he restored as much of the old constitution as was consistent with a monarchy; binding himself by oath to observe the laws, reviving the *comitia* for the election of civic officers, restoring freedom of speech to the senate, and their former authority to the magistrates. Decebalus having sent to claim the tribute granted to him by Domitian, Trajan peremptorily refused to be bound by such a disgraceful treaty, and hastily levying an army, marched against the Dacians, who had already crossed the Danube. A dreadful battle was fought, in which the Romans gained a complete victory; but so great was the carnage on both sides, that linen could not be found to dress the wounds of the soldiers, and Trajan tore up his imperial robes to supply that want. Pursuing his advantages, the emperor soon reduced Decebalus to such distress, that he was forced to purchase peace by giving up all his engines of war, and acknowledging himself a vassal of the Romans. After some time, however, the Dacian monarch, unused to servitude, again had recourse to arms, and was proclaimed a public enemy by the senate. Trajan once more took the field in person. To facilitate the advance of his army, he constructed a stupendous stone bridge over the Danube, fortified with strong castles at both ends; and having thus secured his communications, he marched into the very heart of the country, and made himself master of the capital (A.D. 106). Decebalus, despairing of success, committed suicide; and, after his death, the country was easily formed into a province, and several Roman colonies and garrisons for the first time planted north of the Danube. In the same year Arabia Petræa was subdued, and annexed to the empire by the governor of Syria.

These successes rendered Trajan ambitious of further conquest, and he resolved to contend with the Parthians for the sovereignty of Central Asia. He commenced by subduing Armenia, which he made a new province, and thence he advanced into Mesopotamia. A bridge not less remarkable than that over the Danube was constructed across the Tigris; and the Romans, passing this river to a country where their eagles had never before been seen, conquered the greater part of ancient Assyria. Seleucia and Ctesiphon (*Al Modain*), the capital of the Parthian kingdom, were besieged and taken; after which, the emperor, descending the Tigris, displayed the Roman standards for the first time in the Persian Gulf. Thence he sailed to the southern part of the Arabian Peninsula (*Arabia Felix*), a great part of which he annexed to the empire. He is said to have meditated the invasion of India: but was probably deterred by considering the great difficulties with which he would have to contend in the deserts of eastern Persia.

No permanent advantages resulted from these conquests. No sooner had the emperor returned, than most of the nations which he had conquered revolted, and massacred the Roman garrisons. The Jews, prompted by false prophets, raised a dangerous insurrection in the provinces through which they had been dispersed: after having committed the most shocking excesses, they were subdued, and their treason punished with remorseless severity. Trajan was making vigorous preparations to regain his conquests, when he was attacked by dropsy and palsy, which induced him to return to Italy. He, however, only proceeded so far as Selinus in Cilicia, when the disease assumed a mortal character; and in this little town the best of the Roman monarchs died, in the twentieth year of his reign (A.D. 117). His ashes were carried to Rome, and deposited under the stately column he had erected to commemorate his Dacian victories, though it stood within the city, where no one had ever been buried before. One stain on Trajan's character must not be omitted; he sanctioned the persecution of the Christians, and even when convinced that they were innocent of the atrocious charges brought against them by the pagans, he only forbade inquisitions to be made, but continued the punishment of all who were accused.

Adrian, the cousin-german and pupil of Trajan, succeeded to the empire, it is said, by adoption; but there is some reason to doubt the truth of the assertion. A much stronger claim was the unanimous declaration of the Asiatic armies in his favour, whose potent choice was ratified by the senate. Anxious to preserve peace, he at once abandoned all the conquests made by his predecessors, both in Asia and Europe, destroying the bridges over the Tigris and Danube. On his return to Rome the senate offered him a triumph, which he had the good sense to refuse; at the same time, to shew his moderation and love of tranquillity, he diminished the military establishments, and lowered the taxes throughout the empire. But the virtues of Adrian were not unalloyed; he was a cruel persecutor of the Jews and Christians; he allowed himself to be influenced by unworthy favourites, and too often lent an ear to the tales of slanderers and informers. Deeming that all parts of the empire had a claim to the protection of the sovereign, he resolved to make a tour through the provinces, and began his course by visiting Gaul, Germany, and Britain. He found the Britons far advanced in civilisation; but no longer able to contend with the barbarous Caledonians. In order to check the incursions of these savages, he erected the first Roman wall from the Eden to the Tyne, as has been mentioned in a preceding chapter.

He twice visited Asia, and ordered that a Roman colony should be established at Jerusalem, whose name he changed to Ælia Capitolina (A.D. 131). The introduction of idolatry into the holy city provoked a fierce insurrection of the Jews, headed by an impostor calling himself Bar-Cochab (*the son of a star*), who pretended to be the expected Messiah. After a sanguinary war, which lasted three years, the infatuated insurgents were subdued, but their revolt was punished by the most horrible cruelties, and their name and nation were all but exterminated.

While Adrian continued in the East, Salvius Julianus, the most eminent lawyer in the empire, was employed in compiling the *edictum perpetuum*, a code containing all the laws which had been published by the prætors in their annual edicts. This celebrated statute gave permanence and uniformity to the system of Roman jurisprudence, and in some degree raised law to the dignity of a science. Athens, which had long been neglected, naturally engaged the attention of a sovereign so enthusiastically attached to literature and the arts as Adrian. He completed many of its buildings, which had remained incomplete since the fall of the republic, and added so many new edifices, that a whole quarter of the city was called after his name.

On his return to Rome he fell into a lingering disease, and adopted Commodus Verus as his successor; but he soon repented his choice of a weak, debauched young man, whose constitution was greatly impaired by his guilty excesses. When he was sufficiently recovered, he retired to his magnificent villa at Tusculum (*Tivoli*), where he sunk into the same filthy debauchery as Tiberius at Capreæ. These excesses brought on a relapse; sickness rendered him cruel and jealous, and some of the most eminent men of Rome were sacrificed to his diseased suspicions. On the death of Verus, Adrian adopted Titus Antoninus, on condition of his adopting Marcus Aurelius and Verus, the son of his former choice. Scarcely had this arrangement been completed, when the emperor's ailments were aggravated to such a degree, that no medicines could give him relief; and, through impatience of pain, he made several attempts to commit suicide. Hoping for some relief from bathing, he removed to Baiæ, where he soon died (A. D. 139). A little before his death he composed some verses on the state of the soul when separated from the body, which deserve to be quoted.

> Animula, vagula, blandula,
> Hospes, comesque corporis,
> Quæ nunc abibis in loca,
> Pallidula, rigida, nudula?
> Nec, ut soles, dabis jocos.

They have been thus happily translated by Mr. Prior:—

> Poor, little, pretty, fluttering thing,
> Must we no longer live together?
> And dost thou prune thy hovering wing,
> To take thy flight, thou know'st not whither?

Thy humorous vein, thy pleasing folly,
  Lie all neglected, all forgot;
And, pensive, wav'ring, melancholy,
  Thou dread'st and hop'st, thou know'st not what.

Adrian, by his cruelties towards the close of his reign, provoked public hatred to such a degree, that the senate was disposed to annul all his acts; but the entreaties of Antoninus, and the fear of the soldiers, with whom Adrian had been a great favourite, induced them not only to abandon their intention, but to enrol him in the number of gods, and order temples to be erected to his honour.

Antoninus, immediately after his accession, gave his daughter Faustina in marriage to Marcus Aurelius, procured for him the tribunitian and proconsular power from the senate, and associated him in all the labours of government; but he shewed no regard for the profligate young Verus, whose misconduct he tolerated solely from respect for the memory of Adrian. The mild and merciful reign of this emperor, deservedly surnamed Pius, was undoubtedly the most tranquil and happy to be found in the Roman annals. He suspended the persecution of the Christians throughout the empire, and ordered that their accusers should be punished as calumniators. Peace prevailed through the wide dominions of Rome; the virtues of the sovereign conciliated the affection of foreigners, and distant nations chose him to arbitrate their differences. For the first time the government of the provinces engaged the earnest attention of the sovereign: the lieutenants of the emperor perceiving that their conduct was closely watched, ceased to oppress those entrusted to their charge; and instead of seeing their revenues wasted to support a profligate court, or gratify a degraded populace, the provincials beheld public schools erected for the instruction of youth, harbours cleaned out and repaired, new marts of trade opened, and every exertion made to realise the magnificent project formed by Alexander the Great, of constituting an empire whose parts should be held together by the bonds of commerce and mutual interest. After a useful reign of twenty-two years, the prosperity of which is best proved by its affording no materials for history, he died of a fever at one of his villas, bequeathing nothing beyond his own private fortune to his family (A.D. 163). The Romans venerated so highly the memory of this excellent monarch, that during the greater part of the ensuing century, every emperor deemed it essential to his popularity to assume the surname of Antoninus.

Marcus Aurelius, surnamed the philosopher, on account of his attachment to the doctrines and austerities of the Stoics, succeeded to the empire; but his power was shared by Lucius Verus, to whom he gave his daughter in marriage. He took, however, an early opportunity of sending his unworthy colleague from Rome, entrusting him with the command of the army sent against the Parthians, who had overrun Syria. Verus took up his residence at Antioch, where he abandoned himself to every species of infamy and debauchery, while the conduct of the war was entrusted to his lieutenants. Fortunately these officers were worthy of the high trust confided to them; they upheld the reputation of the Roman arms in four brilliant campaigns, and conquered some of the principal cities of Parthia.

While Verus was disgracing himself in Asia, Rome enjoyed happiness and tranquillity under the merciful but firm administration of Aurelius. But this prosperity was interrupted by the return of Verus, who came to claim a triumph for the victories obtained by his officers. The eastern army unfortunately brought the plague with it into Europe: infection was communicated to every province through which they passed: the violence of the pestilence did not abate for several years, and among its victims were some of the most illustrious men in Rome and the principal cities of Italy.

Scarcely had the affairs of the East been arranged, when a dangerous war was commenced by the Marcomanni on the German frontiers: both emperors took the field; but at the very opening of the campaign, Verus fell a victim to his intemperance (A.D. 171). Aurelius honoured his remains with a magnificent funeral, and even persuaded the senate to enrol this miserable debauchee in the number of the gods. The emperor now devoted his entire attention to the conduct of the

German war; but in the first engagement the Romans were routed with great slaughter; and it was only by the sale of the imperial plate, furniture, and crown jewels, that a sum could be raised sufficient to repair their great losses. Aurelius having by this sacrifice assembled a fresh army, soon restored the fortune of the empire. He took up his résidence at Sirmium (*Sirmich*), and from this central position directed the movements of his officers, whom he had directed to harass and wear out the barbarians, by marches, counter-marches, and skirmishes, rather than peril their armies in pitched battles. Once only he abandoned this prudent policy, advancing beyond the Danube into the territory of the Quadi. This temerity had nearly proved his ruin: the barbarians, craftily pretending flight, drew the Romans into a barren defile, where the army was on the point of perishing by thirst. In this distress the Romans were relieved by a great thunder-storm; the lightning fired the tents of their enemies, and the rain relieved their pressing wants. The barbarians, believing this event miraculous, at once submitted; and Aurelius was, for the seventh time, proclaimed Imperator by the senate. Many ancient fathers ascribe this seasonable shower to the prayers of a Christian legion in the imperial army; but the evidence by which the miracle is supported has been more than once shewn to be a fraudulent falsification.

In consequence of this success, the German nations besought terms of peace, which Aurelius readily granted, as he was anxious to suppress a dangerous rebellion in the East, where his lieutenant, Avidius Cassius, had proclaimed himself emperor. But Cassius, though a formidable rival, had not the prudence necessary for success in a civil war; he disgusted his soldiers by the excessive severity of his discipline, and was murdered by one of his own centurions. Aurelius shewed great regret for the destruction of his rival, lamenting that he had been deprived of an opportunity of shewing mercy. He forbade the prosecution of those who had joined in the revolt, and took the young family of Cassius under his own protection. Having restored tranquillity, the emperor returned to Rome, which he entered in triumph with his son Commodus, whom he had recently declared his successor, and invested with the tribunitian power.

The persecution of the Christians had been renewed in this reign, probably at the instigation of the Stoic philosophers, to whom the superior purity of the Christian doctrines gave great offence; and among the most illustrious victims of imperial bigotry was the celebrated Justin Martyr, whose Apologies for Christianity, addressed to the emperors Antoninus and Aurelius, are among the best, as well as the earliest works, written to refute the calumnies with which in every age the true faith has been assailed. Towards the close of his reign the emperor became more tolerant; some say in consequence of the miraculous shower; others, with more probability, ascribe the change to his having learned the falsehood of the charges brought against the Christians.

Aurelius had not been long in Rome when war was unexpectedly renewed along the Rhine and Danube. The great migration of nations, which was ere long to change the entire face of the civilised world, had now commenced, and the German tribes along the frontiers, pressed forwards by hordes in their rear, were necessarily forced to encroach on the limits of the empire. So formidable was the invasion, whose cause was as yet unknown, that the emperor found it necessary to take the field in person. He gained several important victories, and was preparing to reduce Germany into a province, when he was seized with a violent fever at Vindebona (*Vienna*), to which he fell a victim in a few days (A.D. 180). The glory of the empire may be said to have expired with Aurelius: he was the last emperor who made the good of his subjects the chief object of his government; and he was one of the few princes who attained a high rank in literature. His Meditations, which have come down to our time, contain a summary of the best rules for a virtuous life that have ever been devised by unassisted reason or simple philosophy.

Commodus was the first emperor that was born in his father's reign, and the second that received the empire as a paternal inheritance. He had been spoiled in youth by his mother Faustina, a woman of very violent passions and sanguinary temper, who corrupted her son's mind both by precept and example. His debaucheries exceeded those of all his predecessors in extravagance and iniquity: even his own sisters became the victims of his lust, and one of them, having reproached him, was murdered by his hand. All his sports were cruel: he loved to roam through the streets wounding and slaying the unsuspicious passengers; he frequently contended with the gladiators on the public stage, and delighted to display feats of strength, for his muscular powers were unrivalled. But he shewed no disposition for foreign war; on the contrary, he concluded a peace with the Quadi and Marcomanni, abandoning the territories that had been conquered by his father. An attempt made to assassinate this monster, in the third year of his reign, stimulated his natural cruelty to the most savage excess: his assailant, aiming a blow at him with a dagger, exclaimed, "The senate sends thee this!" and though the murder was prevented by the prompt interference of the guards, the words sunk deep into the emperor's breast, and thenceforward he shewed inveterate suspicion and hatred to the whole body of senators. Scarcely had he escaped this danger, when he was exposed to one more formidable, arising from the war of the deserters. A common soldier, named Maternus, guilty of the unusual crime of abandoning his colours, assembled a band of robbers in Gaul, and being joined by profligates from every part of the empire, pillaged and laid waste that province. Being reduced to great straits by the exertions of Piscennius Niger, Maternus divided his men into several small bands, and marched privately with them by different ways into Italy, designing to murder Commodus at a public festival, and in the confusion seize the empire. The conspirators reached Rome in safety; but just as the plot was on the point of exploding, they were betrayed by their accomplices, arrested, and put to death.

An alarming insurrection of the Roman populace, directed not so much against the emperor as his minister Cleander, was produced by the exhortations of an unknown woman. The prætorian horse charged the multitude, but were defeated with loss, as cavalry generally are when acting against a mob in narrow streets. Commodus, alarmed by the tumult, sacrificed his minister, and the fury of the Romans was appeased.

Having formed the wild project of entering on the consular dignity armed as a gladiator, and marching in procession from the gladiatorial school instead of the palace, he was so enraged by the remonstrances of his concubine Marcia, that he resolved to put her to death. Having accidentally discovered her danger, she determined to murder Commodus, and being aided by some officers of the household, strangled him in his bed (A. D. 192). No sooner was his death known, than the senate, without waiting for the return of day, assembled hastily, annulled his acts, ordered all his statues to be thrown down, and demanded that his body should be dragged through the streets and cast into the Tiber. The latter indignity was prevented by a private and hurried funeral.

SECTION IV.—*Foreign Commerce of the Romans in the age of the Antonines.*

IF the reign of Augustus be justly celebrated for the perfection of Roman literature, those of the Antonines, including even that of the wicked Commodus, deserve to be honoured for the great improvements made in trade and commerce, especially by the opening of new communications with India. Tadmor, or Palmyra, the wondrous city of the desert, distant only eighty-five miles from the Euphrates, and about one hundred and seventeen from the nearest coast of the Mediterranean, was the centre of the trade between Europe and southern Persia, including the countries bordering on the Indus, and the districts now attached to the Bombay presidency. In consequence of the great exports that this trade naturally caused from the harbours of the Levant, great numbers of Syrian merchants settled in Rome, some of whom attained the highest honours of the state. It would appear that some merchants used a more northern route by the Caspian and Oxus; for we find the Roman geographers tolerably well acquainted with the countries that now form the kingdoms of Khiva and Bokhara.

The great caravan-route across Asia, however, commenced at Byzantium (*Constantinople*), which was long the seat of flourishing commerce before it became the metropolis of an empire. Having passed the Bosphorus, the merchant-adventurers proceeded through Anatolia, and crossed the Euphrates near Hierapolis (*Bambúch*); thence they proceeded to Ecbatana (*Hamadan*), the ancient capital of the Medes, and Hecatompylos (*Damghan*), the metropolis of the Parthians. Thence they proceeded circuitously to Hyrcania (*Jorjan*) and Aria (*Herát*). Finally they came to Bactra (*Balkh*), long the principal mart of central Asia. From Bactra there were two caravan routes, one to north India, over the western part of the Himalaya, called the Indian Caucasus (*Hindú Kúsh*), the other towards the frontiers of Serica (*China*), over the lofty mountain-chain of Imäus (*Belúr Tag*), through a winding ravine which was marked by a celebrated station called the Stone Tower, whose ruins are said still to exist, under the name of *Chîhel Sútún*, or the Forty Columns. Little was known of the countries between the Imäus and Serica, which were probably traversed by Bactrian rather than European merchants; but the road was described as wonderfully difficult and tedious.

As the progress of the caravans was liable to frequent interruptions from the Parthians, and the conveyance of manufactured silks through the deserts very toilsome, the emperor Antoninus attempted to open a communication with the Chinese by sea. Of this singular transaction no record has yet been found in any of the Greek or Latin authors; but M. de Guignes discovered it stated in a very old Chinese historical work, that an embassy had come by sea from Antún, the king of the people of the western ocean, to Yan-ti, or rather Han-húán-ti, who ruled over China in the hundred and sixty-sixth year of the Christian era. The name and date sufficiently identify Antún with Antoninus, and the projected intercourse was well worthy the attention of that enlightened emperor; but nothing is known respecting the results of this embassy.

We have already mentioned the great increase of intercourse between Egypt and India, when the former country was governed by the Ptolemies. The navigation was long confined to circuitous voyages round the peninsula of Arabia and the coasts of the Persian gulf; but about a century after the establishment of the Roman dominion, Harpalus, the commander of a ship long engaged in the Indian trade, observing the regular changes of the periodical winds, ventured to steer from the Angustiæ Duræ (*Straits of Bab-el-Mandeb, or "the Gate of Tears"*) right across the Erythræan sea (*Indian Ocean*), and was wafted by the western monsoon to Musiris (*Marján*), on the Malabar coast. This great improvement was deservedly regarded as of the highest importance; and the western monsoon received the name of Harpalus, in memory of the courageous navigator, that had turned it to such a good account.

The route of the Egyptian trade under the Romans has been described with considerable accuracy by Pliny. Cargoes destined for India were carried up the Nile in boats to Coptos (*Ghouft*), thence they were transferred by caravans to Myos Hormus (*Cosseir*), or Berenice (*Hubbesh*). The latter, though the longer, was the more frequented road, because the Ptolemies had raised excellent stations and watering-places at convenient distances along the road. From Berenice the fleet sailed in June or July for Ocelis (*Gella*), at the mouth of the Arabian Gulf, and Cané (*Fartash*), a promontory and emporium on the south-east coast of Arabia Felix. Thence they steered right across the ocean for the Malabar coast, and usually made Musiris in forty days. They began their voyage homeward early in December, and generally encountered more difficulty on their return on account of the unsteadiness of the winds.

The chief imports from India were spices, precious stones, and muslins. There is a singular confusion in the Latin authors between the finer cotton goods and manufactured silks, which has led to their mixing up the Chinese and Indian trade together. The principal exports were light woollens, checkered linens, glass, wine, and bullion.

Commodus, with a providence which could scarcely have been expected from him, made some efforts to open the old Carthaginian trade with the interior of Africa; but the result of his labours is unknown. He also paid some attention to the corn-trade, so essential to the prosperity of his central dominions, when Italy had long ceased to produce sufficient grain for the support of its inhabitants; and he established a company to supply corn from northern Africa whenever the crops failed in Egypt.

The trade of the Black Sea, so flourishing in the age of the Greek republics, appears to have been greatly diminished after the Romans became masters of the countries at both sides of the Ægean; and it seems probable that little or no commerce passed through the straits of Hercules (*straits of Gibraltar*) into the Atlantic ocean. In consequence of this change the amber-trade was transferred from the coasts of the northern sea to the banks of the Danube, and the barbarous tribes who brought it from the shores of the Baltic are said to have been astonished at the prices they received for what seemed to them so useless a commodity. Furs were purchased from the Scythian tribes; but this branch of trade appears never to have been of any great amount. The British tin-trade was rather neglected by the Romans; indeed, it appears to have been monopolised by the Gauls, and consequently was confined to the British channel. From this slight sketch it will be seen that the Romans were not naturally a mercantile people. We must now return to the history of the civil wars and revolutions which frustrated the plans of the Antonines for making commercial pursuits the source of unity and happiness to the empire.

Section V.—*From the Extinction of the Flavian Family to the Establishment of Military Despotism, after the Murder of Alexander Severus.*

FROM A.D. 193 TO A.D. 235.

After the conspirators had murdered Commodus, they proceeded to the house of Publius Helvius Pertinax, and declared that they had come to offer him the empire, as being the person who best deserved sovereignty. Pertinax at first believed that this was some plot for his destruction; but on further inquiry, having learned that Commodus was really dead, he proceeded to the prætorian camp, and was saluted emperor rather reluctantly by the guards. He met a much warmer reception from the senators, who expected that his firmness and virtue would be displayed in checking the turbulence of the soldiers, now the real masters of the empire. Nor did his conduct disappoint their expectations: he diminished the lavish expenditure of the palace, restored the property that his predecessor had unjustly confiscated to the rightful owners, and punished those who, by false informations, had stimulated Commodus to cruelty. These reforms endeared him to the senate and people, but provoked the anger of the turbulent prætorians: three days after his accession, they attempted to make Lascivius emperor, but that senator fled from their violence, and sought shelter with Pertinax himself. Their next choice was the consul Falco, who shewed equal reluctance to accept the precarious station. The emperor, to prevent the recurrence of similar outrages, prepared to restore the ancient military discipline; but this exasperated the mutineers still more, and a party of them, breaking suddenly into the palace, slew Pertinax, after a brief reign of less than three months. The Romans lamented, but did not venture to revenge his death; most of the citizens shut themselves up in their houses, leaving the soldiers to choose a master for the empire at their discretion.

When the prætorians heard that Pertinax was dead, they issued a proclamation, declaring that the empire was for sale, and would be given to the highest bidder. Didius Julianus, the wealthiest man in Rome, offered to become a purchaser: his money, and his promise that he would restore all things to the condition in which they were under Commodus, so pleased the dissolute soldiers, that they proclaimed him emperor, and compelled the senate to recognise their choice. But the Roman populace shewed their indignation at this scandalous traffic by showering curses and reproaches on Didius whenever he appeared in public, and even assailing him with stones and other missiles. The weak emperor bore these attacks with great equanimity, relying for security on the prætorians, whose favour he secured by fresh largesses.

But though Didius, by the favour of the household troops, was able to secure himself in Rome, he could not secure the respect or allegiance of the provinces; and the distant armies, deeming that they had as good a right to confer empire as the prætorian cohorts, offered sovereignty to their commanders. Three competitors together appeared to contest the throne with the ambitious merchant; Clodius Albinus in Britain, Pescennius Niger in Syria, and Septimius Severus in Illyria. Didius prepared to meet the storm with more fortitude than could have been expected; he convoked the senate, and had Severus, the nearest of his rivals, declared a public enemy: he also sent deputies to exhort the Illyrian soldiers to return to their allegiance. But the unfortunate emperor was betrayed by his own officers; the deputies tendered their homage to Severus, and exhorted him to expedite his march towards Rome. The rapid advance of the Illyrians, the capture of Ravenna and the Roman fleet, and the desertion of the troops sent to guard the passes of the Apennines, so alarmed the prætorians, that they resolved to abandon Didius, and make terms with Severus. They communicated their resolutions to the consul Messala, who forthwith convoked the senate. A decree was passed for the deposition and death of Didius, and ere it was enrolled, the band of executioners was on its march to the palace. Didius was found trembling and in tears, ready to resign empire, provided his life might be spared. At sight of the armed band, he exclaimed, "What crime have I committed? whose life have I taken away?" But his remonstrances were cut short by one of the soldiers, who struck off his head. The body was exposed to insult and mockery in the public streets, and thus ended the two months' reign of "the imperial merchant."

Severus, as he approached Rome, issued orders for the execution of all who had shared in the murder of Pertinax, and for disbanding the prætorian cohorts; but he chose new guards, four times as numerous, in the place of those he had dismissed, which filled Rome with soldiers, and proved the fruitful source of many future disorders. Having conciliated Albinus by procuring for him the titles of Cæsar and emperor from the senate, he marched to contend against Pescennius Niger in the east, previously inducing the senate to declare him a public enemy. His progress appears to have been uninterrupted until he reached Cyzicus, where he routed the lieutenant of his rival, and by this victory gained possession of Lower Asia. Niger did not despair, but, collecting a numerous army, occupied the mountain-passes between Cilicia and Syria, posting his main body along the Issus, where Alexander and Darius had long before contended for the sovereignty of Asia. After several engagements, Niger was completely defeated: he attempted to seek safety among the Parthians, but was overtaken near Antioch, and put to death (A.D. 194). Severus made a cruel use of his victory, slaughtering without mercy all who had favoured the cause of his competitor. Byzantium remained faithful to the defeated general even after his death: it sustained a siege of three years' duration; but was finally taken by storm, its inhabitants sold as slaves, and its walls levelled to the ground.

Thus successful, Severus resolved to destroy Albinus, whose suspicions he had calmed while he was engaged in war with Niger. He first attempted to remove him by assassination; but Albinus discovered the plot, and made vigorous preparations for open war. This second contest for empire was decided in Gaul. Albinus, having been completely routed near Lugdunum (*Lyons*), committed suicide; and Severus could only vent his brutal spite on a senseless carcass. The friends of Albinus met the same fate as the partisans of Niger. Severus returned to Rome, where he insulted the senate by pronouncing a laboured eulogy on Commodus; and imitated that wicked monarch's example, by sentencing to a cruel death the most eminent of the nobility.

A war with Parthia recalled the emperor to Asia. He was accompanied by his sons Caracalla and Geta, who were, like their father, learned in camps from infancy. Severus obtained distinguished success; he captured Seleucia, Ctesiphon, and Babylon; but he was compelled to raise the siege of Hatra (*Hadhr*), which had previously baffled the exertions of Trajan. These exploits might have procured the empire all the advantages to be derived from the rule of a gallant soldier, had not

Severus chosen for his prime minister Plautianus, the captain of the prætorian guards; a man of insatiable avarice, whom he entrusted with almost absolute power. The ruin of the premier, however, was occasioned by the very means he took to confirm his security: he procured the marriage of his daughter with Caracalla; but the young prince, disgusted by her imperious temper, became the bitter enemy of her and Plautianus. He soon inspired his father with a suspicion that the minister secretly aimed at empire—a charge to which the conduct of Plautianus gave some colour of probability; and, when Severus called his servant to account, the prince rushed upon him, and slew him in the imperial presence.

A revolt in Britain once more called the emperor into the field. He proceeded to that island, easily quelled the disturbances, and, marching northwards, gained several victories over the Caledonians. He extended the frontiers beyond Adrian's wall, and erected a new line of fortifications between the Firths of Clyde and Forth; but the additional territory was abandoned in the reign of his successor. The fatigues of these campaigns, and the grief caused by the misconduct of his son Caracalla, brought the emperor's gray hairs with sorrow to the grave. He died at Eboracum (*York*), in the eighteenth year of his reign (A.D. 211). Severus deserves to be ranked among great rather than good princes; he was cruel on system, attributing the misfortunes of Pompey and the murder of Cæsar to their excessive clemency: indeed, he wrote a vindication of his excessive severity, which, unfortunately, has not come down to our times.

Caracalla and Geta succeeded their father; but the former was the bitter enemy of his more virtuous brother, and, soon after his return to Rome, he slew him in his mother's arms. To prevent the consequences of this atrocious murder, he gained the support of the prætorian cohorts by large donatives, and then, with strange inconsistency, prevailed upon the senate to rank his brother in the number of the gods. His sole dependence being on the army, he used the most iniquitous means to procure money for purchasing their venal support. The richest men in Rome were massacred under false accusations of treason, their properties confiscated, and their families insulted. He impoverished his subjects in all the provinces of the empire by excessive taxes; yet he gave away such immense sums to his guards, and paid such heavy annuities to the barbarous tribes on the frontiers, that he was forced to debase the coinage. To lower the pride of the Romans, he granted the name and privileges of free citizens to all the subjects of the empire, and soon after commenced a tour through the provinces, to escape from his unpopularity at home. He undertook an expedition against the Catti and Allemanni, but was defeated with great loss, and forced to buy a peace. From Germany he passed into Asia, where he gained some advantages over the Armenians; and then visiting Egypt, he almost depopulated Alexandria, massacring the greater part of its citizens, on account of some lampoons that had been published against him. He was at length assassinated near Edessa by Macrinus, the prefect of the prætorian guard, an officer who, since the time of Severus, ranked next to the emperor (A.D. 217).

The soldiers were greatly enraged at the murder of Caracalla; but Macrinus, by concealing his share in it, procured his election to the empire. Immediately after his accession, he proclaimed his son Diadumenus his successor, giving him the names of Cæsar and Antoninus: when the troops were assembled to witness this ceremony, they demanded, with one accord, the deification of Caracalla; and this disgrace to humanity was actually ranked among the gods. While he was thus engaged, the Parthians passed the Roman frontiers, defeated the imperial armies, and compelled Macrinus to purchase a disgraceful peace by a vast sacrifice of wealth and territory. His extreme severity at length provoked the resentment of the licentious soldiery; they were persuaded by Mœsa, maternal aunt of the late emperor, that her grandson Heliogabalus, a youth of fourteen, was the son of their favourite Caracalla; and a conspiracy was formed to place this young Syrian priest upon the throne. Macrinus, deserted by most of the legions, marched against his competitor with the prætorian cohorts; but he fled from his men the moment that a battle commenced; and the guards, enraged by his cowardice, pursued and slew him

(A.D. 218). His son was at the same time taken prisoner, and executed as a common malefactor.

Heliogabalus being thus victorious sent intelligence of his success from Antioch to the senate, and was immediately acknowledged emperor. Though a mere boy, he was the most infamous monster that ever disgraced a throne. He exceeded Nero in cruelty, Caligula in prodigality, and Commodus in lewdness and debauchery. Soon after his arrival in Rome, he brought his grandmother to the senate, and ordered that she should for the future rank among the members; he also instituted a senate of women, under the presidency of his mother, the subjects of whose debates, consultations, and decrees, were the dresses of the Roman ladies, and the ceremony and etiquette to be observed in visits and entertainments. The lascivious and superstitious idolatry of Syria was established in Rome, and the old forms of the national worship neglected,—a change which gave great offence even to the demoralised guards. Mœsa, foreseeing that the Romans would not long endure the yoke of so contemptible a profligate, persuaded him to nominate his cousin, the virtuous Alexander Severus, heir to the empire; but scarcely had the appointment been made, when Heliogabalus attempted to assassinate the worthy prince. This crime provoked a mutiny of the prætorian cohorts. Heliogabalus, and his mother Sœmis, were murdered by the enraged soldiers, and their bodies thrown into the Tiber (A.D. 222). The senate immediately passed a decree excluding women from their body for ever.

Alexander Severus commenced his reign by revoking all the edicts that had been issued by former emperors against the Christians. It is probable that his mother was a convert to the faith; for he was well acquainted with its principles, and constantly repeated the golden rule, "Do unto others as you would they should do unto you," which he caused to be inscribed on his palace and several other edifices. Supported by the favour of the guards, he introduced many beneficial reforms, restoring the authority of the senate, and purifying the administration of justice.

In the fourth year of his reign (A.D. 226), an important revolution in the east produced a total change in the political condition of central Asia. Ardeshír Babegan, called Artaxerxes by the western writers, restored the ancient dynasty and religion of Persia, or, as it was called by the natives, Irán. His standard was the apron of a blacksmith named Gaváh, who, at an unknown age, had headed an insurrection against the oppressors of his country, similar to that of Wat Tyler in England. Multitudes flocked to the popular flag, and the Parthian, or Arsacid dynasty, was speedily subverted. One great effect of this revolution was to give a sudden and complete check to the progress of Christianity eastwards; it was thrown back upon the west; but it long retained the marks of its contact with the mystic and gloomy doctrines that have from unknown ages prevailed in central Asia. The Magian religion was restored to its pristine splendour; the sacred fire, that had been concealed in the mountains, once more burned on the ancient altars; and the Sassanides, as Ardeshír's dynasty was named, from Sassan, the most celebrated of his ancestors, refused to tolerate any faith but that of Zerdusht, or Zoroaster.

Ardeshír, placed upon the throne of Cyrus, claimed that monarch's empire as his inheritance, and prepared to drive the Romans from Asia. Alexander hastened to Antioch, and marched against the Persians, over whom he gained a great victory; but a pestilence breaking out in his army prevented him from improving his advantages. He returned to Rome, and entered the city in triumph, his chariot being drawn, not, as was usual, by four white horses, but by four of the elephants he had captured. Soon after his return, intelligence arrived that the Germans had passed the Rhine, and were devastating Gaul; upon which the emperor, to the great grief of the senate and people, led his victorious armies to protect that province. He found the legions quartered in Gaul demoralised by a long course of indulgence, and immediately exerted himself to restore the ancient discipline. The licentious soldiers could not endure the change, and their discontents were fomented by Maximin, a Thracian peasant, who had risen from the ranks to high command by his uncommon strength and valour. The prince's guards were bribed to quit their posts; and a band of assassins entering the imperial tent slew him without resistance (A.D. 235). Thus fell this excellent prince in the very bloom of youth, just as his plans for restoring the ancient glory of the empire were beginning to be matured.

SECTION VI.—*From the Murder of Alexander to the Captivity of Valerian, and the Usurpation of the Thirty Tyrants.*

FROM A.D. 235 to A.D. 259.

THE murder of Alexander occasioned a great tumult and confusion in the camp, during which the Pannonians proclaimed Maximin emperor; and the rest of the army, seeing no other candidate come forward, acquiesced in their choice. Great personal strength was the first cause of the new emperor's elevation: it is said he could draw a wagon which two oxen could not move, tear trees up by the roots, and crush pebbles to dust in his hands. But he was a brutal, ignorant barbarian, uniting the cunning to the ferocity of a savage. He commenced his reign by massacring all who had been intimate with the late emperor, or who had shewn sorrow for his death; and he sent orders to the senate to register his sanguinary decrees, without asking that body to confirm his election. The war against the Germans was continued with great success; one hundred and fifty of their villages were burned to the ground; their country, to an extent of four hundred square miles, laid desolate; and an incredible number of prisoners sent to be sold as slaves in Italy. Maximin marched next against the Dacians and Sarmatians, over whom he gained several victories; and it is believed that he would have extended the frontiers of the empire to the northern ocean, had not his avarice and cruelty provoked a civil war. The revolt commenced in Africa, where two young men of high rank being condemned by the emperor's receiver-general to pay a fine that would have reduced them to beggary, conspired to save their fortunes by destroying him: they were joined by several of the legionaries, and so rapid was their success, that they ventured to proclaim Gordian, proconsul of Africa, then in the eightieth year of his age, sovereign of the empire. When news of this event reached Rome, the senators with one accord revolted from Maximin, and ordered all his friends in the city to be murdered. Intelligence of these events being conveyed to Maximin, he made peace with the northern barbarians, and led his army towards Italy, promising his soldiers that they should be enriched by the forfeited estates of his enemies. On his march, he learned that Gordian and his son had been defeated and slain by Capelianus in Africa, but that the senate, undaunted by this calamity, had conferred the empire on Pupienus and Balbinus. This choice did not satisfy the people; a vast multitude assembled while the new emperors were offering the usual sacrifice, and demanded with loud clamour a prince of the Gordian family. After vainly attempting to disperse the mob, Balbinus and Pupienus sent for young Gordian, then only twelve years old, and proclaimed him Cæsar. In the meantime Maximin entered Italy, and laid siege to Aquileia. The garrison made a very brave defence; and the besiegers, hated by the entire empire, suffered more than the besieged, their stragglers being cut off, and their convoys intercepted. Exasperated by their sufferings, the imperialists resolved to remove the cause; a large body marched in the noonday to the tent of Maximin, and slew him, his son, and all his principal favourites (A.D. 238). Though several legions of Pannonians and Thracians were in the camp, they did not attempt to revenge the death of an emperor who had always shewn more favour to the barbarian than the Roman legions.

Scarcely had domestic tranquillity been restored, when the empire was involved in foreign wars. The Carpi and Goths, passing the Danube, ravaged the province of Mœsia; while the Persians renewed their hostilities on the eastern frontiers. It was agreed among the princes, that Pupienus should undertake the defence of Syria, Balbinus march against the Goths, and Gordian remain at the head of the administration in Rome. But while the necessary armaments were in preparation, a dangerous mutiny broke out among the prætorians: Pupienus and

Pupiénus and Balbínus, divided by mutual jealousies, could not unite for its suppression; they were both murdered, and young Gordian remained sole emperor.

Misithéus, captain of the prætorian guards, and father-in-law of the emperor, acted as minister and guardian of young Gordian. He was admirably qualified for such an important office, uniting the valour of a soldier to the wisdom of a statesman. The rapid successes of Shah-púr, or, as he was called by the Romans, Sápor, the second prince of the Sassanid dynasty, directed the attention of the emperor to the Persian war, and he went in person to protect the province of Syria. On his march towards the Hellespont, Gordian was defeated in a tumultuous engagement by the Alans; but the barbarians did not know how to improve their success, and, after a short delay, he arrived safely in Asia. The Persians were defeated in every engagement; and Sápor, forced to abandon Mesopotámia, was pursued to the very gates of Ctes′iphon. But these victories were more than counterbalanced by the death of Misithéus, who showed his patriotism, even in his last moments, by bequeathing all his estates to the Roman people. Gordian, having appointed Philip, the Arabian, his prime minister, continued the war against Sápor, and gave the Persians a decisive overthrow on the banks of the Chab′oras (*Khabúr*), a tributary to the Euphrátes, in Mesopotámia. But while the young conqueror was pursuing the advantages of his victory, a mutiny was excited in his army by the traitor Philip, whom he was compelled to make a partner of his empire. Not content with this elevation, Philip procured the assassination of his youthful benefactor (A.D. 244); but the soldiers soon repented of their crime, and raised a splendid mausoleum to the memory of the youthful hero.

Philip, being elevated to the empire by the army, wrote to the senate, ascribing the death of Gordian to a natural disease: he then concluded a hasty peace with the Persians, and, returning to Syria, made all speed to Rome. Though the senate and people, warmly attached to the Gordian family, at first regarded him with aversion, he soon won their affections by his mild administration and obliging behaviour. He is said to have been

been secretly a Christian, but many of his actions shew that he had little regard for any religion; however, he was a decided enemy to persecution. His reign was rendered remarkable by the celebration of secular games for the thousandth anniversary of the foundation of the city: it was also disturbed by several insurrections, especially in Pannonia, the suppression of which he entrusted to Trajanus Decius. Scarcely had this general reached Illyricum, when his soldiers compelled him, by the threat of instant death, to assume the imperial purple. Philip, leaving his son to protect Rome, marched against Decius, but was defeated and slain near Verona (A. D. 249). His son was massacred by the prætorian guards.

Decius commenced his reign by one of the most sanguinary persecutions that ever oppressed the church. The Christians throughout the empire were driven from their habitations, dragged to execution like common malefactors, and subjected to the most exquisite tortures cruelty itself could invent. The laws of nature and humanity were violated, friend betrayed friend, brother informed against brother, children against their parents, and parents against their children; every one thinking it meritorious to discover a Christian and procure his death. Decius vented his rage chiefly against the bishops. Among his victims were Fabian, bishop of Rome; Babylas, bishop of Antioch; and Alexander, bishop of Jerusalem. Great numbers of Christians betook themselves to mountains, rocks, and deserts, choosing rather to live amongst wild beasts than with men who had divested themselves of reason and humanity. Among these was the celebrated Paul, who withdrew into the deserts of Egypt, where he is said to have lived a solitary life for the greater part of a century. He is usually regarded as the father and founder of the order of anchorets, or hermits, whose superstitious austerities appear to have been derived from the extraordinary penances practised by the fanatics of central and southern Asia.

This persecution was interrupted by an invasion of the Goths, who, for the first time, crossed the Danube in considerable numbers, and devastated Mœsia. Decius marched against them, and gained some important advantages; but in his last battle, charging into the midst of the enemy to avenge the death of his son, he was overpowered and slain (A. D. 251). A great number of the Romans, thus deprived of their leader, fell victims to the barbarians; the survivors, grateful for the protection afforded them by the legions of Gallus, who commanded in the neighbourhood, proclaimed that general emperor.

Gallus concluded a dishonourable peace with the Goths, and renewed the persecutions of the Christians. His dastardly conduct provoked general resentment; the provincial armies revolted, but the most dangerous insurrection was that headed by Æmilianus, who was proclaimed emperor in Mœsia. He led his forces into Italy, and the hostile armies met at Interamna (*Terni*); but just as an engagement was about to commence, Gallus was murdered by his own soldiers (A. D. 253), and Æmilianus proclaimed emperor. In three months Æmilianus himself met a similar fate, the army having chosen Valerian, the governor of Gaul, to the sovereignty.

Valerian, though now sixty years of age, possessed powers that might have revived the sinking fortunes of the empire, which was now invaded on all sides. The Goths, who had formed a powerful monarchy on the lower Danube and the northern coasts of the Black Sea, extended their territories to the Borysthenes (*Dneiper*) and Tanais (*Don*): they ravaged Mœsia, Thrace, and Macedon; while their fleets, which soon became formidable after the capture of the Tauric Chersonese (*Crim Tartary*), devastated the coasts both of the European and Asiatic provinces. The great confederation of the Franks became formidable on the lower Rhine, and not less dangerous was that of the Allemanni on the upper part of that river. The Carpians and Sarmatians laid Mœsia waste; while the Persians plundered Syria, Cappadocia, and Cilicia. Gallienus, the emperor's son, whom Valerian had chosen for his colleague, and Aurelian, destined to succeed him in the empire, gained several victories over the Germanic tribes; while Valerian marched in person against the Scythians and Persians, who had invaded Asia. He gained a victory over the former in Anatolia, but, imprudently passing the Euphrates, he was surrounded by Sapor's army near Edessa, in a situation where neither courage nor military skill could be of any avail, and was forced to surrender at discretion (A.D. 259). During nine years Valerian languished in hopeless captivity, the object of scorn and insult to his brutal conqueror, while no effort was made for his liberation by his unnatural son.

SECTION VII.—*From the Captivity of Valerian to the Resignation of Dioclesian.*

FROM A.D. 260 TO A.D. 305.

GALLIENUS succeeded to the throne, receiving the news of his father's misfortune with secret pleasure and open indifference. He seemed to be versed in every thing but the art of government; "he was a master of several curious but useless sciences, a ready orator and elegant poet, a skilful gardener, an excellent cook, and most contemptible prince."* At the moment of his accession, the barbarians, encouraged by the captivity of Valerian, invaded the empire on all sides. Italy itself was invaded by the Germans, who advanced to Ravenna, but they were forced to retire by the emperor. Gallienus, after this exertion, sunk into complete inactivity; his indolence roused a host of competitors for the empire in the different provinces, commonly called "the thirty tyrants," though the number of pretenders did not exceed nineteen. It would be impossible to describe the various struggles for power between these rivals, which distracted every part of the empire. Far the most remarkable of them was Odenatus, who assumed the purple at Palmyra, gained several great victories over the Persians, and besieged Sapor in Ctesiphon. Though he failed to take the city, he checked for a long time the progress of the Sassanides. Gallienus, hearing of these great achievements, resolved to convert a rival into a friend, and proclaimed Odenatus his partner in the empire. But this great man was murdered by some of his own family: he was succeeded by his wife, the celebrated Zenobia, who took the title of Queen of

* Gibbon.

the East. Gallienus did not long survive him; he was murdered while besieging Aureolus, one of his rivals, in Mediolanum (*Milan*); but before his death he transmitted his rights to Claudius, a general of great reputation (A. D. 268). Most of the other tyrants had previously fallen in battle or by assassination.

Marcus Aurelius Claudius, having conquered his only rival, Aureolus, marched against the Germans and Goths, whom he routed with great slaughter. He then prepared to march against Zenobia, who had conquered Egypt; but a pestilence broke out in his army, and the emperor himself was one of its victims (A. D. 270). Extraordinary honours were paid to his memory by the senate. His brother was elected emperor by acclamation; but in seventeen days he so displeased the army by attempting to revive the ancient discipline, that he was deposed and murdered.

Aurelian, a native of Sirmium in Pannonia, was chosen emperor by the army; and the senate, well acquainted with his merits, joyfully confirmed the election. He made peace with the Goths, and led his army against the Germans, who had once more invaded Italy. Aurelian was at first defeated; but he soon retrieved his loss, and cut the whole of the barbarian army to pieces. His next victory was obtained over the Vandals, a new horde that had passed the Danube; and having thus secured the tranquillity of Europe, he marched to rescue the eastern provinces from Zenobia.

The Queen of Palmyra was one of the most illustrious women recorded in history: she claimed descent from the Egyptian Ptolemies, but was probably of Jewish origin, since she is said to have professed the Jewish religion. She was well acquainted with the principal languages of the eastern and western worlds, skilled in the leading sciences of her day, and so well versed in affairs of state, that the successes of her husband, Odenatus, are generally attributed to his having acted by her advice. For nearly six years she ruled Syria and Mesopotamia, discharging all the duties of an excellent sovereign and intrepid commander. Ambition, however, precipitated her ruin: not satisfied with the conquest of Egypt, she aspired at the sovereignty of Asia, and Aurelian resolved to put an end to usurpations so disgraceful to the Roman fame.

On his march through Thrace, the emperor fought a great battle with the Goths. Not satisfied with a single victory, he pursued them across the Danube, routed their forces a second time, and slew one of their kings. Passing over into Asia, he encountered the forces of Zenobia near Antioch ; the battle was sanguinary and well-contested, but in the end the Romans prevailed. A second victory enabled Aurelian to besiege Palmyra, which the dauntless queen defended with great spirit and resolution. At length, finding that there was no hope of succour, she attempted secretly to fly into Persia, but was betrayed by her servants, and taken prisoner. Palmyra surrendered ; but the citizens soon revolting, this great commercial capital was stormed, its inhabitants put to the sword, and its trade and prosperity irretrievably ruined.

Scarcely had this revolt been subdued, when Aurelian was called upon to quell a formidable insurrection in Egypt. The celerity of his march disconcerted the rebels ; they were speedily conquered ; and the emperor, having thus suppressed all the troubles of the East, resolved to recover Gaul, Spain, and Britain, which had now for thirteen years been the prey of different tyrants. A single campaign restored these provinces to the empire ; and Aurelian, returning to Rome, was honoured with the most magnificent triumph that the city had ever beheld. Far more honourable to him, however, was his generous treatment of his captives,—a suitable estate was granted at Tibur (*Tivoli*) to Zenobia and her children. The princess, reconciling herself to her lot, became a respectable Roman matron ; and her family was not extinct in the fifth century.

Tranquillity was first disturbed by a violent insurrection excited at Rome by the debasing of the coinage. The imperial troops, sent to drive the mob from the Cœlian hill, were routed with the loss of seven thousand men, and it was with the utmost difficulty that the insurgents were reduced. Aurelian punished the principal authors of the tumult with great severity, not to say cruelty ; and, finding that he had thus become unpopular, left the city. He directed his course to Gaul, where he appeased some growing disturbances; thence he marched to Vindelicia, and restored it to the empire; but he abandoned the province of Dacia to the barbarians, withdrawing all the Roman garrisons that had been stationed beyond the Danube.

Aurelian's virtues were sullied by the sternness and severity that naturally belongs to a peasant and a soldier. His officers dreaded his inflexibility, which had been already shewn in his sentencing his own nephew to death. While he was preparing to lead his army against the Persians, he discovered an act of peculation committed by Mnestheus, one of his secretaries, and threatened a severe punishment. The guilty functionary, having no other hope of escape, conspired with several others exposed to legal vengeance: they assailed the emperor, escorted only by a few friends, on his road to Byzantium, and slew him with innumerable wounds (A. D. 275). But the assassins did not escape the punishment due to their crimes; the soldiers, attached fondly to an emperor who had so often led them to victory, tore the authors of his death to pieces. They shewed, at the same time, greater respect for the law than had ever been displayed by their predecessors, cheerfully referring the choice of an emperor to the senate.

After a tranquil interregnum of more than six months, the senate elected Marcus Claudius Tacitus, a member of their own body, in spite of his great age, for he was already passed his seventy-fifth year. Having enacted some useful laws, the emperor marched against the Alans, who had overrun Asia Minor. He defeated the barbarians; but the fatigues of the campaign proved too much for his constitution, and he died in Cappadocia, after a short reign of about seven months.

Florian, the brother of Tacitus, was elected emperor by the senate, but Marcus Aurelius Probus was the choice of the Syrian army; and a civil war soon began between these rivals. But Florian's own soldiers took offence at some part of his conduct, rose in sudden mutiny, and put him to death. Probus, now undisputed master of the empire, led his troops from Asia to Gaul, which was again devastated by the German tribes: he not only defeated the barbarians, but pursued them into their own country, where he gained greater advantages than any of his predecessors. Thence he passed into Thrace, where he humbled the Goths; and, returning to Asia, he completely subdued the insurgent Isaurians, whose lands he divided among his veterans. Alarmed at these victories, Bahram II., king of Persia, called Varames by the western writers, sent ambassadors to solicit peace, and submitted to the terms dictated by the emperor. Three competitors in different provinces were next subdued; but when wars were at an end, the emperor employed his armies in useful public works, which so offended the licentious soldiery, that they suddenly attacked and slew him (A.D. 282). They subsequently repented of the crime, and united to raise a stately monument to his memory.

Carus, the captain of the prætorian guards, was elected emperor by the army; and the senate, not without reluctance, assented to the arrangement. The new emperor gave the title of Cæsar to his sons Carinus and Numerianus, the former of whom was one of the most depraved young men of his time; the latter a model of every virtue. The new emperor signalised his accession by a brilliant victory over the Sarmatians: he would have pursued these barbarians into their native wilds, had he not been summoned to Asia by a new invasion of the Persians. Leaving the care of the western provinces to Carinus, the emperor, accompanied by Numerianus, hastened into Mesopotamia, where he defeated Bahram, and, pursuing the Persians into their own country, besieged Ctesiphon. The city would probably have been taken, had not the emperor fallen a victim to disease, or, as others say, to a thunderbolt (A.D. 283). Numerianus was chosen his successor; but, after a few months' reign, he was assassinated by Aper, his father-in-law and captain of his guards. The crime, however, was discovered, and the murderer put to death by the army.

Dioclesian, said to have been originally a slave, was unanimously saluted emperor by the army. He was proclaimed at Chalcedon, on the 17th of December, A.D. 284; an epoch that deserves to be remembered, as it marks the beginning of a new era, called "the era of Dioclesian," or "the era of martyrs," which long prevailed in the church, and is still used by the Copts, the Abyssinians, and other African nations. When

Carinus heard of his brother's death, he assembled a numerous army, marched from Gaul into Illyricum, where he conquered a usurper named Julianus, and thence advancing into Mœsia, inflicted a severe defeat on the army of Dioclesian, in the plains of Margus (*Morava Hissar*). But in the very moment of victory, a tribune, whose wife he had seduced, seized the opportunity of revenge, and by a single blow put an end to the civil war.

Dioclesian made a generous use of his victory: in an age when death, exile, and confiscation, were the usual fate of the conquered party, the new emperor did not even deprive his rival's ministers of office. The troubles of the empire appearing too great to be managed by a single mind, Dioclesian voluntarily gave himself a colleague, selecting for this high situation his friend Maximian, a brave and skilful soldier, but unfortunately also an ignorant and ferocious barbarian. Scarcely had the appointment been made, when Maximian was called upon to exert his military talents in Gaul, both in suppressing insurrections and checking the barbarians. He effected his purposes with great skill; while his colleague gained several victories over the Sarmatians in the east.

A brief interval of tranquillity was followed by new and more alarming disturbances in every part of the empire. The two sovereigns, in great alarm, resolved on a further division of authority; each chose an associate and successor, with the title of Cæsar, who was to be invested with a considerable share of imperial power: to this new dignity Dioclesian nominated Maximin Galerius; and Maximian, Constantius Chlorus. A division of the empire followed: Dioclesian took the provinces beyond the Ægean sea; Thrace and Illyricum were assigned to Galerius; Maximian received Italy and Africa; Gaul, Spain, and Britain, were entrusted to Constantius.

Although this arrangement appears to have been rendered necessary by the circumstances of the empire, it undoubtedly hastened its decline: four courts, with all their expensive adjuncts, were now to be maintained, instead of one: taxes were multiplied; the inhabitants of several provinces reduced to beggary, and agriculturists, unable to meet the imposts levied on land and produce, left the fields in many districts uncultivated. Italy, which had hitherto borne a very light share of the public burdens, was no longer permitted to claim exception as the seat of domestic empire, and was soon reduced to a deplorable condition.

Britain, which had been usurped by Carausius, early claimed the attention of Constantius: it was, however, necessary to prepare a fleet for the invasion, as the usurper was powerful by sea; and while the naval armament was preparing, Constantius gained several victories over the German hordes. Just as he was about to set sail, he learned that Carausius had been deposed and murdered by a new usurper, named Allectus, far inferior to his victim in talent and popularity. The Cæsar instantly hastened to cross the channel; Allectus was defeated and slain in Kent, the remainder of the province quickly reduced to obedience, and the ravages of the barbarians on the northern frontiers prevented. Galerius was as successful on the Danube as Constantius in Britain and on the Rhine; Maximian subdued the barbarous tribes that had invaded Africa, while Dioclesian quelled a dangerous revolt in Egypt. He was soon summoned to protect the empire from a dangerous invasion of the Persians; Galerius had been sent from the Danube to the Euphrates to check their progress, but he was defeated by the Sassanid monarch Narsí, on the very field which had been so fatal to Crassus and his legions. Dioclesian shewed great indignation at the misconduct of Galerius, to which he attributed the recent calamity; but at length he permitted himself to be mollified, and entrusted the Cæsar with a new army for a second campaign.

In the following year the Romans again invaded Persia; but, profiting by recent and bitter experience, their leader left the plains of Mesopotamia on the right, and led his forces through the Armenian mountains, which were more favourable for the operations of his infantry, in which the principal strength of his army consisted. Masking his course from the enemy, Galerius unexpectedly rushed down from the hills on the Persian lines: the surprise, the impetuosity of the attack, and the desire for revenge which animated the Romans, rendered their onset irresistible. Narsi was severely wounded, but escaped by the swiftness of his horse, leaving his entire family, his magnificent tents, and his sumptuous camp-equipage, as a prize to the conquerors. A bag of embossed leather, filled with pearls, fell into the hands of a private soldier: unacquainted with the value of his prize, he flung the pearls away, keeping the bag as something that might be useful. Galerius treated his royal captives with the greatest kindness and generosity; his conduct produced such an effect on Narsi's heart, that he solicited peace. The great province of Mesopotamia (*Juzîrah*) was yielded to the Romans, together with five districts beyond the Tigris, including the greater part of Carduchia (*Kurdistán*), a country more fruitful in soldiers than grain, but which, from its strength and position, commands the greater part of western Asia. These districts were taken from Tiridates, king of Armenia, the ally of the Romans; but he was indemnified, at the expense of Persia, by the fine province of Atropatenê (*Azerbiján*). When the Armenian took possession of this country, he made its chief city, Tauris (*Tabríz*), the metropolis of his kingdom, and greatly improved that ancient capital.

But these triumphs were sullied by a general persecution of the Christians (the tenth and last), which Dioclesian is said to have commenced at the instigation of Galerius (A.D. 303). It lasted ten entire years, and exceeded all the preceding in its indiscriminate massacres and severities. Such multitudes of Christians suffered death, in all the provinces of the empire, that the emperors believed they had accomplished their purpose, and completely extirpated Christianity. They told the world, in a pompous inscription, that they had extinguished the Christian name and superstition, and every where restored the worship of the gods to its former purity and lustre. But the church triumphed over all their artifices and power; and, in spite of the utmost efforts of tyranny, many years had not elapsed after the publication of this boast, when it reigned triumphant in the very metropolis of idolatry and superstition.

Dioclesian prepared to return to Rome, but was delayed for some time by a strange revolt in Syria. Eugenius, an officer of little or no reputation, had been entrusted with the command of five hundred men in Seleucia, who, being employed all day in cleansing the harbour, and compelled to work all night baking their own bread, resolved to deliver themselves from such insupportable drudgery; and forthwith proclaimed their governor emperor. Eugenius at first refused the dignity; but being threatened with instant death, he allowed himself to be invested with the purple, and, by a rapid march, got possession of Antioch. When the citizens, however, recovered from their surprise, they fell upon the insurgents, and cut them to pieces. Dioclesian, instead of rewarding the people of Antioch for their fidelity, ordered their chief magistrates to be put to death without inquiry or trial—a crime which rendered him so odious to the Syrians, that for more than ninety years they could not hear his name pronounced without a shudder.

Rome, on the return of the two emperors, witnessed for the last time the splendid ceremonial of a triumph; it was less costly than those of Aurelian and Probus, but it commemorated greater and more useful victories. In his triumph, and in the spectacles that followed it, however, Dioclesian having displayed more parsimony than was pleasing to the people, he was assailed by jests and lampoons, which annoyed him so much, that he quitted the city for Ravenna. On his journey a severe storm arose, and the cold which he caught produced a long and lingering disease that affected his reason. After he had begun to recover, he was induced, or perhaps compelled, to resign the empire, by Galerius (A. D. 305). He persuaded Maximian to abdicate also. The two Cæsars became emperors, and chose two other nobles to fill the station they had occupied.

Dioclesian survived his abdication nearly nine years: he resided during this time at his country-seat near Salona (*Spalato*), where the ruins of his palace may still be seen. He never regretted the power he had resigned; and when Maximian and others wrote, inviting him to make a struggle for empire, he replied,—"I wish you would come to Salona, and see the cabbages I have planted: after having once visited my garden, you would never again mention to me the name of empire." The close of his life was embittered by domestic misfortune, by the ingratitude of Constantine and Licinius, and by the calamities which he foresaw that the dissensions of these rivals would bring upon the empire. There are various accounts given of the manner of his death, and it is impossible to discover whether he fell by his own hand or by natural disease.

Section VIII.—*From the Abdication of Dioclesian to the Death of Constantine the Great.*

FROM A.D. 303 TO A.D. 337.

The Cæsars, Severus and Maximin, owed their elevation to Galerius; but they were not quite so subservient to his wishes as he expected, both shewing themselves favourable to the toleration of the Christians. Arrangements were made for the division of the empire; Constantius and Severus received the western provinces; Galerius and Maximin ruled all the territories east of the Adriatic. Constantine, the celebrated son of Constantius, was sick in the provinces assigned to Galerius when the empire was thus divided; some efforts were made to assassinate a prince whose talents and popularity had already rendered him formidable. He escaped the danger by a rapid flight, and came to his father, who was just about to embark at Gessoriacum (*Boulogne*) for Britain. The presence of Constantine was required in that island by a formidable invasion of the Picts, a nation now for the first time mentioned in history; but while on his march against these barbarians, he was seized with a mortal disease, and died at Eboracum (*York*), where his body was honourably interred by his son Constantine (A.D. 306).

Constantine was instantly proclaimed Augustus by the soldiers; but Galerius would only give him the title of Cæsar, declaring that Severus was his partner in the empire. Maxentius, the son of Maximian, indignant at his exclusion from power, caused himself to be proclaimed emperor by the dissatisfied soldiery, and induced his father to abandon his solitude, and remount the throne. Severus led an army against them; but he was abandoned by the greater part of his troops, taken prisoner, and put to death (A.D. 307). Maximian, knowing that Galerius would revenge the murder of Severus, strengthened himself by entering into close alliance with Constantine, to whom he gave his daughter Fausta in marriage. Nor did he dread Galerius without a cause: that emperor hastened from the east with a large army, and attempted to besiege Rome; but failing in this enterprise, he permitted his soldiers to devastate Italy. Maximian had gone to Gaul, hoping to receive aid from Constantine; but finding that prudent prince by no means disposed to encounter the hazards of a dangerous war, and hearing that Galerius had retreated precipitately, he returned to Rome, where he reigned conjointly with his son. In the meantime Galerius conferred the title of emperor on his friend Licinius; and thus the empire was shared between six sovereigns.*

Maximian having quarrelled with his son, returned to Gaul, where he began to plot against the life of Constantine; but his treachery was discovered, and he was deservedly executed (A.D. 310). In the following year a loathsome disease, produced by debauchery, removed Galerius from the stage: his dominions were divided between Maximin and Licinius. It was scarcely possible that peace could long continue between the four princes who now shared the empire. Constantine had won the affections of his subjects by his wise and beneficent administration in Gaul, while the cruelty and rapacity of Maxentius filled Italy and Africa with confusion. But the tyrant was not conscious of the weakness that resulted from his crimes. Under pretence of revenging the death of his father, he ordered all the statues erected in honour of Constantine throughout Italy to be thrown down, and thus provoked a war with the most able prince of the age. Constantine having passed the Alps, defeated the lieutenants of Maxentius at Augusta Taurinorum (*Turin*) and Verona, while the tyrant himself remained sunk in sloth and luxury at Rome. At length he was roused from his lethargy by the rapid approach

* Maximian, Galerius, Licinius, Maximin, Constantine, and Maxentius.

of the victorious army: a dreadful battle was fought at a place called Saxa Rubra, within nine miles of Rome, near the little river Cremera, so memorable for the destruction of the Fabii. The result was fatal to Maxentius; the prætorian guards, on whom he chiefly relied, were broken and cut to pieces by the repeated charges of the Gallic horse. The tyrant himself was drowned in the Tiber, while attempting to make his escape through the crowd over the Milvian bridge (A. D. 312). It was during this campaign that Constantine is said to have seen a miraculous vision of a luminous cross in the heavens, a little before sunset; and to have been warned in a dream to take this sacred symbol as his standard. The principal evidence for the truth of this miracle is the emperor's own account of the event, related many years afterwards to Eusebius: one circumstance, however, greatly weakens his testimony,—the vision was so far from producing the conversion of Constantine, that he did not receive baptism until a short time before his death.

No sooner had the death of Maxentius made Constantine master of Rome, than he removed the great source of all the calamities that had befallen the city under the empire, by disbanding the prætorian guards, and destroying their fortified camp. He restored the authority of the senate and magistrates, recalled all those who had been banished by Maxentius, and dismissed the entire tribe of spies and informers. He revoked all the edicts that had been issued against the Christians, and paid great respect to the bishops and clergy, either on account of the miraculous vision already mentioned, or, as is more probable, through gratitude for the efficient aid he had received from the Christians in the recent contest, and anxiety to secure their assistance in any future struggle.

Maximin was a devoted adherent of Paganism; he viewed the innovations of Constantine with great hostility; and when Licinius married the sister of that prince, he resolved to destroy both. Taking advantage of the war in which Constantine was involved with the Franks, he marched against Licinius, hoping to destroy him before any assistance could arrive from the west. His first efforts were crowned with success; but, being totally defeated near Adrianople, he fled without attendants to Nicomedia, where he soon died of rage and disappointment (A.D. 313). Licinius made a cruel use of his victory, slaughtering without mercy all whom he deemed likely to become competitors for empire: among the most illustrious of his victims were the wife and daughter of Dioclesian.

Constantine, during this war, was engaged in securing the tranquillity of western Europe: he gave an unquestionable proof of his attachment to Christianity by convening a general council of the bishops at Arelate (*Arles*), to suppress the heresy of the Donatists; but before the assembly met, he was forced to take the field against Licinius, who had thrown down his statues in Æmona (*Laybach*), a city of Upper Pannonia. With his usual celerity Constantine hastened into Pannonia, before Licinius could expect his arrival; but he found that prince already in the field. A fierce battle was fought at the little town of Cibalis or Cebalæ (*Sevilei*), not far from Sirmium, in which Licinius was defeated, and forced to fly into Thrace. Thither he was followed by Constantine, vanquished a second time, and forced to consent to an accommodation, by which Illyricum, Macedon, Greece, and Lower Mœsia, were yielded to Constantine (A.D. 314). The conqueror immediately took the most prudent measures to secure his new acquisitions; while Licinius continued to provoke his subjects by repeated cruelties and exactions.

Foreign invasions led to a renewal of the civil war. Constantine having conquered the Sarmatians and Goths, pursued the latter into the territories of Licinius, and that prince immediately declared that the recent articles of peace had been violated (A.D. 322). Great preparations were made on both sides for the renewal of hostilities, but Constantine was the first to take the field, and entering Thrace he found his rival encamped on the Hebrus (*Maritza*), not far from Adrianople. The battle was in some measure a struggle between Christianity and Paganism: Constantine displayed the banner of the cross, Licinius the ancient idolatrous standards of the empire: the struggle was fierce—it ended in the total overthrow of Licinius, who had the further mortification of learning that his fleet had been destroyed in the straits of Callipolis (*Gallipoli*) by Crispus, the eldest son of Constantine. An attempt was made to terminate the struggle by negotiation, but it was frustrated by the insincerity of Licinius: he hazarded a second engagement, and was irretrievably ruined. From the field of battle the defeated tyrant fled to Nicomedia, but he was soon taken prisoner, and put to death (A. D. 324). Constantine being thus sole master of the empire, restored the churches, of which the Christians had been deprived in the eastern provinces, to their respective pastors, and issued several edicts for the suppression of idolatry. New controversies in the church led to the convocation of the celebrated council of Nice, in which the doctrine of the Trinity was fixed and defined, the heresy of Arius condemned, and the spiritual supremacy of the emperor virtually acknowledged (A. D. 325). When the labours of this celebrated assembly terminated, Constantine returned to the western provinces, and paid a visit to Rome. His reception in the city was any thing but flattering; the populace loaded him with insults and execrations for abandoning the religion of his forefathers; and his rage at such injurious treatment is said to have greatly influenced his determination of transferring the seat of government from Rome to Byzantium. At the same time he was harassed by domestic troubles, which led him to commit a horrid crime. Instigated by the Empress Fausta, he put his eldest son, the virtuous Crispus, to death without a trial; and when he too late discovered his error, he caused Fausta and her accomplices to be slain. These horrors aggravated his unpopularity among the Romans; but he no longer regarded their displeasure, having finally resolved to give a new capital to the empire (A. D. 330). Anger and caprice were not the only causes that induced Constantine to make such an important change; indeed, the removal of the seat of government was justified by considerations of the soundest policy. The eastern provinces were exposed to the attacks of a powerful dynasty, the Persian Sassanides, who openly aspired to the ancient empire of Cyrus; the frontier of the Danube was not sufficient to restrain the Goths and Sarmatians; the emperors would therefore have endangered the most faithful and wealthy portions of their dominions, had they continued to reside in western Europe. A metropolis on the confines of Europe and Asia was at once recommended, by the political advantages of its central situation, and the opportunities it afforded for reviving the lucrative commerce of the Euxine and the eastern Mediterranean. A slight glance at the natural advantages of Byzantium will shew that it was worthy of being made the metropolis of an empire by the wise sovereign whose name it bears.

The area of Constantinople is an irregular triangle, whose apex, an obtuse point advancing to the east and towards the Asiatic coast, meets and repels the waters of the Thracian Bosphorus. On the north is a winding harbour, known both in ancient and modern times by the name of Chryso-ceras, or the Golden Horn: it is about seven miles in length, with good anchorage through the greater part of its extent; the entrance is not more than five hundred yards wide, and may be easily defended against a hostile armament. On the south-eastern side the walls of the city are washed by the Propontis (*Sea of Marmora*), and the west forms the base of the triangle which is connected with the continent. Thus situated, the Euxine sea on the one side, and the Ægean on the other, could supply it with the richest productions of Europe and Asia; while its shape rendered it easily defensible against the savage and plundering tribes of Thrace.

Enormous sums were expended by Constantine in embellishing his new capital: unfortunately, there was equal prodigality in the other branches of the administration, and the emperor's rule became grinding and severe. But he did not abandon his warlike character; he severely chastised the Goths and Sarmatians, who invaded Thrace, and compelled them to give hostages for their future good conduct. In the decline of his life, he appears to have adopted much of the pomp and luxury characteristic of Asiatic despots; but when increasing disease warned him of approaching dissolution, he received the sacrament of baptism, and expired ten months afterwards, in the thirtieth year of his reign (A. D. 335). He left three sons to inherit his empire.

The removal of the seat of government consummated the

revolution in the Roman constitution, which had been commenced in the reign of Dioclesian; it became a simple despotism, with more of a political than military character. An entire change was made in the form of administration; the magistrates being divided into three classes, the *illustrissimi*, the *spectabiles*, and the *clarissimi*, (illustrious, respectable, and honourable).

The magistrates of the first class were, the consuls and patricians, the prætorian and metropolitan præfects, the masters-general of cavalry and infantry, and the seven great officers of the household. The titles of consul and patrician were merely honorary. They were conferred by the emperor at his pleasure, and in both cases the distinctions were personal, not hereditary. The power of the prætorian prefects ranked next to that of the emperors. The Roman dominions were divided into four great præfectures, and these were again subdivided into dioceses and provinces. The præfectures were named, those of the East, Illyricum, Italy, and Gaul. To the prætorian præfects was assigned the civil government of these several divisions; but Constantine had taken care that such power should not be rendered too dangerous by being united with military command. To their charge were entrusted the coinage, the highways, the ports, the granaries, the manufactures, and every thing that could interest the public prosperity of their respective districts. They were empowered to explain, enforce, and in some cases modify the imperial edicts. They could remove or punish the provincial governors; an appeal lay to their tribunal from all inferior jurisdictions; and the sentence of the præfect was final.

Rome and Constantinople had præfects of their own. The superior dignity of their tribunals caused those of the prætors to be deserted, and the most ancient title of Roman magistracy soon fell into desuetude. The peace of both capitals was preserved by a vigilant police; and so numerous were the statues with which they were adorned, that a magistrate was specially appointed to preserve them from injury.

The great officers of the state and court were, 1. the *præpositus sancti cubiculi* (lord chamberlain), whose duty it was " to attend the emperor in his hours of state or amusement, and to perform about his person all those menial offices which can only derive their splendour from the influence of royalty." Under him were all the *comites palatii* (lords of the palace), and *cubicularii* (chamberlains), many of whom, at a later age, were eunuchs of great influence. 2. The *magister officiorum* (minister for the home department): to him was entrusted the management of all correspondence between the prince and his subjects, memorials, petitions, letters, and their answers. He was also inspector-general of the civil and military schools, and appeals lay to his tribunal from every part of the empire, in cases where the privileges of the imperial officers were concerned. 3. The *comes sacrarum largitionum* (lord high treasurer) was the chief minister of finance: his duties were not confined to the charge of the exchequer and superintendence of tax-gatherers; he had also the charge over manufactures and commerce, which Constantine, with more wisdom than most of his predecessors, brought under the especial care of the state. 4. The *quæstor* (principal secretary of state) was the representative of the emperor's legislative power, and the original source of civil jurisprudence: some of his functions appear to have been similar to those of the British lord chancellor. 5. The *comes rei principis* (keeper of the privy purse) had the charge of the imperial private estates, which were scattered through the provinces from Mauritania to Britain. 6 and 7. The *comites domesticorum* (commanders of the household guards) presided over the *seven scholæ* (troops or squadrons) of cavalry and infantry that guarded the emperor's person.

The commanders of the army were the *magistri equitum* (generals of cavalry), *magistri peditum* (generals of infantry), and the *magistri utriusque militiæ* (commander-in-chief); those who commanded under them were called *duces* and *comites* (dukes and counts); they were distinguished by wearing a golden belt, and received, in addition to their pay, a liberal allowance, sufficient to maintain one hundred and ninety servants and one hundred and fifty-eight horses. Constantine changed the entire constitution of the legions, diminishing their number to less than one-fourth: to secure a regular supply of young soldiers, he made it one of his conditions, in assigning lands to the veterans, that their sons should be trained to the profession of arms. But the necessity for such a stipulation is not the only proof we have of the decay of military spirit. Such was the dislike the degenerate Romans entertained for a soldier's life, that many young men in Italy mutilated the fingers of their right hand to avoid being pressed into the service. In consequence of this reluctance, the custom of employing the barbarians as soldiers became every day more frequent and more fatal. They were not only enlisted in the ranks, but many of them were raised to the highest dignities of the state.

These changes in the constitution of the civil and military administration of the empire rendered the government more costly, and required an entirely new system of taxation for their support. It is one of the few advantages of an arbitrary government, that it is not tempted to delude its subjects by the onerous and expensive machinery of indirect taxation through the excise and customs, where an apparent choice is left to the purchaser, and his payment of the tax, by buying the taxed article, seems to be voluntary. A despot may venture on direct taxation of property or person; and, though this is apparently more harsh, it is in reality more favourable to the subject. The first of the new taxes was the *indiction*, an annual land-tax, levied proportionate to the fertility of the estates possessed by landed proprietors; and a general census, or survey of property, was made throughout the empire every fifteen years, to regulate this assessment. Hence the name of *indiction* is given indifferently to the tax and to the cycle of registration. Trade and commerce were subjected to an impost called the *aurum lustrale*, which was collected every fourth year. "The honourable merchant of Alexandria, who imported the gems and spices of India for the use of the western world; the usurer, who derived from the interest of money a silent and ignominious profit; the ingenious manufacturer, the diligent mechanic, and even the most obscure retailer of a sequestered village, were obliged to admit the officers of the revenue into the partnership of their gain: and the sovereign of the Roman empire, who tolerated the profession, consented to share the infamous gain of prostitutes."* The last imposition that need be noticed was originally a free gift, called *aurum coronarium*,—being a compensation for the crown of gold presented by the allies of the Romans to generals who had been the authors of their deliverance, or who had conferred upon them any remarkable favour. This spontaneous offering was at length exacted as a debt, whenever the emperor announced any remarkable event which might give him a real or apparent claim to the benevolence of his subjects; such as his accession, the birth of a son, or a victory over the barbarians. To these must be added, the municipal expenses, which fell almost wholly on the civic officers. Instead of having a system of local taxation, the richest citizens were obliged to take in turn the duty of providing for the administrative wants of the towns in which they resided; but our information respecting the practical operation of this plan is too limited for us to pronounce any opinion upon its efficiency.

It must not be supposed that evil alone resulted from these changes; on the contrary, under the circumstances of the empire, Constantine's innovations were for the most part useful reforms. The great curse of the Romans during several centuries had been military despotism; but the license of the turbulent soldiery was checked and restrained by "the pride, pomp, and circumstance," with which the civil administration was surrounded. The despotism of a court was put in place of the despotism of a camp; and it needs not to be told, how vast was the improvement that must have resulted from such an alteration.

Under Constantine, Christianity became the established religion of the empire. He found the constitution of the church already organised—its form of government firmly established. Even in the reign of Dioclesian the bishops held an honourable rank in their respective provinces, and were treated with proper respect, as men of high and sacred station, not only by the people, but the magistrates themselves. Constantine saw clearly

* Gibbon.

the advantages that would result to the extent and stability of his power by cementing the union between the church and the state; he therefore appropriated a great portion of the revenue of cities to the endowment of churches and the support of the clergy. Thus religion came to the aid of police in checking turbulence, and, but for the crimes and follies of the rulers, the Roman empire might have enjoyed a long course of prosperity under the constitution of Constantine.

Section IX.—*From the Death of Constantine to the Re-union of the Empire under Theodosius the Great.*

FROM A.D. 337 TO A.D. 394.

Constantine bequeathed portions of his dominions to his nephews Dalmatius and Hannibilianus; but no notice was taken of their claims by the army or the Roman senate, the late emperor's three sons being proclaimed unanimously heirs of his dominions. These princes had been educated with the greatest care; the most pious of the Christian teachers, the most celebrated professors of Grecian philosophy and Roman jurisprudence, were engaged to superintend their instruction; but the youths, Constantine, Constantius, and Constans, resembled their mother Fausta more than their illustrious father, and were as similar in depravity of disposition as they were in name. Some portion of their faults must, however, be attributed to paternal weakness. Ere they had emerged from boyhood they were successively invested with the title of Cæsar, and invited to share in the administration. Such injudicious indulgence necessarily surrounded them with a crowd of flatterers, ready to take advantage of the warm passions and confiding dispositions of youth; they were summoned too early from their studies, and were permitted to exchange the pursuit of knowledge for the enjoyment of luxury and the expectation of a throne.

Constantius was the nearest of the brothers to the capital when their father died; he hastened to take possession of the palace, and, to remove the apprehensions of his kinsmen, who justly suspected his jealous temper, he took a solemn oath to protect them from all danger. In a very few days a forged scroll was placed in his hands by the bishop of Nicomedia, purporting to be the genuine testament of the late emperor, in which Constantine was made to declare that he had been poisoned by his brothers, and to exhort his children to vengeance. The soldiers, secretly prepared to second this incredible charge, loudly demanded the punishment of the accused; all legal forms were violated; a promiscuous massacre was made of the Flavian family. The two brothers of the great Constantine, seven of his nephews, the patrician Optatus, who had married his sister, and his chief favourite the præfect Ablavius, were butchered, without being permitted to speak a word in their own defence. Gallus and Julian, the youngest sons of Julius Constantius, were with difficulty concealed until the rage of the assassins had subsided.

A new division of the empire was made by the princes. Constantine, the eldest, took possession of the capital; Constantius received Thrace and the Asiatic provinces; the western dominions were assigned to Constans. Ere long, the enemies of Rome, that had been daunted by the fame of Constantine, began to harass his successors; but far the most dangerous of the wars in which they had to engage was that waged by Shah-púr II., king of Persia, against Constantius.

Shah-púr's previous history deserves to be noticed. His father Hormúz (*Hormisdas*) died, leaving no son (A.D. 310): the kingdom was on the point of being thrown into confusion, when it was announced by the principal mobeds, or priests, that one of the ladies in the harem was pregnant, and that, from certain indications, they knew that the child would be a male. A strange ceremony of coronation was performed for the unborn infant. From the hour of his birth the whole nation watched over his progress with the most affectionate interest, and the early proofs he exhibited of spirit and ability spread universal joy through Persia. He had not emerged from boyhood, when the fierce Arab tribes from the neighbouring peninsula took advantage of his minority to desolate his kingdom; the royal youth marched against them, routed their forces, slew many, and took a greater number prisoners. To terrify their countrymen from renewing such an invasion, he caused the shoulders of his captives to be pierced and then dislocated by a string passed through them; and from this circumstance he received the formidable title of *Zúlaktáf*, or "Lord of the Shoulders."

Shah-pûr, or Sapor as he is called by western writers, inherited the pretensions of the Sassanides to the empire of Cyrus; but he was particularly anxious to recover the five provinces that had been ceded to the Romans beyond the Tigris, and to assert the ancient supremacy of his family over Mesopotamia. Constantius hasted to the banks of the Euphrates on the first news of the approach of so formidable an invader; but the war long continued to be a series of petty skirmishes and predatory incursions. Nine sanguinary but indecisive engagements were fought; but at length the Romans, by their own imprudence, received a decisive overthrow in the plains of Singara (*Sinjar*), not far from the ruins of Babylon (A. D. 348). Sapor, encouraged by this victory, laid siege to Nisibis (*Nisibin*); but, after he had lost more than twenty thousand men before the walls, he was forced to relinquish the enterprise, and hasten to the defence of his eastern provinces, which were invaded by the fierce tribes from beyond the Oxus. This war induced him to propose terms of truce to Constantius, which that prince readily accepted (A. D. 350), as the troubled state of the empire rendered his presence necessary in Europe.

Three years had scarcely elapsed from the partition of the empire, when the ambition of Constantine kindled the flames of civil war (A. D. 340). Not content with wresting the African provinces from Constans, he invaded that prince's dominions through the Julian Alps, and devastated the country round Aquileia. But, advancing with great imprudence, he fell into an ambuscade near the little river Alsa (*Ansa*), and was slain with the greater part of his followers. Constans took possession of his brother's provinces, and shewed no inclination to reserve any share for the absent Constantius.

During ten years Constans remained master of two-thirds of the empire, which he plundered by his rapacity, and disgraced by his vices. He usually resided in Gaul, whose forests afforded him opportunities for hunting, the only manly sport to which he was addicted. While pursuing game in a neighbouring forest, Magnentius, who commanded the imperial forces stationed at Augustodunum (*Autun*), caused himself to be proclaimed emperor, and closed the gates of the city. Tidings of the revolt were, however, conveyed to Constans; he fled towards Spain, but was overtaken at Elliberis (*Elne*), or, as it was then called, Helena, in memory of the mother of Constantine, and put to death.

The usurpation of Magnentius in Gaul was followed by that of Vetranio in Illyria; but the latter general assumed the purple very reluctantly, being compelled by the clamours of his soldiers, and urged by the princess Constantina, who placed the crown on his head with her own hand. This ambitious woman had been the wife of Hannibilianus, her cousin, whose sad fate has been already mentioned. She was eager to possess power, and so unscrupulous about the means, that she persuaded Vetranio to form an alliance with Magnentius, whose hands yet reeked with the blood of her brother Constans.

Constantius, having concluded a truce with Sapor, entrusted the care of the east to his lieutenants, but afterwards to his cousin Gallus, whom he thus raised from a prison to a throne. He then hasted to Europe, deceived Vetranio by offering to make him his colleague, and obtained admission into Constantinople. In a public assembly of the army and people, the artful prince, in a studied address, asserted his claims to the empire; a unanimous burst of applause was followed by shouts for the deposition of the usurpers; Vetranio quietly submitted, and, taking the diadem from his head, tendered his homage to Constantius. The prince not only spared his rival's life, but assigned him a considerable pension. Vetranio retired to Prusa (*Brúsa*), where he spent the rest of his life in retirement, without ever expressing a desire to resume the sceptre. Magnentius foresaw that he would be the next assailed, and he led his army into Lower Pannonia, which became the theatre of a fierce and sanguinary war. The armies finally met for a decisive battle on the plains of Mursa (*Essek*); the heavy cavalry of Constantius, sheathed in full panoply of plates of steel, decided the fate of the day, the very weight of their onset breaking the lines of the western legions, while the light archers of Asia harassed the naked German auxiliaries, on whom Magnentius chiefly relied, and reduced them to such despair, that battalions threw themselves into the rapid stream of the Drave. Still, so obstinate was the battle, that fifty-four thousand fell in the field, and the victors suffered more severely than the vanquished. It has been justly observed, that the destructive plains of Mursa absorbed the strength of the empire; for never again could the Roman rulers collect such noble bands of veterans as perished there by mutual slaughter.

Magnentius fled to Italy, whither he was followed by Constantius in the following spring. The peninsula soon submitted to its legitimate sovereign; but the usurper escaped into Gaul. Finding, however, that he could not long protract resistance, he baffled the vengeance of Constantius by suicide; his associates were reduced either to follow his example, or suffer the penalties of treason.

Constantius had given Constantina in marriage to his cousin Gallus, invested him with the title of Cæsar, and entrusted him with the administration of Asia. The Cæsar, naturally of a sullen and morose temper, had been soured by the sufferings of his early youth, and his evil passions were stimulated by the ambitious intrigues of the princes to whom he was unfortunately united. His excesses at length compelled Constantius to send commissioners to investigate the state of the east: these officers proceeded to Antioch, where they seem to have conducted themselves with unnecessary and offensive haughtiness; but their faults afford no sufficient excuse for the crime of Gallus, who urged the populace of Antioch to put the commissioners to death with torture and insult, and then ordered their bodies to be thrown into the Orontes (*Aaszy*). Constantius, instead of openly resenting the outrage, invited Gallus to visit him: the Cæsar delayed until further procrastination was impossible; he proceeded on the road to Milan through Asia and Thrace, in safety; but when he passed the frontiers of Pannonia, he was placed under arrest, hurried to a distant castle in Istria, and secretly put to death (A. D. 354). Julian, the only surviving descendant of Constantius Chlorus, except the reigning emperor, would have shared his brother's fate, but for the generous interference of the empress Eusebia. She procured him permission to prosecute his studies in Athens, where, dazzled by the false philosophy of the schools, he forsook Christianity for Paganism, and earned for himself the unenviable title of Apostate. After he had been more than a year in retirement, he was summoned to court, united to Helena, the sister of the emperor, and appointed to govern the countries north of the Alps, with the title of Cæsar.

Constantius himself had gained several victories over the Germanic tribes; but he delayed in the west after the departure of Julian, to support the cause of the Arians against the orthodox prelates. Before returning to the east, he resolved to visit the ancient capital of the empire; and Rome, after an interval of thirty-two years, was gladdened with the presence of its sovereign. Constantius was so pleased with his reception, that he presented to the city the splendid Theban obelisk, with which his father had intended to adorn Constantinople. He was compelled to hurry his departure by intelligence of the Sarmatians having invaded Pannonia. Constantius soon appeared on the Danube: he gained several important victories over the barbarians; but scarcely had he secured the tranquillity of his northern frontiers, when he was threatened with more dangerous hostilities on the side of Persia.

Having subdued the fierce tribes of Turkestán, Sapor renewed his attacks upon the Roman empire, and, guided by a deserter, entered Mesopotamia. Irritated by the insolence of the inhabitants, he laid siege to Amida (*Diarbekr*); and though he captured that strong city, he lost the favourable season of invading Syria, and was forced to content himself with reducing Singara (*Sanjar*) and Bezabdé (*Jezîrah*). Constantius made an effort to recover Bezabdé, but was compelled to raise the siege. He returned to Antioch, where his mortification was increased by intelligence of the brilliant achievements of Julian in Gaul. The young prince had vanquished the Allemans, the Franks, and several other formidable tribes; he had pursued his victorious career beyond the Rhine, and by his rapid conquests filled Germany with confusion; while the prudence of his civil administration raised Gaul to unexampled prosperity. Constantius resolved to weaken the strength of the Cæsar, and summoned his best legions from Gaul to defend the east; the soldiers refused to obey, and proclaimed Julian emperor. Preparations for civil war were made on both sides; but its calamities were averted by the death of Constantius (A.D. 361). During this entire reign the Christian church was scandalised and distracted by fierce disputes arising out of the Arian heresy: Constantius was the avowed partisan of the Arians, and encouraged them in their persecution of the orthodox, especially sanctioning the efforts made for the destruction of the celebrated Athanasius, bishop of Alexandria.

When Julian reached Heraclea (*Ezekli*), though he was still sixty miles distant from the capital, the whole population of Constantinople came out to welcome his arrival, and he made his triumphal entry amid general acclamations. One of his earliest measures was to constitute a court at Chalcedon (*Scutari*) for the trial of such ministers of Constantius as might be accused of peculation. Many of them indeed well deserved punishment; but the ostentatious mode in which they were brought to trial was an ungenerous attack on the memory of the late emperor, and the inquisitions were conducted with such indiscriminate severity, that many innocent persons suffered with the guilty. He then commenced a complete reform of the court, banishing the eunuchs and other ministers of luxury; but with the idle parade of pomp, Julian discarded many of the decencies of life, ostentatiously exhibiting a disregard for personal cleanliness, as if filth was a necessary element of philosophy. But the great object of his ambition was to restore ancient paganism; he revoked the edicts that had been issued against idolatry, under the plausible pretext of granting freedom of opinion to all his subjects; he encouraged the philosophers to veil the most revolting fictions of mythology under allegorical explanations; he shewed a marked dislike to the Christians who visited the court; and finally, he closed the schools which were kept by the clergy.

But the most remarkable of his enterprises for the overthrow of Christianity was his celebrated attempt to rebuild the temple of Jerusalem, which appears to have been miraculously defeated. Seeing that the condition of the Jews was a standing miracle in proof of Christianity, he resolved to weaken or destroy its effect, by restoring to that people their ancient city and national worship, erecting for them at the same time a temple on Mount Moriah, whose splendour should surpass that of the church of the holy sepulchre. This measure was frustrated, after great expense had been incurred in making preparations for its execution, as most historians declare, in consequence of balls of fire that burst from the earth, and scared the workmen employed to dig the foundation. Whether these phenomena were supernatural, or whether they ever had existence, is really of little importance in the great weight that the occurrence gives to the evidence in favour of the divine origin of Christianity: the most powerful monarch of the earth attempted to erect a building in one of his cities; he was aided by a wealthy and zealous people; pride, passion, and interest equally urged him to persevere; yet was he forced to abandon the enterprise. Assuredly we must say, "the finger of God is here!"

While Julian, by withholding his countenance from sincere believers on the one hand, and placing every possible impediment in the way of instruction on the other, was using all his efforts to check the progress of Christianity, he was summoned to take the field against the Persians, who had renewed their incursions. Julian invaded their dominions, and gained several great triumphs, though he was unable to bring the enemy to a decisive engagement. At length, deceived by treacherous guides, he burned his boats, and advanced into a desert country, where his army was soon reduced to great distress from want of provisions. Under these circumstances he resolved to retreat; but his retrograde march was greatly impeded by the light cavalry of the Persians, who hovered round the flanks and rear, discharging showers of darts and arrows; but retreating, like the Parthians their predecessors, whenever any effort was made to bring them to a regular engagement. At length Julian himself was mortally wounded, in a skirmish that proved favourable to the Romans. He died the same night (A. D. 363), about twenty months after his becoming sole master of the empire.

Jovian, the first of the domestics, was saluted Augustus by the army; and his first care was to conclude a dishonourable peace with the Persians, resigning to Sapor not only the five provinces beyond the Tigris, but the whole of Mesopotamia, including the fortified cities of Nisibis and Singara, which had so often baffled the most vigorous efforts of the Sassanides. His next enterprise was more glorious: he restored the Christian religion to its ancient supremacy; but he calmed the fears of his pagan subjects by a wise edict of toleration, in which he prohibited no rites, however idolatrous, save those of magic. On his journey towards Constantinople, he slept in a damp room, which his attendants had heated with charcoal; he was suffocated by the mephitic vapour, and found dead in his bed (A. D. 364).

For ten days after the death of Jovian, the empire remained without a sovereign. At length the Count Valentinian was chosen by the council of ministers and generals, and the army unanimously acquiesced in their decision. Soon after his election the new emperor divided his dominions with his brother Valens, to whom he assigned the eastern provinces, reserving to himself Illyricum, Italy, Gaul, Spain, Britain, and Africa. The emperor of the west made Milan the seat of his government; Valens established his court at Constantinople. This division of the Roman dominions into eastern and western empires was so manifestly required by the necessity of the times, that it provoked neither observation nor remonstrance. From henceforth their histories require separate consideration; and we shall, in the first place, direct our attention to the reign of Valentinian.

The emperor had scarcely reached Italy, when he was summoned to cross the Alps by an invasion of the Germans, who devastated all northern and western Gaul, defeating two Roman armies that had been sent to check their inroads. Valentinian made the most vigorous efforts to retrieve the fame of the empire, and succeeded; but his exertions brought on a disease that nearly deprived him of life. The angry disputes respecting the succession that had taken place during his illness filled him with just alarm; and immediately after his recovery, he took care to have his son Gratian recognised as his heir, and proclaimed Cæsar in the presence of the army. The piracies of the Saxons in the northern seas first began to attract attention in the reign of Valentinian; and so severely did they harass the northern coasts of Gaul, that it was necessary to appoint a maritime court for their protection. At the same time the province of Britain was invaded by the Picts and Scots: so rapid was the progress of the barbarians, aided probably by some of the discontented natives, that Britain would have been lost to the empire, but for the heroic exertions of Theodosius, to whom Valentinian entrusted the pacification, or rather the recovery of the island. This able commander not only restrained the barbarians, but in some measure restored the ancient prosperity of the province: he was rewarded by the emperor with the office of master-general of the cavalry, and appointed to protect the frontier of the Upper Danube from the inroads of the Allemans, until he was chosen to a more important station, and entrusted with the suppression of the formidable revolt of Africa.

Count Romanus, the military governor of Africa, had provoked general resentment by his avarice and exactions; complaints were made of him to Valentinian, and a commissioner appointed to investigate his delinquency; but the count bribed the imperial ministers and commissioners, purchased security from a venal court, and severely punished those who had been guilty of the treason of complaint. Provoked by such accumulated wrongs, the Africans revolted, choosing for their leader Finnus, the son of the wealthy Nabal, who had been summoned to appear before the governor's tribunal on a charge of murdering his brother. Numidia and Mauritania were already in possession of the insurgents, when the entire face of the war was changed by the arrival of Theodosius: from the moment of his landing, the revolters seem to have lost all courage; after a weak struggle, Finnus abandoned his army, to seek refuge with the prince of a native tribe in the interior; but he was betrayed to the Romans, and could only escape a public execution by committing suicide. Scarcely had this war terminated, when Valentinian died suddenly, while waging war against the Quadi (A. D. 375). He had conquered these savage warriors, and deputies had been sent to deprecate his resentment; but while reproaching the ambassadors with national perfidy, he worked himself into such a passion, that he burst a blood-vessel, and instantly expired. Valentinian was naturally cruel and severe, but he was disposed to be inflexibly just; and the many unmerited executions that he sanctioned must be attributed to the artifices of corrupt ministers. He was warmly attached to the orthodox faith, and readily gave shelter to the bishops and clergy who sought refuge in his court from the persecutions of his brother Valens.

The emperor of the east, soon after his accession, went into Syria, which was threatened by a Persian invasion; but before he could complete his preparations for war, he was alarmed by the revolt of Procopius, a kinsman of the emperor Julian, but possessing no other merit, whose pretensions were acknowledged by a considerable body of the army and the citizens of Constantinople. Valens was defeated in his first efforts to overthrow the usurper; but Procopius soon disgusted his supporters by excessive haughtiness and tyranny: he was deserted by those who had been foremost in placing him upon the throne, and was taken prisoner almost without a contest. His fate involved that of many others, for Valens was a stranger to mercy. The emperor was soon more honourably engaged in a war with the Goths, whom he completely subdued, and compelled to submit to humiliating conditions of peace.

The dangerous schism in the church caused by the heresy of Arius was greatly aggravated by the intemperate zeal, and, in some instances, by the unhallowed ambition of rival prelates. Valens declared himself a patron of the Arians, and caused no fewer than eighty orthodox ecclesiastics to be murdered, for maintaining the election of a bishop of their creed to the see of Constantinople. Armenia was at the same time invaded by the Persians; but Sapor, having received a severe defeat, and the Armenian prince Paras, on whose aid he relied, having been treacherously murdered by the Romans, the truce was once more renewed.

In the western empire Valentinian had been succeeded by his sons Gratian and Valentinian II.; the latter, a child only five years old, was added as a colleague to Gratian by the general council of the army. Gratian II. commenced his reign by punishing those ministers and senators who had been guilty of extortion; but, yielding to the suggestions of envious courtiers, he sanctioned the execution of the gallant Theodosius, who had just completed his conquest of the Moors: the emperor, after some time, discovered by what gross misrepresentations he had been led to commit so great a crime, and bitterly repented of his guilt. He made several laws favourable to the interest of the church, ordaining that all controversies respecting religion should be decided by the bishop and synod of the provinces in which they occurred; that the clergy should be free from personal charges; and that all places where heterodox doctrines were taught should be confiscated.

The western empire was enjoying profound peace, the eastern provinces were beginning to taste the unusual sweets of repose, when a people more ferocious than any barbarians hitherto known appeared for the first time on the north-eastern frontiers. The Huns, crossing the Tanaïs (*Don*) and Palus Mæotis (*Sea of Azov*), drove before them the nations that dwelt north of the Danube; and these fugitives, hurled one upon another, were forced to invade the Roman provinces, and commence the dismemberment of the empire. The earliest accounts of the Huns are to be found in the Chinese historians, who call these savages "Huíng Nú," and describe them as masters of the country between the river Irtish, the Altaïan mountains, the Chinese wall, and Mantchew Tartary. Their personal appearance was almost a caricature of humanity; so that the Romans compared them to a block of wood that had been only partially trimmed: this is said to have been in some degree caused by the strange custom of flattening the nose of male infants the moment they were born, in order that the vizor which they wore in battle should fit closer to the face, and also to their plucking out the beard by the roots as soon as it began to grow. They lived on raw flesh, or at best only sodden by being placed under their saddles and pressed against the backs of their steeds during a sharp gallop: devoted to war and the chase, they left the cultivation of their fields to women and slaves; they built no cities; they erected no houses; any place encircled by walls they looked upon as a sepulchre, and never believed themselves in safety beneath a roof. About the commencement of the second century of the Christian era, the southern Huns, aided by the Chinese and the eastern Tartars, expelled their northern brethren from their ancient habitations, and compelled them to seek refuge in the territories of the Bashkírs. Here they were brought into contact with a fiercer but less warlike race, the Alans, whom they gradually drove before them, being pressed forward themselves by fresh hordes from the east, until they took possession of the plains between the Rha (*Volga*) and the Tanaïs.

Joined by the Alans and other barbarous tribes that they had conquered, the innumerable cavalry of the Huns passed the lower Tanaïs, and swept the rich fields of the Ostrogoths. The Gothic armies were defeated, and at length the greater part of that nation abandoned the country that they had laboriously brought to a high state of cultivation, and retired beyond the Borysthenes (*Dneiper*) and the Danastus (*Dneister*). The Huns made a horrible carnage of those who remained, sparing neither women nor children; and all who did not save themselves by a precipitous flight, perished by the edge of the sword. The conquerors soon passed the Danastus, and inflicted the same calamities on the Visigoths to which they had already subjected their eastern brethren. Athanaric, the Gothic monarch, after having suffered a severe defeat, saw no better mode of defence than to fortify himself between the Hierassus (*Pruth*) and the Danube, by a wall extending from one river to the other, leaving the rest of his country exposed to the ravages of the dreadful Huns.

The whole Gothic nation was reduced to despair; their warriors, who had so often maintained a fierce struggle against the legions, now appeared as suppliants on the banks of the Danube, petitioning for permission to cultivate the waste lands of Thrace. Their request was granted, on condition of their resigning their arms; but the officers sent to see this stipulation enforced were bribed to neglect their duty: most of the Goths retained their weapons, which they regarded as the means of obtaining more valuable possessions than those they had lost.

About the same time, Arianism was established among the Goths by the exertions of their bishop, the celebrated Ulphilas, who invented the Gothic alphabet: this subsequently aggravated their hostility to the Romans; for the enmity of rival sects had, towards the close of the fourth century, become greater than that between Christians and Pagans. The officers whom Valens chose to superintend the settlement of the Goths were the most profligate extortioners even of his corrupt court: instead of supplying provisions to the fugitives until their new lands would yield a harvest, as had been promised, they closed the magazines, and charged exorbitant prices for the worst and most revolting kinds of food. At length Lupicinus attempted to murder Fritigern and the other chiefs of the Goths, at a banquet in Marcianopolis (*Pravadi*), to which they had been treacherously invited. The plot exploded prematurely; the Gothic leaders escaped; and their followers took revenge for the atrocious breach of hospitality by massacring the greater part of the Roman legions. In the mean time the Ostrogoths, pressed forward by the Huns, had crossed the Danube and re-inforced Fritigern just as the war was about to commence: thus supported, the irritated sovereign devastated Thrace, Macedon, and Thessaly, approached the walls of Constantinople, and destroyed its suburbs. Valens wrote to Gratian for aid; and the young emperor, though harassed by wars with the Germanic tribes and the Alans, marched to his assistance. He was delayed, however, by illness at Sirmium; and before he could resume his march, Valens was no more. The eastern emperor, baffled by the artifices and enraged by the boldness of Fritigern, hazarded a decisive battle near Adrianople, in which he was defeated and slain (A.D. 378). The Romans had not suffered so severe a loss since they were overthrown by Hannibal at Cannæ: two-thirds of the legions, including thirty-five tribunes and commanders of cohorts, fell in the fatal field.

Gratian was incapable of remedying this disaster without the aid of a colleague, for he could not advance against the Goths without leaving the western provinces a prey to the Germans. He chose as his associate Theodosius, afterwards named the Great, son of the elder Theodosius, whom he had unjustly put to death.

The accession of Theodosius was hailed with delight by all the eastern provinces: he defeated the Goths in the field; but, what was of still greater importance, he won their affections by his justice and moderation; so that they voluntarily promised not only to abstain from hostilities, but to protect the frontiers of the Danube. Being himself sincerely attached to the orthodox faith, he summoned a general council at Constantinople to check the progress of heresy, and issued several edicts to restrain the teachers of erroneous opinions. While he was thus engaged, Maximus, the governor of Britain, revolted against Gratian, and was joined by the whole of the western legions. The emperor seeing himself abandoned by his troops, fled towards Italy, but was overtaken at Lugdunum (*Lyons*), and put to death (A.D. 383). St. Ambrose, bishop of Milan, courageously went into Gaul, claimed the body of the deceased emperor from the usurper, obtained it after some delay, and honourably interred the remains of Gratian in the sepulchre that had been raised for the Valentinian family in the Milanese cathedral.

Maximus, to support his usurpation, had brought with him the flower of the British youth; but the Roman province, thus deprived of its defenders, was exposed to the ravages of the Picts and Scots, who broke through the Roman wall, and pushed their excursions far into the south. Theodosius, harassed by the attacks of the barbarians in the east, at first entered into a treaty with Maximus: but the usurper, encouraged by impunity, soon meditated depriving Valentinian II. of Italy, though that prince had shewn little inclination to revenge the murder of Gratian, his brother and benefactor. Valentinian, unable to defend his territories, fled to Theodosius, who instantly marched against Maximus. The usurper was defeated in two decisive battles; he sought shelter in Aquileia; but he was arrested by his own soldiers, brought in chains to Theodosius, and executed (A.D. 388). It is said that his death was hastened by the imperial ministers, who feared that he might extort a pardon from their master's compassion.

The generous conqueror not only restored Valentinian to his ancient dominions, but resigned to him the provinces that had belonged to Gratian. Having visited Rome, and sanctioned some severe measures for extirpating idolatry in that city, he returned to the east, where he made similar efforts to crush pagan superstitions and Christian heresies. The young Valentinian did not long retain his throne; he was murdered by Arbogastes, a Frank whom he had unwisely admitted to too great a share of sovereign power (A.D. 392). The Frank did not dare to assume the purple himself, but he conferred the empire on one of the royal secretaries, named Eugenius, whom he trusted that he could make the mere instrument of his ambition.

Theodosius refused to enter into any negotiation with the usurper, but made preparations for war. Having levied a powerful army, he forced the passes of the Alps (A.D. 394), and encountering the forces of Eugenius on the banks of the Frigidum (*Wibach*), put them to the rout. The usurper was murdered by his own soldiers, and Arbogastes committed suicide. Theodosius, in consequence of this victory, became master of the whole Roman empire, which was thus once more re-united under a single head.

SECTION X.—*The Overthrow of the Western Empire.*

FROM A.D. 394 TO A.D. 476.

THEODOSIUS was well aware that the partition of the empire originally made by Valentinian was rendered necessary by the condition of the Roman dominions in Europe and Asia; he therefore invited his younger son Honorius to receive the sceptre of the western empire, appointing Arcadius the elder his successor on the throne of Constantinople. He did not long survive this arrangement; the ease and luxury in which he indulged after his victory proved fatal to a constitution already enfeebled by the fatigues of a severe campaign: he died universally lamented by his subjects, who knew too well that they "ne'er should look upon his like again."

Arcadius and Honorius ascended the thrones bequeathed to them by their father, but both abandoned the cares of empire to their ministers Rufinus and Stilicho. There are few greater stains on the character of Theodosius than his elevation of such an unworthy favourite as Rufinus, a wretch whom all parties describe as stained with every crime. He was the scourge of the east, and was universally hated: aware of his unpopularity, he resolved to secure his power by uniting Arcadius in marriage with his daughter; but some courtiers, jealous of his influence, took advantage of his absence to persuade the young emperor to share his throne with Eudoxia, universally regarded as the most beautiful woman of her age. Though disappointed in this darling object of his ambition, the wealth and power of Rufinus enabled him to triumph over Arcadius and his courtiers; but he dreaded more justly his great rival in the western empire.

Stilicho, the minister and master-general of the west, was worthy of the eminent station to which he had been raised by Theodosius. On his death-bed the emperor recommended to him the charge of both empires; but some pretext was necessary for assembling a force sufficient to depose Rufinus, without giving such alarm as would put that wary statesman on his guard. The Gothic war furnished the desired excuse; Stilicho led his forces round the Adriatic; but he had scarcely reached Thessalonica, when he received orders to return, with a threat that his nearer approach to Constantinople would be considered a declaration of war. Leaving the army in the charge of Gainas, Stilicho returned to Italy; and Rufinus, believing all danger past, went to review the western troops. As he passed along the ranks, he was suddenly surrounded by a chosen band, and, on a signal from Gainas, pinned to the earth by a lance, and mangled with a thousand wounds. If Stilicho had contrived this murder, he derived no advantage from it. Gainas, the eunuch Eutropius, and the empress Eudoxia, combined to exclude him from Constantinople; their puppet Arcadius procured a decree from his obsequious senate, declaring him a public enemy, and confiscating all his property in the east.

Instead of hazarding a civil war, Stilicho exerted himself to suppress the revolt which Gildo, the brother of Firmus, had excited in Africa. He entrusted the command of the forces raised for this purpose to Mascezel, the brother and deadly enemy of Gildo. Accident left the Romans an almost bloodless victory. Before giving the signal to engage, Mascezel rode to the front of the lines with fair offers of peace and pardon; he encountered one of the standard-bearers of the Africans, and, on his refusal to yield, struck him on the arm with his sword. The weight of the blow threw the standard and its bearer prostrate. This was regarded by the rest as a signal of submission, which all the African legions hastened to imitate; they flung down their ensigns, and, with one accord, renewed their allegiance to their rightful sovereign. Gildo attempted to fly, but he was arrested by the citizens of Tabraca (*Tabarca*), and thrown into a dungeon, where he committed suicide, to avoid the punishment of treason. Mascezel was subsequently murdered by Stilicho, who feared the hereditary enmity of the house of Nabal.

The Goths were now become more formidable than they had ever been. Instead of being guided by several independent chiefs, they were united into a compact body under the renowned Alaric; and the withholding of the subsidy paid them by Theodosius, afforded a plausible pretext for war (A. D. 396). Disdaining to ravage the exhausted lands of Thrace, Alaric led his soldiers into Greece, passed the straits of Thermopylæ without opposition, devastated Bœotia, Attica, and the Peloponnesus, while Athens, Corinth, Argos, and Sparta, yielded to the barbarous invaders without opposition. Stilicho hastened to repel the Goths from Greece. His masterly movements drove Alaric into a corner of Elis, whence his extrication appeared impossible; but the Goth, perceiving that the watchfulness of his enemies was relaxed, gained the gulf of Corinth by a rapid march, passed over the narrow strait between the headlands of Rhium and Antirrhium (*Dardanelles of Lepanto*), and was master of Epirus before Stilicho could renew his pursuit. The Romans were preparing to pass into northern Greece, when they received information that Alaric had not only made his peace with the Byzantine court, but had been appointed master-general of Illyricum by the feeble Arcadius.

Stilicho returned to Italy, and was soon compelled to defend that peninsula against Alaric, who forced a passage over the Julian Alps, and advanced towards Milan. Honorius fled from his capital, but was so hotly chased, that he was forced to seek refuge in Asta (*Asti*), which the Goths immediately blockaded. Stilicho hastened to the relief of his sovereign, and gained a complete victory over Alaric at Pollentia (*Polenza*); but the Gothic sovereign having rallied his shattered forces, crossed the Apennines, and made a sudden rush towards Rome (A.D. 403). The capital was saved by the diligence of Stilicho; but Alaric's departure from Italy was purchased by a large pension.

Honorius went to Rome, where he enjoyed the empty honour of being received in triumph; but after a short time he removed to Ravenna, which from this time began to be regarded as the most secure seat of Italian government. Scarcely had Alaric departed, when Italy was invaded by new hordes of Vandals, Suevi, Burgundians, and Goths, under the command of Radagaisus. Once more the peninsula was saved by Stilicho: he allowed the barbarians to lay siege to Florence, which was well garrisoned and provisioned; then securing all the passes, he blockaded them in their turn, and reduced them to such distress, that they surrendered at discretion (A.D. 406). Radagaisus was put to death; his followers were sold as slaves; but about two-thirds of the hordes fell back upon Gaul, and laid waste that province from the Rhine to the Pyrenees. The provincials, receiving no aid from the court of Ravenna, proclaimed Constantine, the governor of Britain, emperor, who gained some advantages over the Germans, and wrested Spain from Honorius. Stilicho entered into a treaty with Alaric against the usurper; but before it could take effect, the able minister was treacherously murdered by his unworthy master (A.D. 408), and the wretched Olympus was appointed premier in his stead. The first measure of the new minister was as impolitic as it was monstrous. He ordered a promiscuous massacre of the families of the barbarians throughout Italy, instead of retaining them as hostages for the fidelity of his mercenary cohorts. The barbarous edict was too well obeyed; and thirty thousand of the bravest soldiers in the Roman pay invited Alaric to head them in avenging the slaughter of their wives and children.

Alaric was not slow in obeying the summons: he hastened into Italy, and, disregarding meaner prizes, marched directly against Rome (A.D. 408). "The eternal city" was closely besieged: plague, pestilence, and famine, raged within its walls. The emperor at Ravenna made no effort to relieve his hapless subjects; and the senate at length purchased temporary safety by paying an enormous ransom. Alaric led his forces into Tuscany, and was joined on his march by forty thousand Goths and Germans, whom his victorious career had enabled to burst the bonds of slavery. Honorius refused to ratify the treaty that had been concluded by the Romans; and in the following year Alaric appeared once more before the city. He took possession of Ostia, where the magazines were established for the corn that supplied the capital; and having thus deprived the citizens of all means of sustenance, summoned them to surrender. They complied, with great reluctance: Alaric raised Attalus to the empire, but soon deposed him, and renewed his negotiations with the court of Ravenna. Once more Honorius refused to treat, and once more Alaric marched to punish the Romans for the crime of their sovereign (A.D. 410). He marched against Rome; the Gothic slaves in the city opened to him one of the gates, and the city became the prey of the barbarians. The horrors of the pillage that ensued were in some degree alleviated by the piety of the Goths, who spared the churches and religious houses. Alaric himself was unwilling that a city which had been so long the mistress of the world should be so totally ruined; and on the sixth day after its capture evacuated the place, and took the road for southern Italy. He was preparing to invade Sicily, when he was seized with a mortal disease, which brought him prematurely to his grave. His remains were interred in the bed of a small rivulet near Consentia (*Cosenza*), and the captives who prepared his grave were murdered, in order that the Romans might never learn the place of his sepulchre.

Adolphus succeeded his brother Alaric, and concluded a peace with the empire, on condition of receiving the princess Placidia as his bride. He led his forces into Gaul, re-united that province to the dominions of Honorius, and then passed into Spain, which had been invaded by hordes of Suevi, Vandals, and Alans. He was murdered; but his successor Wallia established the supremacy of the Visigoths in Spain and the east of Gaul. About the same time, the Franks, the Burgundians, and other barbarous tribes, established themselves in Gaul; while Britain and Armorica, neglected by the emperor, became independent.

In the meantime, the reign of Arcadius in the east was dishonoured by the profligate administration of the eunuch Eutropius and the empress Eudoxia, to whose cruelty the most illustrious persons, and among others St. Chrysostom, were victims. After his death (A.D. 408), the young Theodosius succeeded to the purple; but the administration was usurped by his sister Pulcheria, who ruled the east with singular energy and ability for more than forty years. During a great portion of this period, there was little sympathy between the courts of Rome and Constantinople; but the family intercourse was renewed when Placidia, the widow of Adolphus, was banished by her brother, after the death of her second husband Constantius. She sought refuge in the court of Theodosius, bringing with her Valentinian and Honoria, her infant children. She had scarcely time to enjoy the hospitality with which she was received, when news arrived of the death of Honorius (A.D. 423), and the usurpation of the western empire by John, his principal secretary. Theodosius levied an army to support the claims of his relative; John was deposed and slain; Valentinian III. was proclaimed emperor of the west, under the guardianship of his mother Placidia; and thus two women wielded the destinies of the civilised world.

Placidia, seduced by the interested counsels of her minister Ætius, recalled Count Boniface, the most faithful friend of the imperial family, from Africa; but that governor, deceived by the same crafty adviser, refused obedience, and invited Genseric, king of the Vandals, to his aid. That nation occupied the Spanish province, called from them Vandalusia, a name which it still retains, with but slight alteration. They were still restless, eager to seek further conquests and fresh plunder, so that nothing could have been more grateful to Genseric than such an invitation. Boniface had soon reason to lament the effects of his precipitate resentment. When it was too late, he attempted to check the progress of the Vandals, and returned to his allegiance. Auxiliaries were sent to his aid from the eastern empire; but the unfortunate count was irretrievably defeated. He returned to Italy, where he engaged in a civil war with Ætius, and was slain by his rival. Placidia having discovered the double treachery of Ætius, proclaimed him a traitor, and that general found it necessary to seek shelter in Pannonia with the Huns. Attila, justly called "the Scourge of God," was now the ruler of the formidable Hunnish hordes: he extorted vast sums, as the price of his forbearance, from the Byzantine empire. On the death of Theodosius II. he threatened war against Marcian his successor, the nominal husband of Pulcheria; but the victories of Ætius over the Franks and Vandals, when restored to Placidia's favour, induced the fierce barbarian to turn his arms against the western empire (A.D. 451). He had an additional pretext, through the malice of the princess Honoria, who secretly offered him her hand, to revenge her exclusion from power; and the barbarian monarch, though he already had several wives, proclaimed himself her champion. When the Huns appeared in Gaul, Ætius entered into an alliance with the Visigoths, aided by whom he gained a great victory over Attila, and drove him beyond the frontiers. But in the ensuing spring (A.D. 452) the Huns poured like a torrent into Italy, and laid waste the peninsula. The death of Attila, who fell a victim to intemperance, and the civil wars between his followers, delayed the utter ruin of the empire; but the murder of Ætius by the ungrateful Valentinian, and the unchecked ravages of the barbarians, rendered all the provinces miserable and wretched. Valentinian himself was murdered by the patrician Maximus, whose wife he had debauched (A. D. 455), and the injured husband assumed the imperial purple.

Maximus had scarcely been three months upon the throne when the fleet of the Vandals appeared in the Tiber. His subjects, attributing this new calamity to his supineness, stoned him to death; but ere a successor could be chosen, Genseric marched his soldiers into the defenceless city, and pillaged every thing that had been spared by the piety or mercy of Alaric. Many thousands of the unfortunate citizens were transported as slaves into Africa; but their condition was in some degree alleviated by the generosity of Deogratias, bishop of Carthage, who sold the gold and silver plate of his churches to purchase the redemption of his brethren.

By the influence of Theodoric, king of the Visigoths, Avetus, a Gaul of noble family, was installed emperor; but he was soon deposed by Count Ricimer, the principal commander of the barbarian auxiliaries entrusted with the defence of Italy. He did not long survive his fall; he died on his way to the Alps, as he was about to seek refuge among the Visigoths. Majorian received the degraded sceptre from Ricimer, and made some vigorous efforts to remedy the disorders of the state. His virtues were not appreciated by his subjects. He was dethroned by a licentious soldiery (A. D. 461), and died in a few days after.

Ricimer chose one of his own creatures, Severus, to be nominal emperor, retaining all the power of the state in his own hands; but the superior strength of the Vandals compelled him to have recourse to the court of Constantinople for aid, and to offer the nomination of a sovereign for the west to Leo, the successor of Marcian. Leo appointed the patrician Anthemius to this high but dangerous station, and sent a large armament against the Vandals in Africa. The imperial forces were completely defeated, and when the shattered relics of the armament returned to Constantinople, Ricimer deposed Anthemius, put him to death, and elevated Olybrius to the throne (A. D. 472). Both Ricimer and Olybrius died within a few months; and Leo, after some delay, appointed Julius Nepos his colleague.

Glycerius, an obscure soldier, trusting to the aid of the Burgundians, attempted to dispute the empire with Nepos; but finding his strength inadequate to the contest, he resigned the sceptre for the crosier, and became bishop of Salona. Nepos himself was soon driven from the throne by Orestes, the successor of Ricimer in the command of the barbarian mercenaries. He fled into Dalmatia, where he was assassinated by his old rival Glycerius.

Orestes gave the throne to his son Romulus Momyllus, whom he dignified with the title of Augustus, or, as he is more frequently called, Augustulus. Odoacer, the leader of the German tribes in the Roman pay, persuaded his countrymen to take arms against the usurper. Orestes was made prisoner, and put to death. Augustulus was sent into captivity, but was allowed a pension for his support; and the conqueror, abolishing the name and office of emperor, took the title of king of Italy (A. D. 476). The Ostrogoths finally conquered Italy (A.D. 492), deposed Odoacer, and founded a new empire.

APPENDIX.

No. I.

CATALOGUES OF THE EGYPTIAN KINGS.

Herodotus is the first author who has given us a catalogue of the Egyptian kings. Heeren has shewn, that though it differs from the list given by Diodorus Siculus, the inconsistency is not so great as to render either incredible, because both seem to have given fragments of a series derived solely from public monuments. Let us compare the two historians, and we shall see that this account of the discrepancy is far from being improbable.

Herodotus.	Diodorus Siculus.
Menes, the first man who reigned in Egypt; but he is said to have been preceded by the gods Osiris, Horus, and Typhon.	*Menes.* Fifty-two unnamed successors. *Busiris I.* Seven successors.
Three hundred and thirty kings in succession, including one queen (Nitocris) and eighteen Ethiopians. The names of all these were told to Herodotus; but the only one he mentions is	*Busiris II.*, founder of Thebes. *Osymandias.* Seven successors. *Uchoreus*, founder of Memphis. *Ægyptus*, his grandson. Twelve generations.
Mœris, who built the vestibule to the temple of Vulcan, and dug the lake that bears his name. Great importance attaches to the date of this reign assigned by Herodotus, namely, 900 years before the historian visited Egypt, consequently between B.C. 1500 and B.C. 1450.	*Mœris.* Seven generations.
Sesostris, the conqueror of Palestine, Scythia, Thrace, Ethiopia, and the neighbouring countries. By means of his captives, he formed the trenches by which Egypt was intersected and irrigated.	*Sesostris*, or *Sesoosis.*
Pheron, son of Sesostris.	*Sesostris II.*; an interval of several generations, during which we meet the names of *Amasis* the Ethiopian, *Actisanus* and *Mendes*, or *Manes*, builder of the labyrinth.

Proteus, in the time of the Trojan war.	*Proteus*, or *Cetes*, in the time of the Trojan war.
Rhampsinitus, the richest of the Egyptian kings.	*Remphis*.
	Seven generations.
Cheops, who closed the temples, forbade sacrifices, and made all the people of Egypt work at his favourite structure, the great pyramid.	*Chemmis*, or *Chembes*, builder of the great pyramid.
Chephres, brother of Cheops, builder of a pyramid.	*Cephren*, brother of Chemmis, builder of a pyramid.
Mycerinus, son of Cheops, builder of a pyramid.	*Mycerinus*, son of Chemmis, builder of a pyramid.
Asychis, the legislator, builder of a pyramid.	*Bocchoris*, the legislator, builder of a pyramid.
Anysis, the blind king.	Several generations.
Sabaco, the Ethiopian.	*Sabaco*, the Ethiopian.
The blind *Anysis* restored.	
Sethos, a priest of Vulcan.	
Dodecarchy.	Dodecarchy.
Psammetichus of Sais.	Psammetichus of Sais.

Manetho was an Egyptian priest, who lived under Ptolemy Philadelphus: he wrote a history of his native land, but only some fragments, in a very corrupt state, have been preserved; these contain little more than a list of kings' names, arranged in dynasties; but we are not told in what order the dynasties succeeded each other, nor which reigned at the same time in different parts of Egypt. It is from Manetho's fragments, verified by existing monuments, that the list of kings in the chapter on Egypt has been taken.

No. II.

CYRUS.

We have four different accounts of Cyrus; that of Herodotus, that of Xenophon, that contained in the Jewish Scriptures, and that given by Mirkhoud and Firdausi. All these narratives vary so much, that in some parts they cannot be reconciled: it may be interesting, if not useful, to investigate the cause of the discrepancy. No greater source of error to western writers can be found than the oriental custom of confounding epithets and proper names. The same habit, indeed, existed in Europe, and especially among the Celtic nations. It has been gravely stated, that Brennus, after having sacked Rome, invaded Macedon; an error arising from the circumstance of Brenn, or Brennus, being the old Gallic name for "a leader." Cyrus, or, as the Hebrews write it, Khoreesh, is simply an epithet of dignity, derived from the old Persian *Khor*, or *Khorshíd*, which signifies "the sun," whence eastern Persia at the present day is called *Khorassán*, or "the province of the sun." In like manner Darius, or rather *Darawesh*, is derived from the Persian *Dará*, which, like the modern *Sháh*, signifies "a monarch." Most of the objections urged against the Scripture narrative rest on what the writers are pleased to term the anachronism of making Darius contemporary with Cyrus. But who told them that the Darius of the prophets was the Darius Hystaspes of profane history? The sovereign who threw Daniel into the lions' den is described in Scripture as the "Median Darawesh, son of Achash-werosh;" that is, "the Median monarch, the offspring of a vigorous hero." So that the Darius mentioned by Daniel may have been either Cyrus, Cyaxares, or Cambyses. Neither are we helped to a decision by the mention of the capture of Babylon, because the break between the narrative of Belshazzar's death, and that which tells us of Daniel being cast into the den of lions, clearly includes a considerable space of time; but there are no means of determining its duration. The epithet "Median" would seem to point at Cyaxares; and we shall presently see that some oriental traditions confirm this theory.

The comparative value of the histories of Cyrus given by Xenophon and Herodotus, has been the subject of countless controversies. Xenophon himself settles the question in a single sentence, declaring that his work was derived from the traditionary songs of the Persians. A history of Spain founded on the ballads of the Cid, would consequently be just as authentic as the Cyropædia. Besides, if he collected all the ballads in which a Khorésh was mentioned, he would probably have procured more relating to Jemshíd than to the son of Cambyses. This, indeed, seems likely to have been the case. It is exceedingly probable that Xenophon's philosophical romance is founded as much on the traditions respecting Jemshíd and Rustem, as upon the notorious facts in the history of Cyrus.

The leading fact in the history of Cyrus is, that he subverted the Median dynasty, and established the superiority of the Persians. "The Medes," says Herodotus, "were formerly called Arii." It has been now well established, by the labours of eminent orientalists, that both the Zendic and Pehlví dialects of Persia present a strong similarity to the Sanscrit; a circumstance that proves a connexion in origin between the Persians and Hindús. *A'rya* in Sanscrit signifies "honourable;" Hindustán itself is in the old Indian writings named *A'rya-ávarta*, or "the country of honourable men;" and the Brahmins divide the inhabitants of the earth into A'ryas and Mlechas, as the Greeks did into Hellenes and Barbarians. The name, then, would seem to indicate that the Medes were an ascendant caste, and also the professors of an idolatrous creed similar to the Brahminical. Cyrus, or Khusrau, is described by the orientals as a religious reformer; he is said to have overthrown the tyranny of the idolatrous Afrasiáb, and enforced the worship of the Divine Unity. He is made to exclaim,

> "We shall make the world too narrow for the wicked,
> And bring destruction on the prosperity of Afrasiáb."

Herodotus describes the young hero as beginning his expedition by a solemn sacrifice, which appears from his narrative to have been of an unusual nature; and it is not obscurely hinted in Scripture that the Jews owed the favour he shewed them to their being worshippers of the one true God. It appears, therefore, to us no improbable conjecture, that Cyrus was the leader of a religious as well as a political revolution, similar in its principles to that attempted by the Buddhists in Hindustán. That caste existed in Persia, is sufficiently evident from the narrative of Herodotus, whose account of the Persian Magi would, with little alteration, form a tolerably correct description of the Indian Brahmins: we know also that the Magi were the enemies of the Kaianian dynasty, to which Khusrau belonged; and we regard the story of Smerdis as the perverted account of a struggle made by the priests to recover their superiority. The persecution of the Magi by Gushtasp, or Darius Hystaspes, is mentioned both by eastern and western writers; it is declared to have been a punishment for rebellion; that is, for an attempt to establish the supremacy of the priestly over the regal race. The difficulty of getting at any thing like a chronological arrangement of the Hindu traditions prevents us from inquiring whether this revolution was contemporary with a similar struggle between the priestly and warrior castes beyond the Indus; but it is notorious that such contests were frequent in Hindustán.

It has been long a tradition among the orientals, that Zerdusht, or Zoroaster, was the disciple of a Jewish prophet; some say Jeremiah was his instructor, some Ezekiel, but the majority give that honour to Daniel. Now, it is known to most Rabbinical scholars that the Jews view Daniel with great suspicion, asserting that he refused to return to Jerusalem with his countrymen, and that he became the vizier of Cyrus at Persepolis. They further declare that he broke through the exclusive principle, so conspicuous in the Jewish creed, and that he communicated to the Gentiles a knowledge of Jehovah and of the laws given to Moses. Indeed, in the Talmud of Jerusalem, Daniel is described as little better than a renegade, and his claims to rank in the first class of prophets are discussed very unceremoniously. We have here something like a clue to the persecution of Daniel by the Median Darawesh, whoever he was: the priests, like the Indian Brahmins, persuaded their sovereign that he was an incarnation of the Divinity, and therefore entitled to worship,—a line of conduct which we know to have been by no means unusual in central Asia. They directed his wrath principally against Daniel, because the religion which he taught threatened to subvert the dynasty of their caste; and but for Divine interference, they would have succeeded in destroying their capital enemy.

If Daniel became the vizier of Cyrus, and we see nothing improbable in the tradition, the great favour shewn by this monarch to the Jews becomes perfectly intelligible, and we discover a probable cause for the high compliment paid by Ezekiel to his countryman, whom he ranks with Noah and Job. There may be some who would assert that a Persian monarch would not nominate a foreigner his premier, nor a Jew hold eminent rank under a strange government; but the undoubted history of Nehemiah shews us that such an event, so far from being improbable, was not even unusual or infrequent.

We have now gone through the examination of the character and actions ascribed to the Khoreesh of Scripture, and shewn that all the light which the examination of oriental traditions has enabled us to collect, serves to confirm, not merely the historical verity, but the strict accuracy, of the Old Testament.

No. III.

COMMERCIAL TREATY BETWEEN ROME AND CARTHAGE,

CONCLUDED B.C. 509.

BETWEEN the Romans and their allies on the one part, and the Carthaginians and their allies on the other, peace and alliance shall be established on the following conditions:

Neither the Romans nor their allies shall sail beyond the Fair Promontory (a cape north of Carthage), unless compelled by bad weather or an enemy. And should they happen to be forced beyond it, they shall not be allowed to take or purchase any thing, except what is absolutely required for the repair of their vessels, or for sacrifice. They shall not tarry longer than five days.

The importers of goods for sale into Sardinia, or any part of Libya, shall pay no customs beyond the usual fees to the registrar and the salemaster; and the public faith shall be pledged as a security to the merchant for all he shall sell in the presence of these officers.

Should a Roman land in that part of Sicily belonging to the Carthaginians, he shall not suffer injury or violence in any thing.

The Carthaginians engage not to offer any injury to the people of Ardea, Antium, Laurentium, Circeii, Tarracina, or any other people of the Latins that have submitted to the Roman jurisdiction; nor shall they seize upon any city of the Latins, though it may not be under the Roman supremacy. Should any such be taken, it shall be restored to the Romans uninjured and entire.

The Carthaginians engage not to build any fortress in the Latin territory; and should they be compelled to land, they promise not to remain a single night.

No. IV.

RULING HOUSES OF CARTHAGE.

House of Mago.

- Mago † B.C. 500.
  - Hasdrubal, general in Sicily and Sardinia.
    - Hannibal.
    - Hasdrubal.
    - Sappho.
    - (Generals in Africa.)
  - Hamilcar † in Sicily, 480 B.C.
    - Hamilco, general in Sicily.
      - Hamilco † B.C. 395.
    - Hanno.
      - Hamilco † B.C. 395.
    - Gisco, an exile.
      - Hannibal † B.C. 406.

House of Hanno.

- Hanno, executed B.C. 340.
  - Gisco.
    - Hamilcar, put to death in Syracuse, B.C. 309.
    - Anonymous.
      - Bomilcar, executed B.C. 308.

The Barca family consisted of Hamilcar Barca; his three sons, Hannibal the Great, Hasdrubal, and Mago; and his son-in-law Hasdrubal.

No. V.

THE PERIPLUS OF HANNO

ROUND THOSE PARTS OF LIBYA WHICH ARE SITUATED BEYOND THE PILLARS OF HERCULES; A NARRATIVE OF WHICH VOYAGE HE DEPOSITED IN THE TEMPLE OF SATURN.

It was decreed by the Carthaginians that Hanno should undertake a voyage beyond the Pillars of Hercules, for the purpose of establishing Liby-Phœnician cities; and he sailed, taking with him a fleet of sixty galleys, of fifty oars each, having on board a multitude of men and women, to the number of thirty thousand, and provisions and other necessaries.

When we had passed through the pillars, and sailed beyond them for two days, we founded the first city, and named it Thymiaterium. Below it lay an extensive plain. Proceeding thence towards the west, we came to Solocis, a promontory of Libya, a place densely covered with wood, where we erected a temple to Neptune; and again proceeded, for the space of half a day, towards the east, until we arrived at a lake not far from the sea, producing

† This mark denotes the date of each person's death, where it is of historic importance.

an abundance of large reeds. Here elephants, and a great number of other wild beasts, were feeding.

Having made about a day's sail beyond the lake, we founded cities near the sea, called Cariconticos, and Gytte, and Acra, and Arambys. Thence we came to the river Lixus (*Al Haratch*), which flows from Libya. On its banks the Lixitæ, a shepherd tribe, were feeding flocks, amongst whom we remained some time on very amicable terms. The unhospitable Ethiopians dwelt beyond the Lixitæ: they pasture a wild country, intersected by large mountains, from which they say the river Lixus flows. The Troglodiitæ dwelt close to the mountains, men of great variety of appearance, whom the Lixitæ described as swifter racers than horses.

Having procured interpreters from them, we coasted southwards two days along a desert country, and thence eastwards for a single day. Here we found a small island in a recess of a certain bay, on which we established a colony, and called it Cerné (*Suana*). We judged, from our voyage, that this place lay in a direct line with Carthage; for the length of our voyage from Carthage to the Pillars was equal to that from the Pillars to Cerné.

We then came to a lake, which we reached by sailing up a large river called Chretes (*Nún*). This lake had three islands larger than Cerné; from which, proceeding a day's sail, we came to the extremity of the lake. It was overhung by huge mountains, inhabited by savages clothed in the skins of wild beasts, who drove us away with stones, and hindered us from landing. Sailing thence, we came to another river that was large and broad, full of crocodiles and hippopotami (probably the *Senegal*); whence returning back, we came again to Cerné.

Thence we sailed towards the south twelve days, coasting the shore, the whole of which is inhabited by Ethiopians, who would not wait our approach, but fled from us. Their language was not intelligible even to the Lixitæ who were with us. Towards the last day we approached some large mountains covered with trees, the wood of which was sweet-scented and variegated. Having sailed by these mountains for two days, we came to an immense opening of the sea, on each side of which, towards the continent, was a plain: from this, at night, we saw fire, sometimes more and sometimes less, arising in all directions.

Having taken in water there, we sailed forward five days near the land, until we came to a large bay, which our interpreters informed us was named the Western Horn (apparently the mouth of the *Senegal*). In this was a large island, and in the island a salt-water lake; and in this another island, where, when we had landed, we could discover nothing in the day-time except trees; but in the night we saw many fires burning, and heard the sound of pipes, cymbals, drums, and confused shouts. We were then afraid, and our diviners ordered us to abandon the island. Sailing quickly away thence, we passed a country burning with fires and perfumes, and streams of fire supplied from it fell into the sea. The earth was impassable on account of the heat. We sailed quickly thence, being much terrified; and passing on for four days, we discovered a country full of fire. In the middle was a lofty fire, larger than the rest, which seemed to touch the stars. When day came, we discovered it to be a large hill called "the Chariot of the Sun" (some place in the neighbourhood of Cape Verd, but the description is applicable to the greater part of the coast of *Senegambia*). On the third day after our departure thence, having sailed by these streams of fire, we arrived at a bay called the Southern Horn (probably the river *Gambia*), at the bottom of which lay an island like the former, having a lake, and in this lake another island full of savages, the greater part of whom were women, whose bodies were hairy, and whom our interpreter called Gorillæ. Though we pursued the men, we could not seize any of them; but all fled from us, escaping over the precipices, and defending themselves with stones. Three women were, however, taken; but they attacked their conductors with their teeth and hands, and could not be prevailed upon to accompany us. Having killed them, we flayed them, and brought their skins with us to Carthage. We did not sail farther, our provisions failing us.

No. VI.

HEEREN'S ACCOUNT OF THE CONDITION OF THE FEMALE SEX IN THE HEROIC AGES OF GREECE.

"The internal regulations of families were simple, but not without those peculiarities which are a natural consequence of the institution of slavery. Polygamy was not directly authorised; but the sanctity of marriage was not considered as violated by the intercourse of the husband with female slaves. The noble characters of Andromache and of Penelope exhibit, each in its way, models of elevated conjugal affection. It is more difficult for us, with our feelings, to understand the seduced and the returning Helen; and yet, if we compare Helen, the beloved of Paris in the Iliad, with Helen the spouse of Menelaus in the Odyssey, we find truth and harmony in the character, which could err indeed, but never lose the generosity and nobleness of its nature. It is a woman, who, having become in youth the victim of sensuality, first repented, and returned to reason, before she was compelled to do so by age. Even after her return from Troy she was still most beautiful (for who would think of counting her years?). And yet even then the two sexes stood to each other in the same relation which continued in later times. The wife was a housewife, and nothing more. Even the sublime Andromache, after that parting, which will draw tears as long as there are eyes which can weep and hearts which can feel, is sent back to the apartments of the women, to superintend the labours of the maid-servants. Still we observe in her a conjugal love of an elevated character. In other instances, love has reference, both with mortals and with immortals, to sensual enjoyment; although in the noble and uncorrupted vestal characters, as in the amiable Nausicaa, it was united with that bashfulness which accompanies maiden youth. But we meet with no trace of those elevated feelings,—that romantic love, as it is improperly termed,—which results from a higher regard for the female sex. That love and that regard are traits peculiar to the Germanic nations; a result of the spirit of gallantry, which was a leading feature in the character of chivalry, but which we vainly look for in Greece. Yet in this respect the Greek stands between the east and the west. Although he was never wont to revere women as beings of a higher order, he did not, like the Asiatic, imprison them by troops in a harem."

No. VII.

THE REIGNING HOUSES OF MACEDON.

House of Alexander the Great.

Philip † 336, married, 1. Olympias. 2. Cleopatra.

Alexander the Great † 323, married, 1. Roxana. 2. Barsine. — Cleopatra. — Philip Anhidæus † 317, married Eurydice. — Thessalonica, mar. Cassander.

Alexander † 311. — Hercules † 309.

House of Antipater.

Antipater † 320.

Cassander † 298, married Thessalonica.

Philip † 297. — Antipater † 294. — Alexander † 294.

House of Antigonus.

Antigonus † 301.

Demetrius Poliorcetes † 284.

Stratonice, married, 1. Seleucus I. 2. Antigonus I. — Antigonus I. Gonnatas † 242.

Demetrius II. † 233. — Alcyoneus.

Philip II. † 179. — Antigonus II. Doron † 221.

Perseus † 166. — Demetrius † 180.

No. VIII.

GENEALOGICAL TABLE OF THE SELEUCIDÆ (*from Heeren*).

SELEUCUS I. NICATOR † 281,
married, 1. Apame. 2. Stratonice, daughter of Demetrius Poliorcetes.

1\. ANTIOCHUS I. SOTER † 262, married, 1. Stratonice, his mother-in-law. 2. Anonymous.

2\. Phila, married Antigonus Gonatas, king of Macedon.

1\. ANTIOCHUS II. THEOS † 247, mar. 1. Laodice, his sister-in-law. 2. Berenice, da. of Ptol. Philad.

1\. Apame, married Magas of Cyrene.

2\. Laodice.

1\. SELEUCUS II. CALLINICUS † 227, married Laodice, daughter of Andromachus, father of Achæus.

1\. Antiochus Herax.

1\. Stratonice, married Ariarathes IV. of Cappadocia.

SELEUCUS III. CERAUNUS † 224.

Stratonice, married Mithridates IV. of Pontus.

ANTIOCHUS III. THE GREAT † 187, married Laodice, daughter of Mithridates IV. of **Pontus.**

Antiochus † 192.

Laodice.

SELEUCUS IV. PHILOPATER † 176, married his sister Laodice.

ANTIOCHUS IV. EPIPHANES † 164.

Cleopatra, mar. Ptolemy V.

Antiochis, mar. Ariarathes V. of **Cappad.**

DEMETRIUS I. † 150.

Laodice, married Perseus, king of Macedon.

ANTIOCHUS V. EUPATOR † 161.

DEMETRIUS II. NICATOR † 126, married, 1. Cleopatra, da. of Ptol. Philom. 2. Rhodogyne.

ANTIOCHUS SIDETES † 131, married his daughter-in-law, Cleopatra.

SELEUCUS V. † 125.

ANTIOCHUS GRYPHUS † 97, married Cleopatra Selene, daughter of Ptol. Phys.

ANTIOCHUS CYZICENUS † 96, married Cleopatra, daughter of Ptol. Phys.

Seleucus Epiph. † 94.

Antioch. Epiph. † 93.

Philippus Epiph. † 83.

Demetr. Eucar. † c. 87.

Antioch. Dionys. † 89.

ANTIOCHUS EUSEBES † c. 90, married Cleopatra Selene.

ANTIOCHUS ASIATICUS † 58.

SELEUCUS CYBIOSACTES † 57, married Berenice, daughter of Ptol. **Auletes.**

No. IX.

GENEALOGICAL TABLE OF THE PTOLEMIES. (*From Heeren.*)

PTOLEMY I. son of LAGUS † 284,
married, 1. Eurydice, daughter of Antipater. 2. Berenice. (3. Concubines.)

1. Ptol. Ceraunus † 279, king of Macedonia.

2. PTOL. II. PHILADELPHUS † 246, married, 1. Arsinoe, daughter of Lysimachus. 2. His sister Arsinoe.

2. Arsinoe.

3. Magas of Cyrene. | Berenice.

PTOL. III. EVERGETES † 221, married Berenice, daughter of Magas. — Berenice, married Antiochus Theos.

PTOL. IV. PHILOPATER † 204, married, 1. His sister Arsinoe. (2. Agathoclea.) — Magas. — Arsinoe.

PTOL. V. EPIPHANES † 181,
married Cleopatra, daughter of Antiochus the Great.

PTOL. VI. PHILOMETER † 145, married his sister Cleopatra. | Cleopatra the younger.

Cleopatra.

PTOL. VII. PHYSCON † 117. married, 1. His sister Cleopatra. 2. Cleopatra the younger. (3. Irene.)

2. PTOL. VIII. LATHYRUS † 81. married, 1, 2. his two sisters. (3. Concubines.)

2. Cleop. Selene.

2. PTOL. ALEXANDER I. † 88. married Cleopatra, daughter of Ptol. Lathyrus.

2. Cleopatra.

3. Ptol. Apion, king of Cyrene, † 97.

Children of Ptol. VIII. Lathyrus:

2. Cleopatra † 88, married Alex. I.

2. Cl. Berenice.

3. PTOL. AULETES † 51, mar. 1. his sister Cleop. 2. unknown.

3. Ptol. of Cyprus, † 57.

3. Cleopatra.

Children of Ptol. Alexander I.:

PTOL. ALEXANDER II. † 80, married Cleop. Berenice.

† † † PTOL. ALEX. III. † 66.

Children of Ptol. Auletes:

1. BERENICE † 55, married, 1. Seleucus Cybios. 2. Archelaus.

1. CLEOPATRA † 30, mar. 1, 2. her brothers. (3. Jul. Cæsar.) 4. Anthony.

2. PTOL. DIONYSIUS † 47, married Cleopatra.

2. PTOL. the younger † 44. married Cleopatra.

Arsinoe † 43.

No, X.

THE REIGNING HOUSES OF THE JEWS. (*From Heeren.*)

House of the Maccabees.

- Mattathias † B.C. 166.
  - Judas Maccabæus, general of the army, † 161.
  - Jonathan, high priest, † 143.
  - Simon, high priest and ethnarch, † 135.
    - John Hyrcanus † 107.
      - Aristobulus I. † 106, king and high priest.
      - Alex. I. Jannæus † 79, married Alexandra.
        - Hyrcanus II. † 30, high priest and ethnarch.
          - Alexander II. † 49.
            - Aristobulus † 34.
            - Mariamne † 28, married Herod the Great.
          - Antigonus † 37.
        - Aristobulus † 49.

House of Herod.

- Antipater † 43.
  - Salome.
  - Herod the Great † A.C. 3. married, 1. Doris. 2. Mariamne. 3. Many others.
    - Antipater, † A.C. 3.
    - Alexander, † B.C. 5.
    - Aristobulus, † B.C. 5.
      - Herod II. Agrippa, † A.C. 44.
        - Herod Agrippa, † A.C. 100.
    - Archelaus, ethnarch, deposed A.C. 6.
    - Antipas, tetrarch, deposed A.C. 39, married Herodias.
    - Philip, tetrarch, † A.C. 34.

No. XI.

GENEALOGICAL TABLE OF THE CÆSARS. (*From Heeren.*)

I.

C. Julius Cæsar, prætor, † 84.

- C. Julius Cæsar, dictator, † 44.
  - Julia † 52, married Pompey.
- Julia † 52, married Accius Balbus.
  - Accia † 42, married C. Octavius.
    - Octavia the elder, married M. Marcellus.
    - Octavia the younger, married, 1. C. Marcellus. 2. Pompey. 3. M. Antony.
    - C. Octavius (Cæsar Augustus) † a.c. 14 (see No. II.)

II.

Cæsar Octavianus Augustus † a.c. 14.
married, 1. Scribonia. 2. Livia, widow of Tiberius Claudius Nero.

- 1. Julia † a.c. 17, married, 1. M. Cl. Marcellus. 2. Agrippa. 3. Tiberius.
  - 2. C. Cæsar † a.c. 4.
  - 2. L. Cæsar † a.c. 2.
  - 2. Agrippina † a.c. 35, mar. Germanicus.
  - 2. Julia † a.c. 30.
  - 2. Agrippa Posthumus † a.c. 14.
- Tiberius Nero † a.c. 37, married, 1. Vipsania. 2. Julia.
  - Drusus Cæsar † a.c. 25.
- Nero Claudius Drusus † 9. married Antonia the younger.
  - Germanicus † a.c. 19, married Agrippina.
    - Nero † a.c. 29.
    - Drusus † a.c. 35.
    - Caius Caligula † a.c. 41.
    - Agrippina, married, 1. Cn. Domitius. 2. Claudius.
      - 1. Domitius Nero † a.c. 68, married, 1. Octavia. 2. Poppæa Sabina.
  - Claudius † a.c. 54, married, 1. Messalina, 2. Agrippina.
    - 1. Britannicus † a.c. 34.
    - 1. Octavia † a.c. 59, married Nero

No. XII.

GENEALOGICAL TABLE OF THE HOUSE OF CONSTANTINE. (*From Heeren.*)

- CONSTANTIUS CHLORUS † 306, married, 1. Helena. 2. Theodora.
  - CONSTANTINE the Great † 337, married, 1. Minervina. 2. Fausta.
    - 1. CRISPUS † 326.
    - 2. CONSTANTINE † 340.
    - 2. CONSTANTIUS † 361.
    - 2. CONSTANS † 350.
  - Constantia, married C. Valer LICINIUS, Cæsar, † 324.
    - Fl. Valer. Licinius † 326.
  - Jul. Constantius † 337, married, 1. Galla. 2. Basilina.
    - 1. Gallus † 354.
    - 2. JULIAN (the apostate) † 363.
  - Annibalianus.
    - Dalmatius Cæsar † 339.
    - Annibalianus † 338.

ANALYTICAL AND CHRONOLOGICAL

INDEX.

END OF PART FIRST.